The Indian Economy

Published in cooperation with
the Center for Asian Development Studies,
Boston University

The Indian Economy

Recent Development and Future Prospects

edited by
Robert E.B. Lucas
and Gustav F. Papanek

DELHI
OXFORD UNIVERSITY PRESS
BOMBAY CALCUTTA MADRAS

Oxford University Press, Walton Street, Oxford OX2 6DP

OXFORD NEW YORK
ATHENS AUCKLAND BANGKOK BOMBAY
CALCUTTA CAPE TOWN DAR ES SALAAM DELHI
FLORENCE HONG KONG ISTANBUL KARACHI
KUALA LUMPUR MADRAS MADRID MELBOURNE
MEXICO CITY NAIROBI PARIS SINGAPORE
TAIPEI TOKYO TORONTO
and associates in
BERLIN IBADAN

Published 1988 in the United States of America
by Westview Press, Inc.; Frederick A. Praeger, Publisher;
5500 Central Avenue, Boulder, Colorado 80301

First Indian edition 1988
by arrangement with Westview Press, Inc.
Oxford India Paperback 1989
Fifth impression 1996

ISBN 0 19 562419 X

Printed at Rekha Printers Pvt. Ltd., New Delhi 110020
and published by Manzar Khan, Oxford University Press
YMCA Library Building, Jai Singh Road, New Delhi 110001

Contents

Introduction

The Conference on the Indian Economy, held at Boston University in October 1986, was a modest attempt to help reverse the declining interest and knowledge of Indian economic development which has characterized U.S. business, academic and government circles for the last twenty years. This neglect was in sharp contrast to earlier American interest in India.

In the 1950s and early 1960s India was central to U.S. thought on the countries then called "less developed." Of all the countries in Asia, Africa and Latin America, India seemed the one most likely to achieve rising incomes and greater industrialization and was therefore of particular interest to those groups in America that concerned themselves with the countries outside the industrial, developed Organization for Economic Cooperation and Development (OECD) area. India was seen as potentially a major economic and political power. It had a stable and effective government machinery; a mature and democratic political process; a large and experienced business and industrial sector; and an intellectual, professional and technical group matched or exceeded by few countries. With the other giant of the less developed world, China, suffering from the aftereffects of war, civil war and revolution and essentially withdrawing from the world economy, India was seen as both a political and economic leader of the "Third World." As such India was of interest to American government officials, some elements of the business community, and those in the academic world concerned with economic development.

The Vietnam war accelerated the gradual decline in U.S. interest in the less developed world in general and South Asia in particular. Ethnic and business ties kept interest alive in parts, at least, of Latin America and Africa. East Asia's phenomenal growth led to growing interest in the "four little tigers," as well as Japan. The more modest, but still growing, economic relations with Southeast Asia, combined with traditional U.S involvement in the Philippines, kept alive some interest in that region. None of these factors applied to South Asia. The contrast between the 1950s and early 1960s on the one hand and the last decade on the other was especially vivid with respect to India.

Academic involvement is one index of the extent of interest in and knowledge of a country. Twenty-five years ago there was significant work on South Asian economies, and especially on India, in several U.S. universities. At present, no university has a group of economists working systematically and jointly on economic issues of the region. There are probably fewer than a dozen individual academics doing serious and consistent work on the Indian economy in the United States. American business has been equally neglectful.

Yet India remains a major actor in the world economy, one whose economic potential is truly awe inspiring. One simple indication of this potential is that outside the centrally planned economies India is second only to the United States in its number of "professional and scientific" personnel. There are nearly 400,000 engineers in India with at least a Bachelor's degree and nearly one million if those with diplomas are also counted. Salaries for professional, engineering and technical personnel are one-half or less of those in other mixed economies with a large pool of such personnel. As a result, India is potentially the lowest cost producer in the world of many high technology goods.

That a significant number of India's engineers have been unemployed at one time is only one indication that the country's economic potential is far from having been fully realized. Statistics on the underutilization of industrial capacity support the same point. But it is the slow growth rate of India over most of the past thirty-five years, compared to other Asian countries, which provides the most telling evidence that its economic potential has not been fully developed.

Recent years have seen some important and positive changes in the Indian economy. Effective Government action has resulted in a more rapid growth of food production, which has turned India from a major importer of food to a country with growing food reserves. The industrial growth rate has increased as well, and industry has become more diversified. A new generation of entrepreneurs and managers has made it more likely that industrial growth will continue. Most important, the Government has recently made some important changes in policies, which raise the hope that yet more of the country's economic potential will be brought into play. With greater reliance on price incentives and on the world market, the external environment facing India has become more important.

There has been inadequate recognition in the United States of the changes that have taken place in India in the last decade and especially in the most recent past. One of the purposes of "The Conference on the Indian Economy: Successes, Current Policies, and External Links" was to analyze the Indian economy, its economic potential and the significance of recent changes for the Indian and the world economy and for bilateral economic relations. Another was to increase American knowledge and understanding of Indian economic development and especially of recent economic changes. Yet a third was to strengthen the professional ties among those in India, the United States and elsewhere who work on the Indian economy.

Organized and sponsored by the Asian Center of Boston University, in collaboration with the Indian Center for Research on International Economic Relations (ICRIER), the Conference had important support from a number of sources. The American Institute for Indian Studies, with a grant from the Ford Foundation, and Boston University were the first to offer financial assistance. Major support also came from the U.S. Agency for International Development (AID), New Delhi Office, and the National Organizing Committee for the Festival of India in the United

States. The Government of India covered travel expenses for nearly all Indian participants in the Conference program and made available an unusual number and range of participants from among its officials. The Smithsonian Institution and also a number of Indian manufacturing enterprises helped support travel. We are naturally deeply grateful for all this support, without which the Conference could not possibly have taken place.

Discussion at the Conference was wide ranging and remarkably frank, with a great diversity of opinions expressed. Needless to say, none of the sponsoring organizations is in any way responsible for what were, in all cases, the personal views of the participants.

Our greatest debt is to the many exceptionally busy individuals who accepted the invitation to participate: government officials, businessmen, academics, journalists and others involved in public affairs. Whatever value the Conference and this volume may have is due to the knowledge, and indeed wisdom, about the Indian economy brought to the discussion by this truly remarkable group of participants. We hope, as a result, that the Conference and this volume will contribute to reversing the unfortunate trend in the United States toward largely ignoring a major economy, which could well become a considerable force in world economic relationships.

Lovraj Kumar,
Chairman of the Conference Steering Committee, ICRIER

K. B. Lall,
Chairman of the Board, ICRIER

Robert E.B. Lucas,
Chair of the Conference Committee, Boston University

Gustav F. Papanek,
Director of the Center for Asian Development Studies,
Boston University

PART ONE

Past Performance and Current Issues

1

The Indian Economy:
Past Performance and
Current Issues

P. N. Dhar

Performance of the Economy

Background

To understand the goals of the Indian planners and their policies and methods of implementation it may be useful to recall the political and intellectual milieu in which their thinking took shape. As India was among the first colonial countries in Asia to become independent, it had no experience to draw upon except its own under foreign rule. The lessons of this experience were understood in terms of contemporary thought on problems of development before a relevant strategy was evolved.

In the course of the freedom struggle a nationalist economic platform had emerged in India. The nationalist leadership was acutely aware of the need for industrialization to modernize the economy and was convinced that Government support and involvement were essential for the task. They were impressed more by Friedrich List and Alexander Hamilton than by Adam Smith.

The first cotton mill, the first jute mill and the first railway track had been established in India around the same time as the Japanese started their industrial development after the Meiji Restoration in the second half of the nineteenth century. But while Japan became an industrial country, the Indian effort did not go beyond a small sector dominated by a few consumer goods industries. The rapid industrialization of the Soviet Union was widely acknowledged as an even greater achievement than that of the Japanese: Jawaharlal Nehru was fascinated by what he saw when he visited the U.S.S.R. in 1927.

The author is grateful to Dr. Manmohan Singh, Professors Mrinal Datta-Chaudhry, K. Krishnamurty and Suresh Tandulkar for their comments on an earlier draft.

The leadership of the freedom movement therefore pressed hard for industrial development even while the political struggle was going on. The "Swadeshi" or buy-Indian-goods campaign was as much a weapon in the battle for political freedom as it was a substitute for a protectionist policy. The regeneration of the Indian economy became a pronounced aim of the freedom struggle with planning as the effective way of achieving it. Towards this end, the nationalist leadership made its intellectual preparations alongside the struggle. Thus the Congress Party established a national planning committee under the chairmanship of Nehru nearly a decade *before* the country became free. The Committee established a number of subcommittees which issued reports on different sectors and subsectors of the economy very much like the reports of the Working Groups in the post-Independence period under the Planning Commission. The enthusiasm for planning spread to other parties and groups, besides the Congress Party. Even Indian businessmen prepared a national plan in 1944, known as the Bombay Plan, but what is more important is that they had no objection to the central role of the state in the process of industrialization.

Besides industrial development, the national leadership had other concerns like the removal of age-old social inequalities with which Indian society was riddled. To alleviate the widespread poverty in the country and to make economic growth consistent with social justice, Government intervention on an increasing scale was believed to be necessary. In a country as large and diverse as India, an active government policy was held to be essential for reducing regional disparities and bringing about national consolidation. A competitive democratic political system based on universal adult suffrage articulated these requirements increasingly and forcefully.

At the same time, Indian planners led by Mahalanobis were more outgoing in informing themselves of the "state of art" in understanding the nature of the development process and the means of promoting it. Before finalizing his well-known strategy for economic development and social change, he organized a vast intellectual effort of consultations with the best-known economic experts of the country as well as from the West and the East, whose opinions and beliefs ranged from liberal right all the way to the Marxian left.

In the early fifties, development economics was itself at its early experimental stage. The Keynesian analysis of the determinants of the level of activity as extended by Harrod-Domar models was being taken up by economists for elaboration and application to developing countries. This analysis laid heavy emphasis on increase in capital stock as the key element for economic growth. There were, of course, some other thoughts and discussions which dwelt on sociological and cultural aspects of the development process. But there was not much empirical data available on which to test these hypotheses. Predominance was therefore held by the idea that underdevelopment was the result of deficiency of capital and, consequently, there was need for the Government to promote capital formation and allocate it according to priorities. Since the low level of per capita income acted as a constraint, the need for mobilizing domestic

savings a███████████████oreign aid become major requirements fo███████████████order to finance investment and
generate ███████████████Another element in professional
thinking and judg███████████he outlook for the exports of the
developing countries. The ███████bout the growth of Indian exports,
consisting mostly of goods of inelastic demand, were endorsed by the
more general and theoretical analyses of economists like Raul Prebisch
and Ragnar Nurkse which were also based on "export pessimism." Indeed
economists in general had not imagined the magnitude of the trade boom
that the postwar world would witness. In these circumstances the concepts
of "Big Push" and "Balanced Growth" gained wide acceptability, under-
scoring the need for planning an investment program on a closed economy
basis.

For Indian policymakers the ideas which had been historically inherited
appeared to be wholly in accord with contemporary professional opinion.
At the same time the vast exercise of working out the details of a consistent
set of policies and implementing them appeared quite manageable to the
Indian administrators. The Indian Civil Service prided itself on its efficiency
and honesty and was confident of its ability to implement the plans even
though its experience in economic matters was confined to the administration of a few wartime regulations and controls. Nurtured in the
traditions of the colonial civil service, it felt no diffidence about its ability
to handle the economic future of the country in preference to the Indian
businessmen, the "banias" for whom it had inherited an attitude of
hauteur.

This was the political and intellectual background to the Indian plans
for economic development and social change. The major aims of these
plans were a high growth rate, national self-reliance, full employment
and reduction of income inequalities. To achieve these goals a capital
goods sector was given high priority in the process of industrialization
that was launched. This was based on the proposition that many basic
industries, the transport system and other social overheads would be
necessary before the secondary manufacturing industry could get started.
Investment in such industries takes place in large lumps or not at all.
For some time therefore, it was argued, that the growth of the investment
goods sector must anticipate and be independent of the growth of
consumption. This anticipatory and independent expansion of investment
sector or capital goods industry would lay down the basis of rapid
industrialization. This meant that during the period of basic industrialization the flow of goods would be not from the investment goods sector
to the consumption goods sector but within the investment sector itself:
More coal to produce more steel, to produce more machinery to mine
more coal and ores and more transport to relate one to the other. The
briefest description of this process of industrialization current at that
time was "machines to produce more machines."[1]

Recognizing that these industries were going to be capital intensive
and not likely to generate much employment in the short run, expansion
of small and cottage industries was to be encouraged as a means of

providing employment and also to meet the increased demand for consumer goods.

The plans were implemented in the framework of a mixed economy with an increasing role for the public sector and a state-regulated private sector. Thus Government policy focused on (1) increasing a public sector share in the total capital stock through the allocation of new investments between the public and private sectors; (2) reservations of new investments in basic and heavy industries, mostly for the public sector; (3) regulation of industries in the private sector to secure their development in conformity with the Plan objectives; and (4) agrarian reforms, rural institution building and improvement of farm practices. This strategy was fairly clearly articulated for the decade covering the Second Five-Year Plan (1956–61) and Third Five-Year Plan (1961–66), the First Five-Year Plan (1951–56) being essentially a period of preparation.

Period: 1951–52 to 1965–66

The growth achieved since 1951 was significant but not impressive. For the fifteen-year period of the three Plans ending in early 1966 GDP increased by 3.8 percent per annum. Agricultural output rose annually by 2.8 percent per annum and industrial output by 7.3 percent per annum.[2] These achievements were below the Plan targets and below the average for the developing countries taken together. However, the Plans did succeed in significantly extending land under cultivation and irrigation, abolishing intermediary and rent-receiving tenures and conferring rights of ownership on some groups of tenants. Similarly, in the field of industry a diversified industrial structure with greatly enlarged capacity in basic sectors, particularly metals and machine building, heavy chemicals, transport and communications, was established. Equally important was the development of new managerial skills, technical know-how and designing capacity.

But while the Third Plan was still in progress, events took place which imposed unforeseen burdens on the economy. The sharp increase in defense expenditures consequent on armed conflicts with China and Pakistan and the leveling off of foreign aid, all in the short span of three years (1962–65), put the economy under severe strain. These strains reached crisis proportions when two consecutive droughts hit the country in 1966 and 1967. GDP in these two years fell in absolute terms. The sharp deterioration of economic circumstances and the security environment demanded adjustments in policy and reflection on the direction of changes needed in the structure of the economy. The multifaceted crisis India was facing in the mid-sixties demanded a politically self-assured leadership. However, it was precisely at this difficult time that India lost two Prime Ministers, leading to loosening of the political structure and particularly the governmental decisionmaking process.

Period: 1965–66 to 1973–74

The impact of adverse circumstances brought into view two principal weaknesses of the economic strategy which had been followed. One was the intersectoral imbalance between agriculture and industry, and the other was the underestimation of foreign aid requirements. It became clear that some changes in policy were required to make the plans more viable.

The relative neglect of agriculture, which had become feasible because of the availability of U.S. Public Law 480 supplies, was sought to be rectified with the introduction and spread of new seed-cum-fertilizer technology made possible by breakthroughs in research in plant genetics just around that time. The adoption of new agricultural technology combined with increased investment in irrigation and incentive farm prices was a major shift of policy.

The main adjustment to lower levels of foreign aid was made by economizing on imports and implicitly therefore by reducing the aggregate and sectoral growth targets. There were at the same time other shifts of emphasis in policy to encourage growth. These shifts covered a wide range: a greater role for price incentives, relaxation of some controls on the private sector to enable it to play a larger part in the economy and a greater effort at export promotion. Resources were concentrated on the completion of the ongoing and quick-yielding projects of shorter maturity. This was the doctrine of growth with stability.

The longer-term planning exercise was suspended while three Annual Plans were executed with a view to consolidating the short-run gains before the next phase of growth could be initiated. For that phase, preparations had to be made for mobilization of resources and setting an appropriate policy environment. But the general direction of policy was towards the strengthening of the process of liberalization that had been initiated under the stress of circumstances. The decision to devalue the rupee in 1966, which was not meant merely to correct the overvaluation of the rupee, was expected to reinforce this process. Around the decision was also woven an aid package that was expected to underwrite the liberalization program and to enable the country to dismantle much of the regulatory system, especially in the area of trade and industry policies.

In the event, however, devaluation did not push up the exports as its proponents had hoped. The export earnings for 1966–67 declined in 1967 by 8 percent. In 1968–69 they were a mere 4 percent above the level of 1964–65.[3] Nor did the aid package that was to accompany the decision materialize. The economic analysis on which the decision was based turned out to be off the mark as did the economic diplomacy on the question of aid. The straits to which the Government was reduced are described in a Finance Ministry note to the members of Parliament explaining why the decision to devalue the rupee had to be taken. The note said that

the action could not be postponed as all further aid negotiations hinged on it. It is extremely doubtful whether, without demonstrable evidence of our determination and capacity to push up our exports and improve the internal viability of our economy, we shall continue to get external credits. Particularly as we are already at a stage when we have to incur fresh debts in order to pay off old ones. Without reasonable prospects of aid forthcoming on the

scale contemplated by us, the finalization of the Fourth Plan will be still
further postponed.[4]

Evidently the mood of the donors had changed. It was no longer the
mood of the early sixties when they had endorsed the general framework
and priorities of the Third Plan before it commenced and made a
declaration of intent to provide on soft terms the foreign exchange for
the gap in the resource budget.[5] The deterioration on the foreign aid
front in the wake of devaluation was indicated by the decline in aid from
U.S. $1.3 billion in 1965–66 to under $1 billion in 1967–68. The anticlimax
to the high expectation of aid was reached in 1972–73 when there was
an outflow of $120 million as a result of the famous "Nixon tilt." Thus
finally ended the effort to mobilize aid to do away with aid after "crossing
the hump" as it was called at that time.

The immediate economic consequences and political fallout of the
devaluation episode were disastrous. Worse than that, it cast a long shadow
on economic policymaking in the country. The formulation of the Fourth
Plan (1969–74) had to be postponed till 1969. The interval as noted
earlier was covered with three annual Plans, popularly described as the
"Plan holiday" period.

The Plan holiday, however, coinciding as it did with rapid changes in
the political leadership at the Center and in several States, had an important
political impact. The Nehruvian consensus on the management of the
long-run course of the economy broke down in the wake of political
fragmentation after the general election of 1967 and more particularly
after the split in the Congress Party in 1969. In the political rivalry that
followed the party split, economic policies became a major arena of the
political battles.

The disappointment caused by slow growth, growing population pressure
and rising unemployment had generated a widespread feeling that poverty
could not be reduced as a by-product of the normal growth of the economy.
As early as 1962 the Planning Commission had prepared a paper on the
"implications of planning for a Minimum Level of living" which directed
attention to the issues of poverty alleviation. But it was in the political
turmoil five years later that a direct assault on poverty acquired strong
political support, especially among the left-leaning sections of the Congress
Party and their allies.[6] Their demands more than anticipated what later
in the seventies became a general disappointment with the "trickle down
theory" the world over. Their demands gave a radical turn to the
Government's economic policies in a manner that resulted in the reversal
of the earlier liberal trends. The consequences of the new turn were
mixed. While it stopped political fragmentation, it imposed certain political
imperatives on economic policy, making demands on additional resources
for short-term amelioration of chronic economic problems, alongside a
more stringent licensing policy which was adopted in 1970. The sentiment
against concentration of economic power translated itself into more
restrictive measures against big business: Large business houses were put
under the jurisdiction of the Monopolies Commission to monitor and
approve their new investment proposals.

The problems posed by the resource constraint, especially of foreign exchange, for the framers of the Fourth Plan were made more difficult by an uncertain political situation. The Plan went through several versions but the planners failed, for lack of political support, to find any viable solution to the resource constraint. Nor did the Planning Commission come up with a set of policies that would have yielded a higher growth rate by the improved use of available resources such as those locked up in the public sector. It suffered from a kind of schizophrenia: a split between an ideological longing for economic mobilization associated with authoritarian regimes and a real democratic compulsion for conciliation and compromises. This created a hiatus between promise and performance and between policy and implementation.

In its basic approach the Fourth Plan was not much different from its predecessors. It drew up its resource position on the usual optimistic assumptions and postulated a growth rate of 5.5 percent per annum. Not unexpectedly, the rate hovered between 3 percent and 3.5 percent per annum. The target rate had to be revised downwards in a mid-term appraisal. Thus the eight-year period, i.e., the three years of Plan holiday and the Fourth Plan period, did not show an improvement in the performance of the economy. In fact, some key indicators showed deceleration which was particularly marked in gross domestic as well as fixed capital formation and GDP originating in the manufacturing sector. From 1966 to 1970 the real public investment declined even in·absolute terms. Thus, not only was growth not picking up but the bases for future growth were in fact getting eroded. The most notable exception to this gloomy picture was provided by agriculture which registered improvement in its growth performance, particularly in food grain production.[7]

To conclude the assessment of this period it can be said that disappointment with aid and aid givers introduced an added element of realism and caution into Indian policies. The current account deficit was significantly reduced and, to a greater effect, the imports of food grains were brought down from their earlier high levels. These results gave substance to the political stance of "self-reliance." The economic costs of the adjustment to lower levels of foreign exchange availability were apparent in terms of deceleration of economic growth and of employment.

Period: 1973–74 to 1984–85

We now turn to the third and the last phase. Before the Fourth Plan was completed, India had to face the Bangladesh crisis of 1971. This was followed by the drought in 1972 and the first oil shock in 1973. The sharp increase in inflation and the consequent political turmoil exacerbated the country's formidable development problems and complicated the preparation of the Fifth Plan (1975–80). Although the Plan was formulated with the usual 5.5 percent per annum target growth rate, it was overshadowed by the compelling necessities of short-term adjustments even before its implementation. Keeping the balance of payments manageable, curbing inflation and preventing drastic cuts in the investment programs became the dominant concerns of policy.

The sudden deterioration in the balance of payments was handled with the help of large drawings on the International Monetary Fund, including the Fund's Oil Facility, and larger aid from the India consortium and the World Bank supplemented by oil purchases on deferred payment, a million-ton wheat loan from the Soviet Union and an export promotion drive.[8] The export drive yielded handsome results: an over 20 percent growth rate (7–8 percent in volume terms) from 1973–74 to 1977–78: an impressive performance by Indian standards. The export earnings plus the unforeseen expatriate remittances played a key role in sustaining the balance of payments during this period. Indeed, for a couple of years, 1976–77 and 1977–78, a surplus emerged in the current account which encouraged the Government to take measures to liberalize imports and reduce controls.

Inflation, which had reached an annual rate of 23 percent in 1973–74 and escalated further to about 30 percent by the middle of 1974, became politically unacceptable. Consequently, a two-pronged attack was vigorously mounted on it. This consisted of an effort to increase essential commodities in short supply, on the one hand, and strong measures to curb demand, on the other. These measures were further helped by a bumper crop. The anti-inflation measures proved very successful. At the end of January 1976, wholesale prices were 8 percent below the previous year. The effective control of domestic inflation, well below the rate of international inflation, had also a favorable effect on export growth.

Thus, by 1976–77 the economy had adjusted to the oil price hike and other disturbances attendant on it. The effort at export promotion had succeeded. And more than that, while keeping imports at the same level, in volume terms, the GDP growth rate accelerated. Compared to other oil-importing countries, India handled the crisis reasonably well and its policymakers could think of steering the economy in a longer term perspective. In fact the investment rate went up from 18.1 percent to 22.6 percent between 1975–76 and 1978–79 in constant terms. But then came the second oil price hike in 1979, followed in the early 1980s by the severest recession in the world economy since the Great Depression. Once again, the adverse impact of the new oil price hike was compounded by a severe drought. However, the impact on the balance of payments of further deterioration in the terms of trade and the need to import some food grains was moderated by increases in expatriate remittances. But more than that, the balance of payments was restored to manageable limits by import substitution in two very important commodities: food grains and petroleum.

Had India's terms of trade not deteriorated sharply during the period between the two oil shocks, its capacity to import and to accelerate growth would have improved significantly. Even so, the Sixth Plan (1980–85) was by and large successful. GDP increased at the annual rate of 5.5 percent for the Plan period (target 5.2 percent). The growth rate is somewhat exaggerated because the base year (1979–80) was a drought year and therefore one of poor performance. However, if we make allowance for this, the growth rate was around 4.5 percent a year, which is a percentage point above the traditional growth rate of about 3.5 percent. Even for the decade of the Fifth and Sixth Plan, the actual growth rate has been about a percentage point above the traditional level.[9]

Even more important than the improvement in the aggregate growth rate are the changes in some key sectors of the economy. Agriculture appears to have become more resilient and less vulnerable to bad weather. There was also a marked increase in the output of petroleum, power generation, use of natural gas, cement, fertilizer and coal. During the Sixth Plan period there was also some decline in the incidence of poverty. According to the Planning Commission, the percentage of people below the poverty line declined from 48.3 percent in 1977–78 to 37.4 percent in 1985.[10] There is, however, some misplaced emphasis about the causes for this decline. The credit for this is given to expanded programs of the Integrated Rural Development Program and other antipoverty programs. But there is considerable evidence to suggest that, apart from some useful elements in these programs their contribution to employment expansion is limited and their financial and administrative costs are heavy. The decline in the incidence of poverty is perhaps better explained by the remarkable progress made by agriculture whose growth exceeded the target of 3.8 percent.

This generally creditable performance is lessened by that of the manufacturing sector, which has never really regained the momentum it lost in the mid-sixties. During the Sixth Plan period this sector grew at a meager 4.3 percent rate, well below the modest target of 6.5 percent set in the Plan. All in all, the Sixth Plan can be said to have marked a transition to a slightly higher growth path for the Indian economy.

A more important, and hopefully more enduring, contribution of the Sixth Plan may turn out to be the confidence it has given the Government to pursue more consistently the policy changes that were made under the compulsion of circumstances brought about by external turbulence, particularly those emanating from the two oil shocks.

An Overall Assessment

In the context of the development experience of India as narrated above, what have been its achievements and failures? Given the multiple objectives of planned economic development, it is not possible to draw up a balance sheet of its achievements and failures which would be acceptable to all. The task is made even more complicated by the fact that in the course of the last three-and-a-half decades there has been a constant need to arrange and rearrange priorities between development objectives to adjust to circumstances as they evolved. Some of the circumstances were no doubt the result of policy failure, but there were other circumstances over which the policymakers had no control but which were even more unsettling. Nevertheless, some of the more obvious achievements and equally obvious failures may be noted without attempting to strike a balance.

The most impressive achievements have been in the field of agricultural development, in the rising rate of domestic savings and in the creation of a large pool of skilled manpower.

Agricultural production has moved to a higher growth path in the 1980s compared to the 1970s, from 2 percent to about 3 percent, using three-year moving averages. Expansion of irrigation has made agricultural growth less vulnerable to the vagaries of monsoons. Dependence on large-scale imports of food grains has been almost eliminated, and large, perhaps too large, grain reserves built up. Agricultural development has also directly helped in alleviating poverty since two-thirds of the poor derive their income from this sector.

Against these successes are to be noted the problems that remain. Agricultural performance has suffered from imbalances in production between rice and wheat and between cereals and pulses as wheat output expanded more rapidly than rice output and cereals grew more rapidly than pulses. These imbalances are further reflected between States and regions. These are serious problems and constitute the major development issues to be faced now. Better management of agriculture, particularly the removal of the imbalances, will have far-reaching effects on India's income growth and eradication of poverty and even on the balance of payments if efficient import substitution takes place in oil seeds, which is currently a heavy item of imports.

The domestic savings rate has steadily increased in the last three decades. In the seventies the rate accelerated sharply. From 10 percent in the early 1950s the rate climbed to over 24 percent in 1978–79 and was over 22 percent in 1984–85. The data on savings are not entirely reliable nor is there a wholly satisfactory explanation for the increase in the savings rate. It is also true that a substantial percentage of the household-sector savings, which are estimated in the Seventh Plan (1985–90) to constitute 71.5 percent of the total savings, consist of physical asset formation in the household sector itself and are not therefore available for development elsewhere in the economy. But they constitute savings nonetheless. Furthermore, the physical component is a declining proportion of the total savings. In comparison with other low-income countries, barring China, the Indian achievement has been very impressive.

An important feature of the Indian Plans right from the beginning has been the attention paid to the creation of skilled manpower needed for the modernization of the economy. Large investments have been made in higher education, technical training, engineering institutions and scientific research laboratories. As a result, a vast pool of skilled manpower, trained in a wide variety of skills, has come into existence. In fact, the supply has outstripped the demand and some of the best trained leave the country and become part of the brain drain. Owing to the slow growth of the economy and even slower rate of technological progress, this asset has not been fully used. But if the modernization of the economy is to take place as envisaged in the Seventh Plan and as indicated by Government pronouncements, it is a great asset available to India, unlike many other developing countries.

We now turn to the shadow side of the Indian development process: areas of relative failure. The performance of Indian industry in terms of growth and employment generation has been very disappointing. The emphasis given to the capital goods sector in the original Indian strategy was based, among other things, on the expectation that once this sector was in place, the pace of industrialization would quicken. Instead, after the Third Plan or mid-sixties, the pace slowed and has not picked up in any substantial way since then. There has been an extensive debate on this question in India and it is now generally agreed that besides the infrastructural constraints arising out of the slowdown in public investment, industrial growth has been inhibited by policies which seek to serve multiple objectives and rely on excessive regulations and controls.

Another area in which efforts have not met with adequate success has been that of family planning, even though Indian planners had recognized right at the beginning a potential population problem. The family planning program started in 1951 with a narrow clinical approach which was later broadened into an extension education approach. It is only in the late seventies that the program developed into a service network in which family planning services are combined with overall health services, particularly maternal and child health care.

India's own experience in the State of Kerala has demonstrated the effectiveness of socioeconomic factors like health, education and literacy programs, particularly of women, in reducing fertility and curbing population growth. But the large and densely populated states like Uttar Pradesh, Madhya Pradesh and Bihar are the States where progress in social development has been the least.

During the 1970s the birth rate declined from 40 to 34 per 1,000 but in recent years it has stagnated around 33.[11] An integrated family program has been worked out and a "two child" family norm has been adopted at the policy level and a revised strategy is being evolved. But the effectiveness of the strategy is yet to be demonstrated, particularly in the socially backward States.

Current Issues

Against the background of successes and failures as noted above we now turn to the current policy stance of the Government. We first describe the policy measures adopted or promised and then attempt an evaluation of these measures.

Government Initiatives

With small beginnings in policy changes required to absorb the first oil shock to experiments with some import liberalization since the early 1980s, the process of economic reform has gathered momentum. The Government set up several committees to examine its fiscal, monetary, industrial and trade policies.[12] The general outcome of their findings and recommendations can perhaps be simply expressed in two sets of inter-related propositions.

1. Requirements for accelerating growth:

a. Accelerated growth will require increased imports.

b. Owing to decreases in concessional aid and risks of onerous debt burdens connected with large-scale commercial borrowing, it is absolutely necessary to increase exports to pay for increased imports.

c. To increase exports it is necessary to enhance the competitive advantage of exportables.

d. The competitive advantage for exportables requires changes in industrial, trade and fiscal policies.

2. *The domestic resource situation:*

a. The Government budget is no longer a source of finance for investment. Current revenues are less than current expenditure because of sharp increases on account of defense, subsidies and interest payments.

b. Reducing defense expenditure is not an option available to the Government.

c. Subsidies, especially the larger food and fertilizer subsidies, can be reduced only very gradually to avoid major social and political upsets.

d. The only way, therefore, to raise additional resources for increasing the growth rate to even a modest 5 percent level as envisaged for the Seventh Plan is to make the tax system more responsive and to make the public sector enterprises generate resources through greater efficiency.

Apart from the rationale for policy changes as stated above, an additional factor of liberalization is that some domestic controls simply fail to achieve their stated objectives.

On the basis of an extensive policy review the Government has started a process of economic reform. Since the budget of 1985–86 some changes in policy have been introduced and several others announced in broad terms in the statement on Long Term Fiscal Policy and in the Seventh Plan document. The major premise in the reform is based on the consideration that since the investment rate can be raised only marginally, the acceleration in growth has to be squeezed out through greater efficiency in the use of capital and other resources. And the sector that has to lead this acceleration is the industrial sector.

It is now widely recognized that the regulatory regime imposed on industry has lasted much longer than was required and that public sector enterprises which control a major part of investment in industry and infrastructure have failed to "augment the revenues of the State and provide resources for further development in fresh fields" as was expected in the Industrial Policy Resolution of the Government of India adopted in 1956.

The broad purpose of policy changes now is to move away from directives, regulations and controls to a greater role for market incentives and to indirect policy instruments as against direct physical controls. Thus restrictions on the use and expansion of industrial capacities, price controls and reservation of production of certain commodities in favor of small-scale industries are being relaxed. Greater importance is now being attached to productivity, competitiveness and technological modernization with a view to promoting more rapid growth of manufactured exports. Similarly, quantitative limits on imports are being replaced by tariffs to expose domestic industry to a reasonable amount of external competition.[13] Some more items have also been added to the open general license.

In view of the resource constraint limiting the expansion of the public sector, the private sector is expected to play a greater role than in the past in industrial development. A number of industries have been freed from the requirement of licensing and the number of big business houses whose growth is restricted under the Monopolies and Restricted Trade Practices Act has been reduced. New fields such as electronics and communications have been opened for the private sector. Enlarged private participation is now allowed in restricted sectors such as refineries, petrochemicals, oil explorations and steel. The number of industries not subject to licensing has been increased and more incentives have been offered to promote exports.

Several measures have been taken to rationalize the tax system and to improve its buoyancy, efficiency and administration. Measures are also being taken to reduce tax evasion and tax exemptions which are no longer necessary. These changes along with others to reduce the multiplicity of rates for direct taxation, depreciation, etc., are expected not only to make tax administration easier and simpler but also to help remove some of its distorting economic effects. To help improve the administration of the tax system and also build a more predictable climate for investment, the tax rates are to be stable for at least for five years of the Seventh Plan.

Similarly reform has been undertaken in the area of indirect taxes, i.e., excise and import duties which provide the bulk of Government revenues. The Government recognizes that the "multiplicity of forms in which excise duties are levied complicates the structure, makes it very difficult to assess the final burden and requires elaborate accounting and monitoring."[14] The complicated system of exemptions and deductions provided a fertile ground for corruption and tax evasion.

Several steps have been taken to bring order in this chaotic system. The number of basic rates in the Central excise has been reduced. A modified value-added tax has been introduced covering a large segment of industry in order to reduce the cascading effect of excise duties by relieving inputs from excise and countervailing duties. The coverage of the value-added tax will presumably be extended after experience is gained in the current exercise. The concessions in excise duties given to small-scale industries are also likely to be rationalized into some sort of a uniform system.

A major piece of reform has been in the field of the indirect taxes on imports. Its object, as noted earlier, is to reduce the use of discretionary quantitative controls and the high levels of protection and to strengthen the impact of export incentives. A simpler and more uniform tariff structure with only a few basic rates is being set up to replace the present multiplicity of rates. This is expected to improve resource allocation and efficiency in the economy, transfer economic rents from the present recipients to the Government and reduce the scope for misclassification and therefore for corruption. The lower tariffs should also discourage smuggling.

Besides better tax yields as a result of the tax reform, the Government expects to mobilize additional resources for the Seventh Plan by increasing its nontax revenues. This expectation is based on: (1) better performance of public sector enterprises and (2) control of nondevelopmental current expenditure, particularly expenditure incurred on account of interest payments and subsidies. According to the Long Term Fiscal Policy calculations the contribution of public sector undertakings is expected to be 3.6 percent of the GDP projections of the Seventh Plan. This target compares with 2.1 percent of the likely actuals for the Sixth Plan. A successful realization of this target assumes an unprecedented increase in the efficiency of the public sector in just five years. So far, the bulk of this sector has been incurring losses. The only notable exception has been oil companies. It is not clear how this situation will change as dramatically as is implicitly assumed in the estimates of the Planning Commission.

Profitability in the public sector has been low for several reasons. Besides the low demand for many of its products arising out of cutbacks in public investment and some supply bottlenecks such as power, public sector profitability has suffered from uneconomic pricing policies and political interference in management. Public sector profitability is further eroded by its being saddled with a much larger labor force than is required and the unviable units which the Government has been taking over from the private sector from time to time.

To make the public sector generate resources for development will be an operation which will involve not merely change in price policy and management practices but also political readjustments. We will come back to this question in the latter part of the chapter.

If there are doubts about the generation of additional resources from the public sector for the Plan, is it possible to bring down the growth of non-Plan expenditure or current expenditures? This expenditure has risen both absolutely and relative to GDP in recent years—from an average of 17.7 percent in 1977 to 19.7 percent in 1984–85. Subsidies and interest payments are principally responsible for this. The list of subsidies is long but food and fertilizer subsidies are the most important and most rapidly growing ones. So far no policy has emerged on how to tackle these questions. The Seventh Plan suggests in general terms the need for formulation of an adequate expenditure policy which will lay down priorities, hold certain items of expenditure as a constant percentage of GDP and allow only items of high priority to increase relative to GDP. This again is an area where important political questions have to be sorted out if a feasible policy is to emerge. These problems are discussed in the latter part of this chapter.

The other item in the non-Plan expenditure which has emerged as a major element in current expenditure is interest payments. In 1984–85 these payments were 3.0 percent of GDP as against 1.7 percent in 1975–76. The rise is due to the increase in the absolute size of the debt and the increase in the interest rates. Since the market borrowings are not expected to decline in the Seventh Plan, the burden of interest payments on the

Central budget will not lessen. Indeed it may increase still further if the Government agrees to pay market rates of interest on its borrowings.

We now turn to the prospects of the State Governments in mobilizing additional resources for the Plan. In their case too, success will depend on their will and ability to improve the financial performance of their public sector enterprises, particularly those supplying irrigation water and electricity. The Planning Commission hopes that water rates will be reviewed periodically "so that they are adequate to meet the cost of operation and maintenance of providing a reasonable return on investment."[15] While the rates vary from State to State, they are on the whole so low that they will have to be increased very steeply if the expectation of the Commission is to be met. The same is the case with electricity rates. Here too the performance varies from State to State. But if the performance of the poorly run State Electricity Boards could be raised to the level of the best-run boards, the resources generated by them for their States would increase significantly. But to reverse the trend of rising losses in these enterprises is more than a question of revising water rates and electricity tariffs and improving the management of these operations. It is also a political question because the current practices benefit certain entrenched interests in the governmental and administrative structures of these States. Thus the projections of the Planning Commission are based on assumptions some of which implicitly assume shifts in political power in the States.

Prospects for Recent Policy Initiatives

We have not covered all the initiatives that have been taken recently by the Government to reorient its economic policies to promote greater efficiency and higher growth in the economy. We have confined the narration to some changes in industry, trade and fiscal policies and the proposed measures to mobilize resources for the Plan. But even the partial account does indicate how earnest the Government is to revamp its economic policies. But how far will it go to make a success of the exercise it has undertaken? Obviously a lot will depend on how committed it is to the new policies, on how efficient it is in executing them and, above all, on how much political support it is able to generate in their favor.

An important feature of the new policies is that they have not been revealed as a single package so that they could be judged as a whole. There is no self-contained statement which would relate the changes being effected to their economic consequences and to each other. For that, one has to put together and interpret different measures adopted in the last two budgets and those sketched out in broad terms in the Long Term Fiscal Policy and the Seventh Plan documents.

Bearing in mind the fate of the earlier attempt at policy changes, one can understand and sympathize with the tentative and experimental manner in which individual policies are being presented and implemented. However, this has imposed on the Government a defensive posture, and its policy initiatives are being described as piecemeal, hesitant and ad hoc. Every single policy measure has to be justified within its own limited context and not in a broader perspective which could be done only in a larger integrated policy framework. A fuller and bolder reform program articulated in greater detail and related to overall goals would not only have led to greater clarity in the public mind but would have probably secured much greater political support for the reforms. It would also have brought out the true nature of political resistance to the reforms. To illustrate, the budget of 1985–86 which announced reductions in tax rates on income and wealth was attacked as a rich man's budget while the significant increase in the funding of antipoverty programs came in the budget of 1986–87 and was with some plausibility described by the critics as a sop to the poor and as a contrary signal by some supporters of the reforms who believe that these programs are not cost effective.

To present the reforms as a pragmatic necessity is right up to a point, but to avoid a forthright critique of some of the old policies and institutions is to hand over the ideological weapons to the critics of the reforms. They do not have to suggest solutions to the problems; in order to defend the status quo, they persist in complaining of a betrayal of old ideology. Indeed, for some of them the failure of old policies seems to have enhanced their political appeal.

The case for reforms in India is based on the ground that the new policies will accelerate growth, promote employment and reduce poverty without weakening the country politically or in any other sense. Therefore the new or revised policies have a better chance of achieving the original goals which the nation had set for itself.

A reform of the kind under way involves several interest groups which have benefited in the past and stand to lose if the reforms are pursued vigorously. Their attack on the reforms so far has been on ideological grounds and it has been met by denials or silence. Economic reforms must have a positive political appeal and a political strategy to gain acceptance. Without such a strategy, the reforms will end up with some minor changes and marginal improvements or be even abandoned if they run into transitional problems like a sudden deterioration in the balance of payments.

For illustration, let us take the case of some interest groups that might have to surrender some of their economic privileges in the larger interest of the economy.

It has been indicated that there is a need for a fresh look at the policy of reserving a large number of items of production for the small-scale sector. The review has not taken place so far. But if and when it is undertaken, it is likely to be of a minor nature unless a powerful case is made for it. Small industry has spawned a vast complex of interests thanks to indiscriminate protective policies over and above the more legitimate developmental ones, and it is politically very powerful.

Again, the expectation that public sector enterprises would generate more resources than they actually had was a regular feature of the financial estimates in the past. For the first time now the estimates have been underlined with suggestions that might improve the financial performance of these enterprises. And they very well might if a more appropriate price policy is followed and management practices are improved.[16] But the combined impact of these measures is likely to be inadequate in the absence of the solution of the more serious problems that afflict them.

The public sector enterprises cannot show substantial improvements without facing the problem created by militant trade union leadership that has succeeded in generating a labor aristocracy, high wage islands and a work ethic which is antithetical to the normal concepts of productivity. It is encouraging to note Prime Minister Rajiv Gandhi's observation in Parliament that "Government would not allow the personal interests of trade union leaders to hold the country to ransom or to vitiate the country's interests and the investment of the people in the public sector." But the test will come when wage negotiations which have been pending for some time take place.

Likewise the new approach to sick units is better than the earlier one. During the last two years the Central Government has shown some resistance to the takeover of sick mills and passed the Sick Industries Act of 1985 to speed up the takeover, merger, rehabilitation or liquidation of such units. But the political and trade union pressure against closing down insolvent private sector companies continues unabated. To improve the performance of the public sector or to reduce the deadweight of sick units will not work without squarely facing some of these issues related to trade unions.

The dog-in-the-manger policies of trade union leadership have encouraged substitution of labor by capital and have therefore been a retarding factor in the growth of employment. But it has been difficult to resist the trade unions without a well-worked-out employment plan by the Government.

According to the Planning Commission, "the central element in the development strategy of the Seventh Plan is the generation of productive employment." At the end of the Seventh Plan, according to the Commission, employment will have increased sufficiently not only to offset the net additions to the labor force but also to reduce the backlog of unemployment for the first time in India. This is a shadowy part of the Commission's projections.[17] If the basis of these expectations were established more concretely and more convincingly, it would go some way in creating a favorable environment for more cooperative trade unionism. Without convincing evidence of a significant increase in employment opportunities it is difficult to change trade union attitudes and practices. Without the cooperation of the trade union leadership public sector performance can improve only marginally.

Again, the replacement of quantitative import restrictions with tariffs is a step in the right direction but the problems will arise when the tariffs are allowed to drop low enough to bite the high-cost domestic industry. The liberalization of imports so far has been mostly in noncompeting areas. But even so, the spokesmen of the capital goods industry have already started complaining against freer imports. Unless the consequence of freer imports on domestic industry are worked out in detail and anticipated consequences taken care of, there will always be a danger of sudden reversals of policy. There is no indication in the policies announced so far about any restructuring of industry that may be required in the wake of freer imports. If the economy is to move to a tariff-based and more competitive environment, the policies will have to be worked out beyond the first steps.

Thus, it is still unclear how far the reforms will go. A clear distinction is yet to be established between minor, though important and useful, corrections of past policies and the development of new policies.

While examining the question of mobilization of resources for the Seventh Plan, it has been noted that a vast potential is available to the States if they decide to raise water and electricity rates. If these rates were raised to the level that would yield a reasonable return on capital invested in these undertakings without imposing any hardship on the beneficiaries, the State resources will be augmented substantially and would enable the States to provide irrigation and power to the poorer farmer who cannot have these much-needed inputs for lack of resources. Minor revisions of these rates may reduce the losses somewhat and to that extent will no doubt be useful, but the real issues go beyond such tinkerings and touch on the political power structure, especially in large States like Uttar Pradesh and Bihar. Those who expect much greater resource mobilization in reality are asking for radical changes which will hurt the vested interests of the rich farmers and dominant peasant castes. It is their power rather than the supposed technical difficulties that have made the Governments in the past reluctant to impose an income tax on agricultural incomes or any other substitute of such a tax. There is no indication from the ruling Congress Party that it will make an effort to contain and curb their power. On the contrary, sacrifice of State revenues to favor the rich farmer continues as before. To illustrate, the Haryana Government proclaimed in a November 1986 newspaper advertisement that "the entire recovery on account of lining of water courses has been completely waived. This will mean a loss of Rs 113 crores (1130 millions) to the Government. However, this has been done in the *larger national interest*(!)" (emphasis added). The Haryana Government is not the only State government that indulges in such handouts.

The low-growth syndrome of India has benefited powerful interests spread over big farmers, small industrialists, trade union elite and several business groups operating in sheltered markets or trading in scarce commodities. Together they wield enormous political power and so far there is no countervailing force of sufficient strength to challenge them. To be sure, the new policies of the Government will, if successfully implemented, reach out and benefit those who have so far been bypassed by the development process and would widen the class base of the States and lead to a more meaningful radicalism than we have ever had so far. But that cannot be achieved if the economic reforms are looked upon as a administrative matters only.

On the purely economic front, the next few years that will mark the transition to new policies will be of crucial importance. The success or failure of the new policies will depend essentially upon what happens to the balance of payments in this period. The payments situation is dependent on several imponderables; deterioration in any one of them can widen the trade deficit. A slower growth of exports than envisaged, a decline in expatriate remittances or further decline in concessional aid flows can create a situation which will compel the Government to reduce imports and herald a retreat from the liberalization program. Contrariwise, improvement in the balance of payments, such as the recent fall in oil prices occasioned, will reduce the uncertainty and risks surrounding the new strategy.

So once again, after two decades, India's economic reforms have become crucially dependent on foreign exchange availability. This time the external environment for aid as well as trade is distinctly less favorable than the one that prevailed in the mid-sixties. The challenge for the Indian policymakers is therefore all the greater.

But if the balance of payments remains manageable and consistent with the requirements of the Seventh Plan growth rates, the industrial growth rate picks up substantially and the new agricultural technology spreads to the eastern region of India where the majority of the poor lives, reforms would gain much greater political acceptance. In a mutually reinforcing process of economic success and political desirability, the restructuring of high-cost industry and redeployment of displaced labor which are the necessary consequence of the reforms will become easier.

Notes

1. See P. N. Dhar, "Heavy Industry in a Growing Economy," in *A Decade of Economic Development and in India*, edited by M. R. Sinha (Bombay: Asian Studies Press, 1962), 74–79.

2. Growth rates are obtained by estimating semilog trend equations.

3. *Economic Survey, 1966–67* (New Delhi: Government of India, n.d.), 42; and *Fourth Five Year Plan 1969–74* (New Delhi: Government of India, Planning Commission, 1969), 93.

4. K. Sundaram, "Political Response to the 1966 Devaluation" *Economic and Political Weekly*, 2, no. 37 (9 September 1972).

5. See I. G. Patel, *Foreign Aid*, Lal Bahadur Shastri Memorial Lectures (New Delhi: Allied Publishers, 1968).

6. See the *Report of the AICC Panel* (New Delhi, 1969) and documents of Congress Forum for Socialist Action.

7. The index of food production (base trinium ending 1969–70), which was generally below 90 until 1966–67, reached a higher plateau of about 110 by the early seventies.

8. The export promotion drive consisted mainly of liberalization of industrial and import policies insofar as they related to export industries. These industries were allowed to increase their capacity automatically without prior permission. They were also given licenses automatically for the import of raw materials and components.

Additionally, the level of cash incentives was raised and extended to cover a larger number of products such as engineering goods, chemicals and allied products, synthetic fabrics and garments, coir, marine products, carpets, leather goods and processed foods. The export sector was also provided finance at concessional rates of interest.

Export control was modified through selective abolition of export licensing and simplification of procedure. The licensing formalities were abolished for nearly

200 out of 300 items subject to export licensing earlier. In the remaining cases the procedure was simplified.

For a summary of changes in trade policy in 1975, see *Report on Currency and Finance* vol. 1 (Bombay: Reserve Bank of India, 1975–76).

9. The growth rate estimated by semilog trend for the period 1950–51 to 1984–85 was a little over 3.5 percent.

10. *Seventh Five Year Plan 1985–90,* vol. 1 (New Delhi: Government of India, Planning Commission, 1985), 10.

11. *New Strategy for Family Planning* (New Delhi: Government of India, Ministry of Health and Family Welfare, 1986). See also, T. N. Krishanan, "Population Growth and Indian Planning" (Trivandrum: Centre for Development Studies, 1987, Mimeographed).

12. *Report of the Committee to Examine Principles of a Possible Shift from Physical to Financial Controls,* Narasimhan, Chairman (New Delhi: Government of India, 1985); *Report of the Committee on Trade Policies,* Hussain, Chairman (New Delhi: Government of India, Ministry of Commerce, 1984); *Report of the Committee to Review the Working of the Monetary System,* Chakravarty, Chairman (New Delhi: Reserve Bank of India, 1985); and *Long Term Fiscal Policy,* (New Delhi: Government of India, Ministry of Finance, 1985).

13. *Long Term Fiscal Policy.*

14. Ibid.

15. *Seventh Five Year Plan,* vol. 1.

16. For a discussion of the issues see *Administered Price Policy* (New Delhi: Government of India, Ministry of Finance, 1986).

17. *Seventh Five Year Plan,* vol. 2, chap. 5.

Statement:
Current Major Issues in India's Economic Policy
David Hopper

The issue confronting India now is how fast can India change policies that have evolved over forty years of independence without destroying the political balances of the country. This is one of the essential elements that both the political leadership as well as their economic advisors have to struggle with, and I think that P. N. Dhar has sketched, in his chapter in this volume, the challenges before these advisors.

From my vantage point, that of World Bank lending and the functioning of the consortium for assistance to India, I am obviously deeply concerned with the role of the foreign exchange constraint on Indian development. The foreign exchange constraint is not new, it was there right from the beginning of the Independence period. The First Five-Year Plan (1951–56) that India drew up, before the Malhalanobis Second Plan (1956–61), underscored foreign exchange. Those plans that were drawn in the Malhalanobis mode—the Second, Third (1961–66) and the first draft of the Fourth Plan (1969–74)—had a very real focus on this issue of the foreign exchange constraint. Indeed, it is interesting to note that it was the very deep foreign exchange crisis, following the drought of 1957, that led to the founding of the India consortium. It led also to a massive expansion in the use of the U.S. Public Law 480, which had been on the books before, to provide food aid to India, and it led ultimately in 1960 to the founding of the International Development Association (IDA) in order to provide the poorest countries with concessional assistance from one of the World Bank affiliates.

Until the early 1980s, 1981 or 1982, very large concessional capital transfers to India continued. It was these concessional capital transfers that permitted India to sustain a level of investment and pursue a level of policies which insured at least the lower level of economic growth, which Raj Krishna called the Hindu rate of growth, of around 3.5 or 3.8 percent throughout the period of the 1970s. In 1981 India was receiving 1.6 billion dollars from the World Bank through the IDA concessional window. The total generated from the consortium at that time in concessional resources transferred to India was very close to 2.8 billion dollars. International Bank for Reconstruction and Development (IBRD) lending, that is, World Bank hard-window lending to India, in 1981 was about 450 million dollars. In other words, this represented a transfer arrangement of primarily concessional lending. In contrast, in 1987 India will receive about 600 million dollars from the IDA window, that is, the concessional window, and about 1.7 or 1.8 billion dollars from the IBRD window. The total consortium support for India will approach 4 billion dollars. But in terms of the net aid transfer, that is, net of repayments, the consortium by coming through with about a billion or a billion and a half in new commitments will transfer only between 300 and 500 million dollars in net terms.

We are indeed deeply concerned in the World Bank with the foreign exchange constraint; we are deeply concerned with the hardening of terms that India now confronts in her handling of external debt. And this logically leads us to an examination of the other sources of foreign exchange for India. We are troubled by the potential decline in remittances. Should these begin to fall off, one of the unexpected sources of assistance to India's foreign exchange budget would be lost. India *will* benefit from lower oil prices, but simultaneously the commodities markets have tightened, India's terms of trade in that area have declined, and many of the major importing industrial countries have toughened their protectionist stances.

So the balances that we are focused on lead us primarily to examine the export potential of India. This is where the World Bank is directing its attention and our prescription for raising exports is not a prescription with which anyone that I have ever met from the Government of India would disagree. Indeed, we give this prescription to almost every country with which we are dealing.

But while it is easy to say, "Exports must rise," and, "India has lost its position in the world market," the fact remains that we do not have any specific solutions for implementing an export drive. Although we have assisted ICICI, the industrial credit organization in India, with resources to provide a special window for exporters, we find that resources provided to that window are not moving substantially. But it is clear, I think, from many cursory analyses of the export scene in India that the exports will have to come from industry, that these exports will have to be very much based upon a regearing of the capital structure of Indian industry, that India has fallen substantially behind in its technology and that the quality of Indian products finds difficult acceptance in most international markets. The interlock of regulations, the interlock of Government controls over the transfers and technological agreements, all contribute greatly to the sluggishness of India's export industry. While we cannot but applaud the lowering of tariffs and the improvement of competition in India, we are deeply concerned with the failure of the Government to look after the infrastructure area and with the Government's continued support of a regulatory environment which looks to be antithetical to expansion in the industrial field and particularly to expansion in the export area.

The agriculture picture appears to be very much in hand. I believe that it will be at least another twenty, perhaps thirty, years before Indian agriculture again begins to brush against the present technological ceiling. As long as investments continue to be made and irrigation expanded, as long as the efficiency in distribution of agricultural inputs and in marketed products are handled, I think India can turn its attention to the development of the other sectors.

Transport, telecommunications and energy (at least energy beyond electricity) are going to *have* to command major investments from the Government in the future. But, in addition, it is vital to remove, in my view, the political interventions that are stifling entrepreneurship in India: to provide greater market access and greater market play. These have to be taken, however, subject to my very first question, namely, how fast can India move without destroying the political balances which provide stability to the nation.

PART TWO

Agriculture and Food

2

Regional Dimension
of Indian Agriculture

Yoginder K. Alagh

This chapter presents estimates of the level of Indian agricultural development and productivity growth with district-, regional- and State-level estimates. It also discusses the factors associated with such growth and speculates on possible causes of the observed developments.

District-Level Agricultural Performance

Table 2.1 shows that in the triennium centered on 1971–72 approximately one-sixth of the districts of India showed productivity levels of above Rs 1,500 per hectare. These districts accounted for a little over a quarter of the agricultural output of India and roughly two-fifths of most purchased inputs. Another one-quarter of the districts were at productivity levels between Rs 1,000 and Rs 1,500 per hectare and accounted for not very dissimilar fractions of output and inputs. The balance of the districts accounted for 60 percent of the cropped area, 40 percent of the output and less than that percentage of all purchased inputs. Table 2.2 shows that districts which accounted for a little less than a third of the districts of India, accounting for roughly the same amount of harvested area, grew above 3 percent per annum in the period 1962–63 to 1971–72. These districts accounted for a little less than two-fifths of agricultural output and around two-fifths of most purchased inputs. There was positive growth in another two-fifths of districts in this period, but input intensities were somewhat lower. The remaining districts had negative growth.

In the sixties a number of studies had documented the causal role of irrigation in spearheading the Green Revolution. Irrigation released the land constraint by bringing additional land under cultivation and by increasing double cropping. It permitted the introduction of the high-yielding varieties (HYVs) which again on account of their photoinsensitivity led to shorter duration crops and therefore increases in cropping intensity. Fertilizer expansion was an associated variable. The spread of this HYV/

irrigation/fertilizer process was initially restricted as Tables 2.1 and 2.2 show.

A number of disaggregated studies had estimated HYV/irrigation/fertilizer impacts. Mukhopadhyay's[1] exhaustive and detailed study of production functions for the agricultural sector in eight wheat regions used variance-covariance analysis and dummy variables to introduce "region" and "time" effects. He introduced a model developed by Balestra and Nerlove, in which the space and time effects were separated from the residual term estimated by ordinary least squares estimates of production function from pooled cross-section and time series data. Mukhopadhyay used for this purpose standard econometric methods of transforming the original variables through a priori specification of a "systematic" compound (space or time effect) of the residual in addition to the "random" component and reestimating the production function after purging the original variables of the "systematic" effect. Mukhopadhyay used aggregate crop output as the dependent variable and cultivated area, irrigated area, fertilizers, tractors, literate labor and illiterate labor as independent variables. Data were for seventy-two districts divided into eight wheat regions and for the period 1959–60 to 1968–69. His main empirical finding was that:

It appears that the coefficients of only land, irrigation and fertilizer remain significantly non-zero at 5 percent level of confidence in the regression on transformed variables. Therefore, in the cross-section time series context of these data, it is difficult to derive any firm conclusion about the quantitative contribution of tractors, education or labor to aggregate output.[2]

Using quadratic (instead of Cobb-Douglas production functions), Mukhopadhyay found another interesting result, namely,

It may be noted that the coefficient for irrigation-fertilizer interaction is both positive and significant. This is consistent with recent changes in Indian agriculture, where new high yielding varieties have been grown; where irrigation facilities are available, because they require both assured water supply and fertilizer application.[3]

The JNU-PPD study completed by Bhalla and Alagh[4] had also documented this role of irrigation in agricultural development. Using cross-section district-level data for the triennium centered on 1971–72, they estimated the following elasticities for agricultural productivity (Table 2.3).

On account of multi-collinearity, the estimates are sensitive to the variables excluded. (See the appendix.) The elasticity of agricultural productivity with reference to irrigation intensity is estimated between 0.15 and 0.27, if the fertilizer variable is excluded. The elasticity of agricultural productivity with reference to cropping intensity is also estimated between 2.31 and 3.19. Further work which estimates parameters through more completely specified systems, first estimating cropping intensity as a function of irrigation and then using estimated cropping intensity figures to estimate land productivity, would improve the estimates.

These features of Indian agricultural experience in the early 1970s were used for Indian agricultural planning. Thus the "Agricultural Sub-Model" of the Fifth Five-Year Plan (1974–79) prepared in 1975 argued:

> that State level data corroborates the findings of earlier disaggregative studies that in certain regions of the country foodgrains growth is primarily explained by factors, such as irrigation or multiple cropping, while in other pockets it is due to the water-seed-fertilizers technology.[5]

and again:

> In the methodology used in this paper, growth of gross irrigated area is also given a critical role in determining the growth of gross cropped area as in the National Commission on Agriculture's Report. . . . For the country as a whole and for all crops it was estimated that a one per cent increase in irrigated area would lead to a 0.20 per cent increase in gross cropped area. . . . The estimate of increase in gross cropped area which is derived from the emphasis on irrigation, using past behavior as indicated above would yield a growth rate of 0.8 per cent per annum in the Fifth Five Year Plan and upto 1980/81 and by about 0.6 per cent per annum upto 1988/89. Given the emphasis on the expansion of irrigation facilities, this estimate is considered to be feasible.[6]

The decade of the seventies witnessed encouraging trends of equalization of agricultural growth performance. In the period 1963–64 to 1971–72, 71 districts accounting for 26.78 percent of area recorded negative growth. However, in the period 1962–65 to 1975–78, only 16 districts accounting for 5.55 percent of area showed negative growth. (See Table 2.4.) This, of course, was a dramatic improvement. Correspondingly, the number of districts showing growth rates between 1.5 percent to 4.5 percent increased from 106 to 162, accounting for 54.24 percent of the area as compared to only 33.47 percent earlier. Districts falling in this modal growth class now account for more than half (51.95 percent) of aggregate agricultural output as compared to around a third (36.48 percent) earlier. The equally interesting aspect of this growth was that it was taking place in regions which were earlier thought of as particularly disadvantaged. Eastern Uttar Pradesh and adjoining areas had been characterized as an area where perverse institutional conditions would hold back growth, and in fact had shown low or negative growth in the period 1963–71, but in the period 1963–76 the following districts move into the 1.5 percent to 4.5 percent annual growth class: Jaunpur, Faizabad, Azamgarh, Barabanki, Varanasi, Bahraich, Sitapur and also Kheri, Unnao, Meerut, Aligarh, Bareiley, Bulandshahar, Gonda and Pratapgarh.[7] Similarly districts in Eastern and Central Rajasthan, for example, Bharatpur, Jaipur, Alwar, Tonk, Kota, Churu, Pali and Sirohi, now show vastly improved growth performance as also dry regions in Maharashtra, e.g., Kolhapur, Wardha, Nagpur, Chandrapur, Sangli, Buldhana, Ahmednagar, Aurangabad, Akola, Yeotmal, Dhulia, Satara, Parbhani, and districts like Medak and Nizamabad in

Andhra and Shimoga, Tumkur, Belgaum and Bidar in Karnataka. The geography of low agricultural productivity and hunger in India has, on the basis of earlier work by Bhalla and Alagh, been described by Kundu and Raza as follows:

One can easily identify three cores of high productivity: (i) Punjab, Haryana-Western Uttar Pradesh, (ii) deltaic West Bengal and (iii) coastal Andhra Pradesh, Tamilnadu, Kerala and coastal and eastern Karnataka. These cores are skirted by medium productivity regions. The areas of rain-fed agriculture in the case of south Deccan, the middle Ganga plains and the Mahanadi basin, Rarh cluster act as transitional zones between the two high productivity cores. The medium productivity zone of Konkan and of the Chattisgarh plains peters out in the aridity of Deccan that constitute the hungry belly of India.[8]

The above listing of districts which now show growth between 1.5 percent and 4.5 percent per annum shows that the geography of low agricultural productivity is now gradually changing. Growth is selectively diffusing in the Gangetic Plain and the Deccan dryland area. Table 2.5 shows that in constant prices eighty-four districts accounting for 25.62 percent of the cropped area show an agricultural productivity level of Rs 1,300 per hectare, or higher, in 1975–78 as compared to forty-eight districts accounting for 12.61 percent of the cropped area in 1962–65.

Regional-Level Performance

The "region" in this chapter is identified as the National Sample Survey (NSS) Region. The NSS regions were delineated in the early 1950s after careful studies of sociogeographic characteristics at the district and subregional level.[9] Changes in agricultural productivity at the NSS region level in the trienniums centered on 1963–64, 1971–72 and 1976–77 are presented in Table 2.6. Agricultural productivity growth higher than 1.5 percent on an annual compound basis has been estimated for the following dry or rain-fed regions with initial low productivity levels: Andhra Pradesh Inland Northern, Gujarat Plains Northern, Gujarat Dry Areas, Gujarat Saurashtra, all the regions of Karnataka, all the regions of Maharashtra, the North Eastern, South Eastern and Western regions of Rajasthan and the Himalayas, Central and Western regions of Uttar Pradesh. A number of low productivity regions, however, still had considerable balance of groundwater potential at the end of the period. Many dry or rain-fed regions in Andhra Pradesh, Maharashtra, Bihar and West Bengal still had available over 40 percent of their balance of groundwater reserves for irrigation purposes. As we shall see below, utilization of groundwater and irrigation is not only a source of output but employment growth in such areas.

The Planning Commission had used NSS data for person-day utilization of labor time and the number of agricultural workers for the Twenty-Seventh Round to estimate the demand for labor. Employment elasticities were estimated for both employment per hectare of land and per rupee of output, for developed and underdeveloped regions and for the country as a whole.[10] Developed regions were selected on a three-pronged criteria of high values of output per hectare, fertilizer consumed per hectare and gross irrigated area per hectare of gross cropped area. In the first place, the productivity per hectare for all the fifty-three regions was arranged in descending order and half of the maximum value was made as the cutout point, giving twenty-seven regions above this dividing point. Further, the regional data in respect of the other two variants were also arranged in descending order. From among these first twenty-seven regions it was found there were sixteen common regions which satisfied all the three criteria simultaneously and as such were termed commercially developed regions. The remaining thirty-seven regions formed the traditional rural regions. In this way a region was considered to be developed when the following three conditions were fulfilled simultaneously:

1. Value of output per hectare: Rs 1,160
2. Fertilizer consumed per hectare: 18 kilograms
3. Area irrigated per hectare of gross cropped area: 0.22 hectare.

Table 2.7 presents estimates for one set of employment elasticities prepared from these exercises: Agricultural employment per rupee of output shows a negative elasticity with output per hectare. Thus even in the early seventies, demand for labor per unit of output would decline as land productivity increased. This is a standard demand for labor profile, but it shows that employment augmentation possibilities with agricultural productivity changes within the agricultural sector were limited. This, of course, does not mean that agricultural employment would decline with additions to agricultural output, since both cropped area growth and agricultural output growth would be positive. In spite of the negative elasticity, employment growth would be positive. The results, however, showed that irrigation and land redistribution were strongly positively correlated with employment growth.

The upshot of this analysis was that, in a Tinbergen policy theoretical sense, irrigation and cropping intensity were policy variables mapping not only the output but also the employment objectives of Indian development policy. Thus "the growth of output per hectare, irrigation facilities, fertilizers application per hectare and related variables, was taken as set in the agricultural planning strategy and the employment implications of these changes estimated for the rural sector."[11] But unlike later employment planning models, which postulated that agricultural employment would grow faster than output (employment elasticity "optimism"?), the Fifth Plan model relying on econometric estimates discussed above was far more conservative on the employment generation possibility of output expansion. Thus "while employment opportunities were generated through production planning strategy by the agricultural sector, they were not enough to absorb the additions to the labor force and the backlog inherited at the beginning of the Fifth Five Year Plan."[12]

Given the estimates in Table 2.7, Indian development policy postulated that a regionally disaggregated agricultural development strategy and a policy focus on land reforms were essential components of employment strategies. Thus

the second policy . . . which has to be underlined for employment generation in the rural sector is the sub-regional dimension of the agricultural planning strategy. It is postulated in the Fifth Five Year Plan that the agricultural regions, which are underdeveloped, shall grow at a rate which is 10 percent higher than the aggregate growth rate of the national agricultural economy. This postulate is substantiated by the fact that regions, which are at present under developed, shall be provided irrigation facilities in the Fifth Five Year Plan period and in the Sixth Plan (1980–85) period. Funds are also being provided for the strengthening of the extension mechanism for this purpose. A concerted drive is also being made to spread fertilizer applications to selected regions which have the other pre-requisites of assumed irrigation and the extension mechanism. Given the analysis indicated in [the quotation from the Agricultural Sub-Model of the Fifth Plan] above, the output generation and input provision facilities being postulated separately for the developed and underdeveloped regions were related with the employment generation aspects of the Plan. It was established that the decomposition of the national rural economy into the two sub-sets added significantly to the employment generation possibilities of the planning focus for the agricultural sector.[13]

And again,

Studies in the Planning commission suggested that if in a phased manner for the country as a whole, an additional 10 percent of the operated area is transferred to small farmers either through proprietary rights or through secure tenurial arrangements by the end of the Sixth Five-Year Plan and if adequate production support is provided to such farmers through the general agricultural planning effort and particularly through the special programs, such as the SFDA and MFAL programs, India can look forward to the successful achievement of the objectives of providing adequate and viable rural employment possibilities for the rural labor force.[14]

Recent Trends

District- and regional-level trends are not available for the 1980s. Yet a number of important changes are taking place. These are explored with State-level data, which are at a higher level of aggregation. Examined together with the earlier disaggregated studies, they give preliminary indications of trends, providing a backdrop for discussion. Table 2.8 shows that in the seventies and early eighties, as noted earlier, agricultural growth is picking up in some of the dryland areas with low irrigation intensities, for example, Maharashtra and Gujarat. Also it has been high in States like Uttar Pradesh and Andhra Pradesh and hence, as seen with disaggregated estimates up to 1977–78, agricultural growth is picking up in selected areas outside the traditional high growth belts of Punjab, Haryana and Western U.P.

In terms of structural change in the agricultural sector, e.g., irrigation and fertilizers, States like Uttar Pradesh and West Bengal are showing fairly rapid changes apart from Punjab and Haryana. Fertilizer consumption per hectare increased from 11.53 kilograms in the triennium ending 1970–71 to 30.70 kilograms per hectare in the triennium ending 1980–81 (Table 2.9). There was considerable variation around this average. Towards the end of the last decade, the States of Punjab, Tamil Nadu, Uttar Pradesh, Andhra Pradesh, Karnataka, Haryana, West Bengal, Kerala and Gujarat showed higher application than the national average, ranging around 35 kilograms in Kerala and Gujarat to over a 100 kilograms per hectare in Punjab. The increase in fertilizer application per hectare was particularly dramatic in Punjab at around 70 kilograms per hectare during the decade of the seventies. Also in Tamil Nadu, West Bengal, Uttar Pradesh, Karnataka and Haryana this increase was over 40 kilograms per hectare. It is interesting to note that in all these States there was a substantial increase in irrigation intensity. This increase was particularly marked in Uttar Pradesh, Haryana and Punjab. In these States there was also a substantial increase in cropping intensity. The growth of fertilizer consumption is therefore no longer a localized phenomenon in India and substantial increases have taken place in States like Uttar Pradesh, West Bengal, Karnataka and Gujarat, which were earlier regarded as laggards in this area. A somewhat dramatic case of the expansion of food grains productivity and fertilizer consumption in the early eighties is reported from Uttar Pradesh. In the period 1973–74 to 1978–79, regarded as a period of fast fertilizer expansion, the average annual consumption went up by 3.12 lakh metric tons in India as a whole during the rabi season. In U.P. alone the expansion of fertilizer consumption has been around this magnitude in the rabi season of 1982–83. The expansion of tube-well irrigation and of wheat yield has been particularly dramatic in the districts of Eastern U.P. This area, conventionally regarded as backward in terms of agricultural development, was showing yield levels of around 10–11 quintals per hectare of wheat in the early seventies. In 1982–83 the reported yield levels were around 18–19 quintals per hectare. The increase in production of wheat in U.P. during the seventies and early eighties almost equals the total production of wheat in Punjab. Output growth and fertilizer use growth in Haryana may now be comparable with that in Eastern U.P. In the early seventies, wheat productivity in Haryana (by then a Green Revolution State) was around existing levels in Eastern U.P.

In the Sixth Plan yield has risen in major crops, apart from cotton, and even in cotton the aggregate statistics hide the dramatic shifts taking place towards the extra-superior long varieties. More important, the Sixth Plan targets for wheat, sugarcane, jute and mesta yields have already been achieved (Table 2.10). The Sixth Plan is perhaps the first Plan in which the productivity targets for major crops have been achieved. Of course, rice yields as well as those of pulses and millets have not increased as postulated. The priority to rain-fed and dryland agriculture has, therefore, had to continue.

The interesting feature to notice, however, is that the area expansion under crops is not taking place at all as postulated in the Plan. This means that cropping intensity and irrigation intensity are probably not increasing at the planned rates, since the expansion of irrigation potential has been considerable. As a matter of fact, cropped area is stagnant in wheat, has only marginally increased in sugarcane and has fallen in other principal crops apart from oilseeds. It is clear that the land augmentation targets of the Sixth Plan will not be achieved.

Apart from an emphasis on raising yields and assuming price support in dryland and rain-fed crops, land augmentation and land development strategies will need to be closely looked at in the Seventh Five-Year Plan (1985–90) and the planning methodologies discussed earlier scrutinized in this connection. In this context, apart from reexamining some of the parameters used in agricultural supply modeling in the Plans, questions of more effective use of water are extremely important and lead to interesting planning choices. It is important to emphasize that the choice available in terms of potential investment decisions to control and conserve water application is extremely large. The following are illustrative of some of the major choices:

1. Improved regulation of main canal and branches to reduce operation losses. Complete automation, for example, could reduce such losses by about 50 percent.
2. Lining of distribution systems at the tail end up to different levels, i.e., lining of branches, lining up to 100 cusecs or lining up to the eight-hectare level. This could reduce losses anywhere between 10 percent and 15 percent of the water released at the headworks.
3. Improved operation techniques for the total system, including careful design of buffer storages at different levels of the conveyance system, but particularly at the lower level. In addition to reducing losses, this would also introduce considerable flexibility in irrigation planning, which may become important particularly in large irrigation commands where the cropping conditions are of diverse type and crop stress requirements are severe.
4. In addition, the administrative and political aspects of water control will need to be solved.
5. Such modernization schemes will be expensive and will need to be selectively pursued.

Equally important questions lie in land/water management questions at the field level. To begin with, more precise estimates are required of the benefits of improved timing and control of water deliveries at the field level. Here a beginning can be made by examining yield levels by number of waterings for each crop. Such data are available in crop-cutting experiments and are required to be retabulated. Illustrative results for Gujarat agriculture where such tabulations have been made for irrigation are shown in Table 2.11.

The economists' skills together with agronomic data are important to get more realistic impacts of irrigation on cropping patterns. Acreage allocation studies with reference to relative prices, irrigation, rainfall variables and/or relative profitability are very common in Indian agricultural economics, but they have been made use of in irrigation planning only recently. Once the crop water requirements are worked out for different areas, the whole question of surface and ground water use needs to be carefully considered, particularly in view of ecological considerations of water-logging effects of indiscriminate applications of surface water. Again here recent advances in the modeling of groundwater aquifers need to be put into practice on a more extensive scale. Finally there are questions of working out the interregional net benefits of water allocation. Given more precise yield estimates (see above) and the cost of delivering water, the use of cost of cultivation studies would give such estimates. Quantified social consideration, e.g., the need to bring in social wage rate objectives in relation to poverty and unemployment considerations, can be brought to bear on the benefits of water allocation interregionally, once such exercises are done. A few examples of such planning exist already,[15] but they need to be applied on a more extensive scale.

It may be noted that a land and water management plan in India will be labor intensive in the sense that land development investments have high labor requirements and, finally, the employment intensity of agriculture will rise with improved water use and control of wastage of water.

An aspect of Indian agriculture which needs to be more carefully studied is the fact that some dryland agriculture regions are showing relatively high value added per worker. Thus, after Punjab and Haryana, States like Gujarat and Karnataka which have very low irrigation intensities are showing relatively high value added per worker. (See Table 2.6.) These regions have benefited from concentrating on "high valued" crops. Behind these "trends," however, are probably organizational and institutional systems which have led to successful commercialization of agriculture, including relatively successful cooperative marketing systems. Improved price support operations for commercial crops and strengthened marketing systems, are important aspects of the strategy of reducing the uncertainty of dryland agriculture and internalizing the benefits of the available technologies. These policies will have to be an important part of the overall strategy as Indian agriculture moves over to a more regionally diversified phase, from its earlier "favored crop-region" pattern.

Conclusions

Recent evidence tends to indicate that the phase of region and crop-specific growth in limited areas is now giving way to a more extensive pattern. Earlier, backward areas in Eastern Uttar Pradesh and in some of the dryland and rain-fed regions are showing positive growth. In the period 1963–73, 71 districts accounting for 26.8 percent of area recorded negative growth, but in the period through 1977 only 16 districts accounting for 5.6 percent of the area showed negative growth. Also, districts showing annual growth rates between 1.5 percent to 4.5 percent increased from 106 to 162, accounting for 54.2 percent of the area as compared to 33.5 percent earlier.

Intensive studies of output and input relations and the spread of agricultural productivity were used to design agricultural investment and development policy in the mid-seventies.

Empirical studies also showed that agricultural output growth and irrigation were also strongly influencing employment and labor demand outcomes in Indian agriculture. In addition, security of tenure and land redistribution, as also regionally differentiated strategies of development, were necessary to achieve improved employment outcomes.

In the Sixth Plan area growth has been close to zero and the entire growth is explained by productivity changes. The Sixth Plan is the first Plan in which the crop productivity targets of major crops were achieved. However, the area constraint is to a major extent related with the requirement of improved land and water management policies. In this context questions of more effective use of water are extremely important and lead to interesting planning choices, some of which were highlighted earlier.

Notes

1. S. K. Mukhopadhyay, *Sources of Variation in Agricultural Productivity* (New Delhi: Macmillan, 1976).

2. Ibid., 38.

3. Ibid., 43.

4. Center for Regional Development, Jawaharlal Nehru University, Perspective Planning Division, Planning Commission Project on *Regional Levels of Agricultural Development in India*, Analysis conducted for nineteen crops. See G. S. Bhalla and Y. K. Alagh, *Performance of Indian Agriculture: A District-wise Study* (Delhi: Sterling, 1979).

5. *Studies on the Structure of the Indian Economy and Planning for Development* (New Delhi: Government of India, Planning Commission, Perspective Planning Division, 1979), chap. 2, "The Agricultural Sub-Model," 21.

6. Ibid., 22–23. Also see *A Technical Note on the Sixth Plan of India* (New Delhi: Government of India, Planning Commission, 1981), chap. 3. For methodologies of the agricultural submodel, see Y. K. Alagh, *Agricultural Development Planning and Policies in the ESCAP Region*, in *Experiences in Agricultural Development Planning in Selected Countries of Asia* (Bangkok: United Nations, ESCAP, 1983), 15–28.

7. Compare the listing of districts by agricultural growth rates in Bhalla and Alagh, *Performance of Indian Agriculture*, 42–54, with S. Mahendra Dev, "Direction of Change in Performance of All Crops in Indian Agriculture in the Late Seventies," *Economic and Political Weekly*, Review of Agriculture (December 1985), Appendix 1, pp. A134–135.

8. Amitabh Kundu and Moonis Raza, *Indian Economy: The Regional Dimension* (Delhi: Spectrum, 1982), 49.

9. See, for example, NSS Report No. 5 (by D. B. Lahiri), Reports No. 27 and No. 70 (by M. N. Murti), Report No. 125 (by A. S. Roy and A. Bhattacharya) (New Delhi: Government of India, Ministry of Planning, Department of Statistics, National Sample Survey), and *Technical Aspects of Designs*, A Collection of Five Papers, National Sample Survey (New Delhi: Indian Statistical Institute).

10. *Studies on the Structure of the Indian Economy*, chap. 3, "The Employment Sub-Model," 43–66.

11. Ibid., 47.

12. Ibid.

13. Ibid., 48.

14. Ibid., 48–49.

15. For example, planning for the Sardar Sarovar Narmada Project concretely applies all these techniques.

TABLE 2.1 Summary Profiles of Levels of Agricultural Development in India at the District Level for the Triennium 1970–71 to 1972–73

Gross Value of Output per Hectare (Rs in All-India prices)	Cumulative Percentage of Total						
	Gross Cropped Area	Aggregate Output	Consumption of NPK	Use of Tractors	Pump Sets Installed	Gross Irrigated Area	Number of Districts in India
	(1)	(2)	(3)	(4)	(5)	(6)	(7)
2,500–2,799	0.70	1.83	2.37	5.39	0.83	2.22	1.08
2,000–2,499	3.04	7.18	10.60	12.89	7.82	8.27	3.56
1,500–1,999	14.48	27.84	38.93	46.81	40.68	34.08	17.73
1,000–1,499	40.30	59.46	67.24	69.90	63.40	64.25	42.91
500– 999	83.96	94.20	93.79	95.88	91.56	95.75	87.94
54– 499	100.00	100.00	100.00	100.00	100.00	100.00	100.00

Source: Centre for Regional Development, Jawaharlal Nehru University-Perspective Planning Division, Planning Commission, Project on Regional Levels of Agricultural Development in India, Analysis conducted for nineteen main crops. See G. S. Bhalla and Y. K. Alagh, Performance of Indian Agriculture: A Districtwise Study (Delhi: Sterling, 1979), Table 4, p. 21.

TABLE 2.2 Summary Profile of Agricultural Development in India at District Level Between the Trienniums 1961–62/1964–65 to 1970–71/1972–73

Annual Compound Growth Rate of Gross Value of Output (percent)[a]	Gross Cropped Area	Aggregate Output	Consumption of NPK	Use of Tractors	Pump Sets Installed	Gross Irrigated Area	Number of Districts in India (percent)
	(1)	(2)	(3)	(4)	(5)	(6)	(7)
11.00 – 11.35	0.62	0.15	0.02	0.84	0.08	0.09	0.36
9.00 – 10.99	1.38	0.98	1.22	2.89	1.26	1.19	1.42
7.00 – 8.99	7.93	9.97	14.13	32.47	12.47	16.28	6.38
5.00 – 6.99	13.89	17.03	20.81	46.46	20.13	24.37	12.41
3.00 – 4.99	29.60	36.13	38.99	67.72	34.68	45.53	29.08
1.00 – 2.99	60.58	67.75	66.24	83.74	66.63	71.90	62.41
0.00 – 0.99	73.09	80.98	81.92	90.74	80.69	83.81	75.18
Negative	100.00	100.00	100.00	100.00	100.00	100.00	100.00

[a] Growth rate has been computed by valuing output in 1962–63 to 1964–65 and 1970–71 to 1972–73, at average of all-India prices for each crop for the triennium 1970–71 to 1972–73.

Source: Centre for Regional Development, Jawaharlal Nehru University-Perspective Planning Division, Planning Commission Project on Levels of Agriculture Development in India. See Bhalla and Alagh, Performance of Indian Agriculture, Table 6, p. 28.

TABLE 2.3 Elasticities of Agricultural Output (per hectare) of Net Area Sown
with Reference to Input Variables

Cropping Intensity (gross cropped area) (net area sown)	Irrigation Intensity (gross irrigated area) (net area sown)	Fertilizer Intensity (fertilizers kilograms) (net area sown)
(1)	(2)	(3)
3.19	–	–
–	0.27	–
2.31	0.15	0.26
1.96	–	0.29
–	0.07	

TABLE 2.4 Direction of Change in Growth at the District Level

| Growth Class | 1962–65 to 1970–73 | | | |
	Number of Districts	Percentage Share of Area 1970–73	Percentage Share of Output 1970–73	Levels of Yield (in Rs) 1970–73
	(1)	(2)	(3)	(4)
High Growth (more than 4.5 percent)	50	18.68	23.04	1,205.50
Medium Growth (between 1.5 to 4.5 percent)	106	33.47	36.48	1,060.40
Low Growth (between 0.0 to 1.5 percent)	62	21.07	21.77	1,005.23
Negative (less than 0)	71	26.78	18.71	679.73
Total	289	100.00	100.00	973.00

Source: Bhalla and Alagh, Performance of Indian Agriculture, for columns (1) to (4), and S. Mahendra Dev, "Direction of Change in Performance of All Crops in Indian Agriculture in the Late Seventies," Economic and Political Weekly, Review of Agriculture (December 1985), Appendix 1, p. A130.

TABLE 2.4   (Continued)

Growth Class	Number of Districts	1962-65 to 1975-78		
		Percentage Share of Area 1975-78	Percentage Share of Output 1975-78	Levels of Yield (in Rs) 1975-78
	(5)	(6)	(7)	(8)
High growth (more than 4.5 percent)	39	14.77	20.84	1,559.00
Medium growth (between 1.5 to 4.5 percent)	162	54.24	51.95	1,058.47
Low growth (between 0.0 to 1.5 percent)	72	25.44	22.78	989.84
Negative (less than 0)	16	5.55	4.43	882.54
Total	289	100.00	100.00	1,111.63

TABLE 2.5   Area, Output and Output per Area for All Crops for the Trienniums 1962-65, 1970-73 and 1975-78 Arranged by Their Respective Yield Levels

Yield Levels (Rs per hectare)	1962-65 Triennium			
	Number of Districts	Area (percent hectares)	Output (percent Rs)	Output per Area (in Rs)
	(1)	(2)	(3)	(4)
High (above 1,300)	48	12.61	25.81	1,746.03
Medium (700 to 1,300)	135	47.85	50.73	946.46
Low	106	39.54	23.46	853.00
Total	289	100.00	100.00	

Source: Bhalla and Alagh, Performance of Indian Agriculture for columns (1) to (4), and Dev, "Direction of Change in Performance of All Crops in Indian Agriculture in the Late Seventies," Appendix 1, p. A130.

TABLE 2.5 (Continued)

Yield Levels (Rs per hectare)	1970–73 Triennium			
	Number of Districts	Area (percent hectares)	Output (percent Rs)	Output per Area (in Rs)
	(5)	(6)	(7)	(8)
High (above 1,300)	70	20.27	36.03	1,729.75
Medium (700 to 1,300)	134	48.37	48.48	979.94
Low	85	31.36	15.49	973.00
Total	289	100.00	100.00	

TABLE 2.5 (Continued)

Yield Levels (Rs per hectare)	1975–78 Triennium			
	Number of Districts	Area (percent hectares)	Output (percent Rs)	Output per Area (in Rs)
	(9)	(10)	(11)	(12)
High (above 1,300)	84	25.62	42.09	1,829.25
Medium (700 to 1,300)	142	51.54	46.61	1,005.03
Low	63	22.84	11.30	1,111.63
Total	289	100.00	100.00	

TABLE 2.6 Output per Hectare: Levels and Growth and Irrigation Potential Through Groundwater by NSS Regions

Region	Output Per Hectare (Rs)			Productivity Growth 1976–77 relative to 1963–64 (percent annual compound growth)	Irrigation Potential Through Groundwater as on April 1, 1977 (percent)
	1962–65	1970–73	1975–78		
(1)	(2)	(3)	(4)	(5)	(6)
Andhra Pradesh Coastal	1,524.5	1,645.8	1,696.6	0.8	68.1
Andhra Pradesh Inland Northern	744.3	652.9	956.5	1.9	44.9
Andhra Pradesh Inland Southern	932.6	1,019.5	1,105.9	1.3	36.0
Assam Plains	1,150.8	1,214.7	1,165.2	0.1	42.9
Assam Hills	1,194.1	1,557.3	1,310.8	0.7	25.3
Bihar Southern	893.6	865.4	960.4	0.5	40.2
Bihar Northern	922.1	976.7	1,013.5	0.7	52.9
Bihar Central	946.6	1,066.5	1,115.4	1.2	47.9
Gujarat Eastern	936.5	1,098.2	1,017.1	0.6	6.5
Gujarat Plains Northern	909.4	1,157.6	1,245.0	2.4	22.3
Gujarat Plains Southern	1,005.2	991.8	1,138.2	1.0	7.4
Gujarat Dry Areas	432.5	625.8	773.6	4.6	10.6
Gujarat Saurashtra	777.0	1,013.0	1,283.4	3.9	17.8
Haryana Eastern	905.7	1,372.9	1,587.3	4.4	37.7
Haryana Western	714.2	911.5	1,017.8	2.8	25.6
Jammu and Kashmir Mountainous	551.1	861.8	1,080.7	5.3	—
Jammu and Kashmir Outer Hills	582.7	856.2	1,408.4	7.0	—
Jammu and Kashmir Jhelem Valley	1,243.3	1,506.3	1,508.9	1.5	—

TABLE 2.6   (Continued)

(1)	(2)	(3)	(4)	(5)	(6)
Karnataka Costal Ghats	1,537.3	1,666.3	1,966.5	1.9	100.0
Karnataka Inland Eastern	1,204.0	1,584.7	1,587.0	2.1	56.9
Karnataka Inland Southern	1,031.4	1,415.3	1,422.5	2.5	19.4
Karnataka Inland Northern	538.2	705.0	846.8	3.5	8.6
Kerala Northern	1,630.1	1,751.9	1,651.6	0.1	100.0
Kerala Southern	1,607.5	1,800.3	1,963.6	1.6	100.0
Madhya Pradesh Eastern	818.7	905.5	919.1	0.9	0.5
Madhya Pradesh Inland Eastern	521.4	592.4	580.5	0.8	31.0
Madhya Pradesh Inland Western	582.4	618.0	621.4	0.5	—
Madhya Pradesh Western	618.1	628.5	667.6	0.6	0.4
Madhya Pradesh Northern	626.3	674.1	742.1	1.3	—
Maharashtra Coastal	1,367.3	1,345.1	1,686.1	1.6	—
Maharashtra Inland Western	709.6	631.9	966.6	2.4	—
Maharashtra Inland Northern	649.1	495.4	856.2	2.1	68.5
Maharashtra Inland Central	479.5	293.2	597.9	1.7	—
Maharashtra Inland Eastern	508.7	398.1	620.2	1.5	—

TABLE 2.6   (Continued)

(1)	(2)	(3)	(4)	(5)	(6)
Maharashtra Eastern	709.6	657.5	999.2	2.6	—
Orissa Coastal	1,169.2	1,067.4	1,166.0	Neg.	51.9
Orissa Southern	1,065.1	974.9	960.9	-0.7	18.7
Orissa Northern	1,067.4	1,011.4	1,042.9	-0.2	30.5
Punjab Northern	1,194.7	1,793.4	2,026.8	4.2	40.3
Punjab Southern	1,121.7	1,734.6	1,951.2	4.3	34.0
Rajasthan Western	159.5	225.8	278.0	4.3	5.2
Rajasthan North Eastern	483.9	684.2	802.8	3.9	9.3
Rajasthan Southern	747.3	775.7	825.2	0.8	12.4
Rajasthan South Eastern	537.8	705.2	800.3	3.1	16.7
Tamil Nadu Coastal Northern	1,588.7	2,030.3	2,537.1	3.6	35.2
Tamil Nadu Coastal Southern	1,488.1	1,818.6	1,887.6	1.8	40.1
Tamil Nadu Coastal Inland	1,381.5	1,562.9	1,097.2	-1.8	29.5
Uttar Pradesh Himalayas	879.4	1,034.9	1,199.7	2.4	5.3
Uttar Pradesh Western	1,115.6	1,354.7	1,575.4	2.7	33.3
Uttar Pradesh Central	935.8	1,015.1	1,163.5	1.7	28.7
Uttar Pradesh Eastern	859.9	927.7	1,053.5	1.6	29.9
Uttar Pradesh Southern	569.8	722.0	688.0	1.4	33.8
West Bengal Himalayas	1,265.7	1,323.6	1,187.8	-0.2	46.9
West Bengal Eastern Plains	1,230.4	1,367.4	1,440.0	1.2	51.7
West Bengal Central Plains	1,533.8	1,616.9	1,766.7	1.1	27.7
West Bengal Western Plains	1,313.7	1,431.8	1,473.5	0.9	44.8
All India	853.0	973.0	1,111.0	2.1	NA

Sources: Studies on the Structure of the Indian Economy, chap. 3 for columns (2) and (3), and Dev, "Direction of Change in Performance of All Crops in Indian Agriculture in the Late Seventies," for column (4).   Also, Draft Sixth Five Year Plan: 1978–83. Revised (New Delhi: Government of India, Planning Commission).

TABLE 2.7 Agricultural Employment Elasticities 1972–73
(dependent variable: agricultural employment of
output measured in All–India, 1972–73 prices)

Variable	All Regions	Developed Regions	Underdeveloped Regions
Output per Hectare	−0.96	−1.86	−0.19
Fertilizer per Hectare	−0.19	0.45	−0.22
Electric Pump Sets and Oil Engines Per Hectare	0.12	—	0.16
Percentages of Area Operated in Small Farms	0.40	0.35	0.36

Sources: <u>Studies on the Structure of the Indian Economy</u>, chap 3, 46, and Y. K. Alagh, "The Importance of Integrating Popular Components into Development Models," in <u>Population and Development Modelling</u> (UN Document ST/ESA/SERA/73) (New York: United Nations, 1981), 120.

TABLE 2.8 Agricultural Growth Rate and Value Added per Worker in Agriculture in Major States

State	Value Added per Worker in Agriculture (Rs)		Agricultural Growth Rate[a]			
	1970–71	1980–81	1970–71 1960–61	1980–81 1970–71	1980–81 1960–61	1969–70 1983–84
(1)	(2)	(3)	(4)	(5)	(6)	(7)
Andhra Pradesh	1,097 (8)[b]	2,111 (8)	1.84	3.72	2.72	3.31
Gujarat	1,876 (3)	3,119 (4)	6.35	2.07	4.18	3.92
Haryana	3,230 (2)	7,266 (2)	6.23[c]	3.22[c]	4.62[c]	3.31
Punjab	3,384 (1)	7,593 (1)	6.23[c]	3.22[c]	4.62[c]	3.92
Karnataka	1,649 (5)	2,508 (6)	4.33	1.56	2.92	2.44
Madhya Pradesh	916 (10)	1,916 (9)	1.43	0.10	0.61	1.65
Maharashtra	877 (11)	2,404 (7)	(−)0.85	5.14	2.13	5.59
Rajasthan	1,680 (4)	308 (11)	3.41	0.65	1.80	2.47
Tamil Nadu	994 (9)	1,445 (10)	3.41	0.65	1.80	1.12
Uttar Pradesh	1,175 (7)	2,800 (5)	2.59	1.46	1.95	3.10
West Bengal	1,317 (6)	3,680 (3)	3.03	1.18	1.95	0.90

[a] Agricultural growth is measured as the weighted average output growth of the given major crops of food grains, oilseeds, raw cotton, sugarcane, jute and mesta in columns (4), (5) and (6). Annual rates are estimated on the basis of triennium average figures. Figures in column (7) are semi–logarithmic trend estimates of an Index of Agricultural Production on time Estimates are from the Commission of Agricultural Costs and Prices. The estimate for Bihar is 0.49 percent, for Orissa 2.28 percent and for India 2.37 percent.

[b] Figures in brackets indicate "Rank."

[c] Separate growth rates could not be computed for Punjab and Haryana.

TABLE 2.9 Selected Indicators of the Agricultural Sector in the 1970s

States	Fertilizer Consumption (kilograms per hectare) Triennium		Irrigated Area (lakh hectares)		Irrigated Area Growth 1980 relative to 1969, percent annual compound growth
	Ending 1970–71	Ending 1980–81	1969–70	1980–81[a]	
(1)	(2)	(3)	(4)	(5)	(6)
Andhra Pradesh	23.76	43.55	39.14	43.42	1.0
Assam	2.79	2.78	5.85	5.72	0
Bihar	9.42	17.97	26.33	36.32	3.0
Gujarat	11.47	34.95	12.16	18.82	5.0
Haryana	13.06	41.31	19.34	28.18	4.2
Karnataka	12.49	42.23	13.00	16.76	2.3
Kerala	20.05	34.99	5.81	3.81	Neg.
Madhya Pradesh	2.86	8.53	13.32	24.53	5.7
Maharashtra	8.31	20.36	15.54	22.77	4.3
Orissa	3.46	8.56	12.51	17.11	2.9
Punjab	36.11	101.84	37.89	52.60	3.7
Rajasthan	2.79	7.54	23.68	37.49	4.3
Tamil Nadu	30.82	65.18	32.80	32.94	0
Uttar Pradesh	18.16	45.33	72.80	113.71	4.1
West Bengal	10.01	36.01	14.99	29.00	7.0
All India	11.53	30.70	381.95	480.90	2.1

[a] Source of data for 1980–81, Reply to Rajya Sabha Unstarred Qustion No. 3402.

Cropping Intensity (gross cropped area) (net area sown)		Irrigation Intensity (gross irrigated area) (gross cropped area)	
1969–70	1978–79	1969–70	1978–79
(7)	(8)	(9)	(10)
1.14	1.14	0.31	0.35
1.23	1.23	0.21	0.17
1.31	1.35	0.24	0.32
1.06	1.09	0.12	0.18
1.37	1.48	0.41	0.52
1.05	1.08	0.12	0.16
1.32	1.32	0.20	0.12
1.11	1.14	0.07	0.10
1.05	1.09	0.08	0.12
1.34	1.30	0.15	0.19
1.36	1.54	0.70	0.82
1.09	1.12	0.16	0.19
1.19	1.22	0.46	0.47
1.26	1.35	0.33	0.43
1.22	1.35	0.22	0.20
1.17	1.21	0.22	0.22

TABLE 2.10 Sixth Plan Targets and Recent Performance

| Crop | Targets for 1984-85 | | |
	Area (million hectare)	Yield (quintals per hectares)	Production (million metric tons)
(1)	(2)	(3)	(4)
Rice	41.27	15.24	63.16
Wheat	25.00	17.50	43.75
Food Grains	131.07	11.47	150.33
Sugarcane	3.48	575.00	200.10
Cotton	8.46	1.89	94.00 (lakh bales)
Jute and Mesta	1.34	12.50	93.06 (lakh bales)
Oilseeds	NA	NA	13.00

	Triennium Ending 1980-81			Triennium Ending 1983-84	
Area (million hectares)	Yield (quintals per hectare)	Production (million metric tons)	Area (million hectares)	Yield (quintals per hectare)	Production (million metric tons)
(5)	(6)	(7)	(8)	(9)	(10)
40.01	12.44	49.78	39.99	13.32	53.38
22.36	15.47	34.60	23.37	17.86	41.80
126.96	9.75	123.82	128.19	10.77	138.12
2.79	514.94	143.67	3.24	569.01	184.29
8.02	1.61	76.30	7.90	1.58	73.30
1.26	10.54	78.13	1.06	12.91	76.50
17.42	5.39	9.40	18.50	6.27	11.63

TABLE 2.11   Crop Yields in Gujarat by Crop Type
and Number of Waterings

Crop	5 Years Average (1969-70 to 1973-74) Output in Kilograms per Hectare
Paddy HVY[a]/6 + Irrigation	2,845
Paddy AV[b]/6 + Irrigation	2,180
Wheat HYV/6 + Irrigation	2,489
Wheat AV/6 + Irrigation	2,379
Bajra HYV/3-5 + Irrigation	1,861
Bajra AV/3-5 + Irrigation	1,843
Tobacco HYV/6 + Irrigation	1,994
Tobacco AV/6 + Irrigation	2,337
Cotton HYV/6 + Irrigation	1,312
Cotton AV/6 + Irrigation	1,308
Groundnut AV/6 + Irrigation	1,456

[a] HYV: High-yielding varieties

[b] AV: all varieties

Source: Crop-Cutting Experiments, Retabulations.

APPENDIX

Determinants of Agricultural Yield

Coverage of data is as in the Jawaharlal Nehru University–Perspective Planning Division, Bhalla–Alagh study, <u>Performance of Indian Agriculture</u>, i.e., nineteen crops valued at all–India prices for each of 278 districts, triennium averages for 1970–71 to 1972–73. Variables are transformed into logs. Estimates[a] are as follows:

1. $$\frac{Q}{NAS} = \underset{(138.90)}{602.14} + \underset{(14.47)}{3.19} \frac{GCA}{NAS}$$

$$\bar{R}^2 = 0.43$$

2. $$\frac{Q}{NAS} = \underset{(64.78)}{1,743.69} + \underset{(2.85)}{0.27} \frac{GIA}{NAS}$$

$$\bar{R}^2 = 0.35$$

3. $$\frac{Q}{NAS} = \underset{(104.75)}{934.12} + \underset{(9.63)}{2.31} \frac{GCA}{NAS} + \underset{(6.87)}{0.15} \frac{GIA}{NAS}$$

$$\bar{R}^2 = 0.52$$

4. $$\frac{Q}{NAS} = \underset{(84.39)}{2,404.95} + \underset{(10.36)}{1.97} \frac{GCA}{NAS} + \underset{(14.86)}{0.26} \frac{F}{NAS}$$

$$\bar{R}^2 = 0.67$$

5. $$\frac{Q}{NAS} = \underset{(64.78)}{4,570.86} + \underset{(2.85)}{0.07} \frac{GIA}{NAS} + \underset{(11.16)}{0.29} \frac{F}{NAS}$$

$$\bar{R}^2 = 0.55$$

Q — Agricultural Output in 1970–71 all–India prices for the triennium average 1970–71 to 1972–73.

NAS — Net Area Sown.

GCA — Gross Cropped Area.

GIA — Gross Irrigated Area.

F — Fertilizer application in kilograms of Nitrogen equivalent.

---

[a] See G. S. Bhalla, Y. K. Alagh, et al. <u>Foodgrains Growth: A Districtwise Study</u>, Report of the Second Phase of the Planning Commission–JNU Project (New Delhi: Jawaharlal Nehru University, 1982, Mimeographed).

3

Food Production, Consumption and Development Strategy

John W. Mellor

Introduction

Agriculture, employment and poverty represent three key interacting and interrelated elements of development. Agriculture produces the wage goods that are the other side of the coin of employment. Agriculture is also potentially the major source of effective demand for low-capital-intensity output from the industrial and service sectors, which in turn must be the cornerstone of a high employment growth strategy. Accelerated growth in employment is in turn necessary to agricultural growth, providing income to that segment of society that has a high marginal propensity to spend additional income on food. And, finally, agriculture provides the principal consumption good the supply and price of which substantially determine whether the poor are in abject poverty or doing somewhat better than that, and employment provides the means by which the poor can purchase food and other commodities necessary to lift themselves above the poverty line.

The record on agricultural production in India has been moderately good. In the early years of Independence, agriculture grew far more rapidly than in the pre-Independence period, due to increased work incentives arising from the significant land reforms associated with zamindari abolition, and the rapid expansion of large-scale irrigation. By the late 1960s, yield-increasing technological changes associated with the Green Revolution further accelerated the growth rate, at least modestly, of the agricultural sector. India's record on the agriculture production front is not extraordinary by international standards, but it is a good, solid performance.

The mystery in this record of agricultural development is not in agricultural performance but rather in the link between production and

I am grateful to Tom Harrington for his efforts in developing data and in preparing the chapter.

consumption. Why is it that, in spite of this modest acceleration in growth of food output, there has been downward pressure on food prices? Why has accelerated growth primarily been used to displace cereal imports, to provide marginal cereal exports and to build massive stocks of cereals? Why is it, in contrast to most developing countries achieving adequate growth in cereals production, that demand for cereals has not grown commensurately with accelerated production? Here India's record is somewhat like that of the People's Republic of China, which until recently had a comparable record in agricultural growth and a poor record on growth of effective demand. Numerous countries, including Indonesia, Thailand, Malaysia, Taiwan, South Korea, and even some sub-Saharan African countries, have seen accelerated growth in food production associated with accelerated growth in both employment and effective demand for food.

This imbalance between growth on the supply side and lack of growth on the demand side has profound implications. It tends to provide a price-depressing effect on agriculture that itself may weaken incentives for further production increase. In order to prevent a price-depressing effect, massive expenditures are required from the public sector to build stocks and subsidize exports. Such expenditure is certainly deleterious to the overall development process because it detracts from the public expenditures needed to complement both agricultural growth and development.

The solution to these imbalances lies either with accelerating the rate of growth of employment and poverty reduction on the one hand or decelerating growth in the agricultural sector on the other. The latter is all too easy to achieve. It simply requires a little less attention to expanding irrigated area, a little saving of foreign exchange on imports of fertilizer, and perhaps some reduction of operational support to the Indian Council for Agricultural Research (ICAR). With such modest changes or relaxations, a return to the old rates of food production growth would be virtually instantaneous.

To address the imbalance on the demand side poses complex questions. Is it possible that India (as is typical of the group of countries with per capita incomes between $250 and $500) is simply at a stage of development in which it can accelerate growth in agriculture but at the same time it is prevented from achieving comparable employment-intensive growth by problems in the nonagricultural sector? If so, it could be argued that it is simply a matter of time before India changes to a somewhat different structure of development; at such time, even with rapid growth in food production, the demand for food derived from rapidly growing employment will increase even more rapidly than domestic food supplies. This pattern of accelerated growth in agriculture and, concurrently, growing net food imports is typical of the developing countries with more than $500 per capita income.

In this chapter I argue that food production could have increased more rapidly than it has in India; that consumption growth could have increased more, not less, rapidly than accelerated growth in production; and that the drag on production growth, and even more on consumption growth, comes from a misallocation of public sector resources, which has resulted in a major inadequacy of infrastructure investment.

In order to explore this argument, I will briefly review the production record and the sources of food production growth in India, followed by a brief consideration of consumption issues, including nutritional status. A discussion of development strategy follows, with its implications for food supply and demand balances. I will conclude with a discussion of an optimal program for agricultural and employment growth.

The Production Record

Acceleration of the growth rate of food production in India by 0.5 percentage point is a major achievement with profound implications for the rate of growth of employment and the economy in general. However, there are insurmountable statistical problems in detecting and substantiating changes of this magnitude in the rate of growth of agricultural production in India. Year-to-year, weather-induced fluctuations in production are very large relative to the economically significant changes in trend we wish to detect. And we attempt to measure these changes in a short period of ten to twenty years which assures that the largest changes in trend that are technically possible will still prove statistically insignificant. Similarly, choosing a period with a few more good or bad years at one end or the other in a time series substantially alters the results. Thus, there is bound to be considerable disagreement as to production trends over periods as short as a decade or two. It follows that judgments about this important variable must be made without the assistance of standard statistical procedures, and that the acceptability of the conclusion must depend largely on the supporting logic.

One means of dealing with this problem is to compute rates of growth across peaks and troughs in production carefully selected for equivalency of weather variables. Table 3.1 and Figure 3.1 provide a perspective on this question. Note the tremendous variation in rates across different years. Note that in Table 3.1 a wide range of growth rates can be generated through the choice of years. I contend that a comparison of the excellent crop years 1964–65 and 1970–71 probably moderately understates the growth rate for that period at 3.3 percent because 1964–65 was an even better year for weather than 1970–71. This compares with a likely much slower 2.8 percent growth rate in the 1950s, comparing the excellent years of 1949–50 and 1960–61. The growth rate decelerated substantially to 2.1 percent in the early 1960s. Again, comparing the excellent crop years of 1960–61 and 1964–65, the latter is probably a better year; hence the growth during that period is slightly overstated. However, it seems plausible that the rate dropped off in the 1970s to 3.0 percent, comparing the excellent years of 1971–72 and 1983–84. That is a modest deceleration from the initial acceleration resulting from the Green Revolution. Perhaps it is more reasonable to take the broad position that the growth rate in food grain production has accelerated in the last decade or so from somewhat under 2.8 percent to about 3.0 percent. Statistically, the conclusion that there has been no change in the growth rate over that period does not contradict this assertion. The argument here is not with respect to statistical significance but economic significance, which depends on logic and careful comparisons, given the problems of large year-to-year variations in production.

The above discussion addresses the critical issue of the degree of acceleration in the overall food grain production growth rate. There has, of course, been an important and indisputable Green Revolution in which improved crop varieties and chemical fertilizers have substituted for an inexorably diminishing land frontier. In this sense, the Green Revolution has been essential even to maintain old growth rates in the agricultural sector. But just substituting new methods of growth for old ones that are no longer available is not adequate to meet an overall growth objective. For that objective, agriculture must make an incremental contribution to the growth rate of the economy despite a diminishing land frontier. Such a contribution requires technological change that increases factor productivity. In my judgment, agriculture has provided that, in a very modest way, and less than was possible.

Accelerated agricultural growth in India has been associated with rapid increase in irrigation (Table 3.2) and extraordinarily rapid increase in use of fertilizer (Table 3.3). This has involved rapid commercialization of agriculture. The process has, however, been substantially inhibited because large areas of the country with high potential for accelerated growth are isolated from commercialization by poor physical infrastructure. For example, the contrast in the State government investments in physical infrastructure between Haryana and West Bengal has resulted in quite different records of agricultural production in the two States.[1]

The key role of infrastructure is made apparent forcefully by preliminary data for Bangladesh. Good infrastructure compared with poor shows rice prices 2 percent higher, fertilizer prices 10 percent lower, wage rates 12 percent higher, fertilizer use 64 percent higher, and use of high-yielding varieties (HYVs) 5 percent greater.[2] Despite poor or nonexistent roads, HYVs have spread and rice has been efficiently marketed, but the use of fertilizer and the demand for labor, key elements of agricultural growth, are sharply constrained by lack of infrastructure. In the study area, poor infrastructure is not associated with poor agricultural regions; infrastructure deficiency is interspersed in favorable areas, limiting overall growth rates.

The impressive feature in India, on the production side, is the extent to which complex processes have been institutionalized so that growth proceeds steadily and persistently. For example, the Indian Council for Agricultural Research is a massive research organization, with a huge number of scientists, which has been able, year after year, to bring about improvements in crop varieties and practices. Of course, as with all institutions, there is scope for increased efficiency.

Similarly, India has institutionalized its capacity to expand fertilizer distribution quantities at a rate of 300,000 to 500,000 additional metric tons of fertilizer each year (Table 3.3). In other words, present annual additions to fertilizer use are greater than the total usage only twenty years ago. Similarly, net irrigated area is expanding at an average rate of 2.7 percent per year, and on the order of a million hectares of land are brought under irrigation incrementally each year. Both figures are averages for 1975–76 to 1979–80 (see Table 3.2).

The remarkable failure in the Indian economy, and one that has had a major effect both on employment growth and on agricultural growth, is electric power generation. India has fared poorly in relation to other developing countries at comparable stages in development in institutionalizing a high rate of expansion in electric power generation. It is a major accomplishment to institutionalize a 15 percent rate of growth, as compared to India's 10 percent rate of growth. Once that is institutionalized, however, it has profound continuing implications for overall economic growth. Indian planners have consistently thought that a 10 percent rate of growth was adequate, but this rate has meant reduced consumption incentives and production in labor-intensive industries that require reliable power, even though electricity costs are only a small proportion of their total costs. The uncertainty and unreliability of electric power has certainly inhibited growth in well irrigation, which tends to be the form of irrigation with the highest rate of return.

Despite an excellent record in most elements of agricultural growth except power, India's performance in agricultural production has been well below its potential. One way to make this point is to look at a set of projections made in the mid-1970s with actual data. Those projections of food grain output to 1984 were an attempt to see what growth of food grain production was feasible on the basis of rates of growth of key inputs already achieved in the past, although not all in the same year. The inputs were fertilizer, irrigation and labor, and, implicitly, an agricultural research achievement consistent with past growth was assumed. Response coefficients for each of these components were calculated and used to estimate a 1984 production level.

Several revealing points can be drawn from this exercise. Perhaps most important, the 1983–84 level of food grain production projected was 22 percent higher than the level actually achieved. Since this was believed to be achievable in terms consistent with input levels, it suggests an underperformance in production achievement—and of course an extraordinary underperformance in consumption, to which I will return later. Equally striking, input levels have gone up considerably more than projected. This means that the marginal productivity of these inputs has been declining. That is a matter on which a number of observers have remarked.

Some have suggested that the declining marginal productivity is simply a reflection of classic diminishing returns to the increased use of agricultural inputs. True, agriculture is the classic case of diminishing returns: returns will diminish unless compensated for by technological change. But agricultural growth is a matter of defeating diminishing returns with technological change. Hence the declining marginal productivity of inputs is a reflection of underlying problems. Deficiencies in agricultural research itself are a probable cause, despite the general effectiveness of the Indian agricultural research systems. Improved varieties and practices should have been developed at a faster rate so that a higher proportion of the crop area could have experienced increased productivity, raising the overall growth rate. But, perhaps even more important, there have been deficiencies in the input supply system. Any retardation of the effective distribution of fertilizer to regions such as central India and the rain-fed areas and to crops such as jowar and bajra results in a lower average response to fertilizer than would otherwise be the case. Growth in fertilizer use, unfortunately, has been achieved less by expanding use in areas with high marginal productivity of the input, and more by raising output prices and expanding use in areas where it is already being used at relatively high levels and hence has a lower marginal product.

Desai has written extensively on problems of fertilizer distribution.[3] We can go a step further, drawing on his work to point out that if technology remains constant, fertilizer use will be pushed to lower and lower returns in old areas of use, and it will require lower and lower relative fertilizer prices to maintain growth, whereas expansion to new areas and crops may occur even with rising fertilizer prices. The latter point suggests that the potential exists to increase returns to fertilizer use without relying on fertilizer subsidies which seem so out of hand (Table 3.4).

Perhaps most of all, we can emphasize the relatively slow progress made in the Eastern States, something which I and my colleagues drew attention to some twenty years ago in the book *Developing Rural India*.[4] Subsequently an Eastern States Commission and many other groups have studied this issue. Whatever the cause, the fact that the Eastern States include a vast area of land with still unexploited potentials for technological change and expansion of double cropping indicates that national average factor productivity is well below its potential. The expansion in production has not been achieved at as high a level of factor productivity as possible because these large potentials are being underutilized.

The declining factor productivity is illustrated at the micro level by the work of my colleagues Ranade, Jha, and Delgado,[5] who are tracing the history of the cost of production in areas of India that have experienced the Green Revolution. The first effect of the high-yielding technologies was a sharp decline in the cost of production: the cost per unit of area increased but yields increased much more than commensurately. That was followed inevitably by a decline in real prices as supply increased faster than demand. Then, as demand continues to expand, prices recover, farmers respond by pushing further along the production function, but the yield-increasing effect of the technology tapers off and marginal costs of production increase. Obviously, with rising cost per unit of output, farmers then search for other means of reducing their cost of production: by changing their cropping pattern, for instance, or perhaps by becoming more sophisticated in their application of the new technology. It is a constant battle between rising production costs caused by moving out on the production function and improving efficiency to increase yields.

To summarize, India has experienced rapid technological change in agricultural production over substantial areas. Through investment in rural infrastructure and the broadening of fertilizer and other input-delivery systems, the breadth of participation in that change has increased both across income groups and geographic regions. Nevertheless, output growth has come increasingly from more intensive use of existing technology with declining marginal returns to inputs and hence with rising costs.

At this moment, the critical problem for Indian agriculture is effective demand, to which we will next turn our attention. But when progress is made on this front, concern will turn again to accelerating production growth. Then the still unexploited potentials for accelerating the pace of new technology generated through continued improvements in the research system and investments in infrastructure for delivery of inputs will need to be realized urgently.

The Consumption Record

We know from the careful work of M. Ahluwalia[6]—measuring the extent to which people fall below the poverty line in India—and from the further work with that data base carried out by Narain,[7] that poverty levels in rural India have fluctuated extraordinarily over time from 40 percent of the rural population to about 60 percent (Figure 3.2). We know that those fluctuations are basically a function of agricultural prices and agricultural production: the latter I interpret as a proxy for employment. Higher agricultural prices cause a decline in nonagricultural expenditure by higher income people, which reduces employment in the service and small-scale industry sectors. A decrease in agricultural production reduces employment directly for agricultural laborers and indirectly for rural nonagricultural laborers through the reduction in consumption expenditures of the peasant farming class on labor-intensive goods and services. Narain's analysis shows that there has been a modest, underlying downward trend in rural poverty, masked at least to the mid-1970s by rising agricultural prices and lack of progress on per capita food production at the all-India aggregate level.

The rural poverty indexes show that real incomes of the rural poor have not been rising because of both a lack of employment growth and a lack of decline in food prices, both of which have been fluctuating substantially. This observation is corroborated by data on per capita net availability of food grain. There has not been an increase in per capita food grain availability in India in the last three decades (Table 3.5).

There has been some increase in domestic per capita food production, but that has been drawn off by reduced imports and increased public stocks (Table 3.6). Real agricultural prices have fluctuated substantially during the past three decades, but there has not been a downward trend. That they have been close to the historic low of the late 1950s in the face of stagnant per capita consumption suggests that incomes of the poor and hence employment have not increased significantly in the recent past.

We can draw a comparison between the recent situation and that of the early 1960s, when agricultural production was growing rather slowly by both past and subsequent measures. However, employment was expanding quite rapidly, largely because of massive investment during the

Second (1956–61) and Third (1961–66) Five-Year Plans and presumably because of a good deal of spillover to industries somewhat less capital intensive than those that were in the Plan. The result was that even with a slow growth rate in agriculture more than balanced by a rapid rate of growth in imports and a consequent rise in per capita food availability, there were substantial increases in the relative price of food. The circumstances in the past decade have been just the opposite: agricultural production has expanded reasonably rapidly, imports have been eliminated, and stocks have grown. Food prices, however, have turned somewhat against the food sector. Indeed, relative food prices have returned to what many consider the unfavorable ratio of the early 1960s. That must mean that the other side of the food-employment coin, growth in effective demand, has been slow.

The macro fiscal policy problems for the Government have reinforced this change. Undoubtedly, as I will indicate later, a good deal of the problem in effective demand for food comes from inadequate public investment in the basic infrastructure of growth in the nonagricultural sector, including electrification, roads, railroads, ports and communications. At the same time, the combination of success in agriculture, lack of growth in effective demand for food, and strong farmer lobbies has resulted in rapid growth in public sector expenditures to provide food storage at levels far greater than optimal for food security (Table 3.4).

Before closing this section on consumption, it is fitting to explicitly draw attention to the food consumption record in the aggregate of countries that have high growth rates in agriculture. An International Food Policy Research Institute (IFPRI) analysis of the twenty-eight countries with the most rapid rates of growth in their basic food staples during the 1960s and 1970s[8] calculated that these countries averaged a 4 percent rate of growth in basic food staples production. This is substantially faster growth than India achieved in the same period. During the period of analysis these countries as a group increased their imports of basic food staples by 265 percent. This means that domestic consumption was increasing much more rapidly than even their successful record of domestic food production growth. One can only conclude that countries that have high growth rates in food production tend to increase their food imports.

It is useful to speculate about the various price relationships that could be consistent with those facts, keeping in mind that food production and per capita food consumption increased at high rates. Consumption could have increased in part because imports kept domestic prices low, which emphasizes the role of cost-decreasing technological change in food production growth: that production grew very rapidly in the face of declining prices can be attributed to the incentive effects of declining production costs from technological change. Alternatively, that consumption grew rapidly in the face of rising prices can only be explained in terms of a shift in the demand schedule, presumably due to rapidly increasing demand for labor and a much larger wage bill.

To understand India's performance in this context, however, it is well to note that, as we project net food trade of developing countries, those projected to become net food exporters, with the exception of Argentina and Thailand, fall largely in the under $500 per capita income level (Table 3.7). Thus one can argue that India is one of a group of countries that structurally are able to get their agricultural sectors moving but before accelerating employment growth. In this perspective, it is only a matter of time and gradual structural change before employment rates increase, and growth in effective demand for food catches up with supply growth. Alternatively, India's capital-intensive industrial growth represents a low-employment strategy that must be reversed before effective demand for food grows at a pace commensurate with the potential for growth in agricultural production.

It is important to note that acceleration of growth in agriculture depends heavily on the public sector, which must provide research, input supply systems, basic infrastructure, extension and other education services, and higher education to provide trained people for institutional development. Except for basic infrastructure, it may be that rapid growth in employment requires a vigorous private sector, particularly in the small- and medium-scale sectors. Thus, the countries which have been predominantly socialist or captured by multinational corporate interests have concentrated their capital on capital-intensive industries that generate little employment.

Development Strategy and Its Implications for Food Production and Consumption

I have long espoused a view of development that is oriented toward agriculture and employment.[9] However, it is not sufficient to develop agriculture and expect it, by a process of income multipliers, autonomously to develop other sectors. Virtually all economies have nonagricultural sectors initially, and these must also develop somewhat independently. But I do emphasize the importance for the overall growth rate of getting the agricultural sector moving and allowing the multipliers to operate to provide for substantial overall growth. As I indicated at the outset of this chapter, in such a strategy agriculture, employment and poverty alleviation go hand in hand. And it pays in public discussion to emphasize agriculture particularly as a leading edge of development because agriculture depends substantially on public sector investment and facilitative public policy. However, it does not receive the attention it warrants because of the urban orientation of so many developing-country governments.

There are two key problems with respect to making agriculture a leading edge in the development process. First, agriculture is the classical case of diminishing returns or, to say it more properly, of increasing costs. Thus, agriculture as a leading edge can only move ahead through technological change which raises factor productivity in the face of the serious problem of diminishing returns. This view requires some modification as we move to the relatively land surplus countries, such as Thailand or much of Africa, but it needs to be modified only a little when we are looking at South Asia.

The second problem of agriculture is that it is not only a sector of inelastic supply but also one of inelastic demand. Thus, if we are to use technological change to increase factor productivity in agriculture and to move the sector ahead rapidly, we must then face the problem of inelastic demand and a need to benefit from increasing factor productivity by shifting resources out of the agricultural sector. It obviously is unfortunate to have to shift resources away from the sector that is most responsive to new technologies for raising factor productivity.[10] Of course, the other side of this coin is that increasing employment and incomes, a high marginal propensity to consume food, combined with an inelastic supply of food, creates an inelastic labor supply.

Fortunately, in the case of developing countries, the problem of inelastic demand for food can be dealt with easily by shifting the demand schedule. That is achieved by increasing employment or, more properly, by increasing the wage pool—through higher wage rates or increased employment— or, even more correctly, by increasing the demand for labor. It is because of this supply and demand inelasticity that we must always talk about an agriculture and employment-oriented strategy and not one or the other alone.

In these days of the ascendency of neoclassical economists and objections to thinking in terms of closed economies I should make an aside here about the possibility of perfectly elastic supplies of food. Again, this is a comment that hardly needs to be made in the Indian context, where one is dealing with large aggregates. However, we should keep in mind that in any low-income country, agriculture represents a large aggregate. If, therefore, one increases employment rapidly so that the demand for food is growing quickly and is not met internally, one can argue initially that can be met by a perfectly elastic supply from international markets. However, we are talking about aggregates that in the neoclassical context will result in a pace of growth of food imports that will soon reach the point where they must affect the real exchange rate. At that point, growth in food imports will cause a devaluation of the currency and therefore a rise in the domestic price of food relative to other prices in the economy, particularly nontradables, which is not matched by an increase in the international price. Thus to think in somewhat closed-economy terms about the demand and supply for food is not unreasonable, whereas it would be exceedingly unreasonable for particular manufactured goods.

A critical problem in an agriculture- and employment-based strategy of growth is the capital constraint. Agricultural growth requires a massive capital investment, particularly in various forms of infrastructure. And then, we encourage employment to grow more rapidly, by releasing the wage goods constraint, which requires even further needs for capital. In a modeling exercise, one simply shows a decline in the capital-labor ratio, but we all know that the big problem in the Indian economy has been the rapid increase in capital-labor ratios over time.[11] It is my argument that that increase has been the product of bimodalism in investment.

It is not the economy generally that has been too capital intensive. How could that be? Capital intensity is the total stock of capital divided by the total stock of labor. The problem is bimodalism, with a high proportion of capital invested in combination with a small proportion of the labor force and, conversely, a small proportion of the capital spread over a large proportion of the labor force. Hicks[12] has made it clear that that is extraordinarily uneconomic behavior, and yet we see it carried out energetically in India, China, the Philippines and a number of other countries that have not been able to match modest growth in agriculture with a commensurate growth in the demand for labor and food.

It is here that agricultural growth has another important role to play. We know that the expenditure patterns of peasant farmers are tuned substantially toward high labor intensity. They wish to consume goods including labor-intensive agricultural commodities (such as livestock products and vegetables), nonagricultural services (such as rickshaw rides and haircuts), and nonagricultural goods (such as housing, textiles and bicycles), all of which can be produced with technologies that are relatively labor intensive. Such industries have another advantage in that being relatively small-scale, they can be located in rural areas. This means that they can not only increase their capital resources by modest increases in prices, but they may also directly tap sources of investment funds in the rural economy. Changes in relative prices can have a direct effect on incentives for such investment.

I draw attention to a simulation model that examines the effects of various rates of growth of food grain production on overall growth and growth in employment, assuming that employment would grow commensurately with expansion in the wage goods supply (Table 3.8). We must also look at consistency with certain subsectors such as the nonfood agricultural sector. Note that those sectors grow extremely rapidly and presumably provide a substantial proportion of the increased employment.

Once we see these potentials we must ask why they are not being realized. We know that Taiwan has been extraordinarily successful in realizing its potentials. This also seems to be the case in Thailand, Malaysia, the Ivory Coast, Kenya and a number of other countries. Why has it not worked well in the Philippines, China and India? One explanation is insufficient infrastructure investment. For example, small- and medium-scale firms require electrification. Although power represents only a small percentage of costs for labor-intensive enterprises, an unreliable power supply greatly increases costs because of wastage and idleness of labor and other resources. Small businesses require good transport and communication because they are a combination of trader and manufacturer; profits are dependent upon quick responses to changing market conditions. India has not moved very well on rural electrification particularly if we consider the reliability of the power supply. Similarly, small- and medium-scale industries in regional areas require good transport, telephone and communications. These have not been invested in in India at a rate anywhere near sufficient to generate rapid growth in the small-scale sector.

Conclusion

I will conclude with an observation of what food production, consumption and poverty would look like in India if an optimum growth strategy were followed.

First, public sector expenditure would be concentrated almost solely on expansion of infrastructure. That would represent a loss of expenditure on social welfare and of course in almost all types of direct industrial production.

Second, we would see a greatly accelerated rate of growth and employment in the economy and rising food prices. Existing rates of growth in the agricultural sector would call for two actions: a greater assiduousness in the pursuit of agricultural growth, including greater attention to agricultural research and larger imports of fertilizer; and more rapid expansion of rural infrastructure, such as electrification for small tube wells. It would require modernizing agriculture in the Eastern States.

Such a scenario would also involve, if we look at the record of other countries, a return once again to imports of agricultural commodities and particularly of food grains. But that would be in the context of rising domestic agricultural pries, further acceleration of growth in domestic food production, and rapid growth in employment.

Within the agricultural sector there would be tremendous demand pressures on the livestock, vegetable and fruit sectors, all of which can be reasonably employment intensive and can distribute benefits somewhat broadly geographically. There would therefore have to be considerable attention to the much more complex problems in marketing in these sectors, as compared to other sectors.

As one can see from the simulation model results in Table 3.8, such a strategy of growth would result in a virtual elimination of poverty among the ablebodied labor force within ten to forty years, depending on how unfavorable the assumptions are. Those who are not ablebodied would remain in poverty, and significant regional pockets of poverty would continue to exist.

Notes

1. *Agricultural Productivity in Eastern India* (Report of the Committee on Agricultural Productivity in Eastern India, S. R. Sen, Chairman) (Bombay: Reserve Bank of India, 1984).

2. Raisuddin Ahmed, "Role of Infrastructure in Rural Development: The Case of Bangladesh" (Paper presented at the Global Development Conference, University of Maryland, College Park, Maryland, 1986).

3. Gunvant M. Desai, *Sustaining Rapid Growth in India's Fertilizer Consumption: A Perspective Based on Composition of Use* (Research Report 31) (Washington, D.C.: International Food Policy Research Institute, 1982); and Gunvant M. Desai, "Fertilizer Use in India: The Next Stage in Policy" (Washington, D.C.: International Food Policy Research Institute, 1986).

4. John W. Mellor and others, *Developing Rural India: Plan and Practice* (Ithaca, N.Y.: Cornell University Press, 1968).

5. C. G. Ranade, D. Jha and C. Delgado, "Technological Change, Production Costs, and Supply Response," in *Agricultural Price Policy for Developing Countries*, edited by John W. Mellor and Raisuddin Ahmed (forthcoming).

6. Montek S. Ahluwalia, "Rural Poverty, Agricultural Production and Prices: A Reexamination," in *Agricultural Change and Rural Poverty: Variations on a Theme*

of Dharm Narain, edited by John W. Mellor and Gunvant M. Desai (Baltimore, Md.: Johns Hopkins University Press, 1985).

7. Dharm Narain and Shyamal Roy, *Impact of Irrigation and Labor Availability on Multiple Cropping: A Case of India* (Research Report No. 20) (Washington, D.C.: International Food Policy Research Institute, 1980).

8. Kenneth L. Bachman and Leonardo Paulino, *Rapid Food Production Growth in Selected Developing Countries: A Comparative Analysis of Underlying Trends, 1961–76* (Research Report No. 11) (Washington, D.C.: International Food Policy Research Institute, 1979).

9. John W. Mellor, *The New Economics of Growth—A Strategy for India and the Developing World* (Ithaca, N.Y.: Cornell University Press, 1976).

10. Uma Lele and John W. Mellor, "Technological Change, Distributive Bias and Labor Transfer in a Two-Sector Economy," *Oxford Economic Papers* 33 (November 1981).

11. Mellor, *The New Economics of Growth.*

12. John Hicks, *Economic Perspectives: Further Essays on Money and Growth* (Oxford: Clarendon Press, 1977), cited in this context in John W. Mellor and Bruce F. Johnston, "The World Food Equation: Interrelations Among Development, Employment, and Food Consumption," *Journal of Economic Literature* 22 (1984).

TABLE 3.1 Estimates of Food Grain Production in India 1949–50 to 1983–84
(in million metric tons)

Year	Official Estimates of Production	Percent Change from Previous Year	Compound Growth Rate	Input Estimates of Total Production[a]
1949–50	60.8	0.0	2.2	60.8
1950–51	55.0	(9.5)		60.4
1951–52	55.6	1.1		61.0
1952–53	61.8	11.2	4.8	64.2
1953–54	72.4	17.2		68.6
1954–55	70.8	(2.2)	2.8	68.7
1955–56	69.4	(2.0)		70.8
1956–57	72.5	4.5	4.1	72.0
1957–58	66.7	(8.0)		73.6
1958–59	78.9	18.3	3.4	76.9
1959–60	76.9	(2.5)		79.2
1960–61	82.2	6.9		80.5
1961–62	82.9	0.9	2.1	82.6
1962–63	80.3	(3.1)		84.4
1963–64	80.7	0.5	2.1	85.7
1964–65	89.3	10.7		87.0
1965–66	72.3	(19.0)	2.1	88.0
1966–67	74.2	2.6		91.8
1967–68	95.0	28.0	2.8	94.9
1968–69	94.0	(1.1)		100.1
1969–70	99.5	5.9		104.7
1970–71	108.4	8.9	3.3	106.7
1971–72	105.2	(3.0)		110.8
1972–73	97.0	(7.8)		111.8
1973–74	104.7	7.9	3.2	115.0
1974–75	99.8	(4.7)		119.7
1975–76	121.0	21.2		125.4
1976–77	111.2	(8.1)		131.9
1977–78	126.4	13.7		139.3
1978–79	131.9	4.4		147.8
1979–80	109.7	(16.8)	3.0	154.1
1980–81	129.6	18.1		161.0
1981–82	133.3	2.9		168.5
1982–83	129.5	(2.9)		176.7
1983–84	151.5	17.0		185.5

[a] Input estimates of production are derived from estimates of input of
fertilizer, irrigation and labor with standard response coefficients.
Note that up to 1975–76 these estimates provide a smoother trend, while
subsequent to 1975–76 the actual production falls increasingly short of
the actuals. See The New Economics of Growth (cited below) for full
details of the calculation.

Sources: Official estimates (1949–50 through 1970–71) and input estimates
as cited in John W. Mellor, The New Economics of Growth—A Strategy
for India and the Developing World (Ithaca, N.Y.: Cornell University Press,
1976), Table II–2, p. 39; Official estimates 1971–72 through 1983–84 from
Area and Production of Principal Crops in India 1981–84 (New Delhi:
Government of India, Ministry of Agriculture, 1984); and Area and Production of
Principal Crops in India 1981–84 (supplement) (New Delhi: Government of India,
Ministry of Agriculture, 1984).

FIGURE 3.1
Comparison of Official and Input Estimates
of Production of Food Grains in India, 1950-51 to 1983-84

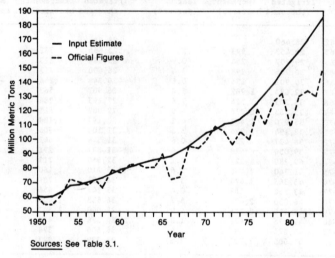

Sources: See Table 3.1.

TABLE 3.2 Gross and Net Irrigated Agricultural Area, India, 1961–62 to 1981–82

Year	Gross			Net		
	Area Irrigated (thousand hectares)	Annual Increment (thousand hectares)	Growth from Preceding Year (percent)	Area Irrigated (thousand hectares)	Annual Increment (thousand hectares)	Growth from Preceding Year (percent)
1961–62	28,460			28,884		
1962–63	29,453	993	3.5	25,665	781	3.1
1963–64	29,707	254	0.9	25,888	223	0.9
1964–65	30,705	998	3.4	26,600	712	2.8
1965–66	30,901	196	0.6	26.344	(256)	-1.0
1966–67	32,683	1,782	5.8	26,907	563	2.1
1967–68	33,207	524	1.6	27,193	286	1.1
1968–69	35,483	2,276	6.9	29,009	1,816	6.7
1969–70	36,970	1,487	4.2	30,197	1,188	4.1
1970–71	38,194	1,224	3.3	31,103	906	3.0
1971–72	38,431	237	0.6	31,546	443	1.4
1972–73	39,059	628	1.6	31,837	291	0.9
1973–74	40,280	1,221	3.1	32,550	713	2.2
1974–75	41,740	1,460	3.6	33,710	1,160	3.6
1975–76	43,363	1,623	3.9	34,491	781	2.3
1976–77	43,552	189	0.4	35,147	656	1.9
1977–78	46,030	2,478	5.7	36,553	1,406	4.0
1978–79	48,306	2,276	4.9	38,060	1,507	4.1
1979–80	49,178	872	1.8	38,478	418	1.1
1980–81	49,875	697	1.4	38,806	328	0.9
1981–82	51,605	1,730	3.5	39,729	923	2.4

a Gross area includes land irrigated more than once during the period.

Source: Fertiliser Statistics 1984–85 (New Delhi: The Fertiliser Association of India, 1985).

TABLE 3.3 Growth of Inorganic Fertilizer Use in India
1961-62 to 1984-85

Year	Total Inorganic Fertilizer[a]	Rate of Growth of Use[b]	Incremental Change from Previous Year
1961-62	338		
1962-63	452		114
1963-64	544	24.1	92
1964-65	773		229
1965-66	785		11
1966-67	1,101		316
1967-68	1,531	14.0	430
1968-69	1,761		230
1969-70	1,982		221
1970-71	2,256		274
1971-72	2,657	13.5	401
1972-73	2,768		111
1973-74	2,839		71
1974-75	2,573		(265)
1975-76	2,894		320
1976-77	3,411		517
1977-78	4,286	11.3	875
1978-79	5,117		831
1979-80	5,255		138
1980-81	5,516		261
1981-82	6,067		551
1982-83	6,386		319
1983-84	7,710		1,324
1984-85	8,211		501

[a] Thousand metric tons of nitrogen, phosphorus and potash.
[b] Trend growth rate of fertilizer use against time for various periods. Calculations used natural logarithms.

Source: Fertiliser Statistics 1984-85 (New Delhi: The Fertiliser Association of India, 1985).

TABLE 3.4   Indian Government Subsidies to Food Grains and Fertilizer
1971-72 to 1984-85

Year	Government Subsidies to Food Grains	Government Subsidies to Fertilizer
	(Rs million)	
1971-72		(200)
1972-73	1,170	(180)
1973-74	2,510	330
1974-75	2,725	3,710
1975-76	4,037	2,420
1976-77	4,000	1,120
1977-78	5,629	2,660
1978-79	5,583	3,420
1979-80	5,895	6,030
1980-81	603	5,050
1981-82	7,610	3,750
1982-83	7,110	6,050
1983-84	8,350	10,420
1984-85	8,500	18,320

[a] Includes total subsidy for consumer cost of buffer stock.
[b] Includes subsidies on imported and domestic fertilizers.

Sources: P. S. George, Some Aspects of Procurement and Distribution of Foodgrains in India (Working Papers on Food Subsidies No. 1) (Washington D.C.: International Food Policy Research Institute); Gunvant Desai, "Policies for Growth in Fertilizer Consumption: The Next Stage" (Paper prepared for the 46th Annual Conference of the Indian Society of Agricultural Economics, Udeapur, December 1986) (forthcoming in the Indian Journal of Agricultural Economics [October-December 1986]).

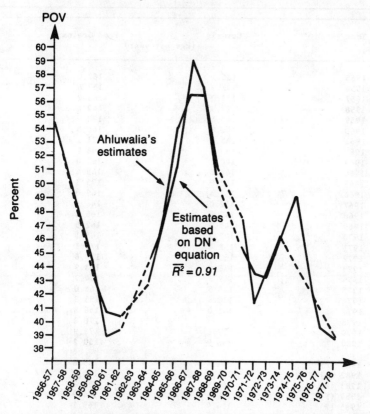

FIGURE 3.2
Changes in the Incidence of
Rural Poverty in India, 1956-57 to 1977-78

* Dharm Narain

Source: John W. Mellor and Gunvant M. Desai, eds.,
<u>Agricultural Change and Rural Poverty — Variations
on a Theme by Dharm Narain</u> (Baltimore, Md.:
Johns Hopkins University Press, 1985), Figure
18.1, p. 196.

TABLE 3.5 Per Capita Net Availability of Food Grains in India 1955 to 1985

Year	Cereals	Food Grains
	(kgs per year)	
1955	136.1	162.0
1956	131.9	157.6
1957	137.0	163.2
1958	127.9	149.2
1959	143.6	170.9
1960	140.6	164.5
1961	145.9	171.1
1962	145.6	168.2
1963	140.2	162.0
1964	146.8	165.4
1965	152.8	175.3
1966	131.4	149.0
1967	132.0	146.5
1968	147.9	168.4
1969	145.2	162.5
1970	147.2	165.1
1971	152.4	171.1
1972	153.4	170.6
1973	138.9	153.9
1974	149.8	164.7
1975	133.5	148.0
1976	136.8	155.3
1977	141.0	156.8
1978	154.2	170.8
1979	157.6	173.9
1980	138.9	150.2
1981 (P)[a]	151.9	165.6
1982 (P)	151.4	165.7
1983 (P)	144.9	159.3
1984 (P)	159.6	174.9
1985 (P)	154.9	169.1

[a] (P) - Provisional.

Source: Selected issues of the Bulletin on Food Statistics (New Delhi: Government of India, Ministry of Agriculture).

TABLE 3.6 Terms of Trade for Food Grains and All Commodities, and Food Grain Stocks, India, 1951–83

Year	Relative Wholesale Prices Food Grains	All Commodities (1970–71 = 100)	Terms of Trade[a]	Public Sector Food Grain Stocks	Net Food Grain Imports (thousand metric tons)
1951	51.9	50.9	102.0		
1952	48.5	44.8	108.3		
1953	48.0	46.7	102.8	1,465	
1954	38.9	44.0	88.4	1,667	
1955	33.6	40.4	83.2	921	
1956	43.2	45.3	95.4	319	
1957	47.5	48.0	99.0	1,175	
1958	49.5	49.0	101.0	906	
1959	49.9	51.0	97.8	1,398	
1960	49.6	54.2	91.5	2,801	
1961	48.0	55.5	86.5	2,636	3,967
1962	51.5	57.5	89.6	2,281	4,160
1963	53.3	59.6	89.4	2,259	4,864
1964	66.5	65.8	101.1	1,016	6,593
1965	73.9	71.2	103.8	2,079	7,930
1966	82.7	70.7	117.0	2,216	10,429
1967	108.8	91.7	118.6	1,965	10,639
1968	100.7	91.3	110.3	3,991	6,050
1969	98.1	93.2	105.3	4,453	4,151
1970	101.4	99.0	102.4	5,569	4,154
1971	102.1	105.0	97.2	8,137	2,347
1972	114.6	113.0	101.4	3,443	323
1973	135.0	131.6	102.6	3,134	3,252
1974	183.6	169.2	108.5	2,730	5,108
1975	187.0	175.8	106.4	8,289	7,567
1976	150.4	172.4	87.2	18,964	6,768
1977	167.2	185.4	90.2	17,364	605
1978	173.3	185.0	93.7	17,160	(882)
1979	179.8	206.5	87.1	17.519	(1,098)
1980	207.3	248.1	83.6	11,739	(953)
1981	236.1	278.4	84.8	11,498	(912)
1982	242.5	285.1	85.1	12,766	663
1983	269.9	307.4	87.8	15,391	2,826

[a] (Relative wholesale price of food grains/all commodities)*100

Sources: Bulletin on Food Statistics 1982–84 (New Delhi: Government of India, Ministry of Agriculture), 24–25; H. L. Chandhok, Wholesale Price Statistics: India 1974–78, vol. 1. (Economic and Scientific Research Foundation, 1978), 1, 75–76; Food and Agriculture Organization of the United Nations, Supply Utilization Accounts (Rome: FAO, 1984).

TABLE 3.7 Relative Shares of Projected Developing Country Net Production
Surpluses by Level of Per Capita GNP (1980), 2000

Level of Per Capita GNP 1980	Net Production Surplus 2000		Percentage of Total Production 2000
	Million Metric Tons	Percent	Percent
Less than $500	50.1	43	61
(China, India, Indonesia, Pakistan)	(42.9)	(37)	(58)
Greater than $500	66.3	57	11
(Argentina, Thailand)	(56.2)	(48)	(6)

Sources: Data set used in preparing Food Trends in the Third World: Past
Trends and Projections to 2000 (IFPRI Research Report 52) (Washington, D.C.:
International Food Policy Research Institute). Projections based on FAO
"Production" and "Agricultural Supply Utilization Accounts" Tapes according to
methodology described in Appendix 1 of IFPRI Research Report 52.

TABLE 3.8 Simulation of the Relation Between the Rate of Growth of Food Grain Production and of Employment Rates[a] (percent rate of growth)

Alternative Food Grain Growth Rates

Assumption Set 1[b] $G_m = 2.75$ $G_d = 1.75$ $G_p = 2.50$ $t = 0.60$			Assumption Set 2[b] $G_m = 3.00$ $G_d = 2.00$ $G_p = 2.50$ $t = 0.60$		
Year	Food Grains	Total Employment	Year	Food Grains	Total Employment
2	2.7	2.7	2	3.0	3.0
5	2.8	2.8	5	3.0	3.0
10	2.9	2.9	10	3.1	3.1
15	2.9	2.9	15	3.2	3.2
20	3.0	3.0	20	3.2	3.2
25	3.0	3.0	25	3.2	3.4
30	3.0	3.1	27	3.3	3.4
35	3.1	3.1			
39	3.1	3.1			

Assumption Set 3
$G_m = 3.00$
$G_d = 2.00$
$G_p = 2.50$
$t = 1.25$

Year	Food Grains	Total Employment
2	3.9	4.0
5	3.9	4.0
10	3.9	4.0
12	3.9	4.0

TABLE 3.8 (Continued)

Alternative Technologies

Assumption Set 4				Assumption Set 5		
$G_m = 3.00$				$G_m = 3.00$		
$G_d = 0.75$				$G_d = 2.80$		
$G_p = 2.50$				$G_p = 2.50$		
$t = 2.00$				$t = 0.70$		
Year	Food Grains	Total Employment		Year	Food Grains	Total Employment
2	4.0	4.4		2	3.8	3.7
5	4.1	4.3		5	3.8	3.8
10	4.2	4.2		10	3.8	3.9
				14	3.7	4.0

Alternative Population Growth Rates

Assumption Set 6				Assumption Set 7		
$G_m = 3.00$				$G_m = 3.00$		
$G_d = 2.00$				$G_d = 2.80$		
$G_p = 2.00$				$G_p = 3.00$		
$t = 1.25$				$t = 1.25$		
Year	Food Grains	Total Employment		Year	Food Grains	Total Employment
2	3.9	4.0		2	3.9	4.0
5	3.9	4.1		5	3.9	4.0
10	3.9	4.1		10	3.9	4.0
				15	3.9	4.0
				19	3.9	3.9

[a] This table shows, under various assumptions, the growth rates of food grain production and agricultural employment in the initial year, at five-year intervals, and at the final year in which full employment is reached.

[b] The g_m – yield growth rate in modern food grains sector; g_d – yield growth rate in traditional food grains sector; g_p – population growth rate; t – rate of transfer of land from the traditional to the modern sector.

Source: John W. Mellor and Mohinder S. Mudahar, "Simulating a Developing Economy with Modernizing Agricultural Sector—Implications for Employment and Growth" (Cornell Agricultural Economics Occasional Paper No. 76) (June 1974), Table 21. As reported in Mellor, The New Economics of Growth, Table VII-5, p. 185.se

4

Agricultural Development and Rural Poverty

A. Vaidyanathan

Main Features of Agricultural Growth in India

There is an extensive literature on various facets of the performance of Indian agriculture since Independence which documents in quite some detail the facts regarding growth and fluctuations in crop production both overall and of specific crops as well as the regional variations therein. The salient features of this record are quite well-known:

1. Aggregate crop output has grown at a much faster rate since Independence than in the first half of the century. The average rate of growth since 1950 has been around 3 percent a year compared to less than 1 percent per annum in the previous fifty years.
2. Though there have been significant technological changes—including the introduction of high-yielding varieties (HYVs)—the overall rate of agricultural growth has not shown any tendency to accelerate. At best, the rate of growth can be said to have remained constant.
3. The rate of area expansion has fallen off pretty rapidly despite some intensification of cropping, but this has been just about compensated for by a quickening in the pace of yield improvement.
4. The rate of yield improvement in different crops is highly disparate: While some crops—notably wheat—have recorded high and even accelerating rates of yield increase, others—including the so-called coarse grains, pulses and major oil seeds—have not. Unlike the case of wheat, HYV technology has not had a dramatic impact on rice yields, except in some pockets and that too outside the traditional rice-growing seasons/tracts.
5. Production growth has been unstable both in terms of the magnitude of year-to-year fluctuations and of variations in the "trend" rate between different segments of the period since Independence. There

I am grateful to S. Guhan and S. Subramanian for comments on an earlier draft.

77

is some evidence of increased instability in the post-HYV period compared to earlier years. But this seems to be more a reflection of greater instability in area and greater synchrony in the movement of area and yields across regions in the post-HYV era rather than a feature inherent to the new technology.

6. There is considerable regional variation in growth: The trend growth rate over the period 1952–78, according to one recent estimate, ranged from less than 1.5 percent per annum in Madyha Pradesh to over 5 percent per annum in Punjab and Haryana. In as many as six major States, output growth was below 2.5 percent a year (Table 4.1).

7. The range of variation is even greater when we consider districts. Between 1962–65 and 1970–73, 100 out of 280 districts recorded a growth of better than 3 percent a year; but 110 others achieved less than 1.5 percent per annum with 64 reporting an absolute decline. While the pattern of regional variation is highly sensitive to the period chosen and the way crop growth rates are estimated, the existence of large variations cannot be doubted.

While the facts regarding agricultural growth are reasonably well documented, it cannot be said that we have anything like an adequate explanation for why growth was not faster and why it varies so much. Some point to the inadequacy of investment (especially public investment) in irrigation and/or its poor quality; others emphasize the inequitable agrarian structure and the failure of land reforms; yet others cite the failure to evolve varieties and techniques for raising yields of dryland crops; while the farm lobby blames it all on lack of incentives. Unquestionably each one of these is relevant but individually none of them provide an adequate "explanation" of observed growth. For instance, if irrigation were the crucial factor, it is difficult to explain why Tamil Nadu, which has a high irrigation ratio—one of the highest in the country—recorded such low growth since the sixties while Gujarat, which has a much lower irrigation ratio and much lower rainfall, achieved such impressive growth. One has to explain why east Uttar Pradesh and Bihar—by all accounts well endowed with groundwater—have been so slow to exploit the resource. That unequal distribution of land and high incidence of tenancy need·not always impede growth is underlined by the experience of Punjab-Haryana where the inequalities in land and wealth are relatively high. If price incentives were the crucial factor, how does one account for the relative constancy of the overall growth rate despite marked shifts in the trends in terms of trade from the period up to the late sixties and thereafter?[1] The highly disparate regional growth patterns, in the context of largely similar trends in the terms of trade, point to the crucial role of environment, technology and other nonprice factors. But their precise role—and relative importance—remains unresearched.

In any case, our concern in this chapter is not so much with the determinants of agricultural growth or explaining the interregional variations as with its impact on rural poverty. Because it is the primary economic activity of rural areas, the performance of agricultural production clearly has an important bearing on the living standards of the rural population.

Trends in Rural Poverty

At a general level there are two divergent hypotheses on the relation between agricultural growth and rural poverty. One school holds that the benefits of agricultural growth trickle down more or less automatically and, sooner or later, to all segments of the rural society. This view implies that it is the rate of agricultural growth which is crucial to the speed with which rural poverty can be eliminated. The other view is that the current strategies of agricultural development have an inbuilt tendency for aggravation of rural inequalities and therefore could well lead to an increase in the incidence of rural poverty despite growth—even rapid growth—in production. The controversy arising from these contending perceptions has stimulated a great deal of empirical work to estimate the incidence of poverty across space and time. While it is not possible to settle the questions definitely, it seems useful to take stock of the available empirical evidence and see where the weight of evidence points.

Broadly speaking, empirical studies on trends in rural poverty fall into two classes: (1) those which quantify the incidence of poverty (in terms of the head count ratio, the Sen index and such other measures) based on the mean per capita consumption levels in rural areas and the distribution of the rural population around the mean at different points of time; and (2) those which focus on the changes in living conditions of rural wage labor which figure prominently among the ranks of the poor.

Studies in the former category are far from unanimous about the direction of change in the incidence of poverty. In an early paper Bardhan[2] concluded that the proportion of rural population in India living below the poverty line had substantially increased during the sixties. Rajaraman[3] estimated that during the sixties the incidence of poverty had risen in Punjab-Haryana despite extraordinarily high agricultural growth rates. In a later and more detailed study, Ahluwalia came to the conclusion that the "NSS [National Survey Sample] data provides no evidence for asserting a trend increase or decrease in rural poverty over the period as a whole"[4] at the national level or for that matter in most states.

More important is Ahluwalia's finding that between 1956 and 1973—the period of his study—the level of agricultural output per capita had a significant inverse relation with the incidence of poverty at the national level. This relation was by no means universal at the State level: It was found to hold in seven of the fourteen major States but not in the rest. Of the six States which recorded a significant trend rise in agricultural output per head of rural population (including Punjab-Haryana), none showed a significant decrease in poverty; at least one (West Bengal) recorded a rise. Further, after netting out the effect of variations in agricultural output per capita there was a trend increase in the incidence of poverty (by the head count measure) in more than half the States suggesting that "there may be factors at work in the rural economy which by themselves tend to increase the incidence of rural poverty." Labor-

NB

displacing technical change was specifically identified as one such factor. In a more recent study Narain found that besides agricultural production and time, the price of food has a significant positive relation to incidence of poverty.[5] The manner in which food price enters as a determinant of poverty, however, remains unclear.

In sharp contrast to the above are the findings of Minhas[6] and recent estimates of the Planning Commission. Minhas estimated that during the sixties—over exactly the period covered by Bardhan—the proportion of rural population living below the poverty line had in fact significantly declined. Gupta and Datta's[7] estimates imply that the incidence of poverty in rural India recorded a trend decline during the period 1960–67 and a mild trend rise subsequently.[8] The Planning Commission in its Seventh Five-Year Plan (1985–90) document estimates the head count ratio to have fallen from 51.3 percent in 1977–78 to 40.4 percent in 1983, well below the level of the sixties. The National Council of Applied Economic Research (NCAER)[9] also estimates the incidence of poverty to have declined substantially between 1970 and 1981 (from 57 percent to 48.5 percent).

Some limitations of the above estimates: Except for the NCAER estimates, which are derived from its own independent survey of "panel samples" at two points of time,[10] the others rely heavily on NSS data. But while some (and in particular Bardhan, Ahluwalia, Rajaraman) rely on NSS estimates for the mean *and* the distribution, others (including Minhas, Gupta and Datta and the Planning Commission) apply the NSS distribution of population around the mean to the mean per capita consumption derived from official national accounts estimates. Given that both sets of poverty estimates use the same estimates of distribution around the mean for each period of time, the divergence between them is entirely due to a different time pattern of behavior in the mean per capita consumption emerging from the NSS and the national income accounts. Thus the divergent conclusions of Bardhan and Minhas about the direction of movement in the head count ratio during the sixties are mostly explainable by the fact that the NSS (used by Bardhan) showed a 10 percent decline in per capita real consumption between 1960–61 and 1967–68, while the Central Statistical Organization (CSO) estimates (used by Minhas) showed a 6.7 percent rise over the same period.[11] Taken over a longer period, the two procedures give rise to quite different time profiles of change in the head count ratio (Table 4.2).

There has been some discussion on the relative merits of the NSS and the CSO estimates as a basis for judging the trends in mean per capita consumption. This question, however, cannot be settled unequivocally. There is a good case for basing estimates of poverty incidence on NSS estimates of both the mean *and* the distribution around it, provided we can be reasonably sure of the comparability of NSS designs, concepts and procedures over the period under review. Unfortunately a careful scrutiny of NSS from this angle raises several doubts.[12]

First, there are questions whether a sample design intended to get a reasonably precise estimate of the mean value of a selected characteristic— in this case consumption—of the population under study will also give an accurate measure of the inequality of its distribution when the latter is highly skewed.

Second, there have been significant changes in concepts, the survey questionnaires and methods of administering them. Examples of these important changes include the switch from the practice of canvassing only consumer expenditure schedules from the selected sample—which used to be in vogue till the early sixties—to the integrated household schedules through the rest of the sixties, the reversion to the original practice in 1973–74 and the combination of consumption and employment/unemployment inquiries from 1977 to 1978. Changes in item coverage and, in some cases, the concept of "consumption" introduce additional elements of noncomparability.

Third, while the comparison of official and NSS estimates of aggregate consumption is fraught with difficulties, for the few items in respect of which there is a reasonable basis to suppose that the official estimates are fairly reliable, the NSS shows very different patterns of change over time from the official series. This is particularly striking in the case of food grains and clothing. Furthermore, in the case of food grains NSS points to a significant decline in per capita intake among the uppermost quartile of the rural population and a near constance in the lowest quartile. These considerations add to the implausibility of NSS for judging time trends.

A fourth reason is that the NSS shows hardly any change in the extent of interregional inequality in consumption: The coefficient of variation in per capita rural consumption across the major States has fluctuated between 15 percent and 17 percent. But other data point to a considerable widening of interregional disparities. Thus the coefficient of variation of crop output per head of rural population is estimated to have risen from 33 percent in 1962–65 to 52 percent in 1970–73. The interdistrict disparities have also increased in this period. A more recent study[13] also reports that disparities in per capita output, computed across fifty-six regions, in 1975–78 was higher than in the early 1960s. While crop production is not the only activity, it is almost everywhere the most important in rural areas; and there is no reason to suppose that regional variations in growth of noncrop activities have been such as to neutralize differences in crop output growth.

Rural Wage Laborers and Their Conditions

More compelling is the evidence that sections of the population which obviously belong to the poorer rungs of rural society have been proliferating in numbers and that their condition has not improved. The most important and striking case is that of rural wage laborers who invariably have a lower per capita income/consumption than the nonlabor classes.[14] Rural labor households as a proportion of all rural households are estimated to have risen from 25 percent in 1964–65 to 30 percent in 1974–75. Those usually working as wage laborers as a proportion of the rural work force have risen from 34 percent in 1972–73 to 40 percent in 1983 among males and 35–38 percent among females. The proportion of casual labor among wage laborers—who in general are poorer than wage laborers with regular employment[15]—has also increased sharply. These tendencies are pretty nearly universal as can be seen from State-level estimates given in Table 4.3.

We have comparable data on employment, wages and incomes of rural wages and incomes of rural wage laborers only for two points of time, namely, 1964–65 and 1974–75 (summarized in Table 4.4). They show that on the average a male worker in the rural labor households had fewer days of wage paid employment in 1974–75 compared to 1964–65 and that real wage rates per day had declined in all states except Punjab-Haryana.[16]

It has been suggested that no inferences on trends can be sustained on the basis of the two rural labor inquiries inasmuch as 1964–65 was a good agricultural year while 1974–75 was below normal. While there is some force in this argument, it is necessary to note that not all States recorded a fall in output and that real wage rates fell even in States which had experienced a significant rise in production. Similar data are not published for other years, but judging from the NSS employment surveys, there are indications that in the aggregate employment has not kept pace with population growth. This is reflected in the fact that the estimated total number of days of employment relative to population shows a progressive decline from 1972–73 to 1977–78 and on to 1983 in seven out of the sixteen major States and that in all cases this index in 1983 is lower than in 1972–73. The earnings of casual labor per day in different operations in 1977–78 as reported by the NSS also show a reduction in real terms compared to 1974–75 which in turn was generally below the 1964–65 levels.[17]

The official series on agricultural wages give a somewhat different picture: Up to the early 1970s they also show a general declining trend in real wage rate for most operations in a majority of States, but in some (Punjab, Kerala, Gujarat and Tamil Nadu) there was a rise in real wage rates. There were also states which experienced a relatively high rise in productivity.[18] More disaggregated analysis of the Punjab also points to a significant rise in real wage rates in several districts and suggests a positive relation between change in real wage rates and the overall growth of crop output.[19] While a more detailed and up-to-date analysis of this body of data would be useful, they are not as representative, comparable or carefully compiled as the NSS. A clearer picture of trends in real wage rates in rural India will have to await the publication of detailed tabulations of data from NSS employment surveys of the past decade.

Other Indirect Evidence

The broad trends revealed by the NSS seem to be generally consistent with what we know about demographic change, output growth and technological progress in rural India. Rural population has been rising at around 1.8 percent per annum even as the extent of arable land has remained practically constant. The area actually cultivated (net sown area) after showing a sizable rise in the fifties and sixties has remained more or less constant in the last decade or more. Even in the absence of any changes in the distribution of operational holdings, this implies a progressive and significant decline in the average size of holdings and a rapid proliferation of relatively small holdings. The tendency would be accentuated if the distribution of operational land holdings gets more concentrated.[20] The increase in the proportion of small holdings will lead to an increase in the proportion of households having to depend on wage labor, at least partly, for their sustenance, unless the increase in net income per unit area in these holdings is sufficient to compensate for the reduction in holding size. The decline in traditional rural crafts under the impact of newer and urban-made products has probably also contributed.

The growth of production relative to population growth has been in general quite low, and scattered evidence points to a relatively faster growth in productivity in relatively larger holdings: For the country as a whole, the rate of expansion of irrigated area at any rate between 1961 and 1971 was positively correlated to holding size. And in some of the rapidly growing areas the inverse relation between size and productivity has been found to have weakened after the introduction of the new varieties, and on occasion even reversed.

A major, at any rate growing, part of the rise in output has come from improvements in yield per hectare of gross cropped area: There is some evidence that labor requirements do not increase in the same proportion as yields following adoption of better varieties and more intensive use of fertilizers, even where there is no change in mechanization of cultivation operation. Where the two types of technical change are combined, there may in fact be an absolute a decline in labor input per unit area.[21] The available data on changes in labor use for crop husbandry in particular—limited to a few regions—suggest that the elasticity of employment with respect to output per hectare is less than 0.5, and in one case negative.[22] The NSS estimate for agricultural employment in 1977–78 is only 4 percent higher than in 1972–73 while crop production was 20 percent higher. At the State level, the increase in agricultural employment is seen to be almost always below the rise in output; in fact, in several cases (including Punjab and Haryana) total labor input declined in absolute terms in spite of a rise in production.[23] However, this may be in part statistical, reflecting changes in the way people report sectoral distribution of their work days.

The NSS shows a significant all-around rise in nonagricultural employment at any rate in the seventies. The share of nonagricultural to total workers in rural India is estimated to have risen from 17 percent in 1972 to 23 percent in 1983 among males and 10–13 percent among females. The reasons for this extraordinary growth in nonagricultural employment are not clear: Elsewhere I have suggested that this may reflect accelerated commercialization of the rural economy; the growth of public spending of all types in rural areas; and greater use of a casual labor force leading to greater discrimination in reporting the nature of work done especially by wage laborers.[24] It is difficult to know the relative importance of these factors in explaining the rising share of nonagricultural employment. Insofar as the last-mentioned factor is significant, the reported rise, or rather a part of it, is more apparent than real. Be that as it may, the fact remains that despite the rapid growth in reported nonagricultural employment, total employment in rural India has grown consistently slower than population and the labor force. This is also true of most States (Table 4.5).

With aggregate demand for labor growing slower than population and the supply of family labor relative to requirements in agriculture rising on account of the progressive reduction in average size of holdings, we would expect the demand for hired labor to have increased considerably slower than the total labor requirements. If this happens, as it seems to have, at a time when the supply of wage labor relative to total labor supply is increasing, both the level of employment and the average daily earnings of wage laborers are apt to be under pressure. There is, as mentioned earlier, some indication of the latter, but the data as published do not permit a categorical assessment of the former: Though the overall unemployment rate (person days) in 1983 is higher than in 1972–73 in a majority of States, it does not show a consistent trend over the period.

Conclusion

The above review suggests that estimates of the overall incidence of poverty derived wholly from NSS consumer expenditure surveys, or by combining the NSS distribution with official estimates of mean consumption, cannot be relied upon to judge the *trends* in poverty incidence. Other evidence—largely relating to the growing importance of wage labor, the growth of employment being slower than population, and a fall in real wage rates—seems to suggest that incidence of poverty may have increased. Being based on observations for two to three points of time, this inference could be questioned. But this evidence gains plausibility when we consider it in conjunction with evidence on the demographic trend, output growth and the responsiveness of employment to output. Slow growth in agricultural output is undoubtedly an important factor working to the disadvantage of the poor. But one cannot take it for granted that moderate improvements in growth per se will make a significant difference unless effective steps are taken to prevent worsening of the distribution of operational holdings (whether due to land transfer or resumption of land by owners for self-cultivation) and to arrest the pace of labor-displacing mechanization.

Notes

1. From 1952–53 to 1964–65 terms of trade moved in favor of agriculture; since then they have steadily deteriorated.

2. P. K. Bardhan, "On the Incidence of Poverty in Rural India During the Sixties," *Economic and Political Weekly* (February 1973).

3. Indira Rajaraman, "Poverty Inequality and Economic Growth in the Punjab 1960–61 to 1970–71," *Journal of Development Studies* 2, No. 4 (1975).

4. M. S. Ahluwalia, "Rural Poverty in India 1956–57 to 1973–74" (reproduced in World Bank Staff Working Paper 279 [Washington, D.C., 1978]), 14. Ahluwalia's

latest study which extends the analysis to 1977–78 reiterates this conclusion at the national level. The study shows a progressive rise in head count ratio up to the 1967–68 and a general tendency to fall thereafter. See M. S. Ahluwalia, "Rural Poverty, Agricultural Production and Prices," in *Agricultural Change and Rural Poverty*, edited by John W. Mellor and Gunvant M. Desai (Baltimore, Md.: John Hopkins University Press, 1985).

5. Mellor and Desai, *Agricultural Change and Rural Poverty*.

6. B. S. Minhas, "Rural Poverty, Land Distribution and Development Strategy," *Indian Economic Review* (April 1970).

7. S.P. Gupta and K. L. Dutta, "Poverty Calculations in the Sixth Plan," *Economic and Political Weekly* (April 1984).

8. The Gupta-Dutta head count ratios are based on a higher poverty line. It is noteworthy that the NSS does not show any significant trend change in the index of relative inequality. Between 1977–78 and 1983, however, there is a marked reduction in the Gini coefficient from 0.34 to 0.30 which accounts for the decline in head count ratio despite near stagnation of real consumption (for further details see S. Subramanian, "Poverty Statistics: Real Phenomena or Arithmetical Illusions?" (Madras Institute of Development Studies, 1986, Mimeographed).

9. National Council of Applied Economic Research, "Changes in Poverty and Consumption Patterns in Rural India between 1970–71 and 1981–82" (1986, Mimeographed).

10. The NCAER data for a panel sàmple is a questionable basis for judging trends in the overall incidence of poverty inasmuch as the set of sample households selected to be representative of the population at one point in time cannot be representative of the population ten years later. Even as a basis for judging what happened to the particular set of households, the NCAER data are of questionable value because a high proportion of the original sample households could not able located in the resurvey. (For a detailed critique see K. Sundaram and S. D. Tendulkar, "Towards an Explanation of Interregional Variation in Poverty and Unemployment in India" (Delhi School of Economics, 1983, Mimeographed).

11. A. Vaidyanathan, "Some Aspects of Inequality in Living Standards in Rural India," in *Poverty and Income Distribution in India*, edited by T. N. Srinivasan and P. K. Bardhan (Calcutta: Statistical Publishing Society, 1974). The relative movements of the two series of per capita private consumption show no consistent pattern over time. Thus the CSO estimate of mean per capita real consumption was below that of the NSS in 1960–61 and 1961–62; the former was 7–8 percent higher in 1963–65 and nearly 20 percent higher in 1967–68. Thereafter the difference progressively narrowed till 1977–78 before widening again. In 1983, the CSO estimate was 20 percent higher than that of the NSS. (See Ahluwalia, "Rural Poverty in India"; and Subramanian, "Poverty Statistics.") Also unlike the CSO, which shows a generally rising trend in mean per capita consumption, the NSS series are quite erratic. (See A. Vaidyanathan, "On the Validity of NSS Consumption Data," *Economic and Political Weekly* January 1986.)

12. For a detailed discussion see Vaidyanathan, "On the Validity of NSS Consumption Data."

13. S. Mahendra Dev, "Direction of Change in Performance of All Crops in Indian Agriculture in the Late 1970s," *Economic and Political Weekly* (January 1985).

14. On the basis of State-level data from the first rural labor inquiry, the per capita consumption of rural labor households in different States is seen to be 16–35 percent less than the average for other rural households. Assam is one exception in that the difference is only 2 percent. It is also noteworthy that Sundaram and Tendulkar ("Towards an Explanation of Interregional Variation in Poverty and Unemployment") found that the incidence of wage labor and the

wage rate were among the factors which had a significant role in accounting for interregional variations in the incidence of poverty.

15. This statement is based on data from the first agricultural labor inquiry conducted in 1950. No data for subsequent periods are published, but it would be surprising if casual laborers' annual income/expenditure exceeded that of regular employees.

16. See also P. K. Bardhan, "Poverty and 'Trickle-Down' in Rural India: A Quantitative Analysis," in Mellor and Desai, *Agricultural Change and Rural Poverty*.

17. Strictly speaking, the estimates for 1964–65 and 1974–75 relate to all wage laborers but it seems a reasonable presumption that averages for particular operations relate to casual labor. There is, however, some question about the comparability of the average daily earnings obtained from the two rural labor inquiries and that obtained from the 1977–78 NSS data.

18. A. V. Jose, "Trends in Real Wage Rates of Agricultural Laborers," *Economic and Political Weekly* (March 1974). Gustav F. Papanek, "Poverty in India" (Boston, 1986, Mimeographed), cites estimates of average real wage rates of agricultural labor in different States for 1954–56 and 1979–80 from the same source as used by Jose. This shows that the national average has remained constant while in seven out of the thirteen States for which estimates are given, the real wage rates show a decline.

19. See for example, S. Bhalla, "Real Wage Rates of Agricultural Laborers in the Punjab 1956–77" *Economic and Political Weekly* (June 1979). This is also borne out in Uttar Pradesh but not in Andhra Pradesh where real wage rates seem to have been stagnant with no association between growth of output and wage rate trends (G. Parthasarathy and Adiseshu, "Real Wages of Agricultural Labor in A.P.," *Economic and Political Weekly* [July 1982]).

20. This seems to have happened only in the Punjab-Haryana region. A detailed scrutiny of district-level data may well show it to be a more widespread phenomenon. But it seems likely that the primary factor behind the burgeoning of the ranks of wage labor in rural India is demographic rather than arising from drastic changes in land distribution.

21. See, for example, W. A. Bartsch, *Employment and Technology Choice in Asian Agriculture* (Geneva: International Labor Organization, 1977).

22. J. N. Sinha, "Employment and Agriculture in the Draft Plan 1978–83," *Economic and Political Weekly* (1979), using farm management survey data for the mid-fifties and the late sixties/early seventies, estimated the elasticity for five districts as follows: Ferozepur, .37; Muzaffarnagar, .30; Ahmednagar, .50; Coimbatore, .40; Hooghly, .40.

23. A. Vaidyanathan, "Pattern of Labor Use in Rural India: A Study of Regional and Temporal Variations" (Madras Institute of Development Studies, 1986, forthcoming).

24. Ibid.

TABLE 4.1 Trends in Growth of Crop Output and Rural Population 1952-78

| | Percentage Per Annum | |
	Crop Production[a]	Rural Population[b]
Andhra Pradesh	2.2	1.6
Assam	1.7	2.9
Bihar	2.0	1.8
Gujarat	3.3	2.3
Karnataka	3.1	2.1
Kerala	2.6	1.9
Madhya Pradesh	1.4	2.0
Maharashtra	1.5	1.9
Orissa	2.6	1.7
Punjab-Haryana	5.1	1.6
Rajasthan	2.9	2.5
Tamil Nadu	2.6	1.2
Uttar Pradesh	2.6	1.7
West Bengal	2.4	2.3

[a] A. V. Jose, "Growth and Fluctuations in Indian Agriculture 1952-53 to 1978-79" (Mimeographed), refers to gross value of output at constant prices.
[b] Computed from census data.

TABLE 4.2 Alternative Estimates of Incidence of Poverty in Rural India

	Ahluwalia	Gupta and Datta
1960-61	38.9	56.8
1961-62	39.4	56.2
1963-64	44.5	53.8
1964-65	46.8	47.4
1965-66	53.8	49.9
1966-67	56.6	49.2
1967-68	56.5	45.2
1968-69	51.0	48.4
1970-71	47.5	46.8
1971-72	41.2	47.8
1972-73	43.1	50.5
1973-74	46.1	47.6
1977-78	39.1	51.5

Sources: Ahluwalia, "Rural Poverty, Agricultural Production and Prices"; Gupta and Datta, "Poverty Calculations in the Sixth Plan."

TABLE 4.3 Trends in Incidence of Wage Labor in Rural Male Work Force and
Composition of Wage Labor

	1972-73[a]		1977-78[b]		1982-83[c]	
	WL/WF[d]	CWL/WL[d]	WL/WF	CWL/WL	WL/WF	CWL/WL
Andhra Pradesh	40.0	68.6	45.8	73.0	46.6	74.2
Assam	23.8	40.0	32.3	49.7	35.9	49.0
Bihar	39.5	60.9	40.9	80.8	42.8	82.2
Gujarat	34.4	64.6	37.1	79.8	40.4	81.5
Haryana	24.0	40.3	28.2	52.8	30.0	52.3
Jammu and Kashmir	9.4	20.9	20.3	39.5	26.8	69.7
Karnataka	37.8	72.1	41.8	81.2	41.5	87.3
Kerala	54.3	72.1	63.8	70.3	54.5	76.7
Madhya Pradesh	27.3	56.8	31.0	71.8	33.7	72.0
Maharashtra	53.5	70.3	48.7	63.8	47.4	71.5
Orissa	39.9	68.3	45.6	74.7	43.7	76.8
Punjab	30.7	52.3	36.0	54.0	33.6	61.7
Rajasthan	10.2	53.5	17.1	65.8	20.5	63.1
Tamil Nadu	42.4	73.8	48.3	73.8	54.2	75.1
Uttar Pradesh	21.6	60.0	24.4	68.7	24.1	73.6
West Bengal	48.1	66.7	49.0	71.3	50.4	75.4

[a] Computed from NSS data for the Twenty-Seventh Round, Sarvekshana (Journal
of the National Sample Survey Organization) (October 1977).

[b] Computed from NSS data for the Thirty-Second Round, Sarvekshana (January-
April 1981).

[c] Computed from NSS data for the Thirty-Eighth Round, Report No. 315 of the
National Sample Survey (New Delhi: Government of India, Ministry of
Planning, Department of Statistics, National Sample Survey Organization,
June 1985).

[d] WF: Work Force
WL: Wage Laborers
CWL: Casual Wage Laborers

TABLE 4.4 Employment and Wages of Male Wage Laborers in Rural India 1964–65 and 1974–75

	1964–65			1974–75		
	Index of Crop Output[a]	Wage Rate[b] (Rs)	No. of Days Worked/ Worker[c]	Index of Crop Output[a]	Wage Rate[b] (Rs)	No. of Days Worked/ Worker[c]
Andhra Pradesh	162.2	.82	242	197.1	.70	209
Assam	117.1	1.50	289	132.2	1.06	291
Bihar	130.7	1.04	222	135.5	.92	201
Gujarat	269.3	.93	294	180.9	.85	240
Karnataka	194.9	.72	248	253.9	.71	228
Kerala	135.2	1.44	184	191.8	1.42	154
Madhya Pradesh	151.9	.76	244	140.3	.56	230
Maharashtra	160.5	.96	264	184.3	.71	240
Orissa	149.7	.85	257	137.1	.61	177
Punjab–Haryana	181.1	1.52	305	291.4	1.89	230
Rajasthan	181.1	1.35	230	196.3	1.01	246
Tamil Nadu	183.2	.85	209	171.5	.76	173
Uttar Pradesh	137.4	.67	230	158.2	.84	216
West Bengal	130.7	1.23	297	156.2	.96	236

[a] Jose, "Growth and Fluctuation in Indian Agriculture 1952–53 to 1978–79". 1952–53 = 100.

[b] At 1960–61 prices obtained by deflating current wage rates by consumer price index for agricultural laborers.

[c] Relates to wage paid employment; 1974–75 figures computed from estimates for wage labor households with land and without land. The wage rate and employment data are taken from Final Report 1964–65 (New Delhi: Government of India, Labour Bureau, Rural Labour Enquiry) and Final Report on Wages and Earnings 1974–75 (New Delhi: Government of India, Labour Bureau, Rural Labour Enquiry).

TABLE 4.5 Number of Working Days Per Day Per 100 Persons in Rural India

| | 1972–73 | | 1977–78 | | 1983 | |
	Male	Female	Male	Female	Male	Female
Andhra Pradesh	63.5	29.8	61.8	35.5	60.4	33.0
Assam	55.7	6.5	53.0	5.8	53.6	7.6
Bihar	55.7	15.8	53.9	13.0	52.9	14.2
Gujarat	57.3	28.3	55.6	25.5	55.6	25.5
Haryana	56.5	22.1	52.4	13.5	55.1	14.4
Jammu and Kashmir	55.3	16.8	56.4	11.0	50.5	3.7
Karnataka	59.2	32.3	58.4	26.8	58.4	28.4
Kerala	41.1	17.7	38.4	14.7	40.6	14.3
Madhya Pradesh	61.5	39.4	59.7	30.1	60.7	32.1
Maharashtra	58.4	36.4	58.2	33.1	56.0	31.4
Orissa	58.3	21.0	55.8	14.4	57.5	18.0
Punjab	60.8	23.5	58.6	12.8	59.4	9.0
Rajasthan	64.2	48.1	60.5	34.7	57.1	37.6
Tamil Nadu	61.6	34.0	57.5	31.0	52.7	28.1
Uttar Pradesh	58.7	19.7	55.7	16.3	56.4	15.5
West Bengal	52.4	9.5	54.5	8.5	50.7	8.6
India	58.0	25.2	56.1	21.6	55.4	21.8

Source: **Sarvekshana** (April 1986).

PART THREE

Employment and Poverty

5

Agriculture, Employment and Poverty

V. M. Dandekar

By any measure, India is a poor country. It was poorer forty years ago when it became independent. According to the 1951 population census, the country had a population of 363.2 million and a net national product (NNP) (at factor cost) estimated at Rs 88,120 million at current prices. This gave a per capita income of Rs 244.6 or about U.S. $65 per annum. In this generally poor population, there were large sections who were poorer still. One of the fundamental problems of development is whether removal or alleviation of so dismal a poverty could be left to the general course of economic development or whether a direct attack would be necessary and successful. The purpose of the present chapter is to delineate the course of public policy and performance in both directions.

There is a certain type of poverty which is institutional. The people are not only poor but they suffer various social and economic handicaps. In this category fall certain castes and tribes in India. It was obvious that the course of economic development would not reach them unless the institutional barriers and handicaps from which they suffered were removed. Hence, the Constitution of independent India adopted by the Constituent Assembly on 26 January 1949 recognized the need to provide certain protective measures and safeguards for these people. They were specifically listed in separate schedules of the Constitution and hence are referred to as Scheduled Castes and Scheduled Tribes. They constitute about 15.5 percent and 7.5 percent of the population respectively. The safeguards included reservations of seats in the Lok Sabha (Union Parliament) and Vidhan Sabhas (State Legislative Assemblies), reservations in services, removal of social disabilities such as untouchability and prohibition of exploitation such as of bonded labor. The Constitution provides for the appointment of a Commissioner for Scheduled Castes and Scheduled Tribes who reports to the President periodically on the working of these safeguards. His reports are placed on the table of the Parliament.

Government Programs for Poorer
and Weaker Sections of Society

A number of steps were taken in pursuance of these objectives with varying degrees of success. However, it soon became clear that institutional reform was only a precondition and that more active steps would be necessary to ensure that the course of economic development reached these people. Hence, in the last few years, particular attention is being paid to secure for these people an equitable share in the benefits of planned development. Strategies adopted for the purpose naturally vary. Scheduled Tribes live as homogenous groups in clearly identifiable but generally inaccessible forest areas. Hence, opening of these areas and bringing them in contact with the mainstream of national life is their greatest need. The strategy for the development of Scheduled Tribes is therefore to formulate and implement Tribal Sub-Plans encompassing the total development effort of the Government in these areas. In contrast, the Scheduled Castes are not so secluded from the rest of the society. But they suffer from social stigma and have been victims of grave injustice in the past. Hence the strategy for their development is to ensure for them an equitable share in the beneficiary-oriented programs in the Central and State Plans. This is done by means of a Special Component Plan which preempts a certain specified portion of the Plan expenditure for the benefit of these people. The Tribal Sub-Plan approach was adopted in the Fifth Five-Year Plan (1974–79) and the Special Component Plan for the Scheduled Castes was formulated in the Sixth Five-Year Plan (1980–85). Their purpose is to earmark allocations for socioeconomic development of the Scheduled Tribes and Scheduled Castes.

Another class poorer than the rest and intolerably oppressed were the tenants of zamindars and other intermediaries who intervened between the cultivator and the Government. At the time of Independence, over 40 percent of the agricultural area was under such tenures. One of the first measures of the Government of independent India was to abolish all intermediary tenures. The implementation has been almost total. More than twenty million tenants of former intermediaries have come into direct relationship with the state and become owners of their land. Besides, in pursuance of the goal "land to the tiller," about three million tenants and sharecroppers in ryotwari (nonintermediary tenure) areas have acquired ownership of over nearly three million hectares.

Other measures of tenure reform such as security of tenure and regulation of rent for the ordinary tenants have not been equally successful. Efforts were also made to legislate ceiling limits on landholdings and to distribute the surplus land to the landless. Reportedly, about one million hectares of land were declared surplus and about half of it was in fact distributed. Moreover, over six million hectares of Government wasteland is reportedly distributed to landless agricultural workers in different States. Success varies from State to State and there are doubts regarding the quality of land distributed and who in fact got it.

While the problem of institutional poverty was thus being attended to, the country was in the grip of acute shortage of food. The problem was immediate and urgent steps were taken to meet it, steps which included massive imports of food and emphasis on food production. This led to the Intensive Agricultural District Program (IADP) in 1960 and subsequently to the Intensive Agricultural Areas Program (IAAP) and the High Yielding Varieties Program (HYVP) in 1965. But again, though these programs led to an increase in agricultural production which came to be known as the Green Revolution, they were by their design focused on areas and farmers with complementary resources, primarily assured irrigation, and soon it became clear that their benefits remained largely confined to such farmers and areas. The problem of poverty of people and whole areas lacking in productive resources came to the surface.

By the early seventies, it became imperative to take special measures for benefiting the poorer sections and for the development of disadvantaged areas. Four categories of programs were initiated: (1) individual beneficiary-oriented programs aimed at Small and Marginal Farmers (SFDA/MFAL) subsequently supplemented by the Integrated Rural Development Program (IRDP); (2) programs for additional wage employment opportunities, such as the Crash Scheme for Rural Employment (CSRE), Pilot Intensive Rural Employment Program (PIREP), and the Food for Work program; (3) programs for the development of ecologically disadvantaged areas such as the Drought Prone Areas Programs (DRAP) and the Desert Development Program (DDP); and (4) the Minimum Needs Program aimed at raising the level of rural living through a greater provision of basic social consumption and rural infrastructure.

The Food for Work program was started in 1977 for creating employment by utilizing the surplus stock of food grains which was accumulating. Its working was reviewed in 1980 and it was restructured and renamed as the National Rural Employment Program (NREP). It aims at generating 300 to 499 million man-days of employment in rural areas every year on works creating durable community assets. During the Sixth Plan period, more funds were provided than could be utilized; Rs 24,846.7 million of cash funds were made available of which Rs 18,078.1 million, that is, about 72.75 percent, were utilized.[1] (Approximate U.S. $1 = Rs 10.[2])

A part of the wage was given in cash and a part in one kilogram of wheat/rice per man-day. In 1980–81, 1.562 million metric tons of food grains were made available of which 1.334 million metric tons were actually utilized. Thereafter, the utilization of food grains has sharply fallen. In the four years 1981–85, only 0.712 million metric tons of food grains could be utilized. The workers in many areas preferred coarse cereals to wheat and rice offered in the program. Moreover, market prices of food grains were often lower than the implied issue price on the works. Hence, beginning in January 1984, the issue of food grains on the works is being subsidized to the extent of about 25 percent. But this has not much improved the offtake of food grains on the works.

The generation of additional employment has been more or less as targeted. During the five years from 1980–81 to 1984–85, the additional employment created was 413.6, 354.5, 351.2, 302.8 and 349.3 million man-days respectively. If we consider the last year, 1984–85, the cash funds utilized amounted to Rs 4,841.7 million. Besides 0.16 million metric tons of wheat/rice was given in part-wages. We may neglect the small quantum of wages in kind. The cash cost of the program turns out to be Rs 13.86 per man-day employed.

In terms of physical achievements, 427,502 hectares were brought under afforestation/social forestry; 51,667 village tanks and 397,062 drinking water wells/community irrigation wells were constructed. Areas benefited by such minor irrigation works amounted to 893,660 hectares; 482,787 hectares were benefited by soil and water conservation and land reclamation works; 429,172 kilometers of rural roads were constructed/improved; and 201,957 school and community buildings of various types were constructed. Besides, 184,723 miscellaneous works were executed.

The Rural Landless Employment Guarantee Program was initiated in 1983–84 with the object of providing employment of up to 100 days every year to at least one member of every landless household. An amount of Rs 1,000 million was provided for 1983–84 and it was expected to generate additional employment of 300 million man-days. The preliminary reports suggest that these targets are overfulfilled.

The IRDP was initiated in 1978–79 in 2,300 development blocks already covered by other special programs like SFDA, MFAL, and DPAP. It was extended to all the 5,011 development blocks in 1980. Its objective is to provide assistance to families below the poverty line to enable them to attain an income level well above the poverty line. This is to be achieved by providing productive assets and inputs to identified families below the poverty line. The capital cost of the asset is subsidized to the extent of 25 percent for small farmers, 33 percent for marginal farmers, agricultural laborers and rural artisans, and 50 percent for Scheduled Tribes. An individual family may receive subsidy up to Rs 3,000. The limit is Rs 4,000 in the DPAP areas, and Rs 5,000 for Scheduled Tribes. Besides, it is stipulated that at least 30 percent of the families assisted are drawn from the Scheduled Castes and Scheduled Tribes.

The program is financed by subsidies provided by the Government and loans from banks. The Sixth Plan allocation for the program was Rs 15,000 million. Besides, the banks were expected to advance credit to the extent of Rs 30,000 million. Thus the total investment in the program during the Plan period would be Rs 45,000 million. A total of 15 million families were expected to receive assistance—600 families per development block per year for five years (600 × 5,000 × 5). The achievements have exceeded the targets: the investment amounts to Rs 47,300 million comprising Rs 16,500 million of subsidy and Rs 30,800 million of bank loans. A total of 16.5 million families have benefited and of these 6.4 million belong to Scheduled Castes and Scheduled Tribes.

We should also mention the program for Training of Rural Youth for self-employment (TRYSEM) which is an integral part of the IRDP. The target is to train about 200,000 rural youth aged 18–35. The selection is made from rural families with annual income of less than Rs 3,5000. Priority is given to Scheduled Castes, Scheduled Tribes and women. Training in appropriate skills is imparted through recognized institutions and master trainers. During the Sixth Plan period, about 900,000 youths have received training in some skill and about half of them are already self-employed.

Besides these Center-sponsored/All India programs, a number of States have special programs for the benefit of the poor, like the employment guarantee schemes, old-age pension schemes, etc.

Thus, the Government of independent India, almost from its inception, has had special programs for the poorer and weaker sections of the society. In the fifties and the sixties, they were directed to the protection of certain socioeconomic classes such as the Scheduled Castes and Tribes and the tenants, particularly of the intermediaries. Some amount of distribution of land to the landless was also done. In the seventies, the programs were more specifically directed to poverty alleviation. The poor were identified by their income and the programs were specifically aimed at giving them either productive assets or direct wage employment. Judged by normal official monitoring and evaluation, these programs seem to have achieved their targets. Hence, we may examine whether the results are also seen in the macroeconomic aggregates such as per capita consumption of food grains. In the following we shall examine the available data.

Macroeconomic Aggregates and Antipoverty Program Results

The Government of India in its *Bulletin on Food Statistics* publishes regularly data on what is called net availability of food grains computed as net production plus net imports minus changes in stocks with the Government.[3] Net production is taken as 87.5 percent of gross production, the balance being allowance for feed seed and wastage. No data on stocks with the public, namely, the producers, traders and the consumers, are available and no adjustment is made for changes in them. Hence, the estimates of per capita net availability cannot be interpreted as per capita consumption; they also show large fluctuations from year to year. In the following we shall suppose that the producers, traders and consumers build up stocks during good years and, in bad years, withdraw from the stocks so that in years in which the production is much below normal the stocks would be low. In particular, we shall assume that at the end of 1953, 1958, 1967, 1975, and 1983, the stocks with the public were zero. It means that if we consider the periods 1951–53, 1954–58, 1959–67, 1968–75, and 1976–83, we assume that there are no changes in the stocks with the public. On that basis, we shall obtain estimates of per capita average consumption in these periods. We shall work with estimates of gross production so that our estimates of consumption are estimates of gross consumption inclusive of feed, seed and wastage. The estimates are given in Table 5.1.

We may neglect the period 1951–53; this was a period of grave food shortage with very low production of less than 60 million metric tons per annum. The production rose to a new level of around 70 million metric tons beginning with 1954. If we consider the gross consumption per capita per annum beginning with the period 1954–58, it increased from 181.80 kilograms in 1954–58 to 185.18 kilograms in 1976–83, an increase of 1.86 percent in thirty years. This is, of course, not much but the achievement lies in the fact that dependence on imports was greatly reduced and brought to zero in the last period. This may be seen from Table 5.2.

Thus, the average annual gross consumption of food grains doubled between the periods 1951–53 and 1976–83, and the dependence on imports declined in the last two decades. The dependence on imports was maximum during the period 1959–67 when 6.8 percent of the gross consumption was met from the imports. It declined to 3.0 percent in the next period 1968–75 and to zero in the following period 1976–83.

The production of food grains in 1984 was an all-time record of 152.37 million metric tons. Nevertheless, as a measure of caution, the Government imported 2.37 million metric tons (net) and added 7.06 million metric tons to the stocks. Production in 1985 was only slightly below that in the previous year, namely, 146.22 million metric tons. There was a small net export of food grains (0.32 million metric tons) and a small addition to the stocks (0.670 million metric tons). The stocks at the end of 1985 amounted to 15.8 percent of the annual production. Clearly, India's dependence on food imports has ended.

There still remains the question whether the production of 150 million metric tons is physically adequate. The provisional estimate of population in 1985 is 750.9 million. If we round it to 750 million, the per capita production of food grains amounts to 200 kilograms. If we allow 12.5 percent for seed, feed and wastage, the per capita net availability of food grains from domestic production amounts to 175 kilograms per annum or 479.45 or, say, 480 grams per day. At the rate of 3.4 calories per gram, this gives 1,632 calories per capita per day.[4] This is 70.96 percent of the recommended norm of 2,300 calories per capita per day. We should therefore consider other items of food.

Other major items of food as sources of calories are edible oils and sugar.[5] The net availability of edible oils including hydrogenated oils in 1984–85 was 6.7 kilograms per capita per annum or 18.36 grams per capita per day. At the rate of 9 calories per gram this gives a supply of 165 calories per day. The net availability of sugar in 1984–85 is estimated to be 10.7 kilograms per capita per annum. But this takes into account only refined sugar. On the basis that only about 45 percent of the sugarcane is used in the production of refined sugar and the rest in the production of raw sugar (gur), we estimate that the net availability of sugar including raw sugar would amount to 23.8 or say 24 kilograms per capita per annum or 66 grams per capita per day. At the rate of 3.9 calories per gram this would supply 257 calories per capita per day. Adding all these together, the per capita per day supply of calories is shown in Table 5.3.

Thus the per capita availability of calories is 2,054 per day. This is 10.69 percent short of the recommended requirement of 2,300 calories per capita per day. We may suppose that this is made up by miscellaneous items of food other than food grains, vegetable fat, and sugar mentioned above. We may therefore say that in 1985 India's population had a diet which, on average, was adequate in respect of calories. But in view of the known inequality in the distribution of purchasing power in the population, the conclusion is inescapable that at least half the population lives on a diet inadequate even in respect to calories. There is enough evidence to show that a large majority of those with consumption of calories lower than the recommended have purchasing power lower than the average. Hence, the low consumption of calories in their case cannot be attributed to what is called interpersonal variation in calorie requirements. The low calorie consumption in most cases must be regarded a consequence of low purchasing power and hence a sign of poverty.

A more disturbing aspect of the situation is that, in spite of a per capita production of food grains of almost 200 kilograms, the gross per capita consumption does not seem to rise much above 185 kilograms per annum. Consumption does not rise in spite of sustained efforts of the Government to unload its stocks and its willingness to import more if people will take it. To see the reasons, let us examine the increase in the per capita net domestic product (NDP) and its distribution among different sectors of the population.

In 1951, India had a population of 363.2 million. In 1985, the population was estimated to be 750.9 million.[6] If we express the NDP at constant (1970–71) prices, the NDP was Rs 167,980 million in 1951 and about Rs 572,000 in 1985.[7] Thus in the period of thirty-four years 1951–85, the population doubled while the NDP in real terms multiplied 3.4 times. The NDP per capita increased from Rs 462.5 in 1951 to Rs 761.8 in 1985, an increase of 64.7 percent. In contrast, if we omit the three years 1951–53 when the shortage of food was acute and consumption was very low, the gross per capita consumption of food grains increased from 181.80 kilograms to 185.18 kilograms, an increase of a mere 1.86 percent. This gives an income elasticity of demand for food grains of 0.03, implying that the consumption of food grains has almost reached saturation while at least half the population remains undernourished. The reason must be sought in the distribution of income.

If we divide the economy into two broad sectors, agriculture and the rest, the net domestic product is distributed as shown in Table 5.4. It will be seen that the NDP from agriculture increased by 95.06 percent while the NDP from the rest of the economy multiplied 4.62 times. In consequence, the share of agriculture in the NDP fell from 58.69 percent in 1950–51 to 37.48 percent in 1982–83.

Of course, it is normal for the share of agriculture to decline as the NDP increases. But the population dependent on agriculture has not declined to the same extent. In fact, the proportion of workers dependent on agriculture, namely, cultivators and agricultural laborers, has declined only slightly. It was 67.5 in 1951, it increased to 69.5 in 1961, remained at 69.5 in 1971 and declined to 66.5 in 1981.[8] In consequence, if we take the population dependent on agriculture and nonagriculture proportional to the number of workers, the per capita NDP in agricultural and nonagricultural sectors appears as shown in Table 5.5.

Thus, the per capita NDP in the agricultural sector has remained more or less the same as it was thirty years ago; actually, it increased 4 percent

during 1954–58 but then during 1959–75 it dropped even below its level
in 1951–53. During 1976–83 it recovered somewhat but not quite to its
level in 1954–58. In the meanwhile, the per capita NDP in the nonagricultural sector more than doubled. In consequence, the differential
between the agricultural and nonagricultural sectors, namely, the ratio
of the per capita NDP's of the two sectors, increased from 1.46 in 1951–53
to 2.93 in 1976–83. The gap between the two sectors more than doubled.

Let us look at this a little more closely. What we have seen above is
that the per capita NDP in agriculture has remained more or less stagnant
over the past thirty years. This is at constant 1970–71 prices, in other
words, in real terms. As noted above, the NDP in agriculture increased

95.06 percent in thirty-two years from 1950–51 to 1982–83. This gives
an annual increase of 2.1 percent. This is not altogether unsatisfactory
considering that this is an annual average growth over thirty-two years.
In any case, it seems unlikely to be exceeded over any long enough period
in the near future. To increase per capita NDP in agriculture, what is
needed is to reduce the burden of population on agriculture. In the rest
of the economy, the per capita NDP multiplied 4.62 times in thirty-two
years from 1950–51 to 1982–83, which is equivalent to an annual growth
of 4.9 percent. The per capita NDP in this sector is now almost three
times the same in agriculture. But this sector does not take in any more
people than it can remunerate at this relatively high level. All the rest
must stay in agriculture and share whatever may grow there. No wonder
that the per capita NDP in agriculture does not increase and that the
gap between agriculture and the rest of the economy is widening.

But, apart from the burden of the population it must bear, the
agricultural sector has also suffered from the recent rise in prices. This
will be evident from Table 5.6 where we give the ratio of per capita
NDP in the agricultural sector and the nonagricultural sector both at
constant 1970–71 prices and at current prices.

Clearly, beginning with the year 1975–76, the gap between the agricultural and the nonagricultural sectors has been wider in terms of current
prices than in constant prices and, though there are fluctuations from
year to year, the difference is progressively increasing. As a result, the
agricultural sector is not only bearing the burden of the residual population
but, in the past eight years, has further suffered from a differential rise
in prices.

To see how the agricultural sector is really at the bottom and how its
position has worsened over the years, we may divide the economy into
two subsectors called the organized and the unorganized sectors. The
organized sector comprises the public sector and, broadly speaking, the
incorporated private sector.[9] The unorganized sector comprises, broadly
speaking, the unincorporated private sector and agriculture (which we
are treating separately). To see the respective size of these sectors, we
show in Table 5.7 the proportion of workers in them in 1971 and 1981
respectively. It will be seen that the proportion of workers in the three
sectors, namely, agriculture, unorganized nonagriculture, and the organized sector are about 70 percent, 20 percent and 10 percent respectively.
Between 1971 and 1981 the proportion in agriculture declined from 69.70

percent to 66.50 percent and was almost fully compensated by a corresponding increase in the unorganized nonagricultural sector. The proportion in the organized sector increased only a little, from 9.68 percent in 1971 to 10.28 percent in 1981.

In Table 5.8 is shown the per capita NDP in the three sectors taking the population in the three sectors proportional to the number of workers. As the estimates of NDP for the organized and the unorganized sectors are not available at constant 1970–71 prices, they are given at current prices. Hence, direct comparison between 1970–71 and 1980–81 is not meaningful. But we may compare the per capita NDP in the three sectors in each year. This is done in the last two columns where the per capita NDP in the other two sectors is expressed as a multiple of the same in the agricultural sector. It will be noticed that the per capita NDP in the unorganized nonagricultural sector in 1970–71 was 1.8 times the same in the agricultural sector and that the gap widened to 2.3 in 1980–81. In the organized sector, the per capita NDP in 1970–71 was already 4.2 times the same in the agricultural sector and the gap widened to 5.7 in 1980–81. As already noted, the agricultural sector accounted for 69.70 percent of the population in 1970–71 and 66.50 percent in 1980–81. All evidence shows that this vast majority has at best remained stagnant, watching the economic development mainly in the organized sector (which accounts for barely 10 percent of the population) and hoping that it might some day trickle down.

Herein lies an explanation why, while food is available and at least half the population lives on a nutritionally inadequate diet, the per capita consumption of food grains does not increase. More specifically, we may return to the growth of per capita NDP in the agricultural and nonagricultural sectors over the three decades 1954–83 and note that the per capita NDP in the nonagricultural sector in 1954–58 was already almost 60 percent above that in the agricultural sector. Hence, it is not unlikely that the demand for food grains there was fully met even then and that further increase in the per capita NDP in that sector would not cause an increase in the consumption of food grains in that sector. On the other hand, the per capita NDP in the agricultural sector has remained unchanged and hence there would be no increase in the consumption of food grains in that sector as well. This is the explanation why in spite of increased production of food grains and availability of imports if needed, the per capita consumption of food grains in the economy has hardly increased over a period of thirty years. In other words, in spite of almost 66 percent increase in the per capita NDP over thirty-four years, the problem of hard poverty remains almost untouched. An increase of 66 percent in the per capita NDP over thirty-four years is not great. What is worse is that these small gains have remained confined to a small section of the population, maybe 20 percent, maybe 25 percent, maybe at most 30 percent. The remaining 70 percent to 80 percent of the population has stayed where it was thirty years ago.

Incidentally, we may note a few important items of which the per capita consumption has increased over the years. The per capita consumption of edible oils, including hydrogenated oil, was 3.2 kilograms per capita per annum in 1955–56. It has more than doubled to 6.7 kilograms in 1984–85. The per capita consumption of refined sugar was 5.0 kilograms per annum. It has more than doubled to 10.7 kilograms in 1984–85. The per capita consumption of cloth has remained almost unchanged; it was 14.4 meters per annum in 1955–56 and 14.5 meters in 1984–85, of course, with some annual fluctuations. But the consumption of cotton cloth declined from 14.4 meters per capita per annum in 1955–56 to 10.6 meters in 1984–85 and was compensated by a corresponding increase in the consumption of man-made fabrics. Consumption of tea more than doubled from 257 grams per capita per annum in 1955–56 to 566 grams in 1984–85. The consumption of electricity for domestic purposes increased eightfold from 2.4 kilowatt-hours per capita per annum in 1955–56 to 20.1 kilowatt-hours in 1984–85. Between 1970–71 and 1984–85 the production of electric fans multiplied 2.79 times, bicycles 2.88 times, motorcycles and scooters 5.19 times, and noncommercial motor vehicles 2.13 times.[10] These and many others in their category are the visible benefits of development. They do not touch three-quarters of the population.

Impact on Poverty

At the outset we pointed out that the Government of India recognized and began attending to the problem of poverty, both institutional and economic, almost from its inception and that at present there are in the field a wide variety of specific antipoverty programs. Reportedly, all of them have fulfilled their annual targets. Why do they not make an impact on poverty? One reason, of course, is that the specific antipoverty programs are only less than ten years in the field and that it must take some time for the results to show. The other and the more important reason is that the size of these programs is too small in relation to the size of the problem they are meant to tackle. In Table 5.9 we give the outlay on the antipoverty program during the Sixth Plan.

These are, of course, large funds. To see that, nevertheless, they are inadequate, we may note that the aggregate of net national product (at current prices) for the five-year period 1980–85 amounts to Rs 6,909,890 million. If we take 45 percent of this as the NNP of the agriculture-forest-fishery and unregistered manufacture sectors, it amounts to Rs 3,109,450 million. The antipoverty programs are expected to benefit primarily people in these sectors. Hence, we may relate the outlay on these programs to the NNP of these sectors. If we do this, the outlay on antipoverty programs is seen to constitute barely 1.2 percent of the NNP in these sectors. Even if we take into account the bank credit amounting to Rs 30,000 million supporting the IRDP, the total outlay would constitute only 2.15 percent of the NNP of the two sectors. Clearly, this is unlikely to make any visible impact on the situation.

The outlay on these programs was greatly enhanced in 1985–86 and particularly large provisions are made in the budget for the current year 1986–87. In Table 5.10 we give the expenditure (revised estimates) on these programs in 1985–86 and the budgeted provision for 1986–87.

These are visibly larger amounts. But, if we relate them to the estimated NNP of the agriculture-forestry-fishery and unregistered manufacture sectors, they do not appear much larger than in the Sixth Plan. The NNP at current prices in 1984–85 is estimated to be Rs 1,732,000 million. Allowing a 10 percent increase per annum (at current prices), the NNP may be estimated at Rs 1,905,200 million in 1985–86 and Rs 2,095,720 million in 1986–87. The NNP in the two poor sectors, at 45 percent of the total, will be Rs 857,340 million in 1985–86 and Rs 943,074 million in 1986–87. The outlay on antipoverty programs, actual in 1985–86 and budgeted for 1986–87, then constitutes 1.43 percent in 1985–86 and 1.59 percent in 1986–87. If we take into account the bank credit supporting the IRDP, being double the Government outlay, the total constitutes 2.08 percent in 1985–86 and 2.50 percent in 1986–87 of the estimated NNP of the two poor sectors. This is only marginally more than the outlay in the Sixth Plan and the impact is not likely to be much greater.

Let us look at the dimension of the problem in a more direct way, namely, the number of persons who are below the poverty line and how much additional income must be given to them in order to lift them up just above the poverty line. This needs data on personal income distribution. However, this is not available. In its absence, we may use the data on personal consumer expenditure which as a substitute are not so unsatisfactory for so poor a population as we are considering. The data are available from the consumer expenditure surveys conducted by the National Sample Survey Organization (NSS) of the Government of India. On the basis of the NSS consumer expenditure data for 1960–61, Dandekar-Rath estimated that, in 1960–61, about one-third of the rural population lived on diets inadequate even in respect of calories. Their reasoning was as follows:

As is to be expected, the consumption of foodgrains increases as we move from the poorest to the somewhat better. . . . In rural areas, the per capita daily consumption of foodgrains and substitutes reaches 616 grams for households with per capita monthly expenditure of Rs. 13–15 or per capita annual expenditure of Rs. 170.8. Calculating at the rate of 3.3 calories per gram of foodgrains (including substitutes), 616 grams of foodgrains give 2033 calories per capita per day . . . other items of food . . . yield some 200 calories per capita per day. Thus the entire food at this level seems to give about 2250 calories per capita per day. Nutritional experts regards this as adequate under Indian condition of climate, etc. It means that, in 1960–61, an annual expenditure of Rs. 170 was essential to give a diet adequate at least in respect of calories . . . the population lying in monthly per capita expenditure classes Rs. 0–8, 8–11, 11–13, and half the population lying in the class Rs. 13–15 had per capita expenditure below this level. These classes add up to 33.12 per cent of the total rural population. Thus, in 1960–61, about one-third of the rural population lived on diets inadequate even in respect of calories.[11]

Subsequently, an expenditure level so defined came to be called the poverty line.

The NSS consumer expenditure data for 1971–72 give directly the per capita calorie consumption in each expenditure class. For the rural population the average calorie consumption per consumer unit reaches 2,734 in the per capita monthly consumer expenditure class of Rs 28–34. This is equivalent to 2,179 calories per capita. To maintain comparability with the Dandekar-Rath estimate for 1960–61, if we take the calorie requirement at 2,250 calories per capita, by proportionate interpolation, the necessary per capita monthly consumer expenditure turns out to be Rs 32.66. A reference to the distribution of the rural population by per capita monthly consumer expenditure given by the NSS survey shows that, in 1971–72, 46.0 percent of the rural population was below the poverty line. Thus, on the evidence of the NSS consumer expenditure data, the proportion of rural population below the poverty line had increased from 32.1 percent in 1960–61 to 46.0 percent in 1971–72.

Beginning with the year 1972–73, the NSS has been conducting the consumer expenditure survey quinquennially. We have now the data for October 1972–September 1973; July 1977–June 1978; and January 1983–December 1983. The data on calorie consumption are not available for these years as it was for 1971–72 (July-June). Hence, we shall revise the poverty line of Rs 32.66 determined for 1971–72 in view of the rise in prices since then. The annual (average of weeks) index numbers of wholesale prices are normally available for the fiscal years April-March. The NSS data on consumer expenditure do not refer to the fiscal year April-March and the reference period has varied from year to year. Hence, we shall obtain the index numbers of wholesale prices for the periods concerned (average of the weeks) by proportional adjustment.[12] In Table 5.11 we give these index numbers, the poverty line consumer expenditure based thereon, and the proportion of rural population below the poverty line in the several periods.

Thus, on the evidence of the NSS consumer expenditure data, the proportion of rural population below the poverty line increased from 46.0 percent in 1971–72 to 53.9 percent in 1972–73 but thereafter declined to 51.9 percent in 1977–78 and to 48.9 percent in 1983. These proportions of rural population below the poverty line are based on poverty lines determined by raising the poverty line of Rs 32.66 in 1971–72 in proportion to the rise in index of wholesale prices. This may not be appropriate for the rural population. For instance, the weights given to the primary food articles, manufactured food articles and other commodities in the wholesale index number (1970–71 = 100) are 29.80, 13.32 and 56.88 percent respectively while the proportion of expenditure on these items in the consumer expenditure, particularly at the poverty line level, are quite different. These proportions are shown in Table 5.12.

It will be noticed that the proportions of consumer expenditure of the rural population at the poverty line level on different items of expenditure are quite different from the weights assigned to these items in the index of wholesale prices. Hence, it will be appropriate to first prepare the index numbers of wholesale prices for the three groups of items, namely, primary food, manufactured food, and other items, and then construct a new index number of wholesale prices giving the three groups of items appropriate weights. We shall take these weights for the three groups to be 62.5, 12.5 and 25.0 respectively. In Table 5.13, we show the revised index number, the revised poverty lines and the revised estimates of proportions of rural population below the poverty lines.

The revision in the index number of prices has actually led to an increase in the proportion of rural population below the poverty line in 1972–73 from 53.9 percent to 54.9 percent but in the next two periods it has caused this proportion to go down somewhat. The proportion of population below the poverty line in 1977–78 has gone down from 51.9 to 49.5 percent. The reduction is substantial in the case of 1983 from 48.9 to 44.4 percent. We may accept these revised estimates. The estimates for 1977–78 and 1983 appear reasonable and in line with the estimate of 46.0 percent for 1971–72. But the estimate for 1972–73 appears to be on the higher side. It seems unlikely that the proportion of rural population increased by almost nine percentage points in one year from 1971–72 to 1972–73.

In view of these doubts and others expressed in the literature regarding the reliability of the NSS consumer expenditure data, it will be worthwhile checking the NSS estimates of consumer expenditure with independent estimates of net domestic product. Estimates of NDP for the rural population are not readily available. Hence, in their place we shall use estimates of NDP for the unorganized sector. The workers in the unorganized sector constituted 90.3 percent in 1970–71 and 89.7 percent in 1980–81. Hence by proportionate interpolation and extrapolation we shall suppose that the proportions were 90.18 percent in 1972–73, 89.88 percent in 1977–78, and 89.60 percent in 1983. We shall apply these proportions to the estimates of total population to obtain estimates of population in the unorganized sector. The estimates of population are available for the midpoint of the calendar years. Estimates of NDP are available for the fiscal year April-March. We have derived corresponding estimates of population and NDP for the periods of NSS consumer expenditure surveys by proportionate interpolation. The results are given in Table 5.14.

Considering the very diverse sources of the data, the estimates of per capita NDP in the unorganized sector and the estimates of per capita per annum consumer expenditure of the rural population, particularly for the years 1977–78 and 1983 appear to be in reasonable agreement. In 1977–78 the per capita consumer expenditure is only 8.5 percent below the per capita NDP. In 1983, the difference is even smaller; the per capita consumer expenditure is less than 5 percent below the per capita NDP. The difference is easily explained. First, the population in the unorganized sector constitutes about 90 percent of the total population while the rural population constitutes about 75 percent. Almost the whole of the rural population is, of course, in the unorganized sector. But the balance of 15 percent is in the urban area and its per capita consumer expenditure would be somewhat higher than that of the rural population. Second, if we allow even a small amount of saving, the consumer expenditure would be that much smaller than the NDP. All in all, it seems that the NSS consumer expenditure data for 1977–78 and 1983 and our estimates of the proportion of the rural population below the poverty line in these years appear reasonable. This cannot be said about the NSS consumer data for 1972–73. It will be noticed that the per capita consumer expenditure in 1972–73 is 16 percent below the per capita NDP. This is a rather large difference and supports our earlier suspicion that the estimate of 54.9 percent of the rural population below the poverty line 1972–73, compared to 46.0 percent in 1971–72, seems too high.

Let us return to our estimate of 44.4 percent of the rural population or of the population in the unorganized sector being below the poverty line in 1983. This estimate is very well supported by an independent estimate of NDP in the unorganized sector. The proportion of population below the poverty line, namely, 44.4 percent in 1983, is, of course, below the same in 1971–72, namely, 46.0 percent. But the decline is too small, only about 1.6 percentage points in 11.5 years, to derive comfort from. The size of the the problem is simply too large compared to the size of the antipoverty programs. Incidentally we may note that the small decline in poverty since 1977–78 is at least partly due to the prices of primary food articles not rising to the same extent as the rise in prices of other commodities, thus partly shifting the burden of the poor on the agricultural sector. We shall return to this point.

To indicate the size of the problem, let us make a hypothetical calculation as to the additional income that would have to be provided to the rural poor in 1983 in order to bring them up just above the poverty line. For this purpose we shall need the distribution of the population by per capita consumer expenditure which, for a poor population, one may take as equivalent to income. The distribution for 1983 is given in Table 5.15.

Consider, for instance, the population in the per capita monthly expenditure class Rs 0–30. The average per capita expenditure in this class is Rs 24.86 per month (thirty days). The poverty line is determined at Rs 88.35 per capita per month. Hence, the population in this expenditure class will need an additional income of Rs 63.49 per capita per month or Rs 772.46 per capita per annum. If we take the total population to be one million, 0.92 percent, that is, 9,200 persons, are in this expenditure class. They will need a total additional income of Rs 7.106 million to come up just above the poverty line. Similarly calculations can be made for the other expenditure classes. The results on the basis of a total population of one million are shown in the last column of Table 5.15.

Thus the additional income needed by the population below the poverty line to come up just above the poverty line is Rs 129.640 million per million population per annum. This is at 1983 prices. At 1986–87 prices this is at least Rs 145 million. The estimated total population in 1986–87 is about 760 million. Taking 75 percent of it as rural, the rural population in 1986–87 may be estimated at 570 million. Hence, the additional income needed by the rural poor to come up just above the poverty line is about Rs 82,650 million in 1986–87. If we may also take into account the urban poor, we may apply the estimate to the population in the unorganized sector. Taking it as 89.5 percent of the total population, the population in the unorganized sector in 1986–87 may be estimated at about 680 million and to bring all the poor just above the poverty line will require annually Rs 98,600 million. The net revenues of the Government of India in 1986–87 are estimated at Rs 290,970 million. Thus, about 28.4 percent of the revenues of the Government of India will be needed for poverty alleviation in the rural areas. To attend to all the poor will take up 33.9 percent of the revenues.

It will be instructive to compare this estimate with the one presented by Dandekar-Rath for 1968–69.[13] To do this, we may note that, for the present purpose, Dandekar-Rath confined their attention to the rural population of which according to their estimate 40 percent were below the poverty line in 1968–69. Further, even among the rural poor, they kept out of their consideration the bottom 10 percent. We may quote:

> One may provisionally agree with the Planning Commission's judgement that the poverty at the bottom, say of the 10 per cent of the poorest of the rural population, is probably due to lack of sufficient earning capacity in the population and hence that it will have to be relieved by special assistance whenever, wherever and in whatever measure this becomes possible. But the poverty of the remaining 30 per cent of the rural population living below the minimum must be attributed to unemployment or under-employment of its working members.

This is a useful distinction to make between destitution and poverty; destitution which needs social relief and poverty which possibly can be tackled by antipoverty economic programs. We may adopt the same procedure.

A reference to Table 5.15 shows that 10 percent of the rural population in 1983 lived on per capita monthly consumer expenditure of Rs 51.9. The additional income needed by this bottom 10 percent of the population to come up just above the poverty line adds up to Rs 56.391 million per million population. This is as much as 43.50 percent of the total additional income needed. Hence, if we leave out of consideration the bottom 10 percent, the previous estimate of Rs 82,650 million for the alleviation of rural poverty in 1986–87 is reduced to about Rs 46,697 million per annum. This may be compared with the Dandekar-Rath estimate of Rs 8,000 million in 1968–69.

The estimate for 1986–87 is 5.837 times the estimate for 1968–69. The reasons are: First, the wholesale prices in 1986–87 are about 3.84 times those in 1968–69. But we have seen that the price index appropriate to poverty line is somewhat lower than the wholesale price index—about 94 percent of the latter. Hence, the prices appropriate to poverty line in 1986–87 may be considered about 3.61 times those in 1968–69. Second, the population in 1986–87 is 1.44 times that in 1968–69. Third, the proportion of rural population below the poverty line in 1986–87, taken at 44.4 percent, is 1.11 times the same in 1968–69. If we multiply the three multiples, we have $3.61 \times 1.44 \times 1.11 = 5.77$. This is as good a tally as one may expect in such exercises.

The main purpose of the exercise and the comparison with the Dandekar-Rath estimate for 1968–69 is to demonstrate that the estimate of additional incomes needed in 1986–87 for alleviation of rural poverty excluding the bottom 10 percent, namely, Rs 46,697 million per annum, is consistent with the earlier estimates and appears to be a reasonable measure of the size of the problem. In comparison, the provision for the antipoverty programs in the budget for 1986–87 amounting to no more than Rs 15,000 million is clearly inadequate. It is less than one-third the requirement. The Plan outlay of the Government of India in 1986–87 amounts to Rs 223,000 million. The outlay on poverty alleviation constitutes a meager 6.73 percent of the total Plan outlay. The rest of the Plan outlay, as past experience shows, does not touch even the fringe of the problem.

Requirements

What needs to be emphasized is that to alleviate poverty of this dimension, with almost half of the rural population or the population in the unorganized sector living below the poverty line, will require substantial transfer of incomes from the urban to the rural sector, from the organized to the unorganized sector or from the nonagricultural to the agricultural sector. In fact, the transfer is not all that large. As we saw, to bring all the poor above the poverty line would require Rs 98,600 million annually at 1986–87 prices. If we restrict attention to the rural poor, the amount needed is Rs 82,650 million. Further, if we exclude the bottom 10 percent, then the amount needed is only Rs 46,697 million. Of course, even this is a large amount. But let us relate it to the NNP in the nonagricultural sector. The provisional estimate of NNP in 1984–85 is Rs 1,732,070 million. Allowing a 10 percent growth per annum, at current prices, it may be put at about Rs 2,095,800 million in 1986–87. Taking 65 percent of it as the NNP of the nonagricultural sector, namely, Rs 1,362,270 million, a transfer of Rs 46,697 million constitutes no more than 3.5 percent of the NNP of the nonagricultural sector. This can be done by a specific tax such as the Government of Maharashtra levies to finance its Employment Guarantee Scheme. If this is not politically feasible, we may forget about it. But what should not go unnoticed is the fact that a transfer of this order, though in the reverse direction, has been going on annually for the past several years through the mechanism of an inflationary price rise. The relevant data are presented in Tables 5.16 and 5.17.

In Table 5.16 are given the deflation factors implied in reducing the NDP of the agricultural and nonagricultural sectors from current prices to constant 1970–71 prices. In other words, it gives the implied price index numbers. It will be seen that beginning with the year 1975–76 the price index for the nonagricultural sector has been higher than for the agricultural sector. If we take 1970–71 as the base, the index in 1983–84 was 2.64 for the agricultural sector and 3.01 for the nonagricultural sector. For the two sectors together, the price index was 2.87.

In Table 5.17 we give the NDP of the agricultural sector at current prices and a hypothetical estimate of what it would be if the price increase were equal in the two sectors. For instance, it will be noticed that the actual NDP of the agricultural sector in 1983–84 was Rs 560,660 million but that it would be Rs 610,650 million if the price increase in the two sectors were equal, namely, 2.87. What the agricultural sector lost is gained by the nonagricultural sector. An amount of Rs 490,990 million was transferred from the agricultural sector to the nonagricultural sector. In the previous two years the amounts so transferred were even larger. It was Rs 57,600 million in 1981–82 and Rs 58,410 million in 1982–83. Similar though somewhat smaller amounts were transferred each year, beginning with 1975–76.

The present transfers of large incomes from the agricultural to the nonagricultural sector are taking place through the price mechanism. Hence, it may be suggested that this could be stopped or even reversed by means of a comprehensive price support to agriculture. But experience shows that, in the absence of demand support, price support involves large subsidies which benefit naturally only the agricultural producers with a marketable surplus while the higher food prices affect adversely the poorer sections. The benefits of higher agricultural prices may eventually percolate to the agricultural labor and other rural poor. But the process takes time.

Poverty alleviation requires a program which will directly and immediately benefit the poor. This means that the transfer of incomes from the urban or the nonagricultural sector must be to the rural or the agricultural poor rather than to the agricultural sector in general. This is what the antipoverty programs seek to achieve. By attending to the rural poor, these programs do not affect the agricultural sector adversely. The additional incomes or purchasing power which these programs create in the hands of the poor also benefit the agricultural sector generally by giving agricultural produce the necessary demand support. Benefits bestowed at the top take time to percolate to the bottom. The process is slow, halting and diffuse. In contrast, the benefits placed at the bottom move quickly to the top.

Apart from their size, let us briefly look at the nature of the antipoverty programs and what one may expect them to achieve. The programs, as we have seen, are mainly of two kinds. One seeks to promote self-employment by providing the poor households with productive assets financed by subsidies and credit. The other seeks to provide wage employment and in the process create community assets. From the standpoint of the poor, the latter is simple and clear. Creation of community assets is a responsibility of the Government and, whether or not they are created, the poor get their wages and that much relief. Of course, the employment program must continue day after day, month after month, and year after year. But that too is a responsibility of the Government. In comparison, the burden of self-employment rests on the poor. It is not easy to decide the scope of self-employment in a district or a development block. The poor man knows little about it and the administrative agencies of the Government know even less. For instance, it is not easy to determine how many sewing machines a development block will support. To ask a poor man to make his judgment and then leave him to the operation of the market burdened with a bank loan is the cruelest thing to do to a poor man. Nevertheless, if the IRDP is overfulfilling the targets, it is because the chosen poor and the administration both have their eyes on the subsidy.

There surely are potentially viable candidates among the poor who with some support will stand on their own. But the identification of the candidates must be left not to the administrative agencies of the Government who have their targets to fulfill but to the banking system which ultimately will bear the liability. The potential viability of the poor cannot of course be judged by the same criteria as the banks will apply elsewhere. But if it is to be a bankable proposition, it must be viable at least at zero rate of interest. If, in the judgment of the banks, it is so viable, the Government may direct the banking system to support all such proposals and agree to subsidize the banking system to the full extent of the interest. To subsidize the beneficiary at the point of purchase of the asset, as is done in the IRDP, is a bad beginning even for a potential entrepreneur.

Hence, while the possibilities of creating self-employment should be explored, the main reliance will have to be on offering wage employment. It is not suggested that the poor should be permanently employed on wage work though there is nothing wrong in that if that is preferred. In fact, a majority of the poor may prefer wage employment to self-employment. Some among them, the more thrifty, provident and enterprising, will save from their wages, and after a period will leave wage employment and set themselves up in small independent businesses. It should be recognized that a poor man cannot easily achieve economic independence in an environment in which he has lived as a poor man for generations. He needs a break from that environment. After a period, he may return home with a small amount of capital or may prefer an urban environment where he is a stranger. With his own initiative and enterprise, he is likely to succeed better than if set up with the support of subsidy and the burden of a bank loan.

One purpose of the hypothetical calculation indicating the size of the problem was to emphasize that the employment program will have to be in the field for many years to come. The present concept of providing employment near everybody's home will therefore not do. Labor will have to move where productive work is. This will require a mobile labor force mobilized in appropriate labor organizations. From this point of view, the present administration of the employment programs is wasteful. Two types of labor organizations are possible and both may be tried. In one, labor may be organized in labor cooperatives with a minimum number of fifty workers as the present law provides. The Government should guarantee continued employment on contractual basis to all labor organized in labor cooperatives provided it is willing to move where work is. Possibly, all small and medium works can be executed through such labor cooperatives. The other form of labor organization is what in the First Five-Year Plan (1951–56) was referred to as the Land Army. Within the provision of Rs 15,000 million made in the budget for 1986–87 for the antipoverty programs, it is possible to raise a Land Army of three million at the cost of Rs 5,000 per worker. The State governments should prepare massive projects of irrigation, afforestation, soil conservation, major road construction and the like with the estimates in man-days and the Land

Army would execute them by employing the labor force as far as possible in the local area but moving it when necessary wherever work is. The country has the necessary organizational ability and it should be possible to set up a Land Army of three million within the current plan period. When that succeeds, it should be gradually expanded to ten million by the end of the century. That is what the country needs to mobilize its vast idle manpower resources for rural development and in the process have a recognizable impact on the poverty situation.

Summary

In the period of thirty-four years 1951–85, India's net domestic product per capita increased 64.7 percent. But the gains of development remained confined to a small section and did not reach the poor. For instance, the NDP in the agricultural sector, which constitutes nearly 70 percent of the population, remained more or less stagnant. As a corollary, even in 1983, 44.4 percent of the rural population was below the poverty line.

The Government of India recognized from the beginning that the alleviation of poverty could not be left to the general course of economic development and that a direct attack was necessary. It has had in the field a number of antipoverty programs but they were too small to make much impact on poverty. For instance, the additional income needed to bring all the rural poor in 1986–87 just above the poverty line is estimated at Rs 82,650 million. Even if we leave out the bottom 10 percent as too poor to be helped by the present antipoverty programs, the additional income needed would amount to Rs 46,697 million. Compared to this, the provision for the antipoverty programs in 1986–87 was Rs 15,000 million, which is less than one-third the requirement. What is needed is an antipoverty program large enough to effect a net transfer of Rs 46,697 million from the nonagricultural to the agricultural sector. This constitutes no more than 3.5 percent of the NDP of the nonagricultural sector.

The evidence is the opposite; a transfer of this order in the reverse direction has been going on for the past several years through the mechanism of inflationary price rise. Hence, it may be suggested that a comprehensive price support to agriculture, rather than an antipoverty program, should provide the solution. But price supports can benefit only the agricultural producers with a marketable surplus. The benefits may eventually percolate to agricultural labor and other rural poor. But the process takes time. On the other hand, additional incomes, which the antipoverty programs can create in the hands of the poor, benefit the poor directly and also the agricultural sector indirectly by giving its produce the necessary demand support. Benefits bestowed at the top take time to percolate to the bottom. In contrast, benefits placed at the bottom move quickly to the top.

The antipoverty programs are of two kinds. One seeks to promote self-employment by providing the poor with productive assets financed by subsidies and bank credit. The other seeks to provide wage employment and in the process create community assets. While the possibilities of creating self-employment should be explored, the main reliance will have to be on offering wage employment. Considering the size of the problem, the employment program will have to be in the field for many years to come and labor will have to move where productive work is. This will require a mobile labor force mobilized in appropriate labor organizations such as a land army. Within the financial provisions presently made for the antipoverty programs, it should be possible to set up a land army of three million within the current Plan period. When that succeeds, it should be gradually expanded to ten million by the end of the century. That is what the country needs to mobilize its vast idle manpower for rural development and in the process make a recognizable impact on the poverty situation.

Notes

1. For the antipoverty programs, sources of data are "Poverty Alleviation Programs, A Status Paper" (Government of India), in *Management of Rural Development Programs* (Pune: Government of Maharashtra, Maharashtra Institute of Development Administration, Mimeographed); *Plan Budget for 1986–87* (New Delhi: Government of India, Ministry of Finance, Budget Division).

2. Exchange rates for Indian rupees to U.S. dollars were as follows:

1981–82:	U.S. $ = Rs 8.97
1982–83:	U.S. $ = Rs 9.67
1983–84:	U.S. $ = Rs 10.34
1984–85:	U.S. $ = Rs 11.89
1985–86:	U.S. $ = Rs 12.16

The last is the average of Reserve Bank's buying rates at the end of each month.

3. For food grains production, imports and changes in Government stocks, figures for 1951–83 are taken from *Bulletin on Food Statistics* (different editions) (New Delhi: Government of India, Directorate of Economics and Statistics, Ministry of Agriculture and Irrigation). For 1984 and 1985, see *Economic Survey 1985–86* (New Delhi: Government of India).

4. For consumer expenditure, calorie intake, etc., sources of data are *National Sample Survey*, Twenty Sixth Round, July 1971-June 1972, Number 238, vol. 1 (New Delhi: Government of India, Ministry of Planning, Department of Statistics, National Sample Survey Organization); *Sarvekshana* (Journal of the National Sample Survey Organization) 9, no. 3 (January 1986); *Report (Provisional) on the Third Quinquennial Survey of Consumer Expenditure*, January-December 1983, Thirty Eighth Round, Number 319 (New Delhi: Government of India, Ministry of Planning, Department of Statistics, National Sample Survey Organization, June 1985).

5. For the availability of edible oils and sugar, consumption of cloth and electricity, production of electric fans, bicycles, motorcycles, scooters and non-commercial motor vehicles, data are taken from *Economic Survey 1985–86*.

6. Population figures up to 1981 are midyear population as estimated by the Registrar General of India. Figures for 1981 onwards are projected on the basis of the observed growth rate between 1971 and 1981. Source of data up to 1983 is *Bulletin on Food Statistics* (different editions). (New Delhi: Government of India, Directorate of Economics and Statistics, Ministry of Agriculture and Irrigation). For 1984 and 1985, see *Economic Survey 1985–86*.

7. For net domestic product and net national product, figures are taken from *National Accounts Statistics* (different editions) (New Delhi: Government of India,

Ministry of Planning, Department of Statistics, Central Statistical Organization);
Economic Survey 1985–86.

8. Workers in different industries are taken from respective population censuses,
Registrar General of India (see note 6).

9. Workers in public/private organized sectors taken from *Economic Survey*
(various editions) (New Delhi: Government of India).

10. See note 5.

11. V. M. Dandekar and Nilakantha Rath, *Poverty in India* (Pune: Indian School
of Political Economy, 1971), 6.

12. For index numbers of wholesale prices, see *Economic Survey 1985–86.*

13. Dandekar and Rath, *Poverty in India,* 138.

TABLE 5.1 Estimates of Gross Consumption of Food Grains
(kilograms per capita per annum)

Period	Kilograms
1951–53	164.64
1954–58	181.80
1959–67	184.87
1968–75	185.41
1976–83	185.18

TABLE 5.2 Average Annual Production, Net Imports, Changes in Stocks, and
Gross Consumption During Given Periods
(million metric tons)

Period	Production	Net Imports Net of Change in Stocks	Gross Consumption	Col. (3) as Percentage of Col. (4)
(1)	(2)	(3)	(4)	(5)
1951–53	57.466	3.346	60.812	5.502
1954–58	70.297	2.021	72.318	2.795
1959–67	79.736	5.803	85.538	6.784
1968–75	100.462	3.063	103.524	2.958
1976–83	123.931	(−) 0.150	123.781	(−) 0.121

TABLE 5.3 Per Capita Per Day Supply of Calories, 1985

Food Item	Availability in Grams	Calories	Percent of Total
Food Grains	480	1,632	79.45
Vegetable Fat	18.4	165	8.03
Sugar	66	257	12.51
Total		2,054	100.00

TABLE 5.4 Net Domestic Product at Factor Cost
(1970–71 Prices, Rs million)

Year	Agriculture	Rest of Economy	Percentage Share of Agriculture
1950–51	98,590	69,390	58.69
1982–83	192,310	320,840	37.48

TABLE 5.5 Per Capita NDP in Agricultural and Nonagricultural Sectors
(1970–71 prices)

Period	Agricultural Sector (Rs)	Nonagricultural Sector (Rs)	Nonagriculture/ Agriculture Ratio
1951–53	405.66	593.13	1.46
1954–58	421.95	677.34	1.61
1959–67	401.91	902.55	2.25
1968–75	398.83	1,068.97	2.68
1976–83	415.61	1,216.78	2.93

TABLE 5.6 Ratio of Per Capita NDP in Nonagricultural and Agricultural Sectors

Year	At 1970–71 Prices	At Current Prices
1970–71	2.68	2.68
1971–72	2.53	2.69
1972–73	2.62	2.65
1973–74	2.87	2.23
1974–75	2.67	2.57
1975–76	2.80	3.00
1976–77	2.60	3.22
1977–78	2.94	3.14
1978–79	2.72	3.37
1979–80	2.82	3.67
1980–81	3.24	3.37
1981–82	2.93	3.65
1982–83	2.94	3.96
1983–84	3.22	3.54

TABLE 5.7 Percentage Distribution of Workers in Different Sectors

Sector	1971	1981
Agriculture	69.70	66.50
Unorganized Nonagriculture	20.62	23.22
Organized	9.68	10.28

TABLE 5.8 Per Capita NDP at Current Prices

Sector	1970–71	1980–81	As Multiple of Agriculture	
			1970–71	1980–81
Agriculture	426.37	859.60	1.0	1.0
Unorganized Nonagriculture	765.15	1,937.05	1.8	2.3
Organized	1,776.74	4,930.75	4.2	5.7

TABLE 5.9 Outlay on Antipoverty Programs During the Sixth Plan (1980–85)

Program	Outlay (Rs million)
Integrated Rural Development Program	15,000
National Rural Employment Program	18,000
Rural Landless Employment Guarantee Program	4,000
Total	37,000

TABLE 5.10 Outlay on Antipoverty Programs of the Government of India
(Rs million)

Program	1985–86 Revised Estimates	1986–87 Budget
Integrated Rural Development Program	2,785.7	4,274.0
National Rural Employment Program	3,372.1	4,426.5
Rural Landless Employment Guarantee Program	6,063.4	6,336.5
Total	12,221.2	15,037.0

TABLE 5.11 Distribution of Rural Population (1983) by Per Capita Monthly
Consumer Expenditure

Year and Period of NSS Consumer Expenditure Data	Index Number of Wholesale Prices Average for Period (1970–71 = 100)	Poverty Line Consumer Expenditure Per Capita Per Month (Rs)	Percent of Rural Population Below Poverty Line
July 1971–June 1972	108.25	32.66	46.0
Oct. 1972–Sept. 1973	127.95	38.61	53.9
July 1977–June 1978	185.80	56.06	51.9
Jan. 1983–Dec. 1983	309.18	93.29	48.9

TABLE 5.12 Percentage Distribuiton of Rural Consumer Expenditure at Poverty
Line Level on Different Items of Expenditure

Year and Period	Expenditure Class (Rs)	Primary Food Articles	Manufactured Food Articles	Other Items
Oct. 1972–Sept. 1973	34–43	66.45	12.42	21.13
July 1977–June 1978	50–60	62.08	12.65	25.27
Jan. 1983–Dec. 1983	85–100	60.12	12.70	27.18

TABLE 5.13 Revised Index Number of Wholesale Prices, Poverty Lines and
Estimates of Proportions of Rural Population Below the Poverty Line

Year and Period of NSS Consumer Expenditure Data	Revised Index Number of Wholesale Prices Average for Period (1970–71 = 100)	Poverty Line Consumer Expenditure Per Capita Per Month (Rs)	Percent of Rural Population Below Poverty Line
July 1971–June 1972	107.52	32.66	46.0
Oct. 1972–Sept. 1973	128.67	39.08	54.9
July 1977–June 1978	179.16	54.42	49.5
Jan. 1983–Dec. 1983	290.85	88.35	44.4

TABLE 5.14 Estimates of Per Capita Consumer Expenditure of Rural Population
Compared with Estimates of Per Capita NDP in the Unorganized Sector

Year	Population in Unorganized Sector	NDP in Unorganized Sector	Per Capita NDP in Unorganized Sector	Consumer Expenditure Per Capita Per Annum
	(million)	(Rs million)	(Rs)	(Rs)
Oct. 1972–Sept. 1973	517.251	288,480	640.0	537.4
July 1977–June 1978	573.869	525,680	916.0	838.2
Jan. 1983–Dec. 1983	645.389	928,090	1,438.0	1,368.1

TABLE 5.15 Distribution of Rural Population (1983) by Per Capita Monthly
Consumer Expenditure

Per Capita Monthly Consumer Expenditure Class	Percent of Rural Population	Average Per Capita Monthly Consumer Expenditure	Additional Income Needed Per Annum Per Million Population
(Rs)		(Rs)	(Rs million)
0 – 30	0.92	24.86	7.106
30 – 40	2.47	35.84	15.780
40 – 50	5.11	45.44	26.678
50 – 60	7.90	55.24	31.824
60 – 70	9.69	65.17	27.328
70 – 85	15.24	77.40	20.303
85 – 100	13.64	92.27	0.621
100 – 125	16.99	111.58	–
125 – 150	10.00	136.56	–
150 – 200	9.78	171.14	–
200 – 250	3.96	221.52	–
250 – 300	1.81	272.12	–
300 +	2.49	437.34	–
All Classes	100.00	112.45	129.640

TABLE 5.16 Implied Deflation Factors for Reducing NDP at Current Prices to NDP
at Constant (1970–71) Prices

Year	Agricultural Sector	Nonagricultural Sector	Total
1970–71	1.00	1.00	1.00
1975–76	1.44	1.63	1.54
1976–77	1.58	1.70	1.65
1977–78	1.60	1.81	1.72
1978–79	1.58	1.87	1.75
1979–80	1.87	2.09	2.01
1980–81	2.06	2.34	2.23
1981–82	2.13	2.61	2.42
1982–83	2.31	2.80	2.61
1983–84	2.64	3.01	2.87

TABLE 5.17 NDP in Agricultural Sector at Current Prices
Actual and Hypothetical in Rs Million

Year	Actual	Hypothetical	Difference
1975–76	258,680	276,720	18,040
1976–77	206,920	278,880	11,960
1977–78	303,960	327,590	23,630
1978–79	309,780	342,460	32,680
1979–80	316,430	339,410	22,980
1980–81	394,610	427,250	32,640
1981–82	425,260	482,860	57,600
1982–83	443,520	501,930	58,410
1983–84	560,660	610,650	49,990

6

Poverty in India

Gustav F. Papanek

For well over twenty years the alleviation of poverty has been a major, if not *the* major, objective of Indian development. But there is no consensus on whether the proportion of the population living in poverty has declined significantly over thirty-five years of planned development. In part this is the result of conflicting and sporadic evidence. Equally important is the absence of a clear, strong and consistent trend. As a result, the recent, careful study by M. S. Ahluwalia,[1] which is more optimistic than most studies, has to be content with the conclusion that there is no basis for the view that the incidence of rural poverty has increased in the period 1956–57 to 1977–78. If the incidence has not increased, while the population has grown, the implication is an increasing number of poor families in India. The Ahluwalia data, limited to the rural population, indeed show a small increase in the absolute number in poverty. This unsatisfactory conclusion is mitigated by Ahluwalia's tentative conclusion that in the decade after the Green Revolution (i.e., from the late 1960s to the late 1970s) there has been a more or less steady decline in poverty. There is a clear and optimistic implication: with continued relatively rapid growth in agricultural output—entirely feasible technically—poverty can continue to decline.

But the limited and sporadic nature of income distribution and consumption data limits the confidence one can place in the empirical foundation of even that limited degree of optimism. The National Sample Survey (NSS) data, carefully milked for all they are worth by Ahluwalia, begin with 1956–57 and end with 1977–78. In the early period from the mid-fifties to the early sixties there was a decline in rural poverty from over 50 percent to less than 40 percent. The decline from the mid-sixties to the late seventies was of comparable magnitude. The recent decline may therefore not have foreshadowed continued improvement any more than did the earlier decline.

Vaidyanathan's careful review of all the evidence he can muster (see his chapter in this volume) leads to the more pessimistic conclusion that the incidence of rural poverty has increased, probably even into the 1980s. Moreover, Bardhan[2] persuasively summarizes evidence from several studies to show that growth and increased productivity do not always "trickle down" to the poor. Indeed some "types of growth processes generate negative forces for the poor," particularly with highly unequal distribution of assets and access to resources. Whether the reduced incidence of poverty accompanying increased production represents a real trend, or a statistical blip, can be established with greater confidence if one can trace the causal mechanism which brought about the change. More importantly, policies to reduce poverty depend crucially on an understanding of the causal connection between poverty and changes in the economy. The rest of this chapter therefore emphasizes the analysis of that causal connection.

The Income of the Poor Is Labor Income

The first step is to establish the facts. The only long and continuous time series useful in tracing the income of the poor are data on agricultural wages. They are available on an annual basis for more than twenty-five years for all of India and for most of the States. It is quite justified to use these data for estimates of poverty in India as in other low-income Asian countries where most of the income of nearly all poor families is derived from the provision of unskilled labor, whether as wage workers or as self-employed in the informal sector. Most of the poor have very little physical or human capital. One can therefore estimate changes in the income of the poor from changes in the income of unskilled workers.

Moreover, the poor do not remain unemployed for any length of time. Since they usually lack significant reserves of liquid assets, most of the poor simply cannot afford to remain unemployed, that is, without income, for long. Indeed, the very poorest sometimes cannot afford to be unemployed for more than a day without dire consequences. That explains the very low rates of open unemployment recorded in surveys. Only 2–4 percent of males and 4–9 percent of females were completely unemployed for a whole week in a compilation by Raj Krishna for a number of years. That is, very few do not work at least some days during a week. Indeed only about 8 percent of days available for work are not taken up by work. Evidence from other countries indicates that many, if not most, of those unemployed for any length of time will be the educated, from middle-income families, looking for an "appropriate" position.

Therefore it is not far wrong to assume that changes in the rate of compensation of unskilled workers reflect and determine changes in the income of the poor. Since they are working most days, if the daily rate increases, that implies that their total compensation increases. Indeed a model of labor compensation for labor-abundant countries[3] implies that the number of hours or days worked and the rate per hour, day or unit of service are likely to move together and to reinforce each other. As a result, any index of per unit compensation will understate the change in income that has taken place: when unskilled workers receive more pay per day, they are likely also to find work for more days.

Finally there is good evidence for India and for other, similarly labor abundant countries that labor compensation in different activities changes in the same direction and by similar magnitudes.[4] Pay rates by day differ substantially, as do actual daily earnings for those compensated per unit of service provided (e.g., shoe shiners, harvesters, bicycle rickshaw pullers), but the direction and rate of change are quite similar in different occupations.[5] Therefore changes in labor income in any unskilled occupation, for which data are available for India, can be taken to reflect changes in income of most unskilled labor, as long as it is not affected by minimum wage laws or labor unions.

Change in the income of workers in "protected" sector occupations may differ from that of other unskilled workers. This sector is one where pay is determined primarily by such factors as government or labor unions. But workers in the protected sector are a small minority of the labor force in such countries as India and most of them are not among the poorest 40 percent, so it is not unreasonable to ignore them in a study of poverty.

The most useful data on labor income are for agricultural workers if they are available. First, with rare exceptions these workers are not protected by either effective minimum wage legislation or by labor unions. Second, there usually are no significant changes in skill composition, which plague data for industry. Third, nearly all of the workers are considered unskilled. Agricultural wage data therefore provide a reasonable approximation of the compensation for poor, unskilled workers, not protected by formal organizations. Indeed Table 6.1 shows that changes in real wages of agricultural workers on the whole parallel changes in the poverty index. On these assumptions, supported by reasonably good evidence, one then has an index, available on an annual basis, of changes in the income of the great majority of the poor.

There is one possible caveat: that the data are too unreliable to be useful. A careful study by Rao examined precisely that question in 1972.[6] He concluded that in comparison with two other sources, gathered with more care and greater coverage, "Agricultural Wages in India," collected by the Ministry of Food and Agriculture, tended to show higher wages and less seasonal variation. He concludes that these a.e systematic errors, but that they do not affect comparisons of wages over time, the purpose for which these data are used in this chapter. In addition to the two biases mentioned he also finds a "few" cases of "flagrantly bad and negligent reporting." But since these do not appear to be systematic, they will only reduce the statistical significance of the reported results, not vitiate the conclusions. His analysis therefore increases confidence in the results presented below.

Trends in the Income of the Poor or in Labor Income

If one compares real average daily wages for Indian agricultural workers for 1954–56, the first two years for which data are available, with those for 1979–81, the last two, there is no change whatsoever over these twenty-five years. (See Tables 6.1 and 6.2. NB: The wage data and the regressions analyzing them are all from Dey.[7]) M. Ahluwalia's (1978 and 1985) regression analysis confirms the absence of any clear trend in poverty, although there were considerable fluctuations on a yearly basis in both wages and poverty.[8] Two brief periods of above-average real wages occurred in 1970–72 and in 1976–79 and one period of below-average wages was registered in 1967–69. The period 1966–68 was also the period of the highest incidence of poverty, with the early and late 1970s showing a decline in the percentage of poor, corresponding to the rise in wages. The early 1960s were another period of low poverty, but of only moderately high wages (Table 6.1). Given these fluctuations, one can support almost any position by judicious selection of initial and terminal periods. But regression analyses incorporating a time variable show no significant trend in either real agricultural wages[9] or in poverty.[10]

Table 6.3 breaks these data down by subperiods and compares them with the change in all-India per capita GNP. It is clear that the direction of change is similar in most States and that real wage changes are related to changes in per capita GNP, although the relationship is far from clear-cut.

Table 6.4 shows a different story for industrial workers. The unweighted all-India index increased by nearly 20 percent over the fifteen years for which data were available (1959–61 to 1974–76). But these data provide much less information about the well-being of the poor. First, during this period the composition of the industrial labor force changed. The proportion of highly paid, skilled, professional and technical personnel increased with a shift to more capital- and skill-intensive industries (see the Lucas chapter in this volume). Second, there was a shift from highly competitive, private sector industries, that pay their workers as little as they can, to Government-owned, capital-intensive industries, that are more concerned with workers' satisfaction and therefore sometimes pay wages above the market. Third, even the unskilled workers in these industries often are not among the the poorest 40 percent in India. For all these reasons overall trends in industrial wages are ignored for the purposes of this chapter. Rather, for reasons given earlier, agricultural wages are taken as an index of the income of the poor.

That wages in so-called large-scale industry are atypical for the majority of workers and the majority of the poor can be seen by comparing them with those in small-scale industry. In general, the latter benefited neither from effective minimum wage legislation nor from labor unions. Like agricultural wages, they reflect rather the play of the market, the bargaining power of labor. As a result, wages for large firms averaged almost twice those in small firms for all of India.[11] Comparing the early 1960s with the early 1970s, we see that wages in all of small-scale industry declined by 8 percent (1960–61 to 1971 and 1973–74) to 13 percent (1960–62 to 1970–71 and 1973–74). This contrasts with the substantial rise for large-scale industry for essentially the same period.[12] The decline in real wages in small-scale industry, where wages are determined by the market, confirms the conclusion derived from agricultural wage data of stagnant real wages over a longer period, rather than the possible conclusion of rising real wages that might be drawn from data on large-scale industry.

Finally, income distribution data are of some help, although they present the analyst with two problems. First, they are quite sporadic. That is a serious problem since all other data show the considerable fluctuations from year to year in the income of the poor (see above) and in income distribution (see time series for India and other countries). Conclusions therefore can depend heavily on the initial and terminal years chosen. Second, indirect evidence indicates that there is massive underreporting by the wealthy. The extent and any time trend in underreporting are unknown. But it is at least conceivable that in India underreporting by the rich has increased as a result of the Government's increasing emphasis on a "Socialist Pattern of Society."

Because of these caveats conclusions about trends in income distribution cannot be firmly stated. I. J. Ahluwalia has summarized the existing data from both National Council for Applied Economic Research (NCAER) and National Sample Survey data. She concludes that there is no evidence of income distribution becoming less equal. According to NCAER, there is a considerable increase in inequality from the mid-1960s to a decade later, but there are only three observations underlying this conclusion. At the same time separate rural and urban coefficients show a small increase in equality from 1960 to the mid-1970s. These results, given the problems with the data, are equivocal at best.

In short, there appears to be no clear trend in poverty over the twenty or so years for which data exist. Most persuasive in my view is the absence of any clear trend in agricultural wages, an appropriate index of what happened to the income of the poor not only in agriculture but also in other nonprotected occupations. For this index the most recent wages are at the same level as twenty-five years earlier in real terms. That is a rather discouraging conclusion and suggests the possibility that income distribution became less equal over this long period. GNP per capita rose during this period about 1.3 percent per year on the average. If unskilled workers, that is, the poor, had no increase in real income, while the average person had a small, but significant increase, then the entire benefits of growth, by definition, must have gone to those with human or physical capital.

Factors in Income Changes: An Alternative Model

What factors caused these distressing results? If, as was argued, the income of the poor depends on the compensation they receive for their labor, it is in the labor market that the answers primarily lie. How that market functions becomes crucial. If it functions on standard neoclassical lines, then an explanation may not be too difficult. Slow and relatively capital-intensive growth in India's modern sector has resulted in little increase in demand for unskilled labor. The supply has grown with population. Stagnation in price therefore is likely. Alternatively, if the Lewis, Fei/Ranis model is applicable to India, then the explanation for stagnation is obvious: real wages remain constant until surplus labor is absorbed. (Readers who accept either of these models can save time by skipping this section.)

But it is unlikely that the Indian labor market conforms to the neoclassical description. For one, there clearly is no single labor market. As Tables 6.2 and 6.3 show, wages for agricultural workers differ greatly among

States and even within the same State unskilled workers in large-scale
and small-scale industry and in agriculture receive quite different wages.
For other countries in southern Asia where more abundant wage data
are available these differences can be demonstrated even more clearly
and it is reasonable that the Indian labor market is rather similar to that
of other labor-abundant countries, such as Bangladesh and Indonesia.
One can also question whether labor compensation equals marginal product
in much of agriculture and the informal sector. Indeed at least one study
for India[13] has shown that it does not, and this is confirmed by evidence
from other countries.[14] Finally, various observers familiar with the labor
market in India describe various aspects which confirm that it does not
conform to the neoclassical paradigm.[15] One therefore cannot simply
assume that the standard neoclassical mechanism of supply and demand
determines wage changes.

The data already provided also show, however, that the widely accepted
model for labor-abundant countries, that described by Lewis, and Fei and
Ranis, does not describe what happened in India: real wages simply do
not remain constant from year to year, much less over a longer period
of time.

An alternative model, already alluded to,[16] provides plausible explanations why labor income and the rate of growth are usually, but not
always, correlated, why rapid growth usually, but not always, is good for
the poor. In that model labor income is influenced in the short term by
the rate of inflation. When inflation accelerates, money or nominal wages
lag changes in prices so the purchasing power of labor income drops.
Conversely, when inflation slows, real labor income tends to rise. The
lag appears to be about two years in many cases. That is, by the end of
the second year real labor income generally has caught up. Therefore
inflation is not a major long-term factor in real labor income unless it
accelerates or decelerates over a long period of time. But in the short
term it can have a powerful effect. The rate of inflation is, of course,
closely related to the rate of growth in real output (or GNP). In an
economy like India's, changes in agricultural output profoundly affect the
rate of inflation. Rapid growth in agriculture, and especially in food
output, by raising real labor income therefore benefits the poor throughout
the economy, not just those working in agriculture.

While the rate of inflation is important in the short term, in the longer
term the crucial variables are the demand for labor in a "commercial"
sector, where wages are determined by labor productivity, and the supply
of labor from a "wage-sharing and income-sharing" sector, where labor
income is related to the average product. The second factor in labor
income is demand for labor from the commercial sector which operates
on neoclassical principles. It is the expanding "modern" sector, and
especially much of industry, which hires workers until their marginal
product roughly equals their wage. Its demand for labor depends on the
rapidity and the labor intensity of its growth. (Largely ignored in the
model are activities for which government or other institutions determine
the wage, the "protected sector," but it accounts for only a small part
of the labor force.) Relatively slow and capital-intensive growth, which

has characterized Indian industry, then means slowly rising demand for labor and therefore little pressure from the demand side for rising labor income.

The reservation wage in the income-sharing sector is the third factor affecting real labor income. The sector consists of thousands of submarkets for labor, characterized by barriers to entry of different magnitude. These barriers enable those inside to derive a rent, which raises their income above their marginal product. The amount of rent varies with the height of the barrier and the average product of those in the submarket. Average product is determined essentially by the value of its output since the number of workers changes only slowly, in response to demand in the commercial sector, already taken into account on the demand side. The largest part of the income-sharing sector is agriculture, the next largest trade and services connected with agriculture. Agricultural prices are largely determined by Government policy and by the world market price. With price thus exogenously given, the value of output is largely determined by the physical quantity produced. When monsoon and policy combine to increase output, then average value product goes up. Since labor compensation is related to average value product, labor income also rises. With it the reservation wage goes up, that is, the supply curve shifts. Wages in the commercial sector have to rise if that sector wants to attract more labor from the only source possible: the income-sharing sector. A higher rate of growth in agricultural output (or elsewhere in the income-sharing sector) then means a more rapid rise in the reservation wage and with it in labor income throughout the economy.

A fourth factor in labor income is a variety of miscellaneous variables which influence labor demand and reservation wage. In India, labor-intensive work programs may be the most important on the demand side. On the supply side any breakdown in work and income sharing will increase the supply of labor seeking work in the commercial sector and drive down the wage. If landlords shift from using sharecroppers, who share in the income from land and benefit from rising output, to self-cultivation, using a smaller number of laborers who receive a fixed wage determined by their marginal product, then surplus workers will be pushed out. They will seek work in other labor submarkets where income sharing still prevails, lowering the average product, or increase the supply to the commercial sector.

In the model labor income in different occupations and regions moves together, but often with a lag. The lag is due to the fact that migration in and out of occupations and areas is needed for labor income in one occupation and region to influence that in another occupation and region. That migration is hindered not only by physical distances and the economic costs of movement but also by the social barriers to entry into different labor markets. But if compensation in a labor market gets too far out of line, then the costs of exclusion rise and, with a lag, additional workers will push in or leave, restoring the previous relationship.

With that model a higher rate of growth, other things equal, has three consequences for the income of the poor:

- a reduced rate of inflation
- a greater demand for labor
- a higher supply price or reservation wage for labor

all of which increase compensation to unskilled workers, by far the largest segment of the poor. Clearly a number of other factors matter besides the rate of growth. The most important in the longer run is the labor intensity of production and factors which undermine income sharing. If a higher rate of growth is achieved only at the cost of greater capital intensity and a breakdown of income sharing, then it could be unfavorable for the income of the poor. In the short run real labor income is affected by various factors other than growth which influence the rate of inflation such as the weather, import policy and the exchange rate.

Empirical Evidence

The wage data for India are quite consistent with this story. One superficial indication is given by the real agricultural wages for different States in Table 6.2: they are highest in those, such as the Punjab, where demand for labor and the average product in agriculture are greatest.

More persuasive than this superficial comparison is the regression analysis in Table 6.5 which tests the variables discussed above or their proxies. For all of India and all of the States prices in the same year or lagged by one year are significantly correlated with nominal wages. For all India wages make up only 30–40 percent of price changes in the first year, but compensate for most of the remainder in the second. The numbers vary among the States, but in all regressions only zero to 80 percent of any price change is compensated in the first year, with 90 percent matched in general by the second. Table 6.1 and annual price data (not reported here) indicate that changes in inflation rates appear to have played a role in the rise in real wages in the early 1970s, the decline in the mid-1970s, the rise from 1976 to 1979 and the subsequent renewed decline.

No good proxy could be found for labor demand in agriculture as a whole, much less for its commercial sector. For demand in the rest of the commercial sector the lagged wage in industry is an excellent proxy. The price of fertilizer was used as a rather unsatisfactory proxy for labor demand in agriculture, on the assumption that it influences the quantity of fertilizer applied, which in turn affects the labor used. As long as the variable is significant, there is some support for the hypothesis, regardless of its sign, since fertilizer can be complementary or substitutive for labor. Average product in agriculture, both current and lagged by one year, serves as a proxy for the reservation wage in the work and income-sharing sector. It should be a reasonably good proxy since agriculture is the largest part of that sector. The wage in industry, lagged by one and two years, tests the assertion that changes in labor compensation are correlated throughout the economy, even if absolute wages differ. It also indicates that changes in labor demand in industry affect labor income in agriculture, the same point from a different perspective.

On the whole, the regression results support the hypotheses, although they are less consistent and significant for India, and especially some of the States, than is the case with respect to other countries for which the same model has been tested (Egypt, Pakistan, Bangladesh, Sri Lanka, Indonesia). There are plausible reasons for this outcome. Fertilizer price data are available only on an all-India basis. Since fertilizer prices are controlled and are supposed to be identical throughout the country, this is not unreasonable, but it is likely that the effective price to cultivators does differ by distance from source of supply. Moreover, the Indian labor market is a complex one. Migration between some States is considerable (e.g., from Bihar to Punjab) and so is temporary migration to other countries (mostly from Kerala) in the recent past. Other States are relatively isolated. Government intervention in wage determination probably affected labor income in both Kerala and West Bengal, and so did Government-sponsored employment programs (e.g., in Maharashtra). None of these factors are captured in the empirical test. In other words, India is far more complex and larger than nearly all other countries. The regional data and knowledge of regional economic relationships needed to capture that complexity are simply not available so analyses for which location matters are likely to be statistically less satisfactory than for other countries. That the results are nevertheless quite consistent with the model permits some confidence in the analysis.

There is also some indirect support from the model tested by I. J. Ahluwalia,[17] M. S. Ahluwalia and others[18] of factors in rates of poverty. The principal variables tested are average agricultural incomes and prices, similar to average product and prices here. The incidence of rural poverty is quite highly and significantly correlated with annual fluctuations in agricultural income. However, the price variables in the I. J. Ahluwalia specification prove not significant.

Note that the relationships tested in these regressions are between annual fluctuations in average product and unskilled worker's wages, and between average agricultural income and poverty incidence. A cogent criticism[19] is that correlation of annual fluctuations does not necessarily mean that over the longer term growth trickles down to the poor. But Table 6.3 shows that the relationship also holds for two-year to seven-year periods. In the two periods when per capita GNP rose rapidly, wages for all-India and all, or almost all, States were rising. For all-India the increase was substantial. Conversely, in the two periods when per capita income declined or stagnated real wages for India and for all States except one fell, often quite drastically.

The most persuasive evidence in support of the model comes from a study of wage changes in five labor-abundant countries in South and Southeast Asia, including India.[20] The details of that study are beyond the scope of this chapter, but given their obvious relevance a few major conclusions are worth summarizing. Covering five countries and about thirty years expands the number of observations to about 150 and the regressions to about 30. More important, the other countries showed far greater variance over time than India in growth rates and real wages. The conclusions are more persuasive since the story is highly consistent.

Whether the analysis covers individual years, or multiyear periods, whether the comparison is a simple one of growth rates with real wages, or a more complex multiple regression, all wage series in a country move together; and the proxies for labor demand and for the reservation wage in agriculture are almost uniformly significant. The principal exception is Indonesia in the 1970s. That exception is explainable because there is good evidence for that period of a pattern of growth that was unusually capital intensive, even by regional standards, and for an erosion of income sharing in the rural areas. With consistent evidence from several sources there is some ground for confidence in the underlying model.

Policies and Poverty Alleviation

Reasons for the persistence of poverty in India can now be identified and related to some of the policies which have been important in this respect. Significant contributions have been made to the alleviation of poverty by India's success in limiting inflation and in creating demand for labor in a variety of labor-intensive, Government-supported programs. But these successes have been balanced by a slow rate of growth in per capita national product and the capital intensity of growth in manufacturing and some other commercial sector activities. Slow and capital-intensive growth in the commercial sector led to stagnation in demand for labor, stagnation of per capita output in the income-sharing sector led to stagnation in the reservation wage. Shrinkage in the income-sharing sector may have contributed to stagnant labor income.

Slow Agricultural Growth and the Stagnation of the Reservation Wage

On the negative side, a major factor has been the very slow growth in average product in agriculture, the dominant element in the income-sharing sector, and with it stagnation in the reservation wage. Over the twenty-five year period from 1950 to 1975 per capita (of the rural population) value added in agriculture (at constant prices) rose by 0.7 percent annually. Near-stagnant per capita agricultural output, in the absence of very rapid growth in other directly productive sectors, principally manufacturing, also meant stagnant average product in other income-sharing activities, principally informal sector trade and services. Whether the specific model sketched above is accepted or not, it does seem reasonable that near-stagnant output per capita, in the absence of a successful radical redistribution of income or assets, is likely to result in little reduction in rural poverty. In terms of the model presented earlier, stagnant average product in most income-sharing activities meant a stagnant reservation wage, resulting in stagnant labor income throughout the economy from the labor supply side.

Slow Industrial Growth and Labor Demand

From the demand side as well there was little impetus for rising wages. In many economies where wages of unskilled workers have risen rapidly the principal reason has been rapid industrial growth. Indian industrial growth, in contrast, has been slow by international standards. While GDP growth in the last twenty-odd years averaged 3.6 percent, manufacturing value added increased at roughly 4.8 percent, or one-third faster. The industrial growth rate in other low-income countries in the same period was about 5.5 percent. But that comparison group includes mostly African countries whose growth was severely affected by a host of noneconomic problems. More appropriate as a standard for India are the middle-income oil importers, most of whom had per capita incomes not significantly different from India in the early 1950s. Their industrial growth rate averaged 6.2 percent, nearly 30 percent higher than India's. If India had achieved comparable growth, employment in manufacturing would have been greater by almost 1.5 million workers in the the 1980s. The other large countries in South and Southeast Asia had an industrial growth rate of about 8 percent, while the newly industrialized countries (NICs) of East Asia achieved well over 10 percent. At these rates of growth employment in India might have been 3–5 million greater.

Capital Intensity and Labor Demand

Moreover, industry employed relatively little additional labor because Indian industry has become progressively less labor intensive. One crude measure is output (value added) per worker. In 1950 each manufacturing worker and complementary machinery and other capital added a bit less than Rs 7,000 (in constant 1970 prices) to the value of output. By 1965 this had increased to about Rs 9,500 and by 1980 to over Rs 12,100, an increase of over 70 percent in capital intensity by this crude measure.

Some reasons for increasing capital intensity have been well recognized.[21] Clearly the fundamental determinant has been *the slow growth of industrial exports.* Even in the 1950s Indian industry could largely supply the domestic market with labor-intensive consumer goods, especially textiles, garments and processed agricultural materials. Planners therefore had the alternative of making it attractive to invest in the production of labor-intensive goods for export, or in increasingly capital-intensive goods for the domestic market. The import substitution strategy, which has been the hallmark of planned development in India, was inevitably accompanied by increasing capital intensity: there simply are no labor-intensive petroleum refineries, chemical plants, or artificial fiber factories; nor are steel mills labor intensive when compared to export-oriented garment, shoe, electrical and electronics factories.

The *relative prices of labor and capital* have also been widely recognized as factors making for capital intensity.[22] Minimum wage legislation has sometimes been seen as a major element in high labor costs. But one can question how important it is since the minimum wage has usually been fixed below the actual wage rate in large-scale firms and is not effective for smaller firms. Instead, risk and the cost of inflexibility seem to be major deterrents to the hiring of more labor. The risk relates primarily to labor troubles, some of which—gheraos—make life especially miserable for managers. For managers of publicly owned enterprises labor troubles can carry the further risk that they will be used by the political leadership as a significant indicator of a poor manager. Of course, the best means for avoiding labor trouble, with these attendant consequences, is to have few, but well-paid workers rather than many poorly paid ones.

Another problem for the manager is the difficulty of dismissing workers, which has resulted in de facto lifetime employment in some factories. Managers may then find themselves saddled with lazy or incompetent workers or with an excess number that cannot be employed productively if demand declines or a new technology requires fewer or different workers. The best solution again is to hire a minimum number of workers.

On *the capital side* the problem, according to some observers, is the low interest rate, which makes it cheap to borrow from Government-sponsored institutions. No doubt this is of some significance, but like the minimum wage, its importance can be overstated. Only a limited proportion of industrial investment is financed by any formal institution. Among those who do obtain such loans some may find that the rent generated by interest rates below those in the open market may have to be shared with those deciding on the loans. If such loans are also troublesome and time consuming to obtain, then the real cost of the loan may not be low. Nor is the opportunity cost of financial capital for the wealthy given by the bank interest rate, but rather by the return on alternative investments. So the subsidy implicit in low interest rates may make capital inexpensive in only a limited number of cases.

Four factors other than low interest rates make for low capital costs and have been less widely discussed. First, a low foreign exchange rate, combined with exemptions from tariffs for capital goods, results in cheap imported capital goods. Second, borrowing for fixed capital, especially the purchase of machinery, is easier and cheaper than borrowing for working capital, needed to hire more workers. Third, much of the investment in public enterprises has come from the budget. The real cost of capital can then be close to zero if the borrowing manager does not expect much pressure to repay during his tenure and even has the possibility of deferring interest and adding it to principal. Fourth, Government lending institutions are usually quite flexible about repayment and may even be flexible about interest payments, during bad times. Borrowing then spreads and reduces risk from the manager's perspective. He can defer payments on the loan when profits are poor.

One thus finds that Indian reality for some large or publicly owned firms stands on their head some standard, textbook assumptions. Instead of machinery and other investment representing a fixed cost it can be a variable cost, adjustable with the profitability of the firm. Labor, conversely, can become essentially a fixed cost, which cannot be reduced significantly even if demand drops sharply. Moreover, at least some managers are less concerned with profit maximization and more with avoiding labor trouble. For both reasons there are strong pressures to reduce the use of labor and to substitute capital to the maximum extent possible.

Add the fact that many industries are not subject to competitive pressures. Decisionmakers then can indulge their preference for the most modern, capital intensive units[23] and for avoiding the messy business of managing large numbers of workers. Finally, for a long period of time import licensing was on the basis of installed capacity, at least in part. Since installed capacity is usually defined in terms of the machinery in a factory, not the number of workers, this provided another reason for capital intensity.

As a result of all these policies managers found it desirable and profitable to shift to increasingly capital-intensive methods for producing particular goods. At the same time the whole industrial sector shifted increasingly to the production of a capital-intensive product mix. The principal reason was mentioned earlier: with exports unattractive, industry was producing for a sheltered domestic market already saturated with labor-intensive goods and able to absorb only more capital-intensive commodities. In addition, the Government fostered capital-intensive capital and inter-mediate goods production and taxed or restricted such labor-intensive consumer goods as cotton textiles. As a result of both a more capital-intensive technology and a more capital-intensive composition of final goods the manufacturing sector became significantly more capital intensive over time. Its demand for labor naturally increased rather slowly as a result. The urban labor force was growing quite rapidly at the same time. The consequence was that industry contributed little pressure for rising wages from the demand side.

The Possible Decline in Income Sharing

There has been a great deal of debate on the effect on the rural labor market of changing agricultural technology, the Green Revolution, and of the threat of land reform. It has been argued that landlords have shifted from the use of tenants and of laborers with a long-term relationship that involved a claim to a share of the output to more commercial arrangements with hired labor. In terms of the model sketched earlier the shift is from work and income sharing, where labor, including wage labor, shares in rising output, to commercial sector relationships, where labor is paid a fixed wage related to its marginal product in agriculture.

Such a shift would have two consequences. First, rapidly rising per capita incomes in agriculture need no longer be accompanied by rapidly rising reservation wages. If labor is compensated in relation to average product, its income rises proportionately with output, by definition. But if it is paid its marginal product and there continues to be surplus labor, then labor income can rise much more slowly than output. Second, the shift could mean that rapid increases in production could be accompanied by declining labor use per unit of output and even per acre. As a result, some workers who no longer have access to the rents derived from income-sharing activities in agriculture would seek employment in activities where income-sharing continues to prevail, or elsewhere in the commercial sector. Either action will put downward pressure on labor income.

The data and their interpretation are quite mixed on the extent of any such shift. On the one hand, there is little doubt that increased output increases labor use. On the other, increased use of commercial inputs has been accompanied in the case of some landlords by increased commercialization of labor relations. The net effect of these conflicting tendencies on labor use and labor relations is not clearly established.[24] But a shift of labor from the income-sharing to the commercial sector with rising agricultural output could explain some puzzling and conflicting trends in real wages and poverty incidence in rural areas. For instance, stagnant real agricultural wages accompanying rapid long-term growth in agricultural output in the Punjab could be due to a combination of in-migration of labor, labor-displacing tractorization and a shift from income sharing to commercial labor relations for a rising proportion of workers.

So much for the policies which tended to depress labor incomes and contributed to their stagnation. But there were policies as well which had positive effects on labor income. In terms of the model sketched earlier relative price stability and special labor-intensive programs made the most important contribution.

Price Stability

The prices of wage goods—especially the crucial food grains—were stable in India by world standards. There were only a few, relatively brief, periods when prices rose rapidly and real wages dropped as a result (by 9 percent from 1964–65 to 1966–67; by 26 percent from 1971–72 to 1974–75; by 18 percent from 1978–79 to 1980–81). Periods of rapidly rising prices seem to have come more frequently in the recent past with unfortunate consequences for workers' income. These recent bouts of inflation, however, were substantially caused by worldwide inflation, primarily as the result of the two oil shocks and not by domestic policies. There is therefore no reason to anticipate more frequent bouts of inflation in the future.

Labor-Intensive Programs

India has been among the handful of countries that have created demand for unskilled labor from relatively successful labor-intensive programs for infrastructure construction. There appear to be no recent studies analyzing the size, impact on employment and consequences for investment of these programs. The superficial impression from casual observation is that such programs have had much less of an impact in federal India, where they differ greatly from State to State, than in unitary Indonesia. Nevertheless they have made some contribution to absorbing some of the increase in the labor force and therefore to preventing a possible decline in real wages from the labor demand side.

But the consequences of relative price stability have been essentially short term and those of labor-intensive programs have been limited. Over the longer term their beneficial effects have been swamped by the negative effects on labor income of slow, capital-intensive growth.

The Potential of Income and Asset Transfers to the Poor: Land Reform, Public Ownership, Subsidies

The discussion so far has been entirely in terms of increasing the earned income of the poor. Nothing has been said about income or asset transfers which have been significant elements in many discussions of poverty alleviation in India and elsewhere. Clearly some aspects of such transfers could be very significant in giving the poor greater control over resources, in the case of asset transfers on a long-term or permanent basis. In fact, however, they have actually proved to be not very significant in India and elsewhere.

Three sets of policies have been advocated most widely to improve income distribution and reduce poverty: land reform, public ownership of major industrial and business enterprises, and fiscal transfers taxing the rich and subsidizing the poor. There are good economic reasons why each should be effective and a few examples of other countries where they have been effective in changing income distribution. All three have been used to some degree in India but, as the evidence advanced earlier makes clear, with little effect in reducing poverty.

The effect of land reform on efficiency and growth has been the subject of dispute, but there has been little argument that effective land reform can increase the income of the poor in the rural areas significantly. But there is also a considerable literature analyzing why it has made only limited progress in India. The reasons are familiar: in India, as in other countries where there has been no revolution to fundamentally alter social and political relationships, the opposition is too great. Land reform is a textbook example of a policy seen as a zero-sum game: some benefit only because others lose. Not surprisingly, policies under which an important group clearly loses are resisted more fiercely than those where everyone gains, or at least no major group loses. Moreover, in this case the potential losers see their losses clearly and are politically powerful, the potential winners cannot be sure of their gains and are politically weak. The usual outcome in a mixed economy is to limit land reform so severely that it does not significantly affect income distribution. India is no exception to this pattern.

Fiscal transfers suffer from the same problem. Again they involve a clear loss to the powerful groups whose taxes are expected to pay for subsidies to the poor. Fiscal transfers to achieve greater equality are quite popular with economists because they can be designed to have a minimum of distortionary effects. But as a result of opposition, as well as some technical problems, there appears to be only one country which has successfully used them to achieve a massive resource transfer. That country is Sri Lanka, and the circumstances which made it possible are not duplicated in India. One study which carefully traced the total effect of taxes and subsidies on different income groups[25] found that in Sind Province of Pakistan the system was neutral or slightly progressive. A food grain subsidy which benefited the poor disproportionately just about offset subsidies for higher education and curative medicine which disproportionately benefited the richer groups. While these results cannot simply be transferred to India, they do suggest the possibility that a detailed analysis would indicate that the fiscal system of India, as of most countries, is not a significant factor in transferring resources from rich to poor.

Public ownership of major enterprises, if achieved by nationalization, is also strongly resisted. If brought about by public investment, or by the takeover of failing enterprises, there is often little or no organized opposition. As a result it is quite widespread in India, as elsewhere. Unfortunately it apparently does not particularly benefit the poor in many cases.[26] Public enterprises traditionally provide better pay and working conditions than many private firms, but since they are usually capital intensive they employ few unskilled workers and most of their workers belong to a labor elite, not the poor. More workers benefit from retaining their jobs in the case of enterprises that would have closed if they had remained in the private sector. In addition to their workers, public enterprises seem to benefit the officials who supervise them and the managers who run them. That is, nationalization often seems to shift benefits from a private commercial elite to a public bureaucratic elite and to provide some additional benefits to a limited number of workers, already among the better off. It provides few direct benefits to the poor. Indirect benefits to consumers via lower prices or indirect costs in the form of higher prices do not have a systematic impact. Some of the consumers may be poor, or they may be primarily among the wealthy (e.g., consumers of electric power or of airplane rides). Even if the poor benefit from low prices, these benefits may be offset if the poor also bear much of the cost of the subsidy which makes these prices possible.

In short, while land reform, fiscal transfers and public ownership can in theory transfer resources from rich to poor, in practice they have failed to do so over the last forty years, not only in India but in practically all nonrevolutionary situations. The wealthy inevitably are also powerful— and vice versa—and they naturally resist such transfers. Once income or assets are in the hands of an elite, they are difficult to extract in any society. It appears to be far easier to adopt policies which provide greater earned income to the poor since such policies do not clearly involve a zero-sum game. Indeed, putting underemployed unskilled workers to work increases total income and can benefit the wealthy as well as the poor. Such a positive-sum policy is clearly easier to adopt than to transfer income after it has been earned.

Framing Policies for Poverty Alleviation: Trade-Offs

Effective and politically feasible policies to reduce poverty then involve an increase in the income of unskilled workers, either by raising the demand for their labor or by increasing their reservation price. Both in turn can be achieved by increasing the rate of growth, if growth is labor intensive. Growth and equity are not conflicting objectives, if equity is defined in terms of increasing the absolute income of the poor, but can be mutually reinforcing: in a labor-abundant economy, like India's, labor-intensive development is likely to be both efficient and equitable.

There may, however, be another difficult trade-off for policymakers, between clear benefits for a limited group of lower-income workers and less obvious, more widespread gains for a much larger but more amorphous group of the very poor. For instance, a higher minimum wage for workers in large-scale, organized industries will clearly benefit the limited number of low-paid, unskilled workers employed by those firms. But by discouraging the hiring of additional workers it can lower the demand for unskilled labor in the economy as a whole and drive down the labor income for all those not effectively covered by minimum wage legislation. Similarly protecting particular lines of cloth production against foreign competition may save the jobs of workers in those firms at the cost of lower demand for labor in the garment industry, handicapped by higher cost inputs, again resulting in lower labor income for the great majority of workers throughout the economy.

There is also a trade-off between the rate of growth in a particular industry and its labor intensity. Investment and growth in most individual industries can be increased by reducing the cost of capital to their investors. Such policies, while widely pursued, have been criticized on efficiency grounds for increasing the social (opportunity) cost of that industry and depriving other, potentially more efficient, industries of capital. In addition to efficiency costs, such a policy also adversely affects equity. Here again higher growth, greater profits and better wages for those in the industry are obtained at the cost of slower growth and reduced income for the poor in the rest of the economy.

In all of these instances the underlying trade-off is between visible, definite and focused gains for a favored few and more diffuse, uncertain and less obvious potential benefits for the many. The first strategy can assure organized political support from important small groups in the short term, while the latter avoids more widespread political opposition in the medium term.

In other words, the poor have a stake in a high rate of growth, but they have even more of a stake in a pattern of growth that makes great demands for their labor. Therefore policies which make it attractive to substitute capital for labor are undesirable. These include a low interest rate for fixed investment and low tariffs, or complete tariff exemption, for machinery imports. But even more important than the relative cost of capital and labor (the wage/rental ratio) is the cost of labor relative to the cost of its products, and especially the cost of labor in relation to the price of labor-intensive exports. Most important are the rules, regulations, permits and licenses which make it difficult to export labor-intensive products. The latter two are important for the same reason: since Indian demand for labor-intensive goods is already largely satisfied by domestic production, a rapid expansion in the production of labor-intensive goods can be achieved only if the goods are exported.

On the basis of the analysis sketched in the early part of the chapter the linchpin of any program of reducing poverty in India is the rapid expansion of labor-intensive exports. Fortunately there is some evidence that India, thanks to its reservoir of highly trained and low-cost technical, professional and scientific personnel, is well placed to compete in relatively high technology and labor-intensive goods[27] but if, and only if, the policy framework is one that permits and encourages such exports.

To sum up, as far as one can tell, there was little reduction in the proportion of poor in India over the last twenty-five years, which implies an increase in the absolute number of poor. The principal reasons were a slow and capital-intensive rate of growth, resulting in little additional demand for unskilled labor, and a slow rise in the reservation wage in agriculture and other informal sector occupations. There is considerable potential for increasing both the rate of growth and its benefits to the poor by shifting to a more labor-intensive pattern of development that would take advantage of India's large pool of low-cost technical and professional, as well as unskilled, labor. But that would require a rapid increase in labor-intensive manufactured exports and would involve some short-term political costs.

Notes

1. Montek S. Ahluwalia, "Rural Poverty and Agricultural Performance in India," *Journal of Development Studies*, April 1978; Montek S. Ahluwalia, "Rural Poverty, Agricultural Production and Prices: A Re-Examination," in *Agricultural Change and Rural Poverty*, edited by John W. Mellor and Gunvant M. Desai (Baltimore, MD: Johns Hopkins University Press, 1985).

2. Pranab K. Bardhan, "Poverty and 'Trickle-Down' in Rural India: A Quantitative Analysis," in *Agricultural Change and Rural Poverty*, edited by John W. Mellor and Gunvant M. Desai (Baltimore, Md.: Johns Hopkins University Press, 1985).

3. Michael Manove and Gustav F. Papanek, with Harendra K. Dey, "Tied Rents and Wage Determination in Labor Abundant Countries" (Boston University, Center for Asian Development Studies, Discussion Paper) (Boston, 1986).

4. Harendra K. Dey, G. F. Papanek, and David Wheeler, "A Labor Income Determination Model for Labor Abundant Countries: Empirical Evidence" (Boston University, Department of Economics, Discussion Paper) (Boston, 1985); and Gustav F. Papanek, "Planning Against Poverty: Wage Data as a Tool," *Economic Bulletin for Asia and the Pacific*, 32, no. 2 (December 1981).

5. Dey, Papanek, and Wheeler, "A Labor Income Determination Model for Labor Abundant Countries"; and Papanek, "Planning Against Poverty."

6. V. M. Rao, "'Agricultural Wages in India'—A Reliability Analysis," *Indian Journal of Agricultural Economics*, July-September 1972.

7. Harendra K. Dey, "Changes in Real Wages: The Effect of Growth, The Consequences for Income Distribution" (unpublished Ph.D. dissertation, Boston University, Boston, Mass., 1984).

8. Montek S. Ahluwalia, "Rural Poverty and Agricultural Performance in India," *Journal of Development Studies*, April 1978; Montek S. Ahluwalia, "Rural Poverty, Agricultural Production and Prices: A Re-Examination," in Mellor and Desai, *Agricultural Change and Rural Poverty*.

9. Dey, "Changes in Real Wages."

10. Isher J. Ahluwalia, *Industrial Growth in India* (New Delhi: Oxford University Press, 1985).

11. B. K. Jain, "Urban Poverty and Industrial Wages" (paper presented at the Fifth Annual Conference of the Society for the Study of Regional Disparities, Udaijana, 1984) (forthcoming in J. L. Sandresh and D. U. Sastry, eds., *Industrialization and Regional Development*).

12. Calculated from Jain, "Urban Poverty and Industrial Wages."

13. Mohammed Sharif, "Labor Supply Behavior of the Poor in Labor Abundant Less Developed Countries" (unpublished Ph.D. dissertation, Boston University, Boston, Mass., 1984).

14. Budiono Sri Handoko, "Productivity, Size of Land and Labor Use in Rice Production in Java and Bali" (unpublished Ph.D. dissertation, Boston University, Boston, Mass., 1982).

15. N. Vijay Jagannathan, *Informal Markets in Developing Countries* (New York: Oxford University Press, 1987).

16. Manove and Papanek, "Tied Rents and Wage Determination in Labor Abundant Countries."

17. I. J. Ahluwalia, *Industrial Growth in India.*

18. M. S. Ahluwalia, "Rural Poverty, Agricultural Production and Prices," and John W. Mellor and Gunvant M. Desai, "Agricultural Change and Rural Poverty: A Synthesis," both in Mellor and Desai, *Agricultural Change and Rural Poverty.*

19. See Bardhan, "Poverty and 'Trickle-Down' in Rural India."

20. Papanek, "Planning Against Poverty"; and Gustav F. Papanek, "Lectures on Development Strategy, Growth, Equity and the Political Process in Southern Asia" (Islamabad: Pakistan Institute of Development Economics, 1986).

21. E.g., Robert E. B. Lucas, "India's Industrial Policy," in this volume; and I. J. Ahluwalia, *Industrial Growth in India.*

22. E.g., Lucas, "India's Industrial Policy."

23. Louis Wells, "Economic Man and Engineering Man: Choice of Technology in a Low-Wage Country" (New York: South East Asia Development Group of the Asia Society, 1973).

24. See Bardhan, "Poverty and 'Trickle-Down' in Rural India," M. L. Dantwala, "Technology, Growth and Equity in Agriculture," and others in Mellor and Desai, *Agricultural Change and Rural Poverty,* and the references on the controversy cited there.

25. Ishrat Hussain, "Impact of Government Expenditure on Income Distribution: An Empirical Study" (unpublished Ph.D. dissertation, Boston University, Boston, Mass., 1981).

26. See Leroy P. Jones, "Public Enterprise for Whom?: Some Perverse Distributional Consequences of Public Decisions," *Economic Development and Cultural Change,* January 1984; and Leroy P. Jones and Gustav F. Papanek, "The Efficiency of Public Enterprise in Less Developed Countries," in *Government and Public Enterprise: Essays in Honour of Professor V. V. Ramanadham,* edited by G. Ram Reddy (London: Frank Cass & Co., 1983).

27. David Wheeler and Ashoka Mody, "Potential for Indian Exports" (Boston University, Center for Asian Development Studies, Discussion Paper) (Boston, 1986).

TABLE 6.1 Agricultural Real Wages and Percent in Rural Poverty

	1) Real Wage of Agricultural Workers		2) Percentage of Population in Poverty
	Rupees (1979–80 Prices)	Index	
1954–55	5.75	97.3	
1955–56	5.53	93.6	
1956–57	5.40	91.4	54.0
1957–58	5.29	89.5	50.0
1958–59	5.33	90.2	46.5
1959–60	5.45	92.2	44.0
1960–61	5.57	94.3	39.0
1961–62	5.88	99.5	39.0
1962–63	5.75	97.3	–
1963–64	5.00	84.6	44.5
1964–65	5.35	90.5	47.0
1965–66	5.13	86.8	54.0
1966–67	4.85	82.1	57.0
1967–68	4.83	81.7	56.5
1968–69	5.74	97.1	51.0
1969–70	5.81	98.3	–
1970–71	6.14	103.9	47.5
1971–72	6.20	104.9	41.0
1972–73	5.76	97.5	43.0
1973–74	5.13	86.8	46.0
1974–75	4.58	77.5	–
1975–76	5.80	98.1	–
1976–77	6.55	110.8	–
1977–78	6.30	106.6	39.0
1978–79	6.55	110.8	—
1979–80	5.91	100.0	
1980–81	5.40	91.4	

Sources: Dey, "Changes in Real Wages"; Ahluwalia, Industrial Growth in India.

TABLE 6.2 Agricultural Real Wage Trends by States
(1979–80 prices, Rs/day)

State	Average 1954–55 and 1955–56	Average 1979–80 and 1980–81	Percentage Change (1954–56 to 1979–81)
Andhra Pradesh	4.82	5.02	4.1
Assam	10.91	6.78	−37.8
Bihar	5.03	5.17	2.8
Kerala	5.84[a]	9.31	59.4
Karnataka	5.17[a]	5.01	− 3.1
Madhya Pradesh	4.83	4.28	−11.4
Mararashtra	5.56[a]	4.56	−18.0
Orissa	4.39	4.36	− 0.7
Punjab	10.03	10.44	4.1
Tamil Nadu	6.34	4.81	−24.1
Uttar Pradesh	4.72	5.95	26.1
West Bengal	7.09	6.43	− 9.3
All India	5.64	5.65	0.002

[a] Kerala is for Travancore Cochin; Karnataka for Mysore and Coorg; Maharashtra for Bombay.

Source: Dey, "Changes in Real Wages."

TABLE 6.3 Average Annual Growth Rates in Agricultural Real Wages
and GNP in India
(percentage)

State	Period					
	1954–55 to 1959–60	1959–60 to 1962–63	1962–63 to 1969–70	1969–70 to 1974–75	1974–75 to 1978–79	1978–79 to 1980–81
Andhra Pradesh	−4.0	5.0	−1.0	−4.5	12.0	−11.0
Assam	−3.0	2.0[a]	−1.0	−6.2	6.0	− 5.0
Bihar	−2.0	0.0	3.0	−7.1	12.0	−11.0
Kerala	−2.0	9.0	2.0	−5.5	7.0	6.6
Karnataka	0.7	1.0	−2.0	−5.0	13.6	−15.0
Madhya Pradesh	−4.0	4.0	−3.0	−4.5	12.3	−12.0
Maharashtra	−0.9	−2.0	1.0	−9.0	8.0	−10.0
Punjab	0.2	3.0	2.0	−5.0	5.0	−11.0
Tamil Nadu	−3.0	3.0	−2.0	−3.3	8.0	−12.0
Orissa	0.8	1.0	−1.5	−5.0	12.0	−12.0
Uttar Pradesh	2.0	4.0	−0.4	−2.0	8.0	−10.0
West Bengal	−3.0	−3.0	0.0	−4.0	11.0	− 8.0
All India	−1.0	2.0	0.1	−5.0	9.0	−12.0
Growth Rate of GNP (1970–71 prices)	3.3	4.1	3.7	2.3	5.8	1.4
Growth Rate of Per Capita Net Product at Constant Prices	1.2	1.7	1.3	0.11	3.7	− 1.05

[a] Initial year is 1960–61 rather than 1959–60.

Source: Dey, "Changes in Real Wages."

TABLE 6.4 Average Per Worker Annual Real Earnings in
Medium and Large Industry
(1960 prices, Rs/year)

State	Average 1959–60 and 1960–61	Average 1974–75 and 1975–76	Percentage Change
Andhra	709	778[a]	9.7
Assam	783	513[a]	−34.5
Bihar	1,847	1,556[a]	−15.7
Kerala	633	775	19.3
Karnataka	886	1,318	48.7
Madhya Pradesh	995	1,583	59.1
Mararashtra	1,472	1,871	27.1
Orissa	1,017	1,755	72.6
Punjab	1,329	1,075	−19.1
Tamil Nadu	1,297	1,457	12.3
Uttar Pradesh	1,098	1,217	10.8
West Bengal	1,282	1,860	45.1
Unweighted Average			19.6

[a] 1974–75 figure only.

Source: Dey, "Changes in Real Wages."

144

TABLE 6.5 Regressions for Agricultural Wages[a]

(dependent variable: nominal wages; 1954–55 to 1980–81 data)

Const	Prices[b] Current	Lagged	Fertilizer[c] Current	Lagged	Avg. Product[d] Current	Lag.	Industry Wage[e] Lagged One Year	Two Year	R^2
Gujarat[f]									
-4.2	-.11	1.07	.01		.2				.98
(-4.4)	(-.7)	(6.5)	(.2)		(3.3)				
-2.0	-.04	.92	.23			.01	.09	.95	
(-1.5)	(-.19)	(4.6)	(-1.6)			(.11)		(3.05)	
Kerala									
-9.4	.79	-.61	.35					.06	.99
(-0.7)	(14.4)	(-6.3)	(1.33)					(2.03)	
Punjab									
-7.7	.27	.50			1.0			.05	.95
(-4.2)	(1.0)	(1.6)			(2.4)			(1.4)	
-6.4		.79	-.18		.94			.08	.95
(2.5)		(4.1)	(-.91)		(1.98)			(3.25)	
Tamil Nadu									
-7.8	.81	.43	.08		.68				.99
(-4.24)	(7.81)	(5.80)	(1.03)		(2.8)				
-3.28	.45	.37	-.27		.38		.06		.97
(-2.36)	(4.18)	(3.71)	(-2.51)		(1.47)		(3.13)		
All India[g]									
-9.29	.41	.56	-.22		.55	.73			.99
(-6.71)	(3.65)	(5.14)	(-2.95)		(2.77)	(3.90)			
-5.5	.31	.60	-.23		.28		.22	.12	.98
(-3.4)	(2.21)	(4.42)	(-2.11)		(1.04)		(1.63)	(3.51)	

[a] Figures in parentheses are t-statistics. All variables are in logarithmic form.
[b] Prices are the rural cost of living index.
[c] The fertilizer price is in real terms, divided by the price of agricultural output.
[d] "Average product" is the per capita value added in agriculture at constant prices. For States this is available as a consistent series only for some States.
[e] The industrial wage is in real terms.
[f] Data for States available for 1959–60 to 1975–6. States are excluded from analysis if needed data not available. Maharashtra results not reported because they involve time trend variable in addition and it could not be fitted into table. Results are comparable to regressions reported.
[g] All-India wage data from State data, weighted by population. Industrial wage data not available for most of the 1950s, so regression for longer period excludes that explanatory variable.

Source: Dey, "Changes in Real Wages."

Statement:
The Poverty of Poverty Analysis in India
A. M. Khusro

Analysts have generally reached the conclusion that in India, between 1951 and the present, the number of people below the poverty line has increased massively and that the proportion of the poor in the total population has remained approximately constant. On close examination, this does not appear to be the case and there is overwhelming evidence to show that the incidence of poverty has been declining.

It has become fashionable to divide the population on the basis of the National Sample Survey (NSS) data between those who consume less and those who consume more than 2,400 calories (rural) or 2,100 calories (urban), and then designate the former poor and the latter nonpoor. Alternatively, a minimum family income or expenditure level, say, Rs 3,500 per annum, is taken as a norm because it accommodates the minimum calorie requirements. Below this norm is considered to be poor. On such a reckoning, the proportion of the poor has stagnated at around 52 percent to 48 percent.

The latest (1983–84) round of NSS data, however, has shown that, even on an expenditure-based or calorie-based reckoning, the poverty proportion has for the first time come down to 37 percent. Thanks to rapid population growth the number of the poor has increased, but the rate of increase of the nonpoor is higher than that of the poor.

The first serious objection to indices of poverty based on calories or on expenditures linked with calorie values is that these indices are totally one-sided, partial and biased in the direction of exaggerating the poverty situation. When people's income increases, their food consumption does not increase proportionately as the income elasticity of demand for food has always been less than one, even for the poor. People are bound rather rigidly by traditional food habits and do not change these very much even when they become more prosperous. Food poverty lingers on a bit longer than other forms of poverty. Indices of poverty based on calories or of food consumption thus have a built-in depressor and fail to note improvements in the nonfood realm of poverty.

The second objection is that there are several other, perhaps equally important, forms of poverty such as the poverty of literacy, education, health, housing and industrial consumer goods, which the calorie- and good-based indices totally leave out of reckoning. And it is here that major improvements have been emerging. People try to get out of these other poverties rather faster than out of food poverty. By concentrating

---

This Statement is based on the Silver Jubilee Lecture at the Institute of Economic Growth, Delhi, 1984.

on an index of poverty which people discard later, analysts reach absurd conclusions about the stickiness of Indian poverty.

The third and perhaps the most critical objection is that people in India purchase their food and many other necessities but typically do not purchase their literacy, education and health goods in this manner. The rich in urban areas do send their children to public schools and some to elite colleges and their ill family members to paid hospitals and clinics. But these are relatively few. Millions of students in schools and colleges and millions of patients in hospitals, primary health centers and subcenters do not pay for these services. These are either heavily subsidized or supplied entirely at the State's expense. And personal expenditure data do not capture this massive consumption. Personal expenditure data thus grossly understate the reduction of poverty through public goods.

Glaring instances can be seen in the realm of literacy and of public health. Literacy has increased from 17 percent in 1951 to 36 percent in 1981 and to about 40 percent in 1986. In the context of growing population, the absolute number of illiterates is still increasing but the number of literates is increasing at a much faster rate. Once a correction is made for children of age five and below (amounting to about 100 million in 1981), it turns out that in 1986 about 49 percent of the educable population was literate. For India 1987 is the year of destiny when, for the first time in the country's entire history, the majority of Indian educable people would be literate. Moreover, in 1987 for the first time the absolute number of illiterates would begin to decline. It is true that, the definition of literacy being what it is, many of the literates have a poor level of literacy. But this was so in 1971, 1961 and 1951. Here we are actually comparing comparables.

Similar trends are visible in the realm of formal education. The percentage of young people enrolled in the tenth, eleventh and twelfth class, in relation to the total population in the relevant age group, has been increasing phenomenally—more than 400 percent in thirty years. In the enrollment for the first degree, a similar percentage increase of a startling magnitude is evident. Even after we allow for the decline in quality, there appears to be a massive decline in educational poverty both in absolute and proportional terms.

The most impressive results are with respect to health poverty. Even on a conservative basis, the population served by hospital beds, by doctors and by primary health centers and centers has risen phenomenally. To take only one example, the percentage of the population having access to primary health centers has risen from 19 percent in 1951 to about 45 percent in 1961 and to 76 percent in 1981. Moreover, the absolute number of people without access to primary health centers has been declining for some years. It is clear that all forms of poverty, whether reckoned in terms of illiteracy, lack of education, ill health or nonaccess to industrial consumer goods, are under a severe attack and that the absolute numbers as well as the proportions of the nonpoor have been increasing.

If we probe into the immediate future, an important phenomenon can be discerned. In the first twenty-five years of planned development, a 3.5 percent per annum increase of the gross national product was eaten up to the tune of about 2.3 percent by population growth. The net improvement in per capita income of a little more than 1 percent was too small to involve the poor in the growth process and pull them up above the poverty line. In other words, economic growth was not trickling down—unlike countries such as Thailand, Malaysia and Indonesia where, owing to a 6 percent growth in the gross national product and 3 percent population growth, there was a 3 percent rise in per capita income, and hence the trickle-down process was much more effective. Thus India implemented a host of antipoverty programs in the hope that since economic growth was not uplifting the poor, the programs would. If, however, in the foreseeable future, as in the last ten to twelve years, India's gross national product continues to grow 4.5 percent to 5 percent with a mere 2 percent increase in the population, the net per capita growth would be 3 percent per year and this ought really to pull up the poor much more than in the past.

On top of it all, India's antipoverty programs are now becoming both massive and effective and thus provide another reason why poverty should decline even faster than in the past. The upshot clearly is that the old notion of a chronic persistence of poverty both in absolute and percentage terms has to be given up and alternative methodologies of poverty estimation, focusing on the total quality of life rather than on calorie or food consumption, and including the consumption of public goods rather than personal expenditures alone, have to be evolved.

PART FOUR

Industrial Performance:
Controls, Imports and Technology

7

Industrial Policy and Industrial Performance in India

Isher Judge Ahluwalia

The importance of industrialization as a means for achieving rapid growth and prosperity has all along been recognized in the thinking on development strategy for independent India. Indeed the objective has been not only to achieve rapid growth and prosperity within a framework of self-reliance under the direction of the public sector, but to ensure that this is translated into improved conditions of living for the masses. Quite naturally the policy framework was required to play a central role in bringing about such economic transformation.

It is a very difficult task indeed to provide a definitive assessment of the performance of Indian industry over the past three decades or so with respect to the multiple objectives, e.g., increasing production and productivity, pursuing self-reliance through import substitution-oriented policies of industrial development, carving out a central role for the public sector in the process of development, encouraging small-scale industries with a view to generating employment and fostering entrepreneurial development. An attempt is made here to evaluate the record with respect to the policies and performance of the industrial sector. It is useful for this purpose to divide the period since Independence into that up to the mid-seventies and the subsequent decade.

An Overview of Industrial Performance: 1950–51 to 1975–76

Over the two and a half decades covering the period since Independence to the mid-1970s, *the major achievements of the industrial sector were:* (1) wide diversification of the industrial base so as to be able to produce a very broad range of industrial products; (2) development of a public sector with the potential to cater to the infrastructure needs of development and to provide direction to the process of development within a mixed economy framework; and (3) reduced and limited dependence on imports for the needs of development.

The major failures included: (1) very disappointing performance with respect to the core indicator, e.g., the rate of growth of value added in industry; (2) poor performance with respect to productivity in the industrial sector; (3) slow growth of employment; (4) heavy price paid for "self-reliance" by ignoring the cost and quality issues as well as the technological upgrading of Indian industry; (5) slow growth of exports; (6) failure of the public sector in generating public saving in the course of time so as to keep pace with the growing investment demands of this sector and in meeting the growing infrastructure needs of the economy; and (7) the emphasis on overregulation at the cost of promoting development, thereby breeding corruption and eating into the moral fiber of the society.

Explanations of Poor Performance

Recognizing that something had gone wrong in the industrial economy of India, the period of the second half of the seventies was characterized by "official reflection" as well as an academic debate on the possible explanations of the poor industrial performance. After an extensive and intensive scrutiny of the available evidence,[1] I. J. Ahluwalia identified three principal factors responsible for the poor performance.

These factors were: (1) underinvestment in infrastructure sectors such as power and railways and poor efficiency in the use of resources in these sectors; (2) slow growth in per capita incomes in the agricultural sector limiting the potential for demand of industrial products from that sector; and (3) the industrial policy regime encompassing both domestic controls and trade policy measures.

The setback that public investment received from the resource crunch of the mid-sixties has been documented in Ahluwalia.[2] While the slowdown in public investment was to some extent unavoidable, its disproportionate impact on investment in the infrastructure sectors could have been avoided. Investment in railways (at constant prices) actually declined in seven out of the ten years following 1965–66. Investment in railways, electricity and mining together accounted for over 36 percent of the total public investment in the first half of the sixties. This share had declined to less than 29 percent in the subsequent decade.

The underinvestment in the infrastructure sectors was associated with evidence of growing inefficiency in the infrastructure sectors. In the case of railways the net metric ton kilometers per metric ton of wagon capacity showed a declining trend from 1960–61 to 1973–74. To some extent, this was due to the neglect of replacement associated with declines in investment in railways. But, more generally, the inefficiencies covered the entire spectrum from project formulation to implementation and finally to operational stages. In the power sector, for example, the evidence of poor operational efficiency of thermal power plants throughout this period is overwhelming.[3]

As for the growth of demand for industry emanating from the agricultural sector, the increases in agricultural incomes could barely offset the increases in population. The growth of per capita agricultural incomes was only about 0.5 percent per annum.

The industrial policy regime was designed to pursue the multiple set of objectives outlined earlier. The principal instruments of policy used were an elaborate industrial licensing framework under the Industries Development and Regulation (IDR) Act of 1951 and a protective foreign trade regime. The Monopoly and Restrictive Trade Practices (MRTP) Act became effective in 1970 to ensure against concentration of economic power and check restrictive trade practices. There was a separate policy of reservation for certain lines of production by small-scale producers. The Foreign Exchange Regulation Act (FERA) of 1973 was designed to control foreign investment in India.

The policy regime as it evolved over time, however, not only suffered from undue conservatism and administrative delays but had some serious economic consequences. The latter included (1) barriers to entry (entry into individual industries was restricted through the industrial licensing framework); (2) indiscriminate and indefinite protection from foreign competition (protection was typically granted to whichever industry set up indigenous capacity without any regard for the relative costs of domestic and foreign production or, for that matter, for quality; the restriction of imports through licensing amounted to an open-ended protection from foreign competition); (3) detracting from the choice of the optimum scale of production (side effect of the protection to the small-scale sector and regional dispersal of industry); (4) barriers to exit (no matter how sick and nonviable an industrial unit, it could not close down; the Government's soft policies towards sick units actually tended to have the effect of encouraging inefficiency rather than penalizing it); (5) administrative hurdles inherent in a system of physical controls; (6) the adverse effect on entrepreneurship by providing incentives for rent seeking rather than long-term corporate planning (the system compelled entrepreneurs to turn towards speculation and short-term maximization rather than creative productive activity); and (7) little or no incentive for technological upgrading.

Reorientation of the Policy Framework
After the Mid-Seventies

A process of economic reforms was set in motion in the late seventies and the pace has been escalated in the last two years. Elements of this reform include a much-needed focus on the infrastructure sectors, widening the base of the Green Revolution in agriculture, and a reorientation of the industrial policy framework towards promotion and development of industry rather than an overzealous concern with regulation.

In respect of infrastructure, there was a significant break in the second half of the seventies. Railways faced a prolonged period of neglect with real investment declining for a large part of the sixties and the early seventies. This trend was reversed in the late seventies. Between 1976–77 and 1980–81 real investment in railways increased at the rate of 20 percent per annum. During the Sixth Five-Year Plan period (1980–85) efforts were also made at improving operational efficiency in railways.

This resulted in a steady improvement in the net metric ton kilometers per metric ton of wagon capacity.

In the power sector, the problem was not only of inadequate investment but also of its imbalanced distribution between generation and distribution of electricity. Emphasis was laid in the Sixth Plan on balancing investments to improve efficiency in factor use. Efforts were also made at improving the operational efficiency of the thermal power plants. The plant load factor in these plants, which had declined to as low as 44.5 percent at the turn of the decade, showed a steady increase after that, reaching a level of 52.4 percent in 1985–86, although it is still much lower than the recommended norm of 58 percent for India.

The pickup in investment in the infrastructure sectors was associated with a pickup in the rate of fixed capital formation (at 1970–71 prices) in the public sector—the latter being of the order of almost 7 percent in the decade ending with the mid-seventies, 8 percent in the second half of the seventies, and a little over 9 percent in the subsequent few years, respectively. The overall rate of capital formation (at constant prices), on the other hand, increased from 18.5 percent in the decade ending with the mid-seventies to 21 percent in the second half of the seventies and then remained relatively stable at that level.

In the industrial policy framework, experiments with domestic liberalization began in the mid-seventies. In 1975 a scheme was introduced for fifteen engineering industries which provided for automatic approval for an increase in licensed capacity up to a maximum of 25 percent in a five-year period. The scheme was extended to cover nineteen more industries in 1980 and the facility for the first time was extended to large industrial houses.[4] Other measures included regularization of capacities in excess of authorized capacities for Appendix I industries, some liberalization from controls for units which exported 100 percent of their production, and a more general scheme of reendorsement of capacities (where larger than authorized capacities existed) introduced in 1982. The exemption limit for industrial licensing was also raised from Rs 1 crore[5] as set in 1970 to Rs 3 crores in 1978 and to Rs 5 crores in 1983. Contrary to the spirit of these experiments, the role of reservation in protecting the small-scale sector was widened by increasing the number of items on the reservation list from about 500 in 1977 to over 800 in 1980. Attempts were also made during this period to attract industry to "backward areas" through fiscal incentives.

The process of reorientation of industrial policies has gained further momentum in the Seventh Five-Year Plan period (1985–90). The report of the Committee to Examine Principles of a Possible Shift from Physical to Financial Controls submitted in early 1985 played an important part in intensifying the pace of reform.

A number of policy initiatives have been taken in the last two years or so with a view to limiting the role of licensing, expanding the scope for contribution to growth by large houses, encouraging modernization, raising the investment limits for the promotion of the small-scale sector and providing fiscal incentives for the same, and encouraging existing industrial undertakings in certain industries to achieve minimum economic levels of operations. Some of the important measures are: (1) delicensing of a number of industries: some twenty-five broad categories of industries, e.g., electrical equipment, automotive ancillaries, machine tools, etc., and eighty-two bulk drugs and formulations were delicensed in March 1985, while roller flour mills and some chemical industries were later added to the list; delicensing was also extended to twenty-two out of the twenty-seven MRTP industries exempt under sections 21 and 22 of the MRTP Act (see below); (2) broadbanding of certain industries with a view to providing flexibility to manufacturing to produce a range of products: by January 1986, some twenty-eight industry groups, e.g., metallurgical machinery, earth-moving machinery, auto ancillaries, machine tools, etc., were covered under this facility, and during 1986 the facility was extended to industries such as glass, steel pipes and tubes, synthetic fibers and synthetic filament yarn, electrical cables and wires, ball and roller bearings, specified categories of agricultural machinery, textile machinery and chemical industries; (3) expanding the role of large houses/enterprises by broadening the list of industries (now thirty-two industries) open to them (Appendix I); (4) raising the asset threshold to Rs 100 crores for MRTP houses, thereby enabling a larger number of companies to operate without the restrictions of the Act; (5) permitting MRTP companies in twenty-seven industries, e.g., machine tools, portland cement, machinery for chemical industries, certain types of electronic components and equipment, to directly seek a license under the IDR Act without first obtaining prior and separate clearance from the Department of Company Affairs (exempting the MRTP companies in the twenty-seven industries from sections 21 and 22 of the Act); (6) raising of investment limits for the small-scale sector and providing fiscal inventives for the promotion of the small-scale sector; (7) exempting from licensing requirements increases up to 49 percent over licensed capacity for purposes of modernization/renovation/replacement; (8) announcing national policies relating to specific industries such as textiles, sugar, electronics and computers; (9) making it easier to import foreign technology for purposes of modernization and upgrading of quality; and (10) more recently, instituting a scheme to encourage existing industrial undertakings in certain industries to achieve minimum economic levels of operations.

A significant development has been the introduction of a measure of stability to the policy framework via long-term fiscal policy and medium-term trade policy commitments. There has also been some move away from extensive physical controls and an increase in the role of financial incentives in channeling investments in the desired areas. This, plus the lowering of the tax rates combined with better administration of the revenue-collecting system, should help in attracting a lot of economic activity which had strayed away from the mainstream (constituting the so-called parallel economy) back into the fold. The role of the financial institutions becomes very important in the new regime.

Since the late seventies the trade policy regime has also been continuously streamlined and liberalized with a view to providing access to raw materials, intermediates and components needed for maintenance and enhancement of production. The process was taken further in April 1985 following the recommendations of the Committee on Trade Policies (1984). An important landmark of 1985 was the institution of a three-year import-export policy designed to impart a sense of stability to the policy regime. Another significant development was the liberalization with respect to the import of capital goods.

There are two aspects of recent changes in the trade policy regime which are worth noting. The liberalization in imports was consciously linked to exports. Also, these changes were made at a time when the foreign exchange situation was relatively tight, unlike the situation in the late seventies.

An innovative development in the area of price controls in the second half of the seventies was the price policy for cement, although a broad-based evolution of administered price policy for the industrial sector is yet to emerge. The cement price policy was designed to allow generation of internal funds and make it attractive to invest in cement. The system of total control over price and distribution of cement until the late seventies had created a situation in which there was large excess demand, a rampant black market, and little new investment in cement. Beginning with a policy decision in 1977 to introduce a favorable price formula for new units in cement ensuring a 12 percent post-tax return on net worth, in 1982 a move was made to a uniform price for all units combined with partial decontrol from the price and distribution of cement. The policy was designed to allow the generation of internal funds via allowing the possibility of selling a certain proportion of the production at the market price. The response in terms of increased investment and production was phenomenal as we shall see below.

Industrial Performance Since the Mid-Seventies

The response to the policy initiatives can be seen in a pickup in the growth of value added as well as productivity since the late seventies. The downward trend in the industrial licenses has also been reversed. The growth in disbursements from financial institutions which had slowed down in the early eighties has shown some signs of a pickup in 1985–86. The recovery and the turnaround of the Sixth Plan period, however, has not been associated with better performance.

Table 7.1 gives clear evidence of a pickup in growth after the mid-seventies. The growth of value added in industry, which had collapsed from 6.5 percent per annum during the decade ending with 1965–66 to 3.5 percent per annum during the subsequent decade, began a turnaround in the period after the mid-seventies. A hesitant recovery in the second half of the seventies from the very low rates of growth of the preceding decade was followed by a stronger pickup in the Sixth Plan period (the latest available data are for 1983–84). Much the same was true of the growth in value added in total manufacturing or in its registered subsector. The fact that unregistered manufacturing did not experience any pickup can be attributed to the possibility that growth in this sector has been increasingly underrecorded as its economic activity increasingly moved underground. Another feature of the sectoral growth patterns worth noting is that growth in construction slowed down during the Sixth Plan period.

The performance with respect to productivity growth has also shown a turnaround after the mid-seventies. Estimates based on a recent study by Ahluwalia, D'Souza and Deepak[6] show that total factor productivity growth for manufacturing was negligible in the first half of the sixties but it had declined to −1.5 percent per annum in the decade ending with 1975–76. The period from 1975–76 to 1981–82, the latest year for which such estimates are derivable, records an improvement in the total factor productivity growth (TFPG) for manufacturing to 0.8 percent per annum. While the worsening productivity performance in the earlier period occurred in most industry groups (the major exception being the machinery industries), the recorded improvement was also true for a large number of industries. It is worth stressing that by international standards, the productivity growth of Indian industry is still low, but the fact of relative improvement over the more recent period implies that a turning point has come, and the challenge lies in reinforcing the new trend.

A measure of the response to the new policies can also be had by analyzing the trend in the letters of intent issued and the industrial licenses granted (Table 7.2).[7] Since the data are not available in value terms but only in physical numbers, there is likely to be a downward bias in the trend projected by these numbers if we assume that the average value of the license has been increasing with time. The letters of intent showed a heavy decline from 1,181 in 1974 to 440 in 1978. This was followed by a turnaround beginning in the late seventies and reaching a number as high as 1,457 in 1985, the latest year for which such information is available. For industrial licenses issued, the same was true with a lag, as one would expect. The decline in the licenses issued extended from 1974 to 1982, and a sharp turnaround was experienced after that. From 432 in 1982, the number of industrial licenses increased to 9,895 in 1985. This increase occurred in spite of the fact that delicensed registrations numbered 1,167.[8]

The trend in the disbursements from the financial institutions, on the other hand, suggests that the pickup in the second half of the seventies was followed by a slowdown in the first half of the eighties (Table 7.3). More recently, there seems to have been a pickup in the growth of sanctions from major financial institutions in 1984–85 followed by a strong pickup in the growth of disbursements in 1985–86. Some of the slowdown in sanctions/disbursements in the early eighties may be explained by the switch to direct borrowing in the capital market on the part of the borrowers.

The chain of linkages from the issue of a letter of intent to an increase in production includes not only the issue of the license and the provision of financial resources, but also the availability of inputs, including infrastructure, to translate the capacity into production. It is worth stressing that the reduction in costs which can be achieved by modernization and better utilization of capacities can also release the demand constraint to some extent as prices are lowered. The cement industry in the eighties provides a good example of the working of these processes.

The reorientation of cement-pricing policies began in 1977–78. The results on the ground could be seen by 1984–85. Installed capacity in cement increased from 20 million metric tons in 1980–81 to 42.5 million metric tons in 1984–85. Production of cement in the Sixth Plan grew by over 11 percent per annum, repeating its earlier peak performance in the Second Five-Year Plan (1956–61). As for modernization, from a situation in 1980 when more than half of the cement capacity in the economy employed the obsolete fuel-inefficient wet process technology, the industry had arrived at a stage in 1985 where the share of the wet process technology was less than one-third. Admittedly new problems have arisen which pose new challenges to policymakers. Capacity utilization has been low. Demand for cement needs to be expanded. But the cement industry is a case in point that the policy framework has a crucial influence on performance and that there are time lags involved between a change in policy and its visible impact on performance.

The cement experience also demonstrates that infrastructure emerges as a major constraint as capacities expand rapidly. Providing for the growing infrastructure needs of development must therefore attain top priority in the process of planning. Another lesson learned from the cement experience is that Indian industry has not "psychologically" adjusted to the fact that there may not be a sellers' market. The industry must be made to direct its energies towards finding markets in new areas, including rural areas.

The policy initiatives of the last ten years or so were designed to improve the efficiency in factor use and bring about a technological upgrading of Indian industry, recognizing that increases in investment are necessary but not sufficient to generate growth. In assessing the performance of the industrial sector over the last decade, what emerges very clearly is that the efforts at improving the efficiency in factor use have paid off. The scope for further reforms is large and the challenge lies in consolidating the gains, sustaining higher growth and providing it a further boost.

Conclusions

The analysis of industrial performance and policy as presented above clearly suggests the need for keeping up the momentum of change that has been set in motion.

The first important gap in the policy framework relates to the existence of the barriers to exit. A sick and nonviable industrial unit is not allowed to die under the present set of legislations and regulations. While a firm would not be allowed to "die," it could easily be passed on as a "sick" unit under the care of the Government. The policymakers must recognize that a healthy, growing economy requires that some sick nonviable units must die.

In January 1987, the Central Government set up a Board for Industrial and Financial Reconstruction with wide-ranging powers in respect of approval of rehabilitation packages for sick companies in the private sector. The packages include their reconstruction and revival through a change of management or amalgamation with another company, etc., as well as closing down of the company. It is still too early to judge the effectiveness of the Board, but if the Board is allowed to exercise even half of the powers entrusted to it, it could go a long way in making a dent on the problem of extensive sickness in Indian industry. An atmosphere of growth and dynamism would help in accomplishing this task.

The major problem in removing the barriers to exit is that of displacement of labor. While there are socioeconomic costs of adjustment, in such a process the interests of organized employed labor very often tend to be at variance with those of the unemployed and the larger interests of society. The Government through the BIFR must specify guidelines on the liquidation of assets to pay off labor, "adequate" compensation in the event of retrenchment, and retraining and rehiring of labor in new ventures by the same industrial group.

Another major gap in policy relates to the much-needed reforms of the public sector. Because the public sector has a crucial role to play in our economy, particularly in providing infrastructural services, the weaknesses of the public sector feed into the entire economy and have a magnified effect. The factors behind the poor performance of the public sector are well-known, e.g., lack of autonomy and accountability, and a tendency on the part of our planning process to start too many projects, run out of resources midstream, delay the projects and lock up a lot of capital in the process. The Sen Gupta Committee is only the latest of many committees that have reflected on these problems and made recommendations. What is needed are fast and firm decisions. Our objective should be to develop a strong public sector rather than a large but weak public sector.

As growth takes off, it will lead to higher demands on the infrastructure sectors and larger need for imports of intermediate materials. As regards the former, planning of energy and transport sectors assumes more urgency in this context. As for imports of intermediate materials, it is important to recognize that the increase in imports will reflect the scale effect even if there is no change in the policy towards imports. It is therefore necessary to ensure that exports are stepped up to keep pace with the growing import needs of the economy. The Cabinet Committee on Exports that has been set up recently under the chairmanship of the Prime Minister has a challenging task ahead. It must be seen that the balance of payments is "balanced" at increasing levels of exports and imports.

Finally, the drive for growth and modernization must be accompanied by a parallel thrust to alleviate poverty and unemployment through employment-generating activities like construction, housing and rural industrialization. The state has to shoulder the responsibility of development in a framework which provides growth with equity.

Notes

1. Isher J. Ahluwalia, *Industrial Growth in India: Stagnation since the Mid-Sixties* (New Delhi: Oxford University Press, 1985).

2. Ibid.

3. See ibid.

4. The facility was provided to "Appendix I" industries. Appendix I to the Notification of Industrial Policy of February 1973 lists specific industries in which large houses are permitted to set up capacities.

5. Rs 1 crore = Rs 10 million.

6. I. J. Ahluwalia, A. D'Souza, and V. Deepak, *Trends in Productivity Growth in Indian Manufacturing* (forthcoming).

7. Under the Industries Development and Regulation Act (1951), a license is required for establishing a new undertaking, for substantial expansion of capacity in the existing line of manufacture and for taking up manufacture of a new article. A letter of intent, valid for a fixed period, is issued in the first instance. It is converted into an industrial license when certain "effective steps" are taken for implementing the capacity.

8. While a number of industries were delicensed or exempted from the requirement of obtaining industrial licenses, they still needed to register with the authorities.

TABLE 7.1 Growth Rates of Net Value Added
(percent per annum)

	Compound Growth Rates				Annual Growth Rates		
	1955–56 to 1965–66	1965–66 to 1975–76	1975–76 to 1980–81	1980–81 to 1983–84	1981–1982	1982–1983	1983–1984
1. Agriculture	0.9	3.9	1.0	3.5	4.1	-3.6	10.4
2. Industry	6.5	3.5	4.6	6.2	6.2	7.3	5.1
Manufacturing	6.2	3.3	4.5	5.8	5.8	6.9	4.7
Registered	7.5	3.2	4.9	7.3	7.4	9.4	5.1
Unregistered	4.5	3.4	3.8	3.3	3.2	2.6	4.1
Electricity	12.9	7.8	7.6	7.2	8.0	6.7	6.8
Mining	7.1	3.0	3.3	9.9	9.0	12.3	8.3
3. Construction	6.2	2.5	3.8	1.8	1.3	0.3	3.7
4. Railways	6.4	3.2	1.5	0.1	-2.0	4.2	-1.6
5. Other Services	5.4	4.5	6.0	7.7	7.3	8.3	7.5
Total	3.2	3.9	3.4	5.3	5.3	2.8	7.9

Source: National Accounts Statistics (various issues) (New Delhi: Government of India, Central Statistical Organization).

TABLE 7.2 Trends in Industrial Licenses

	Letters of Intent Granted	Industrial Licenses Issued
1974	1,181	1,099
1975	962	1,027
1976	547	662
1977	533	518
1978	440	348
1979	550	365
1980	946	475
1981	916	476
1982	1,043	432
1983	1,055	1,075
1984	1,064	905
1985[a]	1,457	985

[a] The number of delicensed registrations during this year was 1,167.

Source: Ministry of Industry, Government of India.

TABLE 7.3 Capital Market Financial Assistance Sanctioned and Disbursed by Major Financial Institutions
(Rs crores)

A

Year	1970–71	1975–76	1980–81	1985–96
Sanctioned	226.7	587.7	2,524.4	6,613.8
Disbursed	152.6	407.1	1,602.7	4,919.6
Compound Growth Rates				
Sanctioned	–	21.0	33.8	21.2
Disbursed	–	21.7	31.5	25.1

B

	1980–81	1981–82	1982–83	1983–84	1984–85	1985–86
Sanctioned	2,524.4	2,825.8	3,183,8	4,115.7	5,647.6	6,613.8
Disbursed	1,602.7	3,060.2	2,358.3	2,935.6	3,501.6	4,919.6
Annual Growth Rates						
Sanctioned	–	11.9	12.7	29.3	37.2	17.1
Disbursed	–	28.5	14.5	24.5	19.3	40.5

[a] Data relate to IFCI, ICICI, IDBI, IRBI, SFCs, SIDCs, UTI, LIC and GIC.

Source: Economic Survey (various issues) (New Delhi: Government of India).

8

Technology Acquisition and Application: Interpretations of the Indian Experience

Ashok V. Desai

There arose in the 1960s and 1970s a school of thought on technology transfer to developing countries which, despite its Marxist and internationalist origins, had local roots in developing countries—at any rate in Latin America and India. It had three basic propositions:

1. *Transnational corporations (TNCs)* were the dominant suppliers of technology to developing countries.
2. The conditions of technology supply created *monopolies* in developing countries.
3. The monopolies so created had no technological dynamism of their own, and they were in a relationship of *dependency* vis-à-vis the TNCs.

There are considerable variations amongst developing countries, and these propositions may have fitted some better than others. But evidence has accumulated recently that contradicts this picture for India in important respects. More specifically,

1. TNCs are *not* dominant amongst technology suppliers to India;
2. imports of technology have *not* created monopolies; and
3. technology imports are *not* the only or major source of industrial technology.

In the first three sections of this chapter we shall argue these three negative propositions. However, they still leave something unexplained, namely, the undistinguished technological performance of Indian industry, in terms of the level as well as the growth of output, efficiency and exports. An explanation becomes all the more necessary if, as we shall argue, competition is common and keen in India. Our explanation runs in terms of active protection of inefficiency by the Government—protection built into trade policy in respect of new products with small markets, and protection in more varied and widespread forms in the case of goods whose domestic market is large enough to permit competition within the country. In other words, the poor performance of Indian industry arises from poor management of competition by the Government, and not from lack of competition.

TNCs and Large Firms as Technology Suppliers

The term "transnational corporation" is rather dated and unclear in its definition. But there are two conditions at least that TNCs must necessarily satisfy, namely, (1) they must be large, and (2) they must operate in a global market that is oligopolistic.

World oligopolies are generally based on close control of a scarce resource, which is often, though not always, technology. The classic TNCs were the seven major oil companies whose oligopoly was based on the control of crude oil supply. Although oil majors are still big, their control of the world crude market is considerably weakened. A few firms control a large proportion of the world supply of a number of minerals, for instance, diamonds, gold, platinum, aluminum and copper, but the firms are not always large. Further, their control of the market is weakened by competition from substitutes, threat of new entry or nonessentiality of the product. The indispensability of oil, the absence (rather, high cost) of substitutes and the control of the markets at the retail level gave oil majors extraordinary influence and led economists to overgeneralize about TNCs. Now that their power has waned, the term transnational corporation is a soul in search of a body.

The classic technology-based TNCs were the big United States, Swiss and British pharmaceutical firms. But there is not much that is difficult or appropriable about the old (i.e., chemical, as against the new biological) pharmaceutical technology. The development of new drugs involved costly searches, trials and tests, but once a drug was developed, it was absurdly easy to replicate it. What gave the drug TNCs oligopolistic control of their markets was not their technology, but patent laws which made imitation illegal and the tying in of retail outlets. They could not, in the long run, control markets in countries where patent protection was weak or where big buyers, e.g., public hospitals, pursued even-handed or anti-TNC purchase policies.

Technology-based world oligopolies are extremely common in products whose markets are too small to attract much competition: for instance, rayon spinnerettes, air tunnels or oil-well logging instruments. Their technologies can be imitated, though they are not necessarily as easy to imitate as drug technology. But imitating them (without the help of an existing producer) would require investment in research and development (R&D) that would be disproportionately high in comparison to the market it would command. Specialist oligopolies do not rely solely on the small size of their markets to maintain control of the markets: they also continue to develop their technologies so as to ensure that their product is distinctly superior to that of an imitator who would be as many years behind them as it takes him to reverse engineer a product. Specialist oligopolies are important, though not overwhelmingly so, amongst technology suppliers to India, and nonrecognition of them lies behind some of the most serious errors in Indian Government policy. But specialist oligopolies as such are not TNCs.

Bigness is a necessary though not sufficient characteristic of TNCs. So if we traced the importance of big foreign firms in Indian technology imports, we would overestimate the importance of TNCs. Large firms are easy to identify—and difficult to miss—thanks to the assiduous compilation of lists of the biggest firms in all major countries. We collected such lists of the largest firms in the United States, Western Europe and Japan, ranged them by their sales in 1982 and identified their technology transfer agreements with Indian firms between 1957 and 1983. We similarly took Indian companies quoted on the stock exchanges, classified them by their 1982 sales and identified their transfer agreements. The results, which are preliminary, are given in Table 8.1.

The first notable result is the small proportion of agreements involving *either* large foreign *or* large Indian firms. The proportion of agreements with firms whose size was known was 12.5 percent for foreign firms and 24.9 percent for Indian firms. In neither case do large firms "dominate" technology transfers.

Secondly, there is no evidence of a tendency for large firms in India and abroad to collaborate more frequently, *except* in one respect: the pattern of agreements of the foreign firms whose sales are known is significantly, though not overwhelmingly, more skewed towards larger Indian firms than the pattern of smaller foreign firms whose sales are not known. This pattern is not evident amongst foreign firms of different sizes, nor is it reflected amongst Indian firms; larger Indian firms do not tend to collaborate more frequently with larger foreign firms.

This intriguing and apparently contradictory evidence has, nevertheless, a reasonable explanation. A technology supplier will wish to maximize the market for his technology or product in India. He will have a pecuniary motive for doing so if he gets a royalty on sales; even if he does not, he will have a strategic interest in maximizing his share of the Indian market. Thus most foreign firms would *prefer* a larger Indian partner firm; and larger foreign firms would command a greater *choice* of Indian firms. The two factors acting in combination result in a relationship that is noticeable.

On the other hand, the size of the technology supplier is immaterial to the Indian firm. More precisely, there are potential advantages and disadvantages in collaborating with large foreign firms, and their balance is unclear. A large firm may have greater resources to help a buyer with problems arising from technology transfer; on the other hand, its stake in doing so would be smaller in relation to its size, and its size may enable it to drive a harder bargain. Thus larger Indian firms have no clear preference for larger foreign technology suppliers, and none is reflected in the figures.

Here we have an embryonic relationship with tenuous foundations; we shall try and reinforce it a bit further. We are distinguishing between the supply and demand for technology. Our hypothesis is that the supply of technology from large suppliers will vary positively with the size of the market. At the same time we assert that the demand of large buyers of technology will *not* vary with the size of the technology supplier. Insofar as large technology suppliers can choose amongst buyers, their preference for large buyers will be reflected in the proportion of agreements with such buyers in the total agreements of the suppliers (A). Similarly, insofar as large buyers can choose amongst suppliers, their preference for large suppliers will be reflected in the ratio of agreements between large buyers and large suppliers to the total agreements of large buyers (B). We have no direct estimate of the market share of large Indian firms, but we have a surrogate for it in the proportion of total agreements accounted for by them (C).

If our hypothesis is correct, A should be correlated with C, but not B with C. Figure 8.1 gives a graphical picture of the two relationships. The industries are apparently divided into two groups, in one of which the value of A associated with C is higher than in the other. But by and large there is clearly a positive association between A and C. Equally clearly there is no association between B and C. Thus disaggregation by industry confirms our hypothesis.

Cooper[1] has used industry-mix comparisons to show that the pattern of Belgian technology exports to India was more closely related to the pattern of the Indian than of the Belgian industrial structure, while the pattern of Dutch technology exports was more closely related to the pattern of the Dutch than of the Indian industrial structure. He related this to the greater importance of TNCs in Holland than in Belgium and to the greater frequency of initiative taken by TNCs (rather than Indian firms) in technology transfer, which he confirmed by means of interviews. While we accept the relationship found by Cooper, we would argue that of the two characteristic markets, it is the latter that is relevant to initiative. Paulsson[2] makes this distinction amongst Swedish firms and finds that oligopolies more commonly took the initiative in selling technology to Indian firms. Oligopolies are interested in early entry into markets, for market shares in oligopolistic markets are easier to defend than to attack. Hence oligopolies in general are more prone to taking the initiative in foreign investment and in technology exports than competitive firms. But oligopolistic firms, like others, suffer from constraints on expansion and have to choose markets to enter. Here, large firms will choose large markets and vice versa. Thus TNCs chose first to expand into Western Europe, whose markets were next only to those of North America; then they turned to Brazil and Mexico. India, with small markets in the products produced by TNCs, was neglected by them and got most of this technology from smaller firms. The picture of transnationalization of developing countries is mainly based on Brazil and Mexico and is largely inapplicable to India. But the problem of obtaining technology from oligopolies faces Indian firms much more frequently than the problem of obtaining technology from large firms, and it is addressed with little understanding and competence by the Indian Government.

Market Structures and Technology Supply

The proposition that TNCs were in the process of creating world monopolies (or oligopolies) had a vogue in the 1960s when large U.S. corporations were moving into Western Europe to exploit the unified market created by the European Community. At that time the view was plausible that transnationalization would extend to developing countries and raise market concentration there to levels higher than in developed countries. This view of progressive and irreversible transnationalization of the capitalist world was based on a few industries (e.g., automobiles) and on short-term trends, and no one would argue it seriously today. We shall not address it; instead we wish to argue against the other half of the proposition, namely, that market structures in developing countries must be at least as concentrated as in industrial countries.

As we argued in the previous section, suppliers prefer to sell technology to buyers who will win the largest national market for it. Hence supply of technology to large firms is greater than to small firms. All firms, large and small, would like to monopolize the markets for their products. Both the seller and the buyer of technology have an interest in monopolizing the local market. Thus if all the technology for a specific industry came from the same industry in another country, the market structure in the country that imports technology would be more concentrated than in the exporting country.

Vintages

However, this view of technology transfer is wrong in at least three respects. First, it assumes that every firm has one technology to sell. In fact, an innovative firm will have at least two technologies to sell: the one it is currently using in production, and the one it is planning to commercialize. It may have a third one, which it has abandoned or is on the point of abandoning. The supply price, however, is considerably affected by the fact that the capital costs of developing already commercialized technologies are sunk, whereas those of future technologies are still to be incurred.

Most firms interviewed in the ATW study of technology transfer to India said they had transferred the current vintage; for instance, 76 of the 106 responding West German firms gave this answer. So did 32 of the 39 British firms.[3] Those that transferred an obsolete vintage commonly said that they had sold the vintage current at the time of negotiations but that Indian procedural delays had made it obsolete.

The technology sellers were not asked whether they would have been prepared to sell their prospective vintage. But Bell and Scott-Kemmis explored a broader question in their study, namely, on what terms would British firms have transferred to Indian firms know-how and how to improve technology.[4] About 25 percent said they would not have done so on any terms; 17 percent said they would have extended the transfer in some direction, but not in all. The rest would have been willing, most for higher payments but some in return for a joint venture arrangement.

Thus there are indications that the coming vintage, or the key to it, was available for sale in a certain proportion of cases, and then for a higher price or a higher degree of control. Conversely, of the two vintages, the current vintage was available from more firms, at a lower price and on more liberal terms.

Competition Between Technology Suppliers

We would argue not only that technology suppliers are *in a position* to sell their current or past vintages at a lower price than their future vintages because the costs have already been incurred, but also that they are *forced* to sell technology at the minimum price by competition. This hypothesis needs to be argued rather carefully because of ostensible evidence of excess demand for imported technology.

In all countries studied except France, the initiative in technology imports was more commonly taken by the buyer than by the seller (Table 8.2). There is considerable unquantified evidence that suppliers are approached by many more Indian firms than they are willing to sell technology to. On the Indian side, sixty-four of ninety-two respondent firms said they had approached more than one foreign firm before concluding an agreement.[5] Thus it is a persuasive conclusion that there is excess demand for technology and that sellers are in a position to push up the price. However, there is other evidence that makes us doubt this picture.

First, the profits of technology suppliers. They were high on their own assessment in the majority of the cases, except only in Japan and the United Kingdom. But in over 40 percent of the cases they were not high; and in 14 percent of the cases the suppliers made losses. If the suppliers were being pursued by hordes of potential buyers and were in a strong bargaining position, there is no reason why many of them should have made losses, let alone low profits.

Second, their level of satisfaction. It was the same as the level of profits in the majority of cases: those who made good profits on technology sales were satisfied, and vice versa. But in a significant minority of the cases, the suppliers were less satisfied than their profits would indicate; many fewer were more satisfied than their profits would indicate. The reason for their dissatisfaction was not the profits made on sales of technology, but the profits forgone owing to lack of direct access to the Indian market.

The profits are denied to them in two ways. Firstly, the policy of protecting domestic industry denies to foreign firms profits on exports to India. As soon as a domestic firm starts production, it is assured of a market by means of quotas. The only way in which a foreign firm can then have access to the Indian market is by exporting technology. Secondly, the foreign firm is denied a return on its firm-specific assets in a number of ways. The difficulties placed in the way of foreign investment and the terms on which it is allowed make the exploitation of know-how and reputation through a subsidiary impossible or unattractive. The ban on the use of foreign brand names makes it impossible to build up customer loyalty, and the difficulty of getting approval for agreements lasting more than five years prevents the long-term exploitation of the market through licensees. None of these policies is entirely rigid; exceptions are permitted "on merit." But securing an exception requires lobbying in Delhi which only firms with large resources and stake can afford. Most firms are compelled to sell technology without thereby securing a long-run market because policy has blocked other alternatives.

Why this is unwelcome is shown by the reasons firms gave for selling technology. Expected profits were the commonest reason. But the next *four* reasons were related to markets: to the gaining and retention of market access which had been cut off by import restrictions, and to the protection of those markets against competitors. The reason for dissatisfaction thus lay in the lack of success in' holding on to the market in the long run. This lack of success is due primarily to the insecure hold of the Indian technology importer on his own market; but it is also due to his lack of loyalty to the technology supplier.

Competition in Indian markets intensified considerably in the sixties and seventies. Of the twenty-two products for which we could find comparable evidence, the number of producing firms was lower in 1978–79 than in 1963–64 only in respect of one: the number of bicycle manufacturers fell from seventeen to thirteen. The number of motorcycle manufacturers remained the same at three. In the remaining twenty products, the number of producers went up—considerably in most cases.[6] As the number of competitors increased, the hold of each on his market weakened, and so did the hold of his technology supplier or suppliers.

On the hold of the supplier on the buyer there is some difference of opinion. Baark[7] was impressed by the frequency of renewals of agreements between Danish and Indian firms, and the ease with which they were approved despite official policy of discouragement. Amongst all the agreements approved between Indian and foreign firms, however, only 11.2 percent were between the same two firms, and 7.5 percent between the same firms for the same product.[8] The difference is partly in the basis of comparison and partly in the question being asked. Baark compared the Danish firms which renewed agreements with those that made agreements, both new and renewed, between 1971 and 1980. He thus excluded firms that had made agreements before 1971 and did not renew in 1971–80, including those that were not allowed to renew. The ease and speed of renewal tell us nothing about the frequency with which renewals are allowed. Renewals are liable to be easier and quicker than first-time agreements because the partners know each other and because the Indian firm has greater experience in dealing with the Government. Thus despite the observed frequency and ease of renewals amongst agreements made by Danish and other foreign firms in 1971–80, it is nevertheless true that renewals in general were infrequent.

Besides, there were other indications of a less secure relationship between the seller and the buyer. The proportion of agreements with no duration—and hence no long-term relationship—rose from 13.0 percent in 1951–67 to 28.9 percent in 1977–80, while the proportion of agreements in which there were no outright payments—and in which there was a clear relationship of some duration—fell from 43.1 percent to 27.4 percent. While the distribution of royalty rates remained about the same, the scale of outright payments went up manyfold; the proportion of agreements with outright payments over Rs 500,000 went up from 7.2 percent in 1951–67 to 40.7 percent in 1977–80. Thus the cases in which the buyer and the seller had a strong *common* interest in increasing sales in the Indian market declined in importance.

Nevertheless, a strong common interest in entering the Indian market *early* was given to both the technology suppliers and the buyers by the policy of import substitution. The rule was that any product that was produced for the first time was given protection by means of quotas. The result was that the producer was given protection whatever price he charged and that, provided he could satisfy the entire home demand, he could get imports banned and monopolize the market. The profits were thus high for the first entrant, and he could pay relatively more for imported technology. But once he monopolized the market, the only way foreign firms (other than his technology supplier) could regain access to the Indian market was by selling technology to a new Indian firm. The Indian policy on foreign investment, on the other hand, ensured that the costs to the technology supplier of entering the Indian market were low. For it made foreign investment virtually impossible where Indian firms were prepared to enter without its support, it generally allowed foreign investment only in the form of minority holdings (i.e., under 40 percent equity), and it made returns on investment unattractive by insisting that a direct investor could not get a price on his technology sales to his affiliate. Thus while a technology supplier found it unattractive to invest in India, he could also be sure that his competitors would not invest. Without investment, the entry costs, consisting only of technology transfer costs, were low.

Thus technology suppliers were induced to sell technology early in order to share in the superprofits of Indian firms which entered the market early. Once production was established, they were compelled to sell technology because that was the only way they could compete with technology suppliers already in the Indian market. And at all stages they could enter the Indian market at a low cost and risk since they could not invest. Finally, as we shall argue below, they had to sell their technology cheaply because the competition in the Indian markets forced down the demand price of technology.

Degree of Appropriability

The model in which competition in developing country markets is limited by competition in developed country markets assumes that technology can only be obtained from foreign firms—that each firm has complete control of access to its own technology. In fact, there is a hierarchy of technological elements ranged by appropriability in any industry. At one extreme are elements that are completely secret; at another extreme are elements that are common knowledge to anyone with the minimum training.

Obviously, technology of the next vintage is less accessible to outsiders than current technology. Although Bell and Scott-Kemmis do not address the question of vintages directly, their finding, earlier referred to, is relevant here, namely, that improvements to current technology are available from fewer firms, at a higher price and on more restrictive terms than current technology itself.

Within current technology, product know-how is less appropriable than process know-how, and within product know-how, design is easier to copy than materials and construction. Product know-how is particularly important in engineering, where copying also is rife. The most closely held know-how is characteristic of industries where pronounced economies of scale limit the number of firms and characteristic of industries with extremely precise and sensitive operations.

Clearly, perfectly inappropriable technology is not sold; it is freely copied. Equally clearly, perfectly appropriable technology would be specific to a firm; it would not sell it except under threat of imitation. It is technology between these two extremes—technology whose unaided replication would be costly or cause delays—that is traded; the greater the cost of or delay in imitation, the higher the price. Legal protection of intellectual property would increase the cost of imitation and raise the price of imitable technology.

In India, where patent protection was significantly weakened in 1973, a technology supplier faces competition not only from other potential suppliers abroad, but also from imitators in India. The European researchers occasionally came across firms whose products had been imitated without permission by Indian firms. The threat of imitation is as potent a competitor as other producers are and serves in the same way to increase the supply and reduce the price of technology. The actual extent of imitation and its effect on competition are analyzed in the next section.

Sources of Technology and Market Structure

We have earlier shown the relationship that exists between the sources of technology and the market structure in India.[9] We excluded consumer goods industries for which technology imports were prohibited and divided the rest of the industries into four classes: industries with few and many firms (small group and large group industries), and within each class, industries with a high and a low degree of product differentiation (homogeneous and differentiated industries). Product differentiation was found to be closely related to the coexistence of firms of very different sizes and hence with high coefficient of inequality. Average figures for the four groups of firms are given in Table 8.3.

We found that in industries where most of the output was produced by firms that had imported technology, the number of firms was small; conversely, many small firms were to be found in large group industries which had not imported technology. Thus technology flows within the country were associated with the emergence of a large number of small firms and in that sense with a more competitive market structure. Since there is virtually no organized technology market in the country, these flows of technology were clearly "informal"; they mainly took the form of the movement of technicians from firms that had imported technology,

the movement of technology through consultants, and informal improv-
ization. Further, it was evident that the emergence of these small firms
dated after the mid-sixties; in the subsequent years, the small group
industries had chiefly expanded through an increase in the average size
of firms, while the large group industries had expanded through the
multiplication in the number of firms. Thus the degree and character of
competition was influenced by the appropriability of technology. Where
it was appropriable, a small number of firms that had imported technology
dominated the industry. Where it was not appropriable, technology was
still imported by a small number of large firms, but large numbers of
small firms emerged by imitating technology and successfully competed
with the large firms. In industries where they did, imitation was not just
a threat, as we suggested in the previous section, but it was the basis of
new competition. Thus while Indian evidence suggests that technology
imports on their own would lead to oligopolistic market structures, it also
shows that imports are not the only source of technology.

The effects of R&D are different. R&D was done almost invariably by
firms that had imported technology; however, all firms that had imported
technology did not do R&D, but only the large ones amongst them. The
firms that did R&D were larger than those that did not. But a much
larger proportion of the firms that had imported technology did R&D
in the industries with differentiated products. Our earlier survey of R&D
had yielded direct evidence to confirm this: a high proportion of Indian
corporate R&D was devoted to developing new products on the basis of
imported technology.[10] Thus large firms used R&D, not so much to develop
specific large-scale production techniques to exploit their size advantage,
but to capture new markets by developing new products. However, product
know-how is less appropriable than process know-how; product differentiation created market niches that were invaded by small firms in
differentiated large group industries.

Thus many industries followed a sequence in which a single Indian
firm started production and made superprofits. The situation is depicted
in Figure 8.2. A monopolist has marginal and average cost curves MCH
and ACH and faces demand and marginal curves DD' and EE' respectively.
His breakeven price is OJ. At the import price OF he would make a loss
FG.FJ. On starting production he gets imports banned and makes profits
NK.KL.

Absence of monopoly will change the situation in two ways. First, a
larger number of firms will entail a greater total investment, higher
overheads and higher average costs than under monopoly. Thus even if
all firms collude and maintain the monopoly price ON, their profits will
be lower than NK.KL. This is shown in Figure 8.3, where PO relates
the rate of profit on capital to the number of firms on the assumption
that they collude. Second, if there is no collusion, the price will be lower
than the monopoly price and the profits will also be lower. PR is the
rate-of-profit curve without collusion. If there is a minimum price of
technology OC, OB firms will be able to afford it under monopoly or
collusion; the number OA that can afford it under competition will be

smaller. This is the theory behind the proposition that the supply of technology limits competition in developing countries.

However, this proposition is reversed in many Indian industries where local sources of technology have led to a proliferation of firms: there competition limits the supply of technology from abroad. In terms of Figure 8.3, the number of firms exceeded OA, and most firms' profits were too low to pay for imported technology. As they grew they would start looking for imported technology. But their capacity to pay for it was limited. Thus we find a large number of Indian firms looking for technology, but bargaining over its price, and not being able to strike a bargain. As Table 8.2 shows, the initiative in negotiations was taken in a majority of cases by Indian firms. Before they came to the firm with which they made a contract, many of them had unsuccessfully approached other firms. And the foreign suppliers had often negotiated earlier with Indian firms without reaching an agreement.

However, it would be mistaken to interpret this "excess demand" as an indicator of a disequilibrium in the market. The Government of India does regulate the price paid for technology; it lays down maxima for royalties to be paid and also tries to ensure that technical fees do not exceed a certain proportion of the sales price. Some early entrants and some firms in oligopolistic industries would undoubtedly want to pay more than the Government permits. But firms in competitive industries generally cannot and do not want to pay more; rather they make use of Government regulations in negotiating the price. Thus the pressure to pay less arises from the Indian firms, and at one remove from the markets in which they operate.

The Influence of Blanket Import Substitution

In the previous section we distinguished between the firms which imported technology and the firms which copied their products. These represent not only different classes of firms but also different phases of the production cycle in an industry—a cycle in which trade policy plays an important part.

It has been a principle of Indian import policy that any product newly produced in India is protected by quantitative import restrictions. So long as a producer of a new product can supply the entire domestic market previously supplied by imports, he can get imports banned and charge any price he likes. So initially he can expect superprofits, but these will fall with the passage of time for two reasons. First, new competitors may enter the market and reduce the demand for his product as well as the price. Second, the Government, when giving him permission to import technology, would normally have imposed on him a phased import substitution program. The progressive increase in the local content of the product will raise costs. Thus the trade policy induces firms to enter a market early—and often to get out later, once competition intensifies.

The need to get in early explains a number of features of Indian firms' behavior. First, they take the initiative and approach a number of potential suppliers to be able to secure one quickly. Of course, the flood of inquiries they send off reduces their chances of getting a reply and makes them write even more letters. Second, they try to buy technology in current use, which can be transferred most smoothly, instead of obsolete or advanced technology. Finally, in order to be the first they often accept conditions imposed by the Government—conditions involving rapid import substitution or build-up of exports—that they know they would find it difficult to fulfill.

The profit cycle introduced by the trade policy shortens the planning horizons of firms and militates against a long-term product strategy. For instance, it works in favor of technology imports and against R&D, whose results are slower and less certain. Within R&D, it works in favor of projects that have a shorter horizon, are more certain of outcome and are therefore less ambitious, for instance, import substitution and diversification of product range.

Finally, the profit cycle encourages firms to accelerate their rate of change of product range and makes them more diversified at any point of time. The extreme diversification of Indian firms has been noted by Bell and Scott-Kemmis.[11] In their comparison of the Indian and South Korean producers of machining centers, Edquist and Jacobsson[12] note the extreme diversification of the major Indian producers, Hindustan Machine Tools and Walchandnagar Industries. The result is that their R&D manpower is absorbed by import substitution in components and diversification, and none is devoted to design of new machines.

The inability to devote resources to new designs is related to over-diversification; at the same time, concentration on import substitution makes it unnecessary for Indian firms to develop design capability. In order to develop independent exports, a firm has to have its own distinctive designs which are not copied from other manufacturers abroad. Korean machining center manufacturers, for example, developed new designs and built up substantial exports. Thus trade policy has an influence on the composition, innovativeness and productivity of R&D in engineering industries.

Policies on Market Structure

The Government has four types of policies affecting the market structure: promotion of small-scale industry, industrial licensing, controls on monopolies and restrictive trade practices, and controls on foreign investment.

Promotion of small-scale industry takes a number of forms, e.g., exemption from industrial licensing, exemption from taxes, privileged access to imported materials and reservation of products. The common feature of all these measures is their all-or-nothing character. Small enterprises are defined in terms of a maximum value of total assets. This means that an enterprise abruptly ceases to be small when it exceeds a certain size and loses all its privileges. This creates a powerful incentive to stay small— or to seem small. It is remarkable that almost no enterprise in India voluntarily declares itself to have grown out of the small-unit category, and a good many have to be weeded out, kicking and bawling, by the

Government. Similarly, small enterprises get access to imported materials, while large enterprises do not. The resulting difference in costs is so great that large enterprises simply cannot compete with small ones and vacate entire industries. This effect is even more drastic where a product is reserved for small industry. Thus the panoply of privileges creates a small-enterprise economy within the economy which is entirely exempt from competition from large-scale firms and which cannot benefit from economies of scale. It reinforces the high cost structure of Indian industry.

Industrial licensing was widely believed to promote monopolies in the sixties; the Monopolies and Restrictive Trade Practices Commission[13] placed great stress on the cornering of licenses by big business houses. This was possible when the production of many goods was beginning for the first time in India. Now that most goods are being produced, the effect of industrial licensing is different. In the interests of competition the Government gives licenses to new firms in preference to allowing established firms to expand. The result is that firms cannot plan to grow by accretion or to exploit economies of scale. Further, while the system allows expansion, the timing of that expansion is arbitrary. An application for expansion may be denied for a number of reasons, e.g., that there is overcapacity, that the applicant is undeserving, that small competitors would be hurt, etc. There are also cycles in licensing policy: it is tightened up when the payments situation is bad or when public enterprises are feeling the pinch of competition and liberalized in the opposite circumstances. Hence many enterprises make profits that they are not allowed immediately to invest in expansion, and they invest them instead in diversification. Finally, licensing increases the risks of competition, and for that reason too encourages firms to overdiversify.

Controls on monopolies and restrictive trade practices apply only to the largest firms and business houses, and there they apply in full rigor. In effect, they prevent those firms from entering most industries where other firms wish to enter. The practice is more muddled than the principle; but MRTP controls multiply the uncertainties introduced by industrial licensing. A major difference between India and the Republic of Korea is in the dynamism of the large business houses: South Korean business houses have grown more rapidly, absorbed technology imports more efficiently and exported more successfully.[14] It is difficult to divorce their superior performance from the considerable assistance given them by the Korean government, and the poor performance of Indian business houses from the handicaps under which they suffer.

Controls on foreign investment probably have the least effect because hardly any foreign firm wishes to invest in India: its industrial growth rate is low, and the Government actively manipulates competition and discriminates against high profits. The regulatory framework of India puts off most firms used to freer economies, so the additional effect of foreign investment controls is negligible. But it does perhaps have a significant effect on specialized oligopolies which are concerned about their market share in India. At present they sell each of their vintages separately to an Indian technology importer and aim to make what profit they can within the five years of collaboration they are allowed. If they are given a chance to defend their market share in the long run, they would take a longer view of profits too. However, it is not just foreign firms that need to take a longer-term view of the Indian market, but Indian firms as well if they are to invest in innovation. Thus what is required is not just a change in policy towards foreign investment, but a change in market structures and the policies that shape them.

Conclusions

It is thus our view that the market environment in India shapes the capabilities and the objectives of firms and makes them technologically stagnant. The most important of the factors affecting their capabilities is their small size: on the one hand, size constrains their capacity to invest in innovation; on the other hand, it makes them vulnerable to competition, increases their perceived risks and makes them ignore long-term objectives, which include innovation. Policies that promote small-scale industry militate against technological dynamism through their effect on the size distribution of firms.

Other policies have the same effect on the objectives of large firms. Industrial licensing and antimonopoly policies increase the perceived risks of large firms by making it uncertain whether and when they can follow up prospects of profit. And trade policy which, by building up a high-cost industry, has confined it to the domestic market introduces profit cycles: products yield high profits in early stages of import substitution, which later decline as domestic competition grows. If domestic and international costs were comparable, access to markets abroad would be easier, and profit cycles would be avoided.

Thus until market structure policies and trade policy are changed, little technological dynamism can be expected in Indian industry. But if these policies were changed, then a change in technology import policy could be envisaged that would encourage technological dynamism. At present, both the market structure and collaboration policy act together to force down the price of imported technology. Since the price of the next generation of technology is considerably higher than that of the current vintage, the factors that depress the price also lead to disconnected imports of each successive vintage as well as its imperfect absorption. If, however, domestic competition ceases to force short-term objectives on firms, the role of technology import policy in encouraging repeated imports of cheap technology will come to the fore. That is the point at which its reform will become important.

The reform would have to take two directions, one in respect of technology imports and the other in respect of technology development at home. In the first respect, long-term relationships between foreign and Indian firms would need to be encouraged; so would a long-term stake of foreign firms (especially specialized oligopolies) in the Indian market. This would certainly require that much longer-term technology import agreements must be allowed, with no contraints on royalty; it may also be assisted by a more liberal policy towards foreign investment. The point is that Indian firms should get a long-term flow of technology instead of technology at a certain point so that they can learn how technological development is driven over time.

The possibility of importing technological trajectories instead of snapshots will encourage all firms to take a longer-term view, whether they import technology or not. But in addition they can be encouraged to take a longer view in three ways. In the first place, their perceived long-run risks can be brought down by improving their access to technological developments in the world. Encouraging longer-term, more comprehensive technology agreements is one way; more fully integrating India into the world patent system is another; encouraging and subsidizing access to information through data bases, libraries, business travel, conference participation, etc., is a third one. In the second place, firms should be rewarded for the *results* of taking a long-term view in the form of processes or products that have a technological lead or that are particularly appropriate to Indian conditions. Such processes or products would in any case be rewarded by increasing market shares in the international or domestic market once the restraints on competition are removed. But recognition of indigenous technological advances can play a role in redirecting firms' strategies. Finally, India has an important asset in the form of national laboratories which should be used, not for import substitution in technology as at present, nor for facilitating the indigenization of imported technologies as captive R&D is used by firms, but to support large-scale, long-range cooperative R&D by industries.

Notes

1. Charles Cooper, "Technical collaborations between firms in the Benelux and firms in India," *Economic and Political Weekly* 20, nos. 45–47 (1985): 2,005–22.

2. Gunnar Paulsson, "Exporting industrial technology to India: Strategies and experiences of Swedish firms," *Economic and Political Weekly* 20, nos. 45–47 (1985): 2,023–26.

3. R. M. Bell and D. Scott-Kemmis, *Indo-British Technical Collaborations Since the Early 1970s: Change, Diversity and Forgone Opportunities,* 5 vols. (Brighton, England: Science Policy Research Unit, University of Sussex); Forschungsgesellschaft für Alternative Technologien und Wirtschaftsanalysen mbH, "Problems and perspectives of the transfer of technology between the countries of the European Community and India," 2 vols. (Regensburg, 1984, Mimeographed) (hereinafter cited as "ATW study of the transfer of technology").

4. Bell and Scott-Kemmis, *Indo-British Technical Collaborations.*

5. Ghayur Alam, "The nature of technology imports in India—a study of the main characteristics and trends" (Paper presented at the Conference on Technology Transfer and Investment: European Community-India, Berlin, 1984).

6. Ashok V. Desai, "Market structure and technology: their interdependence in Indian villages, *Research Policy* 14 (1985): 161–70.

7. Erik Baark, "Technology exports to India. Perspectives on the Danish experience," *Economic and Political Weekly* 20, nos. 45–47 (1985): 2,027–30.

8. Ashok V. Desai, "Technology imports in the sixties and the seventies: changes and their consequences" (New Delhi: ICRIER-NCAER, 1982, Mimeographed).

9. Desai, "Market structure and technology"; and Ashok V. Desai, "Technology imports and Indian industrialization" (Paper presented at the Conference on Technology Transfer and Investment: European Community-India, Berlin, 1984).

10. Ashok V. Desai. "The origin and direction of industrial R&D in India," *Research Policy* 9 (1980): 74–96.

11. Bell and Scott-Kemmis, *Indo-British Technical Collaborations.*

12. Charles Edquist and Staffan Jacobsson, "State policies, firm performance and firm strategies: production of hydraulic excavators and machining centers in India and Republic of Korea," *Economic and Political Weekly* 20, nos. 45–47 (1985): 1,053–72.

13. Monopolies and Restricted Trade Practices Commission, *Report of the Monopolies and Restricted Trade Practices Commission* (New Delhi, 1965).

14. Ashok V. Desai. "Indigenous and foreign determinants of technological change in India and Republic of Korea," *Economic and Political Weekly* 20, nos. 45–47 (1985): 2,081–94.

TABLE 8.1 Technology Transfer Agreements Between Indian and Foreign Firms by Size Classes, 1957–83

Sales of Foreign Firm (U.S. $ billion)	Sales of Indian Firm (Rs million)					Total[a]
	Unknown	250 or Less	251– 500	501– 1,000	Over 1,000	
	Number of Agreements					
Unknown	5,311	513	379	241	431	1,569
1 or less	167	11	12	15	16	54
1.1 – 5	231	30	32	17	50	129
5.1 – 10	120	21	26	21	30	98
Over 10	75	25	12	21	50	101
Total[b]	593	87	82	74	146	389
	Percent					
Unknown		32.7	24.1	15.4	27.8	100
1 or less		20.4	22.2	27.8	29.6	100
1.1 – 5		23.2	24.8	13.2	38.8	100
5.1 – 10		21.5	26.5	21.4	30.6	100
Over 10		23.2	11.1	19.4	46.3	100
Total[b]		22.4	21.1	19.0	37.5	100
	Percent					
1 or less	12.1	14.6	20.3	10.9	13.9	
1.1 – 5	34.5	39.0	22.9	34.3	33.2	
5.1 – 10	24.1	31.8	28.4	20.5	25.2	
Over 10	28.8	14.6	28.4	34.3	27.7	
Total[b]	100.0	100.0	100.0	100.0	100.0	

[a] Row totals exclude Indian firms whose size is unknown.
[b] Column totals exclude foreign firms whose size is unknown.

Source: Indian Centre for Research on International Economic Relations (ICRIER)–National Council for Applied Economic Research (NCAER) data base.

FIGURE 8.1

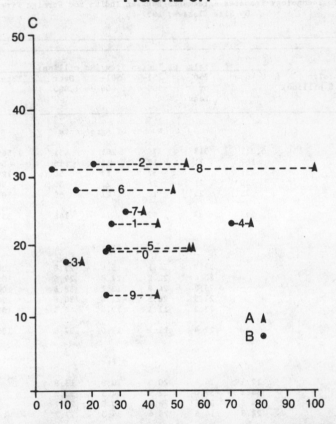

The relationship of (A) the number of agreements between large Indian and large foreign firms as percent of the number of all agreements of foreign firms and (B) the number of agreements between large Indian and large foreign firms with (C) the number of agreements of large Indian firms as percent of the number of all technology import agreements. The points refer to the following industries: (1) chemicals and pharmaceuticals; (2) petroleum products; (3) nonmetalliferous mineral products; (4) basic metals; (5) metal products; (6) machinery; (7) electrical equipment; (8) transport equipment; (9) miscellaneous industries; (0) all other industries (including food, drinks and tobacco, textiles, jute goods, leather goods, etc.).

TABLE 8.2 Foreign Firms' Experience and Expectations: Selected Countries
1983

	West Germany	France	Italy	Denmark	Japan	Total	U.K.
Number of Contracts	113	55	47	9	21	245	44
Initiative							
Supplier	21	30	9	2	2	64	6
Buyer	77	23	24	7	14	145	28
Other	8	2	11	0	5	26	11
Profits							
High	64	27	38	6	1	136	0
Low	25	14	1	2	8	50	23
Negative	12	10	4	1	12	39	2
Satisfaction							
Better Than Profits	0	21	1	0	0	22	13
Same	64	30	14	1	7	116	24
Worse Than Profits	37	0	28	8	14	87	9
Number of Firms	81	28	30	9	15	163	41
Reasons for Selling Technology							
Expected Profits	63	24	22	6	14	129	22
New Markets	59	23	18	5	8	113	18
Import Restrictions	45	17	17	8	10	97	26
Protection of Market	38	11	10	4	2	65	20
Reaction to Competitors	38	11	15	4	9	55	17
Low Labor Costs	16	3	4	0	2	25	

Sources: Bell and Scott-Kemmis, "Indo-British Technical Collaborations"; and
the "ATW Study of The Transfer of Technology."

TABLE 8.3 A Classification of Industries by Market Structure[a]

| | 1978–79 | | | | | | 1963–64 | | |
| | Industry Sales | Sales Per Firm | C (%) | n | H | E | n | H | E |
		(Rs million)							
Homogenous									
Small Groups									
Motorcycles	540	180	100	3	0.36	0.26	3	0.34	0.16
Carbon Black	402	134	100	3	0.38	0.36			
Gears	251	36	62	7	0.23	0.80			
Soda Ash	594	149	100	4	0.43	0.85			
Explosives	410	82	92	5	0.40	0.99			
Scooters	846	106	92	8	0.30	1.17	3	0.50	0.71
Cars	1,193	298	100	4	0.72	1.37	3	0.71	0.85
Mopeds	114	14	89	8	0.36	1.38			
	4,350	104	95	5	0.45	0.96			
Differentiated									
Small Groups									
Cement Machinery	3,211	44	90	7	0.40	1.34	4	0.59	1.17
Commercial Vehicles	5,468	911	95	6	0.57	1.55	5	0.31	0.75
Tractors	2,681	206	64	13	0.28	1.63	4	0.42	0.82
Generators	1,858	372	99	5	0.80	1.73			
Boilers	2,050	136	98	15	0.31	1.92	9	0.30	1.30
Mining Machinery	316	45	99	7	0.69	1.96	2	0.84	0.82
Metallurgical Machinery	784	112	99	7	0.70	1.98	3	0.36	0.30
Electric Machinery	1,014	63	79	16	0.35	2.14			
	14,482	191	89	9	0.50	1.71			
Homogenous									
Large Groups									
Nitrogenous Fertilizers	5,834	389	78	15	0.08	0.45			
Compressors	417	42	63	10	0.14	0.61	7	0.28	0.97
Bicycles	1,400	108	61	13	0.13	0.82	17	0.18	1.41
Synthetic Fibers	8,434	211	44	40	0.04	0.89			
Plastic Resins	2,265	108	47	21	0.09	0.92			
Pesticides	1,280	75	62	17	0.13	1.12			
Refrigerators	900	(60)	57	(15)	0.14	1.03	6	0.44	1.28
Phosphatic Fertilizers	580	11	44	53	0.10	2.06			
	21,110	115	57	27	0.08	0.81			

TABLE 8.3 (Continued)

Differentiated
Large Groups

Sugar Machinery	310	13	35	23	0.07	0.78	9	0.83	2.55
Plastic Products	695	41	52	17	0.11	0.97			
Switchgear	994	58	65	17	0.14	1.15	15	0.28	1.789
Electric Furnaces	150	7	50	22	0.11	1.17			
Chemical Machinery	740	(14)	40	(53)	0.07	1.65	36	0.10	1.65
Earthmoving Equipment	1,300	(23)	53	(57)	0.07	1.70	3	0.46	0.61
Textile Machinery	1,600	(18)	43	(89)	0.07	2.22			
Diesel Engines	2,290	(17)	42	(135)	0.06	2.59	26	0.23	2.24
Motors	1,750	(10)	43	(175)	0.06	3.11	6	0.27	0.77
Transformers	1,300	(7)	52	(186)	0.07	3.53	17	0.26	1.83
Cranes and Hoists	1,100	(12)	81	(92)	0.22	4.41	17	0.25	1.79
Machine Tools	1,220	(7)	48	(174)	0.15	5.01	47	0.24	3.20
Electric Pumps	923	(2)	12	(446)	0.06	5.25	46	0.13	2.21
	14,372	10	48	131	0.09	2.85			

---

[a] For some industries the number of firms was not available, but their total
sales were. It was assumed in such cases that the sales of all firms whose
sales were not known were the same as those of the smallest firm for which
the sales figure was known. The notional number of firms thus arrived at
and the corresponding sales per firms are given in parentheses. In some
industries, the number of firms and their total sales were known, but not
the individual sales figures of all the firms. In those cases it was
assumed that the sales of the firms whose figures were not available were
equal.

Source: Desai, "Market Structure and Technology," and Cooper, "Technical
Collaborations Between Firms in the Benelux and India."

FIGURE 8.2

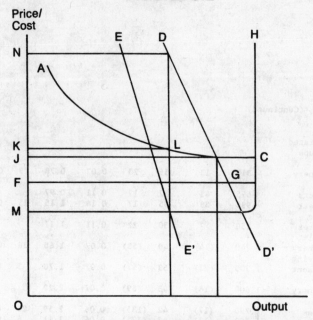

FIGURE 8.3

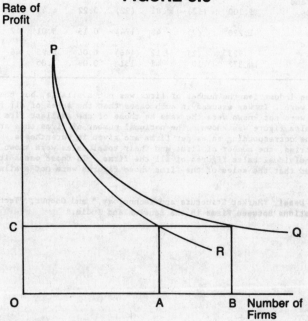

9

India's Industrial Policy

Robert E.B. Lucas

Although many of the essential facts are discussed elsewhere in this volume, it may nonetheless be useful to draw together, at the outset, certain features of India's industrial development, before turning to the three themes of this chapter. Most notably, despite massive investment, industrial growth has been comparatively slow. Since Independence India has made a laudable and generally increasing savings effort, with gross savings in excess of 20 percent of GDP after 1973–74.[1] Much of this accumulated wealth has been directed towards investment in the industrial sector, with capital formation in manufacturing actually exceeding that in the entire agricultural sector in virtually every year in the last two decades. In the latter half of the 1970s, for example, investment in industry, excluding construction, comprised 38 percent of all domestic capital formation. (See Table 9.1.) Yet despite very high levels of investment, industrial growth has been relatively slow with a trend growth rate in net product from registered manufacturing of some 4.5 percent between 1960–61 and 1980–81. Obviously this implies a sharp rise in capital intensity and indeed industrial value added relative to book value of fixed capital fell from 0.67 in 1959–60 to 0.39 in 1977–78.[2]

A large fraction of industrial investments—approximately 50 percent in the 1970s—has been in the public sector. Yet the private sector continued to provide about 78 percent of industrial value added and 68 percent of the employment by 1980. The package of policy instruments adopted to direct industrial development includes a plethora of extremely detailed controls, including industrial licensing, import quotas and widespread use of administered prices, intended to influence industrial performance through restrictions on market behavior rather than relying upon incentives.[3] The upshot has been an almost unique economic system of private ownership combined with widespread regulatory directives—a system of command capitalism as opposed to market socialism. An important objective in intervening in the market processes has been that of generating greater equality of incomes. Yet the resultant industrial performance has not only produced slow growth in output but also in employment, so that by 1981 only 6 million people were employed in the factory sector from a population of some 665 million. This represents the cumulative effect of an annual growth rate in manufacturing employment of 3 percent since 1960, a rate which only marginally exceeds the population growth rate.

India's development strategy, at least until 1974–75, involved across-the-board import substitution in virtually all spheres of manufacturing regardless of comparative cost advantage. The broad scope of this substitution is reflected in Table 9.2, which shows the percentage ratio of imports to factory sector production in 1959–60 and 1969–70 for twenty-two categories of commodities.[4] Only in edible oils did the ratio of imports to domestic production actually rise during this period, and indeed for many industries the ratio fell sharply—notably so in several of the chemicals and engineering goods categories. Quotas restricted imports throughout and the premium levels were very high, averaging some 93 percent on imports of manufactured goods in 1968, for example.[5] Certainly, imports were effectively diminished: the ratio of imports to GNP declined at an exponential trend rate of 3.4 percent per year from 1961–62 through 1973–74, rendering India an extremely closed economy with imports being only 5 percent of GNP by the end of this period.

But after 1974–75 increased exports, remittances and other invisible earnings began to swell foreign exchange reserves and import restrictions began to be relaxed. At first, import liberalization was tentative, but after 1978–79 with the expansion of open general licensing and the second oil price shock, the import bill grew rapidly. Indeed, as may be seen in Table 9.3, the CIF value of imports doubled in just three years from 1978–79 to 1981–82, amounting to some 10.3 percent of GNP by 1981–82. Obviously oil imports dominated this increase, and in fact between 1975–76 and 1980–81—spanning the two oil price shocks—imports of oil actually grew even more rapidly than the world price of oil. After 1980–81 oil imports fell both in nominal and real terms and this has allowed a decline in the aggregate propensity to import to 8.4 percent of GDP by 1984–85, although other components of the import bill have increased rapidly as quota limitations have been relaxed.[6]

Thus, there has been a sharp rise in a broad range of imports, particularly after 1978–79, though certain categories of import have remained unaffected. In fact, under Open General Licensing the former binding quotas have effectively been replaced by tariff barriers in many, though not all, categories. But average protection levels remain both high and widely differentiated. For example, a very recent study by the Association of Indian Engineering Industries estimates that domestic steel prices remain at a premium of 153 percent over world prices. The net result is both emerging pressure on the balance of trade from expanded imports, which increased by some 18 percent in the first nine months of 1985–86, and a structure of effective protection which provides a quite diverse set of incentives for various industries.

Against this background, in this chapter I wish to emphasize three themes with respect to industrial policy.

The Connection Between Import Liberalization and Domestic Regulation

In general, simulations of the consequences of import liberalization in the short run reveal comparatively small efficiency gains across a wide variety of country contexts.[7] The reason is that with capital stock fixed in each activity, the potential room for adjusting production as the relative price structure changes is naturally restricted. The case of India is no exception, and indeed if domestic prices are actually permitted to track world prices, then in a short-run framework industrial production may well fall. The reason is that highly protected industries will dwindle rapidly but those labor-intensive activities in which India has a comparative cost advantage would be barred from major expansion without additional capacity.[8]

But in India a critical additional element influences the consequences of trade liberalization. The distribution of investment amongst different manufacturing activities has been largely influenced by the restrictions of industrial licensing, by the Monopoly and Restrictive Trade Practices Act and by the role of public sector investment. Policy reform in the context of the dual policies of import protection and industrial licensing requires second-best comparisons and it is quite conceivable—and perhaps likely—that relaxation of import restrictions alone may prove counterproductive. Thus, the phases of import liberalization in the mid-1960s and after 1974–75 did little if anything to accelerate industrial growth. On the other hand, the continued import liberalization of the last couple of years has been accompanied by at least a partial relaxation in industrial licensing also—a number of industries having been delicensed entirely—and industrial growth seems to have responded. Preliminary estimates place the industrial growth rate at 6.3 percent for 1985–86 though, of course, it is too early to tell how much of this is attributable to liberalization of the licensing process. Nonetheless delicensing as well as import liberalization remain quite selective in scope and there seems little evidence that this selectivity is being designed to encourage labor-intensive activities specifically or to reflect comparative cost advantage more generally.

The rationale for limiting private investment initiative in the past has included a desire to limit domestic monopoly, to retain key industries in the public sector and to protect the small-scale enterprises. On the other hand, the constraints imposed on plant capacity have limited efficiency by preventing exploitation of scale economies in some industries, leading to recent calls for reform.[9] Other than in spheres of natural monopoly, the chief need to limit domestic monopoly has ultimately stemmed from limited import competition resulting from widespread use of quotas and barriers to entry imposed by industrial licensing requirements. To this extent, the recent removal of many of the quantitative restrictions on trade should obviate the need for much of the antitrust policy. Moreover, the success and merits of promoting small-scale enterprises by limiting capacity in the factory sector have also been quite questionable. Thus, it is not obvious the restrictions on new cotton mill capacity have truly helped the handloom industry.[10] Indeed, if India had taken her textile exports more seriously, rather than focusing on a zero-sum game for domestic demand for cloth, both mill and handloom production could have been promoted.

Thus, much of the argument which has been maintained in favor of industrial licensing has been intimately associated with the trade policy simultaneously adopted. Conversely, both the short- and long-run efficacy of trade liberalization is now inextricably associated with domestic de-regulation, and trade reform with inappropriately phased industrial de-licensing could well prove harmful.

Choice of Technique

The unfortunate net effect of limiting capacity in those labor-intensive industries which compete with small-scale enterprises, of public sector investment leadership in heavy industries, and the structure of import protection has been a focus of manufacturing investment in capital-intensive activities. Thus, the six two-digit manufacturing industries with capital to value added ratios in excess of 4.0 on average between 1960 and 1980—namely, fertilizers, steel, petroleum products, cement, paper and basic chemicals—absorbed some 47 percent of total manufacturing investment over this period.[11] Indeed, this implies a growing fraction of manufacturing capital in these most capital-intensive industries, for their initial portion of fixed capital stock by 1959–60 was "only" some 39 percent. At the opposite extreme the fraction of investment assigned to cotton textiles and jute textiles was less than half their initial share in capital stock, with similar low proportions for such relatively low capital-intensity industries as textile products, tea processing, edible oils, tobacco and wooden products.

This emphasis might have been sufficient to explain the increase in the capital output ratio noted in the introduction, but in fact this has not been the case. Not only has there been an increase in the role of capital-intensive activities but most of the manufacturing industries have also become more capital intensive through time. Thus, in Table 9.4 it may be seen that fixed capital per man-hour worked increased in virtually every manufacturing industry between 1959–60 and 1979–80, and even fixed capital relative to value added increased within most industries.[12]

In fact, the increase in the aggregate fixed capital relative to value added and relative to man-hours worked in manufacturing may be de-composed into a within-industry increase in capital intensity versus an increase in the comparative emphasis on inherently capital-intensive ac-tivities. Between 1959–60 and 1979–80, only some 36 percent of the increase in fixed capital relative to value added and 24 percent of the increase in capital per man-hour are attributable to emphasis on capital-intensive activities: the bulk of the increase in capital intensity is thus a reflection of choice of production technique within the thirty-nine man-ufacturing activites shown in Table 9.4.[13]

This is an important point from a macro policy perspective. It seems that slow industrial growth despite massive investment has been caused, not predominantly by the structure of import protection and the sectoral pattern of investment as dictated by Plan requirements, but by whatever factors have shaped the rapid increase in capital to labor ratios within various activites.

Towards understanding these factors, it is worth noting that the real product wage—the wage rate relative to the producer price index of manufactured products—has increased steadily. Hence Table 9.5 shows that the real product wage rate in manufacturing increased by some 86 percent between 1960–61 and 1979–80. Relative to the national accounts deflator for capital formation the manufacturing wage rate rose by some 47 percent over the same period, and it seems that this rise has indeed significantly encouraged reliance on more capital-intensive techniques in most manufacturing industries. Thus in the appendix to this chapter some simple regressions are reported exploring man-hours worked per unit of installed fixed capital in relation to the wage rate deflated by the price index for capital formation.[14] For twenty-seven of the thirty industries for which regressions are reported, increases in the wage rate relative to price of capital are estimated to have significantly encouraged more capital-intensive techniques on at least a 75 percent confidence level test and in seventeen cases the significance level is 5 percent or better.

This evidence certainly suggests that the rising industrial wage has been a significant factor in the observed move toward more capital-intensive techniques. But why have wages in the manufacturing sector been rising? From Table 9.5 it may be seen that although the real wage in manufacturing has risen fairly steadily over the last two decades, the real wage of agricultural workers has hardly risen at all.[15] Given this evidence and the very obvious gap which exists in earnings between those urban dwellers employed in the organized sector and those who are not, one may generally rule out the pressure of labor demand on the available supply as the cause for wage increases. Wage escalation has not been the result of healthy growth and ensuing demand for labor. Definitive answers to the proximate determinants of manufacturing wage performance through time must await further research. But it is clear that the comparative power of unions in pressing for wage settlements has grown substantially and the incidence of strikes has consequently risen as reflected in the number of man-days lost in strikes and lockouts reported in Table 9.5. To what extent minimum wage laws, recommendations of wage boards and the leadership role of public sector wage policy have also contributed to manufacturing wage increases remains unclear.

But in addition to wage increases, another important element has also served to increase the cost of labor use, and that is the job security laws. In many activities, any worker employed for more than six months in a job is essentially granted tenure for life. Such legislation naturally renders employers reluctant to hire for fear of subsequent difficulties in retrenching the work force. Moreover, labor productivity is almost certainly reduced through at least three mechanisms: (1) by encouraging the use of temporary labor, less on-the-job training occurs; (2) to circumvent the job security laws, work is often put out to small workshops or on piece rate at home, denying the benefits of any scale economies; (3) by removing the threat of dismissal, effort on the job is either diminished or requires costly supervision to monitor. Since the scope and coverage of these job security laws has increased through time, it again seems likely that they have contributed to the trend towards reliance on more capital-intensive techniques within many manufacturing activities.

Domestic Aggregate Demand and Exports

A further plausible explanation for the rise in the ratio of installed capacity to value added is that of increasing excess capacity. Certainly the data on capacity utilization in the Industrial Development Bank of India *Annual Report* indicate substantial excess capacity over a wide range of industries. To what extent such excess capacity might be a result of restricted access to key inputs such as electricity, as opposed to being the result of inadequate demand, is difficult to disentangle.[16] But no matter whether output has been limited by demand at a level below that of installed capacity or whether demand has influenced output through its effects on domestic prices under a quota regime, the level and composition of demand for industrial goods have almost certainly affected industrial growth.

The import substitution strategy adopted by India in the past has focused almost all of the attention on domestic demand for industrial goods, to the neglect of exports. Yet agricultural growth in India has been slower than that of industry itself and so demand for manufactured consumer goods out of agricultural incomes has not been an important source of stimulus for industrial growth. Indeed, at present levels of income, spending on manufactured consumer goods produced by the factory sector is quite tiny in rural areas, with the exception of just a few products such as cotton cloth, bicycles and radios. Most industrial food products are primarily consumed in urban areas, for in the villages a local counterpart good is generally preferred. Thus, unless the income elasticity of rural demand for industrial consumer goods rises considerably, even more rapid agricultural growth is unlikely to provide a significant stimulus to demand in the organized industrial consumer goods sector.[17] Purchases of fertilizer by the agricultural sector have obviously grown, but price controls on fertilizer prevent increased demand in this sphere from being translated into incentives for expanded production.

The industrial wage bill itself is clearly a source of demand for a number of industrial consumer goods, and particularly some of the more labor-intensive consumer goods. But the focus of planned investments in the capital-intensive industries and such factors as the job security laws limit growth in the wage bill and hence the domestic demand for labor-intensive goods.[18]

To rely on domestic markets alone to generate demand for industrial goods, and especially for the more labor-intensive industrial goods, is thus not very promising in the current environment. To achieve the kind of industrial growth targeted in the Seventh Five-Year Plan (1985–90), manufactured exports must be taken more seriously than in the past. A common argument in this sphere is that India is such a large country that exports must always be comparatively unimportant, in contrast to some of the often-cited East Asian success stories. But, although it is true that for large countries exports will always be a smaller fraction of GDP, this does not deny their importance as a source of demand, for what matters is the potential for increasing demand on the margin and the multiplier effects of such increases. Moreover, the comparatively low ratio of exports to GDP in India is not only a result of being a large country but of the neglect of exports in the past.

But export performance has now assumed an importance beyond that of providing demand alone, for the liberalization in imports which has occurred has resulted in a high trade deficit in the 1980s as exports have failed to grow. Preliminary estimates indicate a record trade deficit for 1985–86 of nearly 80 billion rupees and in fact export levels have actually declined in recent months, led by a drop in engineering goods exports over the last couple of years. Although current calculations are not available, it seems almost certain that effective protection for manufactured exports remains negative: the various export incentive schemes, such as cash subsidies and drawbacks, have simply been inadequate to compensate for the high levels of import protection on inputs to manufacturing, the recent increases in drawback levels notwithstanding.

Yet a policy design based on a simple view of infinite price elasticity of demand for all of India's manufactured exports is also inappropriate. Lucas[19] reports a very wide range of estimated price elasticities of world demand for various manufactured exports from India. In cotton textiles and miscellaneous textile product exports an infinite elasticty of world demand cannot be rejected, up to the level of present foreign quota limits. Thus, for example, how effective will be the increase which occurred at the end of June 1986 in the cash compensation rate for textile exports depends entirely upon the ability of the mill sector to respond in product lines where quotas are not now binding. But in other spheres world demand is far less responsive to price cuts by Indian exporters, probably because of nonprice competitive elements in world markets, such as delivery time, reliablilty and quality. This consequently raises serious doubts as to the efficacy of export promotion by across-the-board export incentive schemes or indeed of devaluation, which is again under current debate. Rather, the design of an appropriate export program may require a careful consideration of the price responsiveness of both world market demand and of Indian supply in various export categories. In other words, the current policy of identifying "thrust areas" for export targeting and cost reduction could, if well executed, prove much more effective than a simple devaluation in enhancing export earnings. Though, on the other hand, the dangers in designing a "scientific," highly tuned trade policy package are well-known and the costs of error may be prohibitive.

Closing Remarks

To even approximate the growth rates envisioned in the Seventh Plan, the industrial sector will have to expand rapidly. The combined policies of import liberalization and deregulation seem to have generated a spurt in industrial production in the last couple of years. But it is clear that the balance of payments is now becoming a constraint on further import liberalization. Of course, it is not unusual for exports to lag behind imports during a phase of liberalization, but in India the long history of neglecting exports and the consequential loss of foreign markets even in areas of traditional export will render export promotion particularly difficult.

At least in some spheres, it seems that cost reductions will be effective in expanding export demand. But the key question then becomes whether such cost reductions can be effected in these potential "thrust areas" and whether the supply of exports will then be forthcoming. The current emphasis on the need for high technology in this context is unlikely to provide the answer. Almost no disembodied technical progress has occurred in Indian manufacturing in the last twenty-five years. The early belief in infant industry learning has simply not materialized. Today, the high-tech industries are receiving a similar emphasis to that granted to their basic industry counterparts in the past, again based on infant industry arguments. In the environment of limited export incentives, regulated labor markets and continued industrial licensing which prevails, there seems little reason to believe today's infants will provide an engine for growth consistent with Seventh Plan targets.

Both cost reductions and supply increases in "thrust areas" will require not only access to imports on a competitive basis but other accompanying reforms. Chief amongst these must surely be further relaxation of the industrial licensing system. The barriers to expansion of capacity in the labor-intensive industries have limited factory employment and hence domestic demand, denied the possibility of export expansion in spheres of clear comparative advantage, and had at best a questionable effect in aiding cottage and small-scale industries which might perhaps have been explicitly subsidized at lower cost. In this context, the recent reforms in the textile industry, removing the freeze on the mills' loom capacity which had been in place since the 1950s, may represent a major improvement. But another sphere of needed reform also seems pressing, namely, with respect to job security legislation which raises the effective cost of labor and hence encourages the choice of more capital-intensive techniques, thus limiting industrial employment and hurting export competitiveness in otherwise labor-intensive activities.

Although such a strategy should be employment enhancing, there is, of course, no guarantee that the precise prevailing pattern of jobs would remain viable. Indeed the incidence of sick units in a number of industries has increased in severity in the 1980s, as one might predict as long-standing high levels of protection are selectively dismantled. Attempts to protect jobs by actually restricting exit of firms from such spheres is no doubt currently imposing a substantial resource cost at least in activities which would not be profitable even in shadow price terms.[20]

The restructuring of industry which will be necessary to further industrial growth will hurt some while helping others, thus raising difficult political choices. As a result of the ensuing political pressures some reversals have already happened, such as the protection of some portions of the ailing capital goods industry in July 1986 by preventing international tendering in certain equipment acquisitions. On the other hand, the capital goods industry itself is still hampered, for example, by steel prices well above those paid by their foreign counterparts, as noted earlier.

There are no easy answers to the phasing of reform in an economy starting from the extreme degree of intervention prevailing in India. If that phasing proves wrong, then India could easily face a severe balance-of-payments constraint. In general, we economists are not very good at proffering advice on the phasing of economic reform. But at least if barriers to the expansion of key advantageous areas could be removed at an early stage, this would permit the emergence of a new constituency with a vested interest in reform. Certainly, there is no guarantee that everyone will gain from the process of reform and new political allies may prove crucial to sustained reform. Without continued reform there will be a return to the slow growth and poor employment prospects of the inward-looking strategy of the past.

Notes

1. The Raj Committee Report raises some doubts as to whether the true savings rate has been quite as high as the national accounts data would suggest, but the savings propensity has indisputably been very high (K. N. Raj [chairman], *Capital Formation and Savings in India: 1950-1 to 1979-80*, Report of the Working Group on Savings [Bombay: Reserve Bank of India, 1982]).

2. Derived from *Annual Survey of Industries*, census sector data.

3. See Jagdish N. Bhagwati and Padma Desai, *India: Planning for Industrialization* (New Delhi: Oxford University Press, 1970), or the Dagli Committee Report (Vadilal Dagli [chairman], *Report of the Committee on Controls and Subsidies* [New Delhi: Government of India, 1979]).

4. The only manufactured commodity groups omitted from Table 9.2 are those for which the initial import ratio is below 3 percent. It should be noted that since imports are measured CIF (cost, insurance and freight) in Table 9.2 and factory sector output is in domestic prices, the changes in ratios reported also embody changes in protection levels. However, if both components are measured in constant domestic prices only, the pattern of change in the reported ratios remains essentially the same.

5. This is a weighted average of the implicit tariffs estimated by V. R. Panchamukhi, *Trade Policies of India* (Delhi: Concept Publishing Co., 1978), using value added in the census manufacturing industries as weights.

6. Amongst manufactured items, for example, paper, basic chemicals, plastics, cement, metals (both steel and nonferrous) and machinery imports all increased relatively rapidly. But, on the other hand, such important items as fertilizer and railway equipment remained limited in import through the period covered by Table 9.3, though 1985-86 has witnessed a sharp rise in fertilizer imports also. Certain industrial raw material imports have increased rapidly, including synthetic yarn, pulp, crude rubber, nonmetallic minerals and metal ores. But other industrial raw materials have increased far less quickly and it is notable that imports of cotton and jute fibers fell significantly in nominal terms after 1977-78 even though the agricultural production index for cotton grew at less the 0.5 percent per year thereafter.

7. Kemal Dervis, Jaime de Melo and Sherman Robinson, *General Equilibrium Models for Development Policy* (Cambridge: Cambridge University Press, 1982); John B. Shoven and John Whalley, "Applied General Equilibrium Models of Taxation and International Trade," *Journal of Economic Literature* 22 (September 1984): 1,007–51.

8. Robert E. B. Lucas "Liberalization of Indian Trade and Industrial Controls" (Boston University, January 1986, Mimeographed), undertakes such a simulation for India, using a multiple sector econometric model, and over the period 1960–80 it is found that manufacturing production actually declines if the only change in policy is to liberalize imports such that domestic prices are equated with world prices.

9. Indeed the emphasis on the importance of scale economies has now led to the introduction of "minimum operational capacities" in licensing requirements as opposed to the traditional maximum restrictions.

10. Dipak Mazumdar, "The Issue of Small versus Large in the Indian Textile Industry," *World Bank Staff Working Papers* (No.654) (Washington, D.C., 1984).

11. Capital stock here refers to estimated replacement cost of fixed capital in the census manufacturing sector, measured at constant prices. The estimates are obtained from gross expenditures on fixed capital, derived from the *Annual Survey of Industries*, with initial capital stock for each industry calculated from book value adjusted to replacement cost according to ratios estimated by S. R. Hashim and M. M. Dadi, *Capital Output Relations in Indian Manufacturing: 1946–1964* (Baroda: University of Baroda Press, 1973), depreciated at 5 percent per year. Value added is measured in gross terms and deflated by producer prices for the relevant industry.

12. Fixed capital refers to estimated replacement cost of fixed capital measured at constant prices as before.

13. The percentage effects cited are based on a decomposition of the increase in capital per unit of value added (and per man-hour worked) into a Laspeyres index of sectoral value added, with initial capital relative to value added as weights, and a Paasche index of sectoral capital-value added ratios weighted by current relative contribution to value added. It should be noted, however, that the relative contributions of a within-industry and an across-industry effect are not independent of the level of disaggregation.

14. The specification adopted is:
$\ln(\ell/k) = a + \beta \ln(w/pk) + \lambda \ln(\ell/k)_{-1}$ where ℓ represents man-hours, k is fixed capital, w is hourly wage rate, pk is the price index for capital formation, $\ln$ indicates a natural logarithm and $_{-1}$ indicates a one period lag. This specification is consistent with the first-order conditions for cost minimization in a CES value-added function with a flexible accelerator appended to reflect difficulties in rapid adjustment of inputs. The term pk may be thought of as a proxy for the true user cost of capital, though in the context of credit rationing and the consequent focus on internal financing in Indian industry, any interest rate measures are unlikely to be of much importance. The flexible accelerator term is omitted from equations in which it proves to be insignificantly positive. Regressions for eight industries in which the point estimates for the coefficient on $\ln(w/pk)$ prove positive are omitted from the appendix. All results are obtained from *Annual Survey of Industries* data for the census sector from 1960–61 through 1979–80, using the Cochrane-Orcutt method of correction for first-order serial correlation for discontinuous samples, since ASI data are not available for 1972–73.

15. The real wage rate in manufacturing is derived by deflating the nominal wage by the cost of living index for industrial workers and the real wage in agriculture is deflated by the cost of living index for agricultural workers.

16. Indeed, the precise interpretation of the concept of excess capacity is unclear for there is also evidence to indicate that newly installed capacity has contributed to expansion of value added over a wide range of industries. See, for example, Lucas, "Liberalization of Indian Trade and Industrial Controls." One reason why value added might increase with additional capacity installed, despite excess capacity, arises from the tying of import license issues to creation of new capacity.

17. Nonetheless there remains an important link between agricultural performance and consumer goods industries arising from the availability of raw materials for food processing and textiles. This link is rendered important by limitations on raw material imports—imposed by the responsiveness of the canalized import authorities as well as from quotas—and probably is responsible for at least some of the observed correlation between successful monsoons and industrial production.

18. Whether wage rate escalation has served to limit the wage bill depends upon the elasticity of labor demand. Estimates in Lucas, "Liberalization of Indian Trade and Industrial Controls," indicate an elasticity of labor demand below one, suggesting that wage escalation should actually have served to enhance labor incomes.

19. Robert E. B. Lucas, "Demand for India's Manufactured Exports" (Boston University, April 1986, Mimeographed).

20. Moreover, exit restrictions may well discourage initial entry for risk-averse entrepreneurs and in industries where ability to switch product lines with changing demand conditions is important.

TABLE 9.1 Gross Domestic Capital Formation in Major Sectors
(Rs crores)[a]

	Agri-culture	Manu-fact.	Electricity gas, water	Transp., storage communic.	Real Estate	Other	Total
			At 1960–61 Prices				
1960–61	395	707	122	345	308	667	2,544
1961–62	360	639	199	405	312	434	2,349
1962–63	402	714	281	483	278	574	2,732
1963–64	431	683	293	520	281	707	2,915
1964–65	495	844	277	552	304	734	3,206
1965–66	591	991	324	567	436	628	3,537
1966–67	538	1,261	288	488	634	701	3,910
1967–68	548	812	295	399	653	933	3,640
1968–69	600	595	296	401	732	790	3,414
1969–70	682	832	335	393	804	934	3,980
1970–71	732	839	380	462	569	1,159	4,141
1971–72	722	922	359	505	580	1,047	4,135
1972–73	779	735	410	533	507	1,447	4,411
			At 1970–71 Prices				
1972–73	1,444	1,660	627	984	903	1,457	7,075
1973–74	1,519	2,450	580	995	1,200	2,328	9,072
1974–75	1,230	2,791	627	922	921	1,714	8,205
1975–76	1,217	2,353	876	891	782	2,303	8,422
1976–77	1,807	1,963	910	889	1,206	2,654	9,249
1977–78	1,904	2,493	1,087	994	1,370	2,111	9,959
1978–79	2,413	3,480	1,162	1,071	1,449	2,705	12,280
1979–80	1,963	3,654	1,195	1,065	960	2,298	11,135
1980–81	2,175	3,326	1,320	1,263	1,148	2,909	12,141
1981–82	2,057	3,675	1,429	1,326	1,152	2,886	12,525

[a] Rs 1 crore = Rs 10 million.

Source: National Accounts Statistics (New Delhi: Government of India,
Ministry of Planning, Department of Statistics, Central Statistical
Organization).

TABLE 9.2   Imports Relative to Factory Sector Output
(percent)

	1959–60	1969–70
Dairy Products	9.77	3.75
Edible Oils	3.24	7.56
Beverages	5.64	0.63
Synthetic Textiles	3.70	0.22
Paper	15.24	11.30
Oil Products	129.78	17.70
Basic Chemicals	184.35	29.33
Fertilizer	53.14	42.28
Paints–Dyes	27.78	3.61
Plastics	75.59	6.75
Pharmaceuticals	11.25	5.95
Miscellaneous Chemicals	13.90	4.94
Nonmetallic Mineral Products	9.60	1.81
Steel	41.26	8.24
Nonferrous Metals	73.40	35.13
Metallic Products	12.61	1.87
Agricultural Machinery	52.97	44.06
Nonelectrical Machinery	163.26	45.24
Electrical Apparatus	51.61	11.91
Railway Equipment	29.50	5.21
Motor Vehicles	36.56	3.73
Cycles	10.82	2.72

Sources: Monthly Statistics of the Foreign Trade of India (Calcutta:
Government of India, Directorate General of Commercial Intelligence and
Statistics); Annual Survey of Industries (New Delhi: Government of India,
Central Statistical Organization).

TABLE 9.3 Composition of Imports by Major Category
(Rs millions)

	Wheat, Rice, Flour	Edib. Oils, Sugar	Other Food	Oil, Coal	Cott. -Jute Fibre	Syn. Yarn	Pulp, Rub'r, Nonmet. Min'ls.	Metal Ores	Other Raw Mat'ls.	Paper
1959–60	1192	39	361	780	362	139	164	34	230	97
1964–65	2053	50	434	686	655	127	184	20	234	131
1969–70	2466	180	739	1376	839	23	282	68	455	237
1974–75	7162	138	1383	11570	312	100	262	60	1092	595
1975–76	12702	155	1583	12260	316	100	339	202	657	577
1976–77	8698	1021	930	14121	1363	42	285	311	807	622
1977–78	1298	7137	1018	15564	1989	108	524	446	1118	817
1978–79	1129	5394	1307	16853	280	377	917	673	1113	1047
1979–80	1236	4329	1550	33315	5	415	994	904	1230	1553
1980–81	1261	7715	1665	52909	20	433	698	1152	1764	1865
1981–82	3844	6883	1878	52262	143	794	1467	2024	2009	2454

	Basic Chem.	Fert.	Plas -tics	Other Chem.	Cem't	Metals	Mach., Metal Prod.	Rail Equip., Motor Vehic.	Other	Total
1959–60	405	157	47	242	1	1330	2084	579	631	8874
1964–65	344	268	88	213	1	1690	4190	536	717	12621
1969–70	460	911	102	367	0	1563	3569	241	1791	15669
1974–75	1297	5081	211	728	0	6130	6016	574	2478	45188
1975–76	1222	5507	260	686	0	4149	8282	725	2925	52648
1976–77	1372	2063	578	772	1	3818	8761	433	4113	50110
1977–78	1948	2702	2581	1143	133	4554	9438	446	7281	60242
1978–79	2329	3891	2678	1434	689	7142	10312	456	10087	68107
1979–80	3152	3906	2052	1603	677	11832	11146	688	9608	90195
1980–81	3586	6776	2180	1195	955	13544	14526	957	11691	124892
1981–82	4856	5236	2986	2108	730	16377	18203	817	10407	135476

Source: Monthly Statistics of the Foreign Trade of India.

TABLE 9.4 Change in Capital Intensity Within Manufacturing Sectors

	Fixed Capital Value Added		Fixed Capital Man-Hours	
	1959–60	1979–80	1959–60	1979–80
Dairy Products	2.92	2.56	20.6	17.3
Granary Products	1.70	1.65	4.7	6.9
Sugar	2.74	4.60	10.7	14.1
Edible Oils	0.75	2.16	4.8	10.6
Vanaspati	0.99	1.38	12.2	13.2
Tea Processing	2.65	2.50	9.9	8.1
Other Food Products	1.41	1.42	1.3	2.8
Beverages	1.41	1.35	9.7	12.9
Tobacco Products	0.54	0.71	1.2	2.4
Cotton Mills	2.20	1.68	3.7	5.8
Synthetic Textiles	3.79	1.73	7.6	11.1
Jute Products	1.45	1.07	2.8	2.6
Woolen Products	1.16	2.08	3.8	6.1
Other Textile Products	1.50	1.59	3.2	3.9
Wooden Products	2.04	1.70	2.7	5.0
Paper	4.30	3.93	12.8	20.0
Leather	1.15	3.52	2.2	6.8
Leather Products	0.91	1.24	1.6	4.2
Rubber Products	0.96	2.23	7.4	18.2
Oil Products	3.16	11.98	55.4	109.5
Basic Chemicals	5.10	3.86	24.3	34.8
Fertilizer	7.23	7.79	28.9	154.5
Paints and Dyes	1.49	1.98	17.7	32.1
Plastics	3.35	2.58	15.4	44.7
Pharmaceuticals	1.59	0.99	10.7	17.5
Toiletries	0.84	1.14	7.8	16.1
Other Chemicals	1.12	1.87	4.7	10.5
Cement	4.92	5.63	27.8	30.8
Nonmetallic Mineral Prods.	2.09	2.80	3.0	7.3
Steel	5.71	7.23	25.9	40.2
Nonferrous Metals	1.25	5.52	11.2	51.2
Metallic Products	1.07	1.51	3.3	8.1
Agricultural Machinery	0.81	2.08	1.9	13.9
Nonelectrical Machinery	1.71	1.96	4.1	11.1
Electrical Apparatus	1.51	1.59	5.8	14.2
Railway Equipment	1.67	3.57	3.2	12.8
Motor Vehicles	0.03	2.32	3.4	17.2
Cycles	2.30	1.76	6.1	9.8
Miscellaneous Manufacturing	1.80	1.67	4.5	9.9

Source: Annual Survey of Industries, census sector.

TABLE 9.5 Wages and Industrial Disputes

	Nominal Wage (Rs/day)		Real Wage (1960–61 Rs/day)		Real Product Wage (1960–61 Rs)	Man–Days Lost in Industrial Disputes (1,000)
	Manuf.	Agric.	Manuf.	Agric.	Manuf.	
1960–61	6.40	1.43	6.40	1.43	6.40	—
1961–62	6.88	1.55	6.64	1.51	6.80	6,121
1962–63	7.28	1.57	6.80	1.48	7.12	3,269
1963–64	7.68	1.61	6.80	1.28	7.44	7,775
1964–65	8.48	1.99	6.40	1.37	7.84	6,470
1965–66	9.04	2.10	6.56	1.32	7.84	—
1966–67	10.40	2.38	6.88	1.25	8.40	13,846
1967–68	11.36	2.60	6.64	1.24	8.80	17,148
1968–69	12.16	2.75	6.88	1.47	9.04	17,244
1969–70	13.68	2.90	7.84	1.49	9.76	19,048
1970–71	15.28	3.04	8.32	1.58	10.16	20,563
1971–72	15.84	3.21	8.32	1.59	9.84	16,546
1972–73	—	3.37	—	1.48	—	20,544
1973–74	20.16	3.78	8.80	1.32	10.56	20,626
1974–75	24.72	4.33	8.08	1.18	10.00	40,262
1975–76	27.36	4.69	9.12	1.49	10.96	21,901
1976–77	28.16	5.04	10.00	1.68	11.12	12,746
1977–78	30.40	5.27	9.68	1.62	11.52	25,320
1978–79	33.04	5.41	10.32	1.68	12.08	28,340
1979–80	36.72	5.91	10.80	1.52	11.92	43,854

Sources: Annual Survey of Industries, census sector; Harendra K. Dey, "Changes in Real Wages," (unpublished Ph.D. dissertation, Boston University, 1984 (derived from Agricultural Wages in India.); H. L. Chandhok, Wholesale Price Statistics (New Delhi: Economic and Scientific Research Foundation, 1978); Statistical Abstract (New Delhi: Government of India, Ministry of Planning, Department of Statistics, Central Statistical Organization).

APPENDIX
Capital-Labor Regression Equations for Selected Sectors
Dependent variable: $\ln[\ell/k]$

	Intercept	$\ln[\frac{w}{pk}]$	$\ln[\ell/k]_{-1}$	Rho	R^2	No. obs.
Granary Products	−1.519 (73.85)[a]	−1.248 (19.97)		.067 (0.28)	.96	17
Sugar	−2.199 (15.01)	−.804 (2.27)		.453 (2.09)	.21	17
Edible Oils	−.388 (2.03)	−.603 (2.14)	.811 (7.98)	−.275 (1.11)	.93	15
Vanaspati	−.016 (0.03)	−.197 (1.46)	.942 (4.75)	−.271 (1.09)	.64	15
Tea Processing	−2.105 (55.88)	−.503 (2.60)		.576 (2.90)	.26	17
Other Food Prods.	−1.094 (4.75)	−1.302 (4.16)	.367 (2.74)	.177 (0.70)	.91	15
Beverages	−1.291 (3.33)	−.230 (1.66)	.429 (2.71)	.477 (2.10)	.44	15
Tobacco Products	−.157 (2.97)	−.162 (0.94)	.810 (11.81)	−.620 (3.06)	.91	15
Synthetic Text.	−.871 (4.11)	−.307 (0.95)	.578 (4.37)	.022 (0.09)	.83	15
Jute Products	−.852 (7.19)	−.825 (6.35)		.812 (5.74)	.71	17
Woolen Products	−.686 (2.43)	−.570 (1.66)	.521 (3.41)	.356 (1.48)	.53	15
Textile Products	−.636 (2.10)	−.286 (1.63)	.498 (2.25)	.478 (2.11)	.33	15
Wooden Products	−1.484 (43.36)	−1.837 (9.03)		.039 (0.16)	.83	17
Leather Products	.286 (1.60)	−.608 (1.95)	.993 (24.64)	−.350 (1.45)	.98	15
Oil Products	−.681 (1.68)	−.106 (0.65)	.832 (7.95)	−.580 (2.76)	.86	15

Appendix (Continued)

Basic Chemicals	−2.838 (13.10)	−.850 (3.87)		.723 (4.56)	.47	17
Fertilizer	−1.073 (2.18)	−.781 (2.27)	.559 (2.81)	−.020 (0.07)	.96	15
Paints and Dyes	−2.262 (19.19)	−.907 (8.90)		.131 (0.54)	.83	17
Plastics	−2.063 (3.18)	−.139 (0.74)	.413 (1.90)	−.201 (0.79)	.54	15
Pharmaceuticals	−1.832 (9.70)	−.772 (4.96)		.414 (1.87)	.60	17
Other Chemicals	−.920 (3.44)	−.176 (0.87)	.593 (5.88)	−.294 (1.27)	.71	15
Cement	−.254 (0.48)	−.098 (0.36)	.912 (4.85)	.464 (2.03)	.75	15
Nonmet. Min. Prods.	−.966 (2.89)	−.792 (2.65)	.364 (1.74)	.679 (3.58)	.67	15
Steel	−3.108 (14.15)	−.463 (1.95)		.510 (2.44)	.15	17
Nonferrous Metals	−.562 (2.31)	−.115 (0.28)	.819 (5.48)	−.008 (0.03)	.92	15
Metallic Products	−.863 (5.83)	−1.070 (14.04)	.180 (2.67)	.596 (2.88)	.93	15
Agricultural Mach.	−.347 (4.95)	−.257 (0.81)	.786 (7.34)	−.359 (1.49)	.98	15
Nonelec. Mach.	−1.818 (5.75)	−.769 (2.17)		.774 (5.04)	.19	17
Elec. Apparatus	−.954 (4.51)	−.662 (3.06)	.354 (2.49)	.159 (0.62)	.85	15
Miscell. Manuf.	−.147 (0.75)	−.370 (1.22)	.787 (5.85)	−.239 (0.96)	.87	15

[a] T-statistics for a zero null hypothesis are reported in parentheses.

10

Growth, Controls and the Private Sector

Fredie A. Mehta

Every decade seems to search for a solution in the garb of a slogan. In India the slogan during the decade of the 1960s was Growth with Stability; the slogan during the next decade of the 1970s was Growth with Social Justice; the slogan for the decade of the 1980s seems to be Growth with Productivity. It is significant that, during the lifetime of Mrs. Indira Gandhi herself, she proclaimed the year 1982 as the year of National Productivity. It is also necessary to state, right here, that a number of measures in the direction of liberalization were introduced by Mrs. Gandhi's Government on resumption of power in January 1980. This in no way is to belittle the sharp acceleration in the trend towards liberalization that has been brought about by the new Government under Rajiv Gandhi. Indeed, there have been, in the course of the past one and a half years, forty-six packages of liberalization in the areas of trade, taxation and industrial policies.

It is hardly surprising that some degree of reaction has begun to set in in the evaluation of these new policies of liberalization, simplification and rationalization. The critics fall naturally into different brackets. There are those who feel that the liberalization is not proceeding in its actual implementation as fast as it should be, so that the real benefits are not available to the Indian economy as speedily and as substantially as they should. As against this school, there are those who feel that liberalization, even though beneficial in the short run, will not solve India's long-term problems of growing unemployment and (growing!) inequalities of income and wealth. There are those who feel that liberalization by its very nature goes against the grain of Indian Socialism (howsoever defined) and that the modernization of her society, as indeed of her industries, will have the effect of destroying the "left of center" stance which is so essential, in their views, to the political and economic stability of the country. There is also the view that the "opening" of the Indian economy (through liberal imports of products and technologies) strikes a great blow to the cherished goal of "Self-Reliance." The Prime Minister has been accused of carrying India into the twenty-first century in a car built "on imported wheels and imported vision."

Even if we allow for the rhetoric that must creep into political debates of economic issues, it is quite clear that some sort of a reaction against liberalization has set in. Within a period of ten days, three articles appeared by eminent journalists, all arguing the theme in different language and with different emphasis, that liberalization has not increased industrial production, that it has not improved industrial productivity, that it has certainly not increased exports, and that all it has helped are the growing rich of India on the one side, and the multinational corporations (MNCs) operating in India on the other side.

Liberalization, Not Liberalism

One must confess that part of this reaction was due to the euphoria initially generated; even *The Economist,* as late as December 1985, ran a banner headline, proclaiming that the "two billion people [of India and China] are discovering the joys of the market." It is, therefore, necessary to recognize, in India's case at any rate, that liberalization has not meant economic liberalism in the Western (or more accurately, the European) sense of the term. There has been no instant dismantling of Government controls in any area (recall what Margaret Thatcher did to exchange controls in the United Kingdom!); there has been no denationalization of any erstwhile public sector industry; indeed, to date, there has not even been any privatization in the sense of a major profitable Government company spinning off its shareholding to the public at large, as is currently under contemplation in comparable developing countries like Spain and Brazil.

Without, therefore, in any way belittling the concrete efforts and achievements of the present Government, it needs to be said that liberalization has by no means done away with controls in the critical areas of the Indian economy. To be sure, there have been significant exemptions in specific areas; there have been specific industries in which now no licensing and/or no reference to the antimonopoly legislation has been deemed essential; and certainly on the tax front there has been a very substantive reduction, particularly in the area of direct taxation. Simultaneously, in a number of cases the time period for clearances of necessary licenses has been noticeably reduced, and, even more conspicuously, the attitude of the Government in conducting open-house discussions with managers and industrialists has created an overall milieu of confidence among them.

But to say all this is not to mean that controls have been dismantled, lock, stock and barrel; they still remain a very powerful instrument of Government's economic policies. Nor has privatization in the meaningful sense of the term come into existence; all that privatization has meant till now has been an intention on the part of Government to permit private sector entry into specific areas, which till now were considered as the close (and closed) preserve of the State and Central Governments. Significantly, the reason most often cited for this Indian version of privatization is the scarcity of resources of the public sector, not any inherent managerial superiority of the private sector. Again, it would be reading too much into the present situation to proclaim that relations between Government and industry in India have developed a rapport of the intensity which has allegedly been secured by the economies of Japan and of the Republic of Korea. India, Inc., is a distant goal.

The Change in Psychology

What, however, is certainly true is that both Indian and foreign business enterprises in India no longer operate under the intensely emotional and hostile environment which prevailed during most of the decade of the 1970s. The battle cries of "concentration of economic power," "penetration of the Indian economy by the MNCs," and "goals of nationalization" are seldom heard now. Indeed, those who lived in India during this period of the 1970s can scarce believe that the tidal wave of populism that swept Indian society as a whole, and Indian industry in particular, has currently little attraction for the great masses of the Indian people. Even the critics of the present policies of the Government do not invoke these slogans, except in academic journals. The cry against liberalization is on the grounds that it does not readily and speedily deal with the problems of India's poverty, that the overemphasis on technology intensified the severity of India's unemployment problems, and so on.

This type of criticism can be economically challenged, but it cannot be dismissed as emotional, the very fact that the so-called "pro-rich" Union Budget of 1985 was succeeded by an "antipoverty" Budget of 1986 shows that in a democratic society, both humanity and maturity demand an "equilibrium approach"—the Plimsoll line may still be the best line.

The prevailing slogans in India are not ideological—they are managerial. They are those of "efficiency," "productivity," "technological upgrading," "modernization," and so on. Every fourth page in the Seventh Five-Year Plan (1985–90) has a clarion call for improved technology and increased productivity. It seems that while the Prime Minister's message of taking India into the twenty-first century has invited many sarcastic rebuttals, it has had the effect of inviting a debate on securing the specific managerial solutions to the problems of the Indian economy. This managerial mood coincides with the temper of the emergent and enlarging middle class of India, which is no longer prepared to accept uncritically the slogans of the past decade, still less the slogans of the past century.[1]

The Rewards and Penalties of Productivity

The transformation of the Indian economy as now visualized cannot but invite reactions. As we have noted before (rather colloquially), a lady kept in purdah for thirty years cannot on her thirty-first birthday be asked to participate in a discotheque dance. What is not sought is a transformation so substantive that it is doubtful whether the various parties involved have thought through its various ramifications. This transformation entails a transformation

- from an overregulated economy based on a plethora of physical controls to one based on a few strategic controls,
- from a seller's market to a buyer's market,
- from a relatively low technology, low productivity situation to an eventual stage of high technology and high productivity,
- from a highly protected to a relatively internationally open economy.

All these will bring rich rewards to the Indian economy in the long run. Of this, there should be no doubt.

However, the transitional period, if there is to be no major retreat, must bring certain dislocations and discontinuities. Of this also, there should be no doubt. The injection of new technologies, the introduction of new products and processes, the induction of the risks and benefits of world trade into a relatively protected economy—all these must involve stresses and strains to any economy.

The restructuring of Indian industry—a phrase much in vogue—will, very wisely, not be done at one stroke but in stages. Apart from the legacy of the past, there are in the Indian economic society too many competitive goals to satisfy, the achievement of one goal negating in the short run the achievement of other goals. More specifically, there are a number of old industries about to be overtaken by new technologies and new products; the jute industry is now facing a challenge from the burgeoning petrochemical industries, now not from outside India but from inside India. The erstwhile electrical and mechanical industries are in several areas being short-circuited by the upsurge of industrial electronics.

Again, as it is, Indian industry, and far more so, India's infrastructural industries, are heavily overmanned and yet, in many cases, also heavily capitalized. They have become over the years both labor intensive and capital intensive; and they operate at 55 percent to 75 percent of their installed capacities. If we forget the problem of absorbing new employment seekers (can we afford to forget?), substantial increases in output can be secured with practically the same labor force, and in a number of cases with only marginal additions to capital inputs.

Keynes noted in an oft-quoted sentence that in the long run we are all dead. In a depression-plagued economy, nothing could have been truer; in an economy making a crucial transition of the type India says she wishes to make, we are alive in the long run with the promise of new jobs, through new industries and new technologies. It is in the short run, that we must face the penalties of productivity, the convulsions of change, the travails of transition.

This is where the recent reactions to the policies of liberalization assume significance. This is because liberalization, competition and technology are considered the three principal instruments of the new economic policy. That each of these may carry penalties, particularly in the short run, is no reason why they should be abandoned easily. It can only mean that in order to avoid a quick backlash, the policy of "hastening slowly" should be adopted. The problems of managing change are with us—with a vengeance.

Welcome Reversal in Rates of Industrial Investment

No one single factor explains the prevalence of a prolonged economic trend, and, therefore, we shall be very careful in asserting that the enormous multiplication of controls during the decade of the 1970s in several areas, but particularly in the area of the legislation pertaining to the Monopolies and Restrictive Trade Practices Act (MRTP) and the Foreign Exchange Regulation Act (FERA), have been the principal cause of the tardy growth of industrial investment and production during this period. However, even those who were then at the helm of economic affairs now concede that there is a considerable correlation to be established between the substantive increases in controls and regulations during this decade and the sharply deteriorating rates of growth in industrial investments in the first place, followed by a deceleration in the rates of growth of industrial production.

It would be easy in this area to cite a wealth of evidence from the works on industrial production and productivity of P. R. Brahmananda and I. J. Ahluwalia. Thus, regarding industrial production, the following summation needs recall:

> The overall picture that emerges is one of industrial stagnation in the organized sector after the mid-sixties. Heavy industries, e.g. machinery, transport equipment and basic metals, suffered a major slowdown in growth, while light industries such as food manufacturing and textiles, never experienced a take-off. Analyses of growth of value added and value of output at different levels of disaggregation confirm the presence of this dual phenomenon of deceleration and slow growth.[2]

A major contributory factor was the phenomenon of declining real fixed investments:

> Public real fixed capital formation decelerated from an average annual growth rate of 10 percent between 1956–57 and 1966–67, to 5.8 percent between 1967–68 and 1979–80, while infrastructure investment fell from an annual growth rate of approximately 17 percent in the first half of the 1960s, to an annual growth rate of 2 percent in the next decade. In the same time period, private real fixed capital formation growth also decelerated from 8.2 percent to 2.8 percent.[3]

The declining rates of investments were bad enough; what made their economic impact far worse was the trend, by now conclusively established, of low productivity revealed by a steadily rising capital:output ratio.

By contrast, we now have a situation in which there has been a conspicuous spurt in the capital formation of the private corporate sector; indeed the Seventh Five-Year Plan has placed the annual rate of growth from 1980–81 to 1984–85 in the fixed real capital formation of the private sector industry at no less than 16 percent. In fact, an expert estimate has placed the Gross Capital Formation of the private corporate sector in real terms to have been 17 percent higher than the target set for it by the Sixth Plan (1980–85).[4]

We believe that this picture of a marked turnaround in industrial investments has further improved in the last two years as evidenced by the intensified boom on the stock markets and the sharp increase in the number of new companies floated during the last two years. Significantly, the known investment programs of the major private sector companies are already running into over Rs 22,000 crores[5]; in one industrial house alone which invested (or was permitted to invest) less than Rs 500 crores during the decade of the 1970s, the investment in diversification/expansion/modernization will in all probability be over Rs 5,000 crores during this decade.

It is, therefore, not a small achievement that in this decade of the 1980s we have begun to witness a sharp (and one hopes, a sustained) reversal in the low rates of growth in industrial investment which we experienced during the fifteen years 1965–66 to 1980–81. It is too early to say whether there has been a proportionate improvement in the productivity of invested capital, though there is some evidence of a slight decline in the capital to output ratio of Indian industry in recent years. What can be stated with some degree of confidence is that the investment famine of the 1970s in the private corporate sector has been converted, with the new climate of liberalization, into a veritable flood of investment.

The Beginning of a Reversal in Rates of Industrial Production

While there is abundant statistical proof of a spectacular reversal in the investment climate, current statistics do not seem to suggest correspondingly a noticeable acceleration in the rate of growth of industrial production. Even so, it is significant that the current annual rate of growth of industrial production during the first five years of the decade of the 1980s at 6 percent is higher than the annual rate of 4.3 percent secured during the decade of the 1970s. This is not a small jump, it is indeed an acceleration of almost 40 percent. This rate of 6 percent is still below that of 7 percent targeted for the Sixth Plan and of 8 percent for the Seventh Plan; and certainly in relation to the sharp step-up in the annual rate of investment, this production growth is perhaps not commensurate.

One, however, has to bear in mind that the current Series of Industrial Production does not take into account the entry of a substantial range of new products, particularly in the area of petrochemicals and electronics; for another thing, it does not include the very sizable increases scored by the small-scale sector industry in a number of areas. It needs to be recalled that nearly half of the total gross value of industrial production of India emanates from the small-scale sector, and indeed in several consumer items like cotton and blended textiles, soaps, matches, detergents, radios, television sets, vegetable oils, etc., the small-scale sector, *in terms of volume of production,* is far ahead of the organized industrial sector. The

New Series of Industrial Production will show that the actual rate has been even higher than that indicated.

However, it does not require any specific economic perception to recognize that in a number of core products like cement and fertilizers, India has already achieved spectacular growth. Far more significantly, India is poised for a very major breakthrough in several areas, so much so that the fears of a glut have already been expressed by a number of businessmen and the managers in private sector industry.

Due to the introduction of a liberalized industrial licensing policy in the early 1980s, combined in the case of core products like steel, cement and fertilizers with a liberalized pricing system, private sector investments began to be made almost simultaneously by a number of firms in a wide range of industrial products. While the existing units began to move in the direction of modernization and expansion, a number of new units entered simultaneously the same field. The problem of bunching of investments in one specific industry has occurred in the past, but Indian industry witnessed in the early 1980s an unusual phenomenon of the bunching of massive investments made simultaneously in a wide range of industrial products.

Nowhere is this better illustrated than in the case of cement industry, which during the decade of the 1970s could not invite investments due to the rigid price controls, and, therefore, could secure in the whole decade of the 1970s an increase in production of only 5.5 million metric tons. Once there was a partial decontrol in the pricing of cement, what was a trickle of investment turned into a flood. A number of companies have, in their diversification programs, already entered into the cement industry, while the existing companies have begun a program of modernization with expansion. The result has been that cement production, which was a little less than 20 million metric tons in 1980–81, will, by the end of 1986, touch nearly 38 million metric tons. The current annual rate of growth is about 5 million metric tons, which is only slightly less than the total increase in production during the decade of the 1970s. In fact, fears have been expressed that by the end of next year, unless "saved" by the power shortage, the cement industry may be heading for a production of anything between 45 and 48 million metric tons.

What is true of cement is also true, or about to be true, of another core industry, viz, the fertilizer industry, in which the private corporate sector is committed to an additional investment in the next three years along with about Rs 4,100 crores. In one major industry after another, we are therefore about to witness a sharp, if not steep, increase in the next two years—cement, fertilizer, synthetic fibers, petrochemicals, cars, two-wheelers, electronics and the telecommunication industry.

Significantly, the substantial black market premia that used to be a common phenomenon during the decade of the 1970s in the core products—steel, cement, alkali chemicals, commercial vehicles, paper, synthetic fibers, etc.—have virtually disappeared. It is also ironical to note that as late as November 1984, Jha, in his Foreword to Ahluwalia's book *Industrial Growth in India*, had stated: "As for demand, it is clearly outstripping supply. For a wide range of industrial products such as scooters, passenger cars and trucks, many producers have a long queue of customers who have made advance deposits and have to wait for years to get delivery."[6] Within less than two years the situation has so radically transformed and indeed will transform even further, that not only in the above-mentioned products but in many more, supply will clearly outstrip the demand.

We believe, therefore, that it is only a question of time before the massive investments made by the private corporate sector will translate themselves into a major upsurge in production. Indeed, due to the substantive bunching of investments in several industries made during the last four years, conditions of glut (with savage competition) will soon come to prevail. In a few cases exports may come to the rescue, but in most cases a tough and trying supply-demand imbalance is likely. The logical result of a liberalized licensing policy is the promotion of competition. Those who have proclaimed their faith in liberalization must not now run away from the battlefield of competition.

The Demands of Modernization

While, therefore, we have clear evidence of an upsurge in industrial investment and of a discernible rise in industrial production, there is one gap we need to fill. We believe, though without the benefit of accurate statistics, that anything between 20 percent to 25 percent of the substantial annual capital expenditure of private corporate sector industry is geared towards modernization. This increases the capital investment made, but it increases only slightly the output. Hence, one important reason why the massive investments made are not resulting in increased production lies in the demands of modernization.

Modernization beginning in a very slow way in the late 1970s has not started to account for a large part of the capital expenditure in Indian industries—cotton textiles, sugar, cement, steel and engineering industries. In the biggest private sector steel plant of India the program of modernization alone will absorb something like Rs 2,200 crores. In the cement industry, including the sanctions for modernization already made by the public sector financial institutions, the modernization expenditure will be close to Rs 500 crores. For the textile industry, a special modernization fund of Rs 750 crores has just been instituted by the Industrial Development Bank.

The reason why these programs of modernization have been rendered compulsive lies in the fact that in industry after industry the regime of price controls and industrial licensing (combined with differential excises in some cases) left too low a margin of profits to permit effective modernization, a situation which was further worsened by the fact that normal provision for depreciation did not take into account the demands of replacement costs. Major Indian industries presented a picture of obsolescence, so that it could be said with a slight degree of exaggeration that in several industries of India, there has taken place since 1965–66 an accumulated obsolescence in capital equipment, in technology and in skills.

Modernization programs have show a fair success in raising productivity (and in reducing energy inputs) per unit of output, but they are basically not designed (in most cases, not permitted to) increase output markedly. Hence, one reason why the incremental capital:output ratio of Indian industry is still high, certainly by international standards, lies in the fact that only 70–75 percent of the capital inputs are geared to securing increased output. Yet modernization represents a capital expenditure which Indian industry must incur; with it, output may not increase appreciably—without it, it may perhaps have decreased markedly.

Liberalization Regarding the World Economy

The slow and steady wave of liberalization which began in the early 1980s covered right from its very beginning a corresponding liberalization in the area of trade and technology. At a time when several countries of the world have begun to look to protectionism for salvation, India has opened her economy to substantial imports of both foreign goods and foreign technology.

This is amply revealed by the fact that the nonoil imports of India have risen significantly from Rs 7,280 crores in 1980–81 to Rs 13,670 crores in 1985–86, an increase of 87.7 percent. Noticeably, the imports of capital goods have nearly doubled from Rs 1,820 crores to Rs 3,600 crores. Indeed, it has been, to a large extent, due to what is dubbed the "indiscriminate" imports of capital machinery from abroad. India has been continuously running balance-of-trade deficits of a major order with almost all the industrialized countries of the world, and this has now become a critical issue for calling upon these countries to open their gates to the entry of Indian products.

Likewise, in a significant move away from self-reliance the number of technical and financial collaborations sanctioned has risen sharply from 526 in 1980 to 1,024 in 1985. Predictably, the financial agreements are a relatively small part of the total collaborations, but even so, there has been a sizable increase in the annual flow of direct foreign investment from Rs 89 million in 1980 to Rs 1,259 million in 1985.

Once again, as in the case of other areas of liberalization, there has been a strong emotional reaction against the indiscriminate import of foreign technology on the grounds that it discourages the development of indigenous research and development efforts. The truth is that the whole question of liberalization of trade, technology and finance has several facets which defy a straightforward and simple answer. Each case needs to be treated on its own merits and, by and large, this is what the Government is doing.

Nevertheless, it is the strong contention of this writer that once India has established its priority list regarding the imports of foreign technology, the existing period of the technical collaboration agreements needs to be extended not grudgingly, but more liberally, from the current period of five years to about seven to ten years. Likewise, the quantum of technical fees and of royalties needs to be made more liberal if India has to do the leapfrogging that is now considered so essential to the transformation of the Indian economy. Incidentally, in our view the development of Indian R&D need not axiomatically be taken to be adversely affected by the imports of foreign technology; several cases can be shown of how once foreign technology is imported and rubbed into Indian industry, the latter can proceed to find the necessary adaptation and reorientation in the technology to suit Indian conditions.

Conclusions

It is clear then that for Indian industry not only is there no escape from the triple requirements of competition, technology and liberalization, but there are positive benefits which have already begun to accrue. We have no doubt whatsoever that the decade of the 1980s, with its emphasis on the slow and steady process of liberalization, will show a performance in terms of production, productivity and investments in Indian industry of a type distinctly better than that achieved in the decade of the 1970s.

This does not mean that more should not be done, but bearing in mind the claims of a democratic society, the legacies of the last three decades of development and the mental attitudes so formed, it would be prudent to continue to make these movements in slow and steady measures. To ask for a gigantic leap amounting to a U-turn, would be neither wise nor humane. For the last century, we have talked of Fabian Socialism; for India, it is perhaps necessary now to proceed with Fabian Liberalism.

One has an unhappy feeling, which could be wrongly perceived, that the people of India need to be emotionally groomed to understand both the rewards and the penalties of competition, productivity and technology. That a sophisticated middle class feels at home in this culture of competition cannot be taken to mean that the whole of India is ready to face the type of convulsions which the advanced countries of the world have undergone during the last fifteen years. Everyone seems to be agreed on the benefits of competition, provided it takes place outside his industry; everybody wishes as a consumer to reap the full benefits of competition in the shape of lower prices, better-quality products and shorter delivery dates. The problem arises only when competition forces the exit of an industrial unit. Then neither the Indian Government, nor the Indian private sector, nor the Indian trade union is capable of understanding the true mechanics of competition—its process of "creative destruction." That is why certain obvious contradictions are now making themselves evident in the actual implementation of the policies of liberalization and in the introduction of the mechanism of competition.

Notes

1. It is an interesting and ironical reversal of roles that the most conspicuous attack on most public sector firms comes currently from Cabinet Ministers and the most devastating attack on some private sector firms comes from sources dedicated to free enterprise. The public sector companies are assailed for their low productivity and low profits by the apostles of socialism; the private sector firms are attacked for their dishonesty by the champions of free enterprise.

2. Isher J. Ahluwalia, *Industrial Growth in India* (New Delhi: Oxford University Press, 1985), 7.

3. "India: An Economic Survey" (Prepared for Merrill Lynch by Paul Levy, March 1986), 8.

4. *Economic Outlook* (New Delhi: Center for Monitoring Indian Economy, June 1986), 97.

5. Rs 1 crore = Rs 10 million.

6. Ahluwalia, *Industrial Growth in India.*

PART FIVE

Exports and Foreign Borrowing

11

India's Export Performance, 1970–85: Underlying Factors and Constraints

Deepak Nayyar

The balance-of-payments adjustment in response to the first round of oil price increases, during the mid-1970s, was unexpectedly smooth in India. It was based on a larger inflow of external resources, a dramatic increase in net invisibles other than transfer payments, a phenomenal growth in remittances and, above all, a management of the balance-of-trade situation which transformed a large deficit into a modest surplus within three years.[1] Many of the underlying factors were policy induced although some, which were important, were exogenous. These developments in the external sector of the economy should be viewed in the context of the deflationary package of macroeconomic policies which was adopted at the same time. In retrospect it is clear that our policy response to the crisis was excessively concerned with correcting the payments deficit and preempting the possibilities of inflation in the short run.[2] Levels of output and investment remained low, while little attention was paid to the impact of overall economic performance on the balance of payments.

It is therefore not surprising that the adjustment process has turned out to be much more difficult, in the early 1980s, following the second round of oil price increases. What is more, the factors which had a favorable influence on the balance of payments the first time around waned in their impact. For one thing, there was a substantial squeeze on foreign aid programs which led to an increasing reliance on expensive commercial borrowing in international capital markets. For another, there was a sharp and continuous decline in net invisibles (excluding transfer payments) while there was a marked deceleration in the growth in

For comments on an earlier draft, I would like to thank Krishna Bharadwaj, Nirmal Chandra, Ashok Mitra, Prabhat Patnaik, S. K. Rao and the participants in the discussion at the Conference in Boston. I am particularly grateful to Abhijit Sen for helpful discussion and valuable suggestions.

remittances. And above all, the balance-of-trade deficit which reached a peak level of more than U.S. $7 billion in 1980–81, remained in the range of $5–6 billion throughout the subsequent years, and climbed back to a level of more than $7 billion in 1985–86.[3]

The present balance-of-payments scenario is difficult but manageable, although it has meant an increasing resort to commercial borrowing in international capital markets and now somewhat more expensive private capital inflows originating from nonresident Indians. The situation is likely to get much worse in the late 1980s. There is a further squeeze on bilateral, as also multilateral, concessional aid flows. The surplus on net invisibles other than transfer payments has all but disappeared and is likely to emerge as an increasing deficit as the burden of debt servicing mounts. It would be well nigh impossible to sustain the present level of remittances which are bound to decline with the economic slump in the oil-exporting countries of the Middle East.

The option that remains is to manage the balance of trade, that is, step up exports or curb imports, or ensure that exports increase faster than imports. There is some room for maneuver in terms of trimming the import bill which has burgeoned at least partly as a consequence of import liberalization. The scope for such economies is significant in the short run but limited in the long run, and, beyond a point, curbs on the growth in imports would also curb investment, thereby leading to a sacrifice in terms of output. Hence, exports, which create the capacity to import, are essential to sustain the growth process in the economy. But that is not all. It is imperative that foreign exchange earnings derived from increased exports should finance the payments deficit as far as possible, if India is to keep the size of its external debt and the burden of debt servicing within manageable proportions. The other alternative of a macroeconomic squeeze, often advocated as part of a typical International Monetary Fund (IMF) package of policies, would not only impose excessive social costs in terms of output, income and employment but would also be myopic in its search for external balance at the cost of economic growth.

The preceding paragraphs situate the subject of the chapter in its wider context and highlight the role of exports at the present juncture. The object of this chapter is a limited one. It attempts to evaluate India's export performance in the recent past, examine the underlying factors and assess the relative importance of domestic and foreign constraints. The first section provides a brief assessment of export performance in retrospect. The second section outlines the trends in exports since 1970 and explores the factors underlying the export performance at a macrolevel; in doing so, it makes a distinction between external and internal factors. The third section sketches a profile of the regime of export promotion policies to examine its impact on exports. The fourth section analyzes the foreign and the domestic constraints on export performance in an endeavor to answer the question: What ails Indian exports?

An Assessment of Export Performance

The first decade of planned economic development in India witnessed a stagnation in export earnings during the 1950s. India's export performance during the 1960s constituted a distinct improvement as exports registered a growth of a little more than 4 percent per annum in terms of both value and volume. Over these two decades, however, there was a phenomenal expansion in world trade, which meant that India's share in world export declined continuously throughout the period from about 2 percent in 1950 to 1 percent in 1960 and 0.65 percent in 1970.[4] During the 1970s India's export performance was clearly better than in the earlier decades as the average growth in exports reached a level of more than 6 percent per annum in terms of volume and nearly 16 percent per annum in terms of value. Yet, India's share in world exports continued to decline and, despite a period of stability in the mid-1970s, dropped to its lowest level of 0.42 percent in 1980.[5] A significant proportion, but not all, of this decline was attributable to the increased value of world trade in fuels.[6] Although there has been a marked deceleration in the rate of export growth since 1980, it is worth noting that India has managed to maintain, even marginally recover, her share in world exports during the first half of the 1980s, at a level somewhat less than 0.5 percent, perhaps because of the near stagnation in international trade flows.

In contrast with the earlier period, it is rather difficult to interpr the trends in exports since 1970 for two reasons. First, there was a sharp acceleration in the rates of inflation and, second, the world economy moved from a system of fixed exchange rates to a regime of floating exchange rates. Therefore, data on the value of exports in terms of current prices, at current exchange rates, are somewhat deceptive. In an attempt to resolve this problem, Table 11.1 outlines the trends in exports since 1970 not simply in terms of current rupee values but also in terms of the foreign exchange value measured in terms of U.S. dollars and in terms of special drawing rights (SDRs); the latter is perhaps a better numeraire. The data on the trend in the volume index, as also the average unit value index of exports, since 1970 are presented in Table 11.2. To facilitate a comparison, the trends in the dollar value, the SDR value and the volume index of Indian exports are outlined in Figure 11.1.

At an aggregate level, India's export performance during the period under review reveals two discernible phases in terms of growth. Any temporal line drawn in this manner is always likely to be arbitrary, but the trends outlined in Table 11.1 and Figure 11.1 suggest that 1977–78 represents a watershed. Hence, it is useful to divide the span of fifteen years into two subperiods: 1970–71 to 1977–78 and 1977–78 to 1984–85. A computation of average annual rates of growth, the results of which are set out in Table 11.3, confirms the sharp decleration in export growth whether measured in terms of the rupee value, the dollar value, the SDR value or the volume index. It appears that the average annual rate of growth in exports during 1977–78 to 1984–85 was half of what it was

during 1970–71 to 1977–78. In retrospect, it would seem that the unprecedented export growth in the period until 1977–78 represents a
departure from, whereas the export growth thereafter broadly conforms
to, the earlier trend in exports.

The picture of decleration in export growth would be far more
pronounced if 1985–86 is taken as the end point in this exercise, for it
witnessed an absolute decline in exports over the preceding year as exports
of crude oil dropped very sharply on account of the development of
refining capacity for Bombay High crude within India. In order to place
India's export performance in perspective, it would be more appropriate
to consider the trend in nonoil exports during the 1980s. Exports of
crude oil registered a spectacular growth starting in 1981–82 because of
a mismatch between domestic production and domestic refining capacity.
This was associated with swaps in the world market and matching imports
of crude oil and petroleum products. It was obviously a transient phenomenon which could not provide a sustained basis for export growth
and, as expected, 1985–86 witnessed a slump in oil exports. Table 11.4,
which outlines the trend in exports, excluding crude oil and petroleum
products, since 1980–81, shows that there was a near stagnation in the
dollar value of nonoil exports (partly attributable to the appreciation of
the U.S. dollar), whereas the growth in the SDR value as also the rupee
value of nonoil exports was much less than the growth in the corresponding
figures for total exports. It would, therefore, be reasonable to infer that
the figures in Table 11.3 possibly underestimate the de facto deceleration
in export growth during the period since 1977–78.

On balance, there can be little doubt that India's export performance
since 1970 has been distinctly better than it was in the preceding decades.
At the same time, it is clear that this performance is simply not enough
when considered in relation to the needs of the economy and indeed
poor when placed in the international context.

The evidence presented in Table 11.5 shows that, except for a brief
period in the early 1970s, export performance was on the whole adequate
until 1977–78 when we consider it in the context of the import bill, the
current account deficit in the balance of payments and the burden of
debt servicing. Since then, there has been a steady deterioration as the
capacity of export earnings to finance the import bill has been in the
range of 25 percent ever since 1980–81 and reached a high level of 45
percent in 1985–86. The burden of debt servicing in relation to export
earnings has been manageable during the early 1980s, but it provides
cause for concern at almost 30 percent in 1985–86 particularly as it is
likely to rise further.

Table 11.6 compares India's export performance since 1970 with that
of Argentina, Brazil, China, Hong Kong, Malaysia, Mexico and South
Korea. This group includes not only the East Asian newly industrialized
countries (NICs) but also the large semi-industrialized economies of Latin
America and the continental economy of China. The figures in the table
tell a sad story. In 1970 India's exports of approximately $2 billion were
only slightly lower than the exports of Brazil, China and Hong Kong but
significantly higher than the exports of the others. The disparity in the

export performance of these countries did increase thereafter but was not so large until the mid-1970s. By the mid-1980s, apart from Argentina whose export performance was roughly at par with that of India, the other countries had forged way ahead and, by 1984, the dollar value of their exports was at least double, indeed in most cases nearly treble, the level of exports attained by India. It may be argued that the small East Asian economies, such as Hong Kong and South Korea, are somewhat special, or that exports of crude oil and petroleum products are responsible for the export performance of Mexico and, to a lesser extent, of China, or that the export performance of Brazil has been coaxed by the debt burden squeeze, but none of this can take away from the fact that India's export performance, when placed in the international context, is poor indeed.

An Analysis of Export Trends Since 1970

The evidence presented in the preceding discussion revealed that, during 1970–71 to 1977–78, the average annual rate of growth in export earnings was 20.3 percent in terms of rupee values, 17.8 percent in terms of dollar values and 15.3 percent in terms of SDR values, as compared with 11.0 percent, 6.1 percent and 9.4 percent respectively during 1977–78 to 1984–85. The rapid export growth in the first period was attributable to a very significant increase in the volume of exports (58 percent) and an even greater increase in the unit value of exports (122 percent) between 1970–71 and 1977–78. This is confirmed by the data in Table 11.2 which outlines the trend in the volume index and the unit value index of exports. Unfortunately, the data on index numbers are available only until 1983–84. All the same, it is clear that the sharp deceleration in export growth in the second period was, almost as an analogue, attributable to a much smaller increase in the volume of exports (30 percent) and a marked slowdown of the increase in the unit value of exports (68 percent) between 1977–78 and 1984–85.[7]

The discussion so far has confined itself to an aggregate view. Let me now consider how these overall trends relate to export performance at a disaggregated level in terms of values, volumes and composition.

Table 11.7 outlines the movements in the rupee value of India's principal exports which, taken together, accounted for more than 80 percent of total export earnings, throughout the period under review. It reveals that the trends were rather complex and export performance varied significantly from sector to sector. Nevertheless, a careful examination of the data reveals the following categories of exports: (1) rapid and continuous growth throughout: fruits and vegetables, iron ore, chemicals and allied products, gems and jewelery, carpets and clothing; (2) steady growth until circa 1980, with occasional spurts, but stagnation or decline thereafter: marine products, leather and leather manufactures, handicrafts, metal manufactures and machinery and transport equipment; (3) rapid growth until 1977–78 and near stagnation thereafter: tea, coffee, tobacco, cashew kernels and spices[8]; (4) periods of growth interspersed with periods of stagnation: jute manufactures and cotton textiles (the former characterized by sharp fluctuations while the latter reveals a discernible upward trend); (5) sharp fluctuations with no trend whatever: sugar, rice, oil cakes, raw cotton, iron and steel and, for want of a better category, crude oil and petroleum products, most of which can perhaps be characterized as fair-weather exports that did, in their respective peak years, make a significant contribution to the growth in exports.

These trends in the rupee value of principal exports in current prices and at current exchange rates may be deceptive because of the inflation and the depreciation implicit in the figures. In an attempt to circumvent this problem, Table 11.8 presents the available evidence on the trends in the volume of exports, since 1970, in terms of index numbers for commodity groups at the Standard International Trade Classification (SITC) one-digit level. It reveals much clearer trends: (1) a rapid volume growth in exports of primary commodities (SITC 0–2 and 4) until 1976–77 and stagnation or decline thereafter; (2) a moderate volume growth in exports of domestic resource-based manufactures (SITC 6) until 1977–78, concentrated mostly in the mid-1970s, with stagnation followed by decline thereafter; (3) a steady volume growth in exports of chemicals and allied products (SITC 5), miscellaneous manufactured articles (SITC 8) and, to a lesser extent, machinery and transport equipment (SITC 7) throughout the period under review but, except for chemicals, slackening in the 1980s; and (4) a dramatic volume growth in exports of fuels during the early 1980s.

Table 11.9, which outlines the percentage contribution of the commodity groups (at the SITC one-digit level) in total export earnings, reflects the trends described above. The share of primary commodities in total exports declined from 47 percent in 1970–71 to 41 percent in 1977–78, mostly on account of the drop in the share of raw materials; it stayed at this level until 1980–81 but returned to its earlier level of 47 percent in 1984–85 as the share of fuels rose to 15 percent. The share of manufactures in total exports registered a corresponding increase from 53 percent in 1970–71 to 59 percent in 1977–78, thus sustaining the rapid growth in exports during the period; it stayed at this level until 1980–81, but dropped to 53 percent again in 1984–85. There can be little doubt, however, that there was a steady increase in the share of manufactures in nonfuel exports. More important, perhaps, there was a discernible change in the composition of manufactured exports.

In the period 1970–71 to 1977–78, the share of resource-based manufactures (SITC 6) in total exports remained stable at around 40 percent but declined thereafter to a level of about 30 percent by 1984–85, which means that the growth in these traditional exports of manufactures did not even keep pace with the much slower growth in total exports during 1977–78 to 1984–85.[9] In sharp contrast, the contribution of miscellaneous manufactured articles (SITC 8) to export earnings registered a continuous increase throughout the period under review from 5 percent in 1970–71 to more than 12 percent in 1984–85.[10] The share of machinery and transport equipment (SITC 7) in total exports also increased from about 5 percent in 1970–71 to nearly 8 percent in 1980–81 but declined thereafter as these exports experienced a stagnation in value and a decline in volume.

The steady growth in exports of chemicals (SITC 5), in terms of both value and volume, meant an increase in their relative share particularly after 1977–78 as the growth in total exports slowed down.

What were the factors underlying these trends in exports? Given the diverse commodity composition, it is obvious that a complete analysis of export performance should be based on a systematic study of the underlying factors at a disaggregated level. Such an approach, however, would require more than an essay and is beyond the scope of the present exercise. Instead, I shall attempt to provide a brief explanation of India's export performance during the period under review, at a macro level, making a distinction between external factors and domestic factors.

Consider, first, the period of rapid growth in exports from 1970–71 to 1977–78. In my view, there were three sets of external factors which had a very significant favorable impact on export performance during these years. First, there was a remarkable expansion in world trade, which was associated with an increase in world import demand for most of India's exportables. Second, there was a boom in the prices of primary commodities, which led to a sharp increase in average unit values realized for exports. Third, the oil price increases led to the emergence of new markets in the oil-exporting countries which constituted a net addition, and, in response, the share of the Organization of Oil-Exporting Countries (OPEC) in India's total exports rose from about 6 percent in the early 1970s to more than 17 percent in 1977–78,[11] representing, in one sense, a recycling of petrodollars.

These external developments coincided with a set of domestic factors within the economy which also provided a boost to exports. Beginning in 1974, while the world economy experienced high rates of inflation, domestic prices in India registered relatively little increase. This was, to a significant extent, the result of a few good harvests and an improved performance of the agricultural sector, but it was also a consequence of the macroeconomic squeeze in the mid-1970s arising out of a concern about the balance-of-payments deficit and the fear of inflation. The differential rates of inflation meant that the unit value index for exports rose much faster than the domestic wholesale price index, whether for primary commodities or manufactured goods, during 1970–71 to 1977–78, although the difference was far more pronounced after 1974–75.[12] There can be little doubt that this improved the relative profitability of exports.

Over the same period, starting in 1970, there was a steady depreciation in the exchange value of the rupee, brought out clearly by Figure 11.2, in terms of both the U.S. dollar and the SDR. The data in Table 11.10 show that this yielded a continuous depreciation in the nominal effective exchange rate (NEER) of the rupee throughout the 1970s.[13] Given the lower rate of inflation at home as compared to the outside world, this also meant a sharp downward movement in the real effective exchange rate (REER) of the rupee from 1974 to 1979, once again reflecting the improved relative profitability of exports. The trends in the nominal and real effective exchange rate are highlighted in Figure 11.3. While the depreciation of the rupee was a contributory factor, it is worth noting that the turning points in export performance, whether acceleration or deceleration, did not quite follow the lead of movements in the exchange rate.

The rapid growth in exports was concentrated in the quinquennium 1972–73 to 1977–78, where the volume index for exports peaked in 1976–77, while the unit value index for exports peaked in 1977–78. The growth in exports of primary commodities was a consequence of the growth in agricultural output, an adverse movement in the intersectoral terms of trade at home, and the sharp rise in world prices. The growth in exports of manufactured goods, on the other hand, was a consequence of sluggish domestic demand and the persistent quasi-stagnation in the industrial sector, which made export sales an attractive proposition at the margin[14] when combined with the higher relative profitability of exports.

It would seem, therefore, that the impressive growth in exports until 1977–78 was attributable to an unusual combination of external and internal factors. What accounts for the deceleration in export growth since then? In my view, the changed situation in the sphere of external factors constitutes an important part of the explanation. The rapid expansion in world exports continued through the late 1970s, but the first half of the the 1980s witnessed a near stagnation in international trade flows. In sharp contrast with the earlier phase, there was also a discernible softening of commodity prices in world markets. At the same time, the economic expansion in the oil-exporting countries slowed down during the 1980s, and the recent slump in oil prices is likely to have serious consequences.[15] It would not be surprising if these developments in the world economy, taken together, had an unfavorable impact on India's export performance in the later phase, particularly in the period since 1980.

As we know, however, the turning point in export trends came earlier, during the late 1970s, the explanation for which is to be found in the realm of domestic factors. For one thing, the rate of growth of agricultural production dropped sharply after 1977–78, and it showed signs of revival only as late as 1983–84, which possibly accounts for the stagnation or decline in the volume of exports of primary commodities as also domestic resource-based manufactures. For another, there was a revival in the levels of investment and output in the industrial sector, particularly in manufacturing, which began in the late 1970s and picked up further in the early 1980s. The consequential increase in the domestic demand for industrial goods probably meant that, for individual firms, manufactured exports as a means of recovering variable-costs-plus were no longer as worthwhile as in the earlier period of recession. This is perhaps borne out by the fact that, except for chemicals, the growth in manufactured exports was sustained only through products such as gems and jewelery where the entire output is exported, or clothing, carpets and handicrafts where production for the export market is, for all practical purposes, separated from production for the home market. Apropos domestic factors, the story about the turning point in export performance is complete once we note that the remarkable price stability of the mid-1970s gave way to substantial price increases in 1979–80 and 1980–81 whereafter the inflation rate became moderate. At the same time, however, inflation in the world economy had dropped to much lower levels. Consequently, there was an erosion in the relative profitability of exports as compared with the earlier phase of domestic price stability and rapid export growth. Thus, the slowdown in export growth, which began with these internal factors in the late 1970s, persisted in the 1980s as the adverse impact of external factors also came into operation.

The Impact of Export Promotion

The regime of export promotion policies in India performs two basic roles: First, it seeks to provide compensation for disincentives implicit in domestic economic policies and, second, it attempts to provide an incentive for products and market development. Its principal components are the duty drawback system, cash compensatory support, an interest subsidy on export credit, fiscal concessions on exports, and the import policy for exports. It would mean too much a digression to enter into an analysis of the regime and its impact on export performance, particularly as it has been discussed at length elsewhere.[16] For our purpose in this chapter, it would suffice to sketch a profile and highlight rough orders of magnitude so as to examine how the policy framework influenced export trends since 1970.

(1) The duty drawback system endeavors to reimburse exporters for tariffs paid on imported raw materials or intermediates and central excise duties paid on domestic inputs that enter into export production. While we do not have data on the actual value of exports eligible for it, the duty drawback disbursed, on an average, amounted to approximately 2.4 percent of the free on board (FOB) value of total exports over the period 1973–74 to 1981–82, but this proportion dropped to a level of about 1.4 percent in the subsequent years of the early 1980s[17] as the import policy enlarged the access to duty-free imports for export production.

(2) Cash compensatory support (CCS) is a phase used to describe cash assistance, in effect a subsidy, specified as a proportion of the FOB value of exports for selected products. It has been estimated that two-thirds to three-fourths of CCS is simply a compensation for unrebated indirect taxes which are not reimbursed through the duty drawback system, while the rest of it is an incentive for product and market development.[18] The proportion of total exports eligible for CCS rose from about 20 percent in the early 1970s to a little more than 40 percent in the early 1980s. The rates of CCS, as a proportion of the FOB value of exports, for most of the eligible commodity groups ranged from 5 percent to 15 percent.[19] On an average, the total CCS disbursed, during the period 1974–75 to 1983–84, added up to approximately 12 percent of the FOB value of exports eligible for it; over the same period, as shown in Table 11.11, the total CCS disbursed amounted to about 5 percent of the FOB value of total exports.

(3) In keeping with the practice in most other countries of the world, export credit is made available at a concessional interest rate. During the period under review, the commercial banking system provided preshipment and postshipment credit for 90 and 180 days respectively, at a concessional

rate of 12 percent per annum, for which it received an interest subsidy from the Government at the rate of 1.5 percent per annum;[20] of course, a part of the cost was also borne by commercial banks in terms of interest forgone. The total resource cost of subsidizing export credit, hence the implicit benefit for the export sector, was the equivalent of 0.5 percent of the FOB value of total exports.[21]

(4) Ever since the early 1960s, the regime of fiscal concessions for exports has provided income tax rebates related to export earnings in one way or another; the form has changed on several occasions but the substance has not. In the first half of the 1980s, 1 percent of the FOB value of exports and 5 percent of the incremental export turnover as compared to the preceding year was deductible from taxable income.[22] Assuming that the average rate of income tax paid by exporters was 50 percent and that the average rate of growth in exports was 10 percent per annum (a reasonable approximation of the actual figures), the subsidy equivalent of this concession, in terms of revenue forgone, works out at 0.75 percent of the FOB value of exports.

(5) The import policy allows special facilities for exporters to provide them access to importable inputs at world prices.[23] The system of import replenishment licenses (REP), which are related to the FOB value of exports, is, in large part, a facility insofar as it enables exporters to import inputs where the domestic substitutes are not adequate in terms of price, quality or delivery dates; it is also, in part, an incentive insofar as there is a premium on those REP licenses that are transferable. The replenishment rate and the range of items importable on a REP license are functions of the import content of export production. There are two main categories of licenses in the import replenishment regime. First, there are REP licenses for registered exporters which are issued ex post, after exports have been shipped, where the licenses as also the goods imported are transferable in the marketplace. Second, there are REP licenses such as duty-free advance licenses and imprest licenses which are issued ex ante, in anticipation of export production, and cannot be sold in the market as they are nontransferable. During the period under review, at least two-thirds if not a higher proportion of total exports were eligible for import replenishment facilities.[24] The data in Table 11.11 show that the total value of REP licenses as a proportion of the FOB value of total exports rose from a mere 6 percent in 1973–74 to almost 24 percent in 1983–84, and much of this increase occurred in a relatively short period during the late 1970s. We can infer that as a proportion of the FOB value of exports eligible for these facilities the corresponding figures rose from around 10 percent to about 35 percent. Over the same period, the proportion of ex ante nontransferable import licenses in the total value of REP licenses increased from a negligible level in the early 1970s to almost half in the early 1980s.[25]

It is exceedingly difficult to provide a quantitative assessment of the incentive implicit in the market premium realizable on import replenishment licenses because the proportion of the transferable REP licenses, as also the premium thereon, varied significantly across sectors and over time. At a macrolevel, we can only guess at broad orders of magnitude on the basis of some plausible assumptions. Let us assume that: (1) in the early 1970s (a) the average market premium on REP licenses was 50 percent, and (b) all REP licenses were transferable and sold: (2) in the early 1980s (a) the average market premium on transferable REP licenses was 20 percent , and (b) all the transferable REP licenses, which accounted for half the total in terms of value, were sold while none of the non-transferable REP licenses were. In my judgment, these assumptions represent a reasonable approximation of reality.[26] The implicit subsidy equivalent then works out at 5.2 percent of the FOB value of exports eligible for REP facilities or 3.5 percent of the FOB value of total exports during the early 1970s, and 3.5 percent or 2.3 percent respectively during the early 1980s.[27] It is worth noting that there was no similar decline, or even change, in the implicit subsidy equivalent over the period under review if it is measured as a proportion of the net foreign exchange earnings derived from exports rather than the gross FOB value of exports.[28] It needs to be stressed, however, that these estimates are, at best, a crude aggregate measure of the export incentive implicit in import policy which cannot claim any precision.

The preceding paragraphs have attempted to assess, in quantitative terms, the significance of the export promotion regime, while Table 11.11 outlines the available evidence on the resources and facilities provided to the export sector over the decade 1973–74 to 1983–84. This brief assessment leads to three conclusions. First, the assistance provided through the duty drawback system, cash compensatory support, the interest subsidy on export credit, fiscal concessions on exports and the import policy for exports, taken together, added up to a little more than 10 percent of the FOB value of total exports during the period under review; if we assume that, on an average, exports eligible for such assistance contributed two-thirds, or one-half, of total export earnings,[29] it can be inferred that the subsidy implicit in the export promotion regime added up to somewhat more than 15 percent, or at the outside a little more than 20 percent, of the FOB value of eligible exports.[30] Second, it would appear that there was little, if any, change in this subsidy equivalent of export promotion over the period under review; the incidence of CCS may have been smaller in the early 1970s, as compared with the early 1980s, but the incentive implicit in import policy was correspondingly larger. Third, it is quite clear that a significant portion of the regime of export promotion policies, at least three-fifths of the implicit subsidy, sought to compensate the export sector for the competitive disadvantage arising out of domestic economic policies; the element of incentive, at most two-fifths of the implicit subsidy, was less important in quantitative terms.[31]

How did this regime of export promotion policies influence export trends in the period 1970–85? Insofar as such policies compensated for, or offset, disincentives implicit in other domestic economic policies, ceteris paribus, it is plausible to argue that their presence should have increased the competitiveness of Indian exports just as their absence would have decreased competitiveness, thus affecting export performance. However, it is important to recognize that there were no significant qualitative or even quantitative changes in this regime during the period under review;

most of changes were in the nature of marginal variations which could not, by themselves, have led to any departures from the trend in exports. Therefore, in my judgment, the substantial difference between export performance in the period 1970–71 to 1977–78, as compared with 1977–78 to 1984–85, cannot be explained in terms of the export promotion policies alone.

It would be reasonable to ask if there is a satisfactory explanation in the wider context of the policy framework, which considers the possible impact of import liberalization and exchange rate depreciation on export trends since 1970. I think not. Although several economists have advocated a liberalization of the trade regime and an adjustment in the exchange rate as an integral part of a policy reform that would inter alia, lead to a sustainable improvement in export performance,[32] such a belief is not confirmed by past experience and available evidence.

Consider the question of import liberalization and export performance. The changes in the import intensity of export production, during the period under review, are outlined in Table 11.11. The data reveal a dramatic increase in the average import content of Indian exports. Between 1972–73 and 1984–85, it rose from 6.9 percent to 23.5 percent as a proportion of total exports and from 10.4 percent to 35.5 percent as a proportion of exports eligible for REP facilities. Even if we exclude gems and jewelry, for which the import content was very high, these proportions, albeit lower, more than trebled and registered a slightly larger increase. It must be recognized that this measure of import intensity probably underestimates not only the level of but also the increase in the import content because it does not include imports under Open General License (OGL), by exporters in the domestic tariff area or by exporters in the Export Processing Zones and 100 percent Export-Oriented Units, which are likely to have increased significantly since the late 1970s.[33] Given the paucity of data, however, the estimates in Table 11.11 provide a reasonable approximation.

It would seem that most of the increase in the import intensity of exports, particularly if we exclude gems and jewelry, materialized by 1980–81 and a substantial part of it was concentrated in the period 1977–78 to 1980–81. In view of the fact that, apart from gems and jewelry, there was no noteworthy change in the product composition of Indian exports, it would be reasonable to infer that the rising trend in import intensity was largely attributable to import liberalization.[34] What was its impact on export performance? We find that until 1977–78, when the import content of exports though rising was low, the growth in exports was unprecedented. In sharp contrast, during 1977–78 to 1984–85, when the import intensity of export production rose sharply to much higher levels, the growth in exports was sluggish. The substantial import liberalization for exports, as also otherwise, appears to have done little for export performance, while it did obviously reduce the proportion of net foreign exchange earnings in the gross FOB value of exports. One possible explanation at a macrolevel is that progressive import liberalization simply reduced the average market premium on import replenishment licenses, so that an equivalent implicit subsidy would have required a higher import content. It goes without saying that a reasonable access to imports of inputs, capital goods and technology for the export sector is essential to ensure competitiveness in the world market. Beyond such a point, however, experience shows that import liberalization is neither necessary nor sufficient for an improved export performance.

Let us turn to the issue of exchange rate policy and export performance. The changes in the exchange value of the rupee, the nominal effective exchange rate and the real effective exchange rate, during the period 1970–85, are outlined in Table 11.10 as also in Figures 11.2 and 11.3. The NEER depreciated throughout the 1970s, particularly from 1971 to 1975 when the rupee was pegged to the pound sterling and afloat; it was stable from 1979 to 1982 and, once again, declined sharply thereafter. The REER depreciated very sharply from 1974 to 1979, not so much because of conscious exchange rate policy[35] but because of the lower rate of inflation in India as compared to the outside world; it appreciated significantly between 1979 and 1981, remained stable thereafter at around the 1977 level, dropping once again in late 1985.[36]

It has been argued that export performance during the period under review is closely linked to these movements in the exchange rate.[37] In my view, such arguments which oversimplify a complex reality are not convincing. For one thing, it is futile to search for statistical causality through regression exercises,[38] and argue on a *post hoc ergo propter hoc* basis, because the factors which led to a depreciation of the REER may also have been responsible for the improved export performance. For another, it is misleading to make point-to-point comparisons between exchange rate depreciation and export growth,[39] because the choice of years is an important determinant of these results. As discussed earlier in the chapter, the turning points in export performance did not quite follow the lead of movements in the exchange rate. The period of unprecedented export growth was 1970–71 to 1977–78, or 1971–72 to 1976–77 in terms of volume, whereas the REER began to depreciate after 1974 and continued to do so until 1979 when it reached its lowest level; if the impact of exchange rate depreciation is felt with a time lag, the correspondence would be even less. Thus, a comparison of export performance during 1970–71 to 1977–78 and 1977–78 to 1984–85 with movements in the REER does not reveal a systematic relationship, let alone account for any departure from, or a return to, the earlier trends. Clearly, the depreciation of the rupee in real terms was a contributory factor insofar as it improved the price competitiveness or the relative profitability of exports but, by itself, it cannot constitute an explanation for export performance which was influenced by a wide range of external and internal factors discussed earlier in the chapter. The point of my argument is that one must learn to be skeptical about simple policy prescriptions which suggest that an exchange rate adjustment is all that is necessary to resolve problems on the export front.[40]

Constraints on Export Performance

It is obvious from the preceding discussion that India's export performance since 1970 has been determined by a wide range of internal and external factors which affected the supply of, and the demand for, her exports. While domestic economic policies in general, and trade policies in particular, exercised a significant influence, it is misleading if not wrong to suggest, as some economists have,[41] that the policy regime provides the main explanation of overall export performance. Any systematic analysis of the trends in India's exports reveals the complexity of the process. Indeed, given the diverse commodity composition and the complicated structure of policies, it is exceedingly difficult to generalize about the relative importance of internal and external factors which varied across sectors and over time. Nevertheless, it is essential to distinguish between domestic and foreign constraints on export performance, at least for the purpose of analysis and diagnosis, if not prescription.

Available research on the subject clearly shows that the basic determinants of India's export performance are to be found in the realm of domestic economic factors and policies.[42] In my view, the domestic factors which constrain India's exports are the costs of production, the pressure of domestic demand and the infrastructural or sectoral supply bottlenecks which, coupled with nonprice factors such as quality, have adversely affected the competitiveness of exports. It is possible that domestic policies may have accentuated these problems in the period before 1970 and may not have done enough to alleviate such constraints thereafter. To avoid repetition, I shall consider these issues in a skeleton manner as I have discussed them as length elsewhere.[43]

(1) India's competitiveness in the world market is, inter alia, dependent on export prices which, in turn, are closely related to the costs of production in export industries. The main determinants of costs are the prices of inputs which derive from the structure of costs in the economy, and the levels of productivity which are a function of the scale of output, the technology in use, managerial efficiency and labor skills. India is often at a disadvantage in the world market because its costs of production, hence export prices, are higher than in competing countries. This is attributable in part to the higher prices of importable or nontraded inputs and in part to much lower levels of productivity; to some extent, the origin of both may lie in the failure to realize economies of scale. It is hardly surprising that such problems reduce competitiveness particularly in the sphere of manufactured exports. While these constraints on exports are often perceived as a consequence of the management of the economy at a macro level, they are as much a consequence of the management of firms at a micro level.

(2) A large proportion of India's exports, whether consumer goods or intermediate goods, are exportables that enter into domestic consumption and use. Given the relatively slow growth in output, the pressure of domestic demand squeezes the surplus available for exports and worsens the price competitiveness of exports. There are two basic factors underlying the pressure of domestic demand. First, the rapid growth in population leads to a rapid increase in consumption. Second, the income elasticity of demand for most exportables is quite high in the domestic market. In any case, the gigantic size of the home market means that even small increases in per capita consumption have serious repercussions on the

supplies available for export. Available evidence suggests that, for many exportables, domestic absorption has tended to increase faster than domestic production, and this has often constituted a dominant constraint on the possibilities of export growth, particularly in the sphere of primary commodities and agro-based manufactures where a significant proportion of the total output is exported.[44] Insofar as such a domestic demand pull improves the relative profitability of sales in the home market vis-à-vis exports, it has a further adverse effect on export performance.

(3) Infrastructural constraints in the economy at large and supply bottlenecks in specific sectors influence exports just as much as the performance of the economy. Frequently enough, export supplies are restricted by the inadequate infrastructure or the nonavailability of domestic and imported inputs at the right time. While some scarcities directly affect competitiveness through higher input prices which are reflected in the costs of production, other bottlenecks simply limit the output available for exports. Such supply constraints are common enough in India and examples of how they constrain export performance abound.

(4) The competitiveness of exports also depends, to a significant extent, upon factors which are not reflected in prices. In fact, nonprice factors such as quality and marketing have an important bearing on export performance. This is particularly true for nontraditional manufactured exports where the ability to compete in the world market is, in important part, a function of these nonprice attributes of exports. Apropos quality, Indian exports have been constrained by failures on two counts: the maintenance of quality control at any given point of time and the improvement of quality over a period of time; the former has sometimes tarnished the reputation of Indian firms as reliable exporters, while the latter has often taken away the competitive edge from Indian exports in the world market. It is also possible to discern a serious constraint on export performance in the realm of marketing. There has been little systematic effort to develop products or markets for exports so that, as a rule, India has attempted to sell what it produces rather than produce what it can sell. What is more, the development of brand names, the improvement in designing and packaging, the execution of export orders in accordance with promised delivery dates and the provision of an adequate after-sales service, all of which are an integral part of success at exports, have simply not received the necessary attention.

(5) Many of these constraints were beyond the reach of policy; some others were, or could have been, alleviated by compensatory policies; a few may even have been accentuated by inappropriate policies. The export promotion regime sought to compensate the export sector for the disincentives implicit in domestic economic policies largely by providing access to importable inputs at world prices and reimbursing taxes paid on inputs that entered into export production; it also provided some incentives for product and market development. This constituted a vast improvement over the discrimination against the export sector associated with the pessimistic neglect of exports during the 1950s, and a rationalization of the inappropriate export promotion during the 1960s which concentrated attention on a narrow range of nontraditional exports while it neglected

traditional exports and other promising new exports.[45] All the same, given the level of tariffs on imports and the degree of compensation or incentive implicit in the gamut of export promotion policies,[46] it is likely that the effective exchange rate for import-competing production was significantly higher than that for export production, even during the period under review. Export performance may also have been influenced by the policy framework in its wider context. Industrial policies which placed limits on capacity expansion or capacity creation may have preempted the realization of scale economies or erected barriers to entry for new firms, thus increasing the degree of monopoly and creating an environment where there was no pressure on manufacturers to reduce costs or improve quality. The fiscal regime, which opted out of the difficulties associated with domestic resource mobilization through direct taxes, relied more and more on indirect taxes, both import tariffs and excise duties, so that an escalation of costs across-the-board was inevitable given the cascading effect of such levies, and the export sector was not quite immune.

A study of past Indian experience confirms that the factors outlined above have always acted as constraints on export performance. It is not as if these constraints vanished in the period 1970–71 to 1977–78. It is simply that an unusual combination of internal and external factors, discussed earlier in the chapter, neutralized their impact and led to a rapid growth in exports not witnessed before or after. Obviously, it is difficult to generalize because the relative importance of each factor, or the dominant constraint, can only be determined by sector-specific analysis. Nevertheless, in retrospect, it is clear that export performance in primary commodities and agro-based manufactures (particularly in sectors where a significant proportion of output is exported) was constrained by the pressure of domestic demand, sometimes exacerbated by supply bottlenecks. On the other hand, industrial exports were constrained by the lack of price and nonprice competitiveness, attributable perhaps to the limited size of, and the absence of competition in, the domestic market. In the manufacturing sector, the failure to realize economies of scale has meant high costs while the absence of competitive pressure has meant poor quality. It has not been possible to circumvent the problem by isolating production for exports from production for the home market, because exports are the end of, rather than the beginning of, the typical market expansion path for most firms in India.

Let me now turn to the significance of foreign constraints in India's export performance. It is widely accepted, as also established by existing research on the subject,[47] that external factors have not constrained the growth of Indian exports in the past.[48] Indeed, our analysis of the trends in exports since 1970 shows that external factors had a very favorable impact on export performance during the period 1970–71 to 1970–78. However, in the context of the changed situation in the world economy, it is necessary to reexamine the accepted perception about foreign constraints. In my judgment, external factors, which have always been significant for a few categories among Indian exports, probably became significant for the export sector as a whole during the 1980s, when there was a near stagnation in international trade flows. This view deserves some elaboration.

The orthodox literature assumes that, in principle, external factors should not constrain export performance wherever India is a small or marginal supplier in the world market, which is the case for a large proportion of India's exports. On this presumption, it is often argued that it should be possible for India to increase her share of world exports in such cases irrespective of the growth in world import demand. This proposition is open to question, for it needs to be recognized that restrictions on international trade flows in certain products do impose an external constraint on Indian exports. For example, quantitative restrictions embodied in the Multi Fiber Agreement (MFA) limit the growth in export of clothing. Similarly, nontariff barriers in importing countries constitute a foreign constraint on many of India's exports such as oil cakes to the European Economic Community (EEC), marine products to the United States and meat to the Middle East. But that is not all. The increasing incidence of protectionism in the industrialized countries, embodied in the escalated tariff structure and a range of unquantifiable nontariff barriers, also places a limit on the growth of manufactured exports, even where India is a marginal supplier in the world market because, in practice, such restrictions constrain exports from countries which are either not established as suppliers in the importing country or are new entrants in the world market for a product.

These are, of course, the familiar limits to market access which impose foreign constraints on the export performance of developing countries in general. But countries from the developing world do not have equal access to the markets of industrialized countries. The problem of market access is often compounded for some because international trade flows, which constitute transactions between countries, are intrafirm transactions within transnational manufacturing or trading firms. In many of these sectors, the export performance of individual countries is determined not so much by their competitive ability as it is by the sourcing decisions of transnational corporations. What is more, market access is determined not only by the economics of competitiveness but also by the politics of international relations. In an international trading system where the principles of multilateralism are increasingly violated, the resort to bilateralism means that some countries benefit from a preferential market access as compared to others; this is easily done through a manipulation of nontariff barriers or gray-area measures. These are manifestations of foreign constraints which may have exercised an important influence on India's export performance but are seldom recognized or discussed in the literature on the subject. Such external factors may also constitute a part of the explanation for why Brazil, China or South Korea have succeeded in the sphere of exports but India has not; in an endeavor to explore this issue, further research should examine the comparative export performance of developing countries in the international context.

While it is difficult to provide conclusive evidence, it is plausible to suggest that external constraints on India's export performance have acquired greater significance in the 1980s as there has been a steady increase in protectionism in the industrialized countries and as the near stagnation in international trade flows has led to fierce price and nonprice competition in major markets. The pressure of external factors on manufactured exports from India has continued to mount as Indian firms have been unable to offer the generous terms of export credit or the large price discounts which have become increasingly necessary to circumvent existing market channels. It is likely that these problems would only be accentuated in the remaining years of this decade. Therefore, an assessment of India's export prospects must extend beyond domestic economic factors or policies and also consider the influence of the international trade environment.

Notes

1. For a detailed analysis, see Deepak Nayyar, "India's Balance of Payments," *Economic and Political Weekly* (Annual Number, 1982).

2. See I. G. Patel, "India's External Economic Relations: Challenge of the Eighties," *Reserve Bank of India Bulletin* (August 1980).

3. Calculated from statistics published by the Directorate General of Commercial Intelligence and Statistics (DGCI&S), Calcutta.

4. The data on India's export performance in the 1960s, cited in this paragraph, are from Deepak Nayyar, *India's Exports and Export Policies* (Cambridge: Cambridge University Press, 1976), chap. 2.

5. The figures on India's share in world exports during the 1970s, derived from statistics published by the United Nations, reveal that the share was relatively stable in the range of 0.55 during the period from 1972 to 1977.

6. India's share in world nonfuel exports declined from 0.72 in 1970 to 0.62 in 1975 and 0.55 in 1980; calculated from the UNCTAD *Handbook of International Trade and Development Statistics* (New York: United Nations, 1983).

7. The two series of index numbers reveal almost identical trends. The percentage changes in the volume and the unit value of exports, mentioned in this paragraph, are point-to-point increases.

8. This generalization is subject to one exception, as export earnings derived from tea attained their highest level in 1984–85 largely because of the dramatic increase in the world price of tea.

9. India's principal exports in this category are jute manufactures, cotton textiles, leather and leather manufactures, metal manufactures, iron and steel and gems and jewelry. Had it not been for the phenomenal growth in exports of gems and jewelry during the period 1977–78 to 1984–85, the share of this group of (largely) traditional manufactured exports in total export earnings would have declined even more.

10. The share of SITC 8 in India's nonfuel exports was even higher at 14.7 percent in 1984–85; the principal exports in this category are clothing, carpets and handicrafts.

11. Calculated from statistics published by DGCI&S, Calcutta.

12. For time-series data on the index numbers of wholesale prices, see *Economic Survey 1985–86* (New Delhi: Government of India, Ministry of Finance, 1986). It need to be recognized that the rising trend in the average unit value index for exports was also, in part, attributable to the depreciation in the exchange value of the rupee, the impact of which is discussed in the following paragraph.

13. Estimates of the effective exchange rate of the rupee, both nominal and real, cited in this table, are obtained from Vijay Joshi, "The Nominal and Real

Effective Exchange Rate of the Indian Rupee: 1971–1983," *Reserve Bank of India: Occasional Papers* 5, no. 1 (June 1984). The details about the methodology, the assumptions and the data are outlined in this valuable study. The same methodology was used to estimate the NEER and REER for 1984 and 1985 and these figures are obtained from Vijay Joshi, "Exchange Rate Policy," *The Economic Times* (New Delhi) 31 January 1986.

14. A recent study by the Industrial Credit and Investment Corporation of India (ICICI), based on a sample of sixty-five firms from engineering, textiles and a few other industries, shows that the profitability of exports at the margin, covering only variable costs, was likely to have been an important factor underlying the export performance of the sample firms. In 1978–79, for example, on an average for the sample firms, the gross profit on export sales as a percentage of the FOB value of exports was −15.4 percent, whereas profits before interest, depreciation and overhead (covering only variable costs) as a percentage of the FOB value of exports was −5.4 percent; with export incentives, these proportions become positive at 4.0 percent and 14.2 percent respectively. The relative orders of magnitude were similar for the sample firms in 1979–80 and 1980–81; see *Export Performance of ICICI Financed Companies: 1978–79 to 1980–81* (Bombay: ICICI), 12–20. It is likely that, in a period of slack domestic demand, exports on a variable-costs-plus basis would have been an even more attractive proposition.

15. The significance of the OPEC markets, as a source of growth for Indian exports, began to decline in the late 1970s much before expansion in OPEC slowed down. In the early years, following the first round of oil price increases, exports from India had a competitive edge that was attributable to geographical proximity and traditional trade channels. This edge was steadily lost to increasing competition from Western Europe, Japan and the smaller East Asian countries. The share of India in the total imports of OPEC obviously declined. The share of OPEC in India's total exports also declined from a peak level of more than 17 percent in 1977–78 to 11 percent in 1980–81 and 8 percent in 1984–85 (calculated from statistics published by DGCI&S, Calcutta).

16. See, for example, Deepak Nayyar, *India's Exports and Export Policies* (Cambridge: Cambridge University Press, 1976), chap. 10, 219–66; and Amaresh Bagchi, "Export Incentives in India," in *Change and Choice in Indian Industry*, edited by A. K. Bagchi and N. Banerji (Calcutta, 1981), 297–328. For a more recent discussion on export promotion policies, see *Report of the Committee on Trade Policies* (New Delhi: Government of India, Ministry of Commerce, December 1984), 21–34.

17. Calculated from the data in the *Report of the Committee on Trade Policies*, 109.

18. Ibid., 28.

19. The data about the magnitudes of CCS, cited in this paragraph, are obtained from ibid, 26–27 and 110–13.

20. Following an announcement by the Government in March 1986, preshipment and postshipment export credit is now available at a concessional interest rate of 9.5 percent per annum for a period of 180 days; the interest subsidy has been raised to 3 percent per annum.

21. The annual expenditure on the Export Credit Development Scheme under the MDA, used to finance the interest subsidy, is reported in ibid, 109; during the period 1973–74 to 1983–84, as shown in Table 11.11, it was in the range of 0.20 percent to 0.25 percent of the value of total exports. It is assumed that the implicit cost for the commercial banking system was the same, at the rate of 1.5 percent per annum, as export credit beyond the specified period was then provided at an interest rate of 13.5 percent per annum.

22. The budget for 1985–86 replaced this with a new provision under which 50 percent of the profits attributable to exports, determined by the proportion

of export sales in total sales, were exempted from income tax. The following budget, for 1986–87, modified the situation further. It provided that 4 percent of the net foreign exchange earnings derived from exports (defined as the gross FOB value of exports minus the value of import replenishment licenses obtained for export production whether ex post or ex ante) would be deductible from taxable income; in addition, 50 percent of the profits from exports would be exempt from income tax, subject to the condition that such deductions do not exceed the total profits from exports.

23. For a detailed discussion, see Nayyar, *India's Exports and Export Policies*, 232–36, and *Report of the Committee on Trade Policies*, 30–32.

24. This is clear from the data on selected years presented in Table 11.11. For time-series evidence on the value of REP licenses issued, and the value of exports, in each of the eligible product groups, see *Report of the Committee on Trade Policies*, Table 19, 121–23.

25. In 1983–84, import licenses issued in anticipation for export production (including duty-free advance licenses, imprest licenses and special imprest licenses) accounted for 48 percent of the total value of licenses issued under the import replenishment regime, while ex post REP licenses accounted for the remainder, of which 44.3 percent were issued to registered exporters and 7.7 percent were issued to Export Houses; and Trading Houses see *Report of the Committee on Trade Policies*, 31–32.

26. It is known that the market premium on REP licenses declined with the import liberalization that began in the late 1970s. The assumptions about the average market premium in the early 1970s and the early 1980s are based on my discussion with knowledgeable persons in official circles and in the export sector. The assumption that all transferable REP licenses were sold in the market to realize a premium would obviously tend to overestimate the export incentive implicit in import policy insofar as such licenses were, in fact, used to import inputs that went into export production. All the same, it does provide a measure of the ultimate benefit to the export sector, for two reasons: (1) in the absence of these special provisions in import policy, exporters would have paid market prices for imported or home-produced importable inputs; and (2) even when used in domestic production by exporting firms, REP imports, which were significantly cheaper than their domestic substitutes, enhanced profitability.

27. These estimates of the implicit subsidy equivalent are derived from the stated assumptions and the figures on import replenishment licenses, as a percentage of (1) eligible exports, (2) total exports, presented in Table 11.11 for the years 1972–73 and 1984–85.

28. The implicit subsidy equivalent works out at 5.8 percent of the net foreign exchange earnings from exports eligible for REP facilities or 3.7 percent of the net foreign exchange earnings from total exports in 1972–73, and 5.3 percent or 3.1 percent respectively in 1984–85. For this computation, net foreign exchange earnings are defined as the gross FOB value of exports *minus* the value of import replenishment licenses. The results of the exercise are hardly surprising given the increase in average import content of export production over the period (see Table 11.11).

29. Strictly speaking, these export promotion measures are not perfectly additive because all are not available for the same set of exports. Thus it is quite appropriate to use the value of total exports as the denominator for it does provide an index of how, if at all, the incidence of export promotion has changed over time.

30. It is worth noting that this estimate, which is based on data available at the macro level, is quite consistent with the results of the ICICI study compiled from data obtained at the micro level. Information provided by a sample of 46 firms (drawn mostly from the engineering goods sector with a few from chemical

and textiles) shows that, during the period 1978–79 to 1980–81, export incentives received (duty drawback, CCS and premium in REP licenses) added up to 20 percent of the value of their exports (Rs 276 million per annum as compared with Rs 1,383 million per annum); see *Export Performance of ICICI Financed Companies: 1978–79 to 1980–81,* Annexure 5.2, p. 93.

31. This computation is based on evidence available for the 1980s, assuming that the subsidy implicit in fiscal concessions, the premia realized on REP licenses and one-fourth the CCS constituted the element of net incentive in the regime of export promotion. Insofar as the compensation provided by the regime was not adequate, the quantitative significance of the incentive portion may be over-estimated here.

32. See, for example, Jagdish Bhagwati and Padma Desai, *India: Planning for Industrialization* (New York: Oxford University Press, 1970); Jagdish Bhagwati and T. N. Srinivasan, *Foreign Trade Regimes and Economic Development: India* (New York: Columbia University Press, 1975); and Martin Wolf, *India's Exports* (New York: Oxford University Press for the World Bank, 1982).

33. Following the Alexander Committee Report, the Import Policy for 1978–79 significantly enlarged the access to imports under OGL (which became, for the first time, a residual unspecified category for imports of raw materials, components, spares and consumables) that was maintained, or even increased, in subsequent years. Exports from the two EPZs (at Santa Cruz and Kandla) begin to pick up starting in the late 1970s, while the scheme of 100 percent EOUs was introduced only in 1981.

34. The liberalization of the trade regime began in 1976–77, but it gathered momentum starting in 1978–79 when structural changes in import policy liberalized import replenishment facilities for the export sector and OGL provisions for the economy as a whole.

35. Between 1974 and 1979, there was no discernible trend in the exchange rate of the rupee vis-à-vis the U.S. dollar or the SDR basket (see Figure 11.2), which suggests that there was no conscious exchange rate policy intervention.

36. In the last quarter of 1985, the REER was lower than it was in 1976 and it is likely that in 1986 it dropped to a level lower than the trough of 1979.

37. See, for example, Vijay Joshi, "Exchange Rate Policy," *The Economic Times* (New Delhi) 31 January 1986; Vijay Joshi and I. M. D. Little, "Indian Macro-Economic Policies," *Economic and Political Weekly,* 28 February 1987; and Charan D. Wadhva, "Some Aspects of India's Export Policy and Performance," chap. 13 in this volume.

38. See Wadhva, "Some Aspects of India's Export Policy and Performance."

39. Joshi and Little, for instance, make such point-to-point comparisons and argue that during 1974–79, a period which witnessed a sharp depreciation of the REER, India's exports rose as never before or since, whereas the reverse happened during 1979–83 ("Indian Macro-Economic Policies," 377).

40. For a detailed discussion on this issue, with reference to devaluation of the rupee in June 1966, see Nayyar, *India's Export and Export Policies,* chap. 11, 267–95.

41. See, for example, Wolf, *India's Exports,* 55–76.

42. Manmohan Singh, *India's Export Trends* (New York: Oxford University Press, 1964); Nayyar, *India's Exports and Export Policies;* and Wolf, *India's Exports.*

43. Nayyar, *India's Exports and Export Policies,* 9–15 and 341–50.

44. See Singh, *India's Export Trends,* and Nayyar, *India's Exports and Export Policies.* Much the same is true for the period under review. This is borne out by the fact that exports of jute manufactures, coir products, leather and leather manufactures, tea, coffee, tobacco, castor oil, pepper and cardamom (sectors in which 20–60 percent of total output is exported), taken together, contributed

37.6 percent of India's nonoil exports in 1973–74 but this share dropped to just 17.8 percent in 1983–84; see *Report of the Committee on Trade Policies*, 11.

45. For a detailed discussion and analysis, see Nayyar, *India's Exports and Export Policies*.

46. It has been shown earlier that the subsidy implicit in export promotion policies, during the period under consideration, added up to a little more than 10 percent of the value of total exports. Over the same period the average level of tariffs, as measured by the ratio of total import duties to the total · value of imports, was in the range of 30 percent. If we consider the subsidized exports and protected imports alone, the difference between 20 percent and 80 percent respectively would turn out to be even greater.

47. See Singh, *India's Export Trends*, and Nayyar, *India's Exports and Export Policies*.

48. The exceptions to this conclusion are few because even in traditional exports where India faced an inelastic demand it failed to exploit the limited opportunities that were available, for it was not even able to maintain its market share (see Singh, *India's Export Trends*, and Nayyar, *India's Exports and Export Policies*.)

TABLE 11.1 Trends in India's Exports
(in current prices at current exchange rates)

Year	Rupees Million[a]	U.S. $ Million[a]	SDRs Million[a]
1970–71	15,352	2,031	2,031
1971–72	16,082	2,157	2,102
1972–73	19,708	2,540	2,313
1973–74	25,234	3,232	2,660
1974–75	33,288	4,184	3,444
1975–76	40,263	4,666	3,894
1976–77	51,427	5,755	4,969
1977–78	54,079	6,316	5,322
1978–79	57,260	6,980	5,489
1979–80	64,184	7,924	6,092
1980–81	67,107	8,484	6,594
1981–82	78,059	8,702	7,553
1982–83	88,033	9,104	8,334
1983–84	97,707	9,449	8,931
1984–85	118,552	9,972	9,935
1985–86	110,120	9,000	8,521

[a] The rupee values have been converted into U.S. dollars and SDRs on the
basis of annual average conversion factors compiled by the Reserve Bank
of India.

Source: Directorate General of Commercial Intelligence and Statistics (DGCI&S),
Government of India, Calcutta.

TABLE 11.2 Index Numbers of India's Exports

Year	Series A:[a] 1968–69 = 100		Series B:[b] 1978–79 = 100	
	Volume Index	Unit Value Index	Volume Index	Unit Value Index
1970–71	106.0	106.0	58.9	45.1
1971–72	107.0	108.0	59.4	46.0
1972–73	120.0	120.0	66.7	51.1
1973–74	125.0	146.0	69.4	62.1
1974–75	133.0	183.0	73.9	77.9
1975–76	147.0	197.2	81.7	83.9
1976–77	174.2	210.3	96.8	89.5
1977–78	167.7	235.8	93.2	100.3
1978–79	179.6	234.3	100.0	100.0
1979–80	199.4	236.2	106.2	105.4
1980–81	185.5	266.0	108.1	108.5
1981–82	198.2	291.6	110.1	124.1
1982–83	210.1	310.2	116.7	132.0
1983–84	203.4	354.8	113.0	151.0

[a] Series A was compiled until 1979–80, and the index numbers for the period thereafter have been obtained by using a simple aggregate conversion factor.

[b] Series B was started in 1980–81, and the index numbers for the period before then have been computed by using a more accurate linking factor which makes the figures more comparable.

Source: DGCI&S, Calcutta.

FIGURE 11.1 Trends in India's Exports

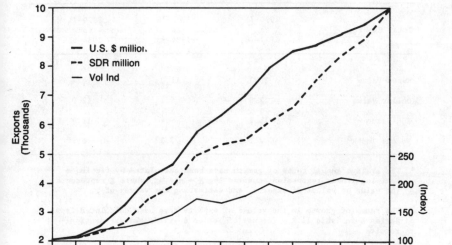

TABLE 11.3 Average Annual Rates of Growth of Exports[a]

Total Exports	1970–71 to 1977–78	1977–78 to 1984–85	1970–71 to 1984–85
Rupee Value	20.3	11.0	14.4
Dollar Value	17.8	6.1	12.0
SDR Value	15.3	9.4	11.9
Volume Index[b]	7.5	3.2[c]	5.7[c]

[a] The average annual rates of growth have been calculated by fitting a semi–log linear regression equation log $X = a + bt$, where X represents the value or volume of exports, and estimating the values of b.

[b] The rates of growth in the volume of exports have been calculated from Series A in Table 11.2. The use of Series B yields almost identical results.

[c] These figures relate to the periods 1977–78 to 1983–84 and 1970–71 to 1983–84 respectively, as 1983–84 is the latest year for which index numbers on the volume of exports are available.

Source: Table 11.1 and Table 11.2.

TABLE 11.4 The Value of India's Nonoil Exports During the 1980s[a]
(in current prices at current exchange rates)

Year	Rupees Million[b]	U.S. $ Million[b]	SDRs Million[b]
1980–81	66,858	8,452	6,569
1981–82	75,810	8,452	7,335
1982–83	75,677	7,826	7,164
1983–84	81,826	7,914	7,479
1984–85	100,323	8,439	8,407
1985–86	103,590	8,467	8,016

[a] The figures below exclude exports of both crude oil and petroleum products.

[b] The rupee values have been converted into U.S. dollars and SDRs on the basis of annual average conversion factors compiled by the Reserve Bank of India.

TABLE 11.5 India's Exports in Relation to Selected Macroeconomic Variables

Year	Exports as a Percentage of GNP	Exports as a Percentage of Imports	Current Account Deficit (Surplus) as a Percentage of Exports	External Debt Servicing[a] as a Percentage of Exports
1970–71	4.2	93.9	21.6	29.3
1971–72	4.1	88.1	25.0	29.8
1972–73	4.6	105.5	12.8	25.7
1973–74	4.7	85.4	14.4	23.6
1974–75	5.3	73.7	19.4	18.8
1975–76	6.1	76.5	(7.3)	17.1
1976–77	7.2	101.4	(29.7)	18.6
1977–78	6.7	89.8	(32.1)	18.1
1978–79	6.6	84.1	3.0	17.5
1979–80	6.7	70.2	3.7	13.3
1980–81	5.9	53.5	24.7	16.1
1981–82	6.0	57.4	29.7	16.2
1982–83	6.1	61.5	26.1	16.4
1983–84	5.7	61.7	23.2	19.1
1984–85	6.3	69.0	24.1	22.4
1985–86	5.2	55.7	45.4	28.6[b]

[a] The data on external debt servicing reported in the Economic Survey are incomplete as they do not include amortization and interest payments on account of: (1) drawings from the IMF, and (2) external commercial borrowing. For the period 1970–71 to 1979–80, debt servicing has been estimated by adding repurchases in transactions with the IMF. For the period 1980–81 to 1985–86, the text of the Economic Survey, each year, provides an aggregate figure for total debt servicing (including transactions with the IMF and external commercial borrowing) as a percentage of current receipts (export earnings plus gross invisibles); starting from absolute values for the latter, I have estimated external debt servicing as a percentage of exports in this table.

[b] The RBI statistics on balance of payments are available only up to 1984–85, and the figure for 1985–86 in the penultimate column is based on my estimate of the current account deficit.

Sources: For data on export and imports: DGCI&S, Calcutta.
For data on GNP and external debt servicing: Economic Survey, various issues (New Delhi: Government of India, Ministry of Finance).
For data on the current account deficit (surplus) in the balance of payments: Reserve Bank of India Bulletin, various issues.

TABLE 11.6 Export Performance of Selected Developing Countries Since 1970
(in U.S. $ billion at current exchange rates)

	1970	1975	1976	1977	1978	1979
Argentina	1.77	2.96	3.92	5.65	6.40	7.81
Brazil	2.74	8.67	10.13	12.05	12.66	15.24
China	2.31	7.69	6.94	7.52	9.75	13.66
Hong Kong	2.51	6.02	8.53	9.63	11.50	15.15
India	2.03	4.36	5.53	6.36	6.65	7.85
Malaysia	1.69	3.83	5.30	6.09	7.40	11.08
Mexico	1.31	2.99	3.36	4.29	5.90	8.82
South Korea	0.84	5.08	7.72	10.05	12.71	15.06

	1980	1981	1982	1983	1984[a]
Argentina	8.02	9.14	7.80	7.84	8.11
Brazil	20.13	23.29	20.18	21.90	27.00
China	18.27	21.56	21.91	22.15	24.98
Hong Kong	19.72	21.74	20.99	21.95	28.32
India	8.38	8.37	8.81	8.71	9.46
Malaysia	12.95	11.77	12.03	14.13	16.49
Mexico	15.30	20.04	20.93	21.01	24.33
South Korea	17.51	21.25	21.85	24.45	29.25

[a] The figures for 1984 are obtained from IMF International Financial
Statistics, June 1986.

Source: UNCTAD Handbook of International Trade and Development Statistics,
1985 (New York: United Nations).

TABLE 11.7   Trends in India's Principal Exports Since 1970
(in Rs million at current prices)

Commodity Group	1970– 1971	1971– 1972	1972– 1973	1973– 1974	1974– 1975	1975– 1976	1976– 1977
Tea	1,483	1,563	1,473	1,460	2,281	2,369	2,931
Coffee	251	221	329	460	516	667	1,260
Tobacco	314	423	611	684	804	931	968
Cashew Kernels	571	613	688	744	1,182	961	1,061
Fruits and Vegetables	80	90	151	181	195	387	570
Spices	388	362	291	557	614	715	750
Sugar	276	302	133	427	339	4,723	1,481
Rice	50	111	35	82	215	130	61
Marine Products	305	414	545	892	662	1,272	1,806
Raw Cotton	140	163	215	324	152	413	270
Oil Cakes	554	402	748	1,792	960	965	2,344
Iron Ore	1,173	1,047	1,098	1,329	1,604	2,139	2,385
Chemicals and Allied Products	294	304	353	503	929	853	1,108
Leather and Leather Manufactures	874	1,031	1,871	1,855	1,652	2,226	2,936
Cotton Textiles	931	953	1,214	2,265	2,040	2,039	3,206
Jute Manufactures	1,904	2,653	2,500	2,273	2,968	2,509	2,011
Metal Manufactures	399	323	383	495	764	958	1,636
Iron and Steel	906	409	418	607	884	1,215	3,984
Machinery and Transport Equipment	833	756	874	1,183	2,155	2,596	3,022
Gems and Jewelery	447	537	810	1,116	1,072	1,569	2,994
Carpets	106	124	196	255	351	417	684
Handicrafts	151	151	183	294	349	549	547
Clothing	302	377	561	996	1,382	2,027	3,058
Crude Oil and Petroleum Products	86	88	133	122	136	200	187
Total Above	12,817	13,415	15,813	20,896	27,249	32,630	41,260
Total Exports	15,352	16,082	19,708	25,234	33,288	40,363	51,427
Principal Exports as a Percent of Total Exports	83.5	83.4	80.2	82.8	81.9	80.8	80.2

Source: Directorate General of Commercial Intelligence and Statistics (DGCI&S),
Government of India, Calcutta.

TABLE 11.7 (Continued)

1977–1978	1978–1979	1979–1980	1980–1981	1981–1982	1982–1983	1983–1984	1984–1985
5,697	3,405	3,678	4,253	3,952	3,698	5,152	7,667
1,944	1,440	1,633	2,142	1,463	1,871	1,817	2,102
1,132	1,107	1,023	1,244	2,049	2,144	1,556	1,505
1,495	802	1,181	1,401	1,815	1,354	1,508	1,797
473	645	635	796	1,060	1,536	1,400	1,831
1,371	1,479	1,494	1,114	988	945	1,168	2,067
198	1,310	1,289	360	632	674	1,753	361
115	387	1,283	2,239	3,679	2,179	1,136	1,692
1,743	2,263	2,534	2,170	2,849	3,695	3,593	3,814
7	160	751	1,649	363	1,091	1,667	597
1,333	1,099	1,276	1,251	1,179	1,486	1,516	1,369
2,404	2,329	2,852	3,033	3,518	3,805	4,016	4,594
1,167	1,481	1,978	2,248	3,641	3,482	3,149	4,650
2,720	3,539	5,195	3,779	4,060	3,930	4,632	6,754
2,850	2,810	3,654	3,648	3,987	3,685	3,954	5,727
2,449	1,169	3,661	3,300	2,580	2,053	1,717	3,413
1,831	2,092	2,166	1,994	2,328	1,962	2,144	2,171
2,801	2,237	1,061	697	791	508	485	757
3,372	3,994	4,488	5,259	6,179	5,850	5,408	6,632
5,596	7,294	5,431	6,184	8,115	10,148	12,941	12,371
832	1,003	1,398	1,639	1,828	1,794	2,076	2,587
685	970	1,151	1,190	1,480	1,096	1,300	1,597
2,999	4,185	4,597	5,150	5,958	3,928	6,919	9,192
⸴ 157	142	213	249	2,249	12,356	15,881	18,229
45,371	47,842	54,322	56,989	66,743	75,266	85,332	101,971
54,079	57,261	64,184	67,107	78,059	88,033	97,707	118,552
83.9	83.6	84.6	84.9	85.5	85.5	87.3	86.8

TABLE 11.8 Index Numbers of the Volume of Exports from India
(by major commodity groups)

Commodity Group	1970–1971	1971–1972	1972–1973	1973–1974	1974–1975	1975–1976	1976–1977
				1968–69 = 100			
Food	112	113	128	121	138	163	162
Beverages and Tobacco	93	120	199	165	157	158	167
Crude Materials	114	108	107	128	129	129	138
Mineral Fuels	100	62	138	85	85	67	70
Animal and Vegetable Oils	45	50	117	86	105	141	232
Chemicals	167	149	185	233	229	208	254
Manufactured Goods	92	94	102	105	94	110	145
Machinery and Transport Equipment	166	144	156	188	386	325	373
Miscellaneous Manufactured Articles	151	171	275	283	341	410	620
General Index	106	107	120	125	133	147	174

[a] The data for the period 1980–81 to 1983–84 are not strictly comparable with
that for the earlier period, 1970–71 to 1979–80, because of the change in the
base year and the associated changes in coverage, classification and weights.

Source: Source: Directorate General of Commercial Intelligence and Statistics
(DGCI&S), Government of India, Calcutta.

TABLE 11.8 (Continued)

			1978–79 = 100			
1977–1978	1978–1979	1979–1980	1980–[a] 1981	1981–[a] 1982	1982–[a] 1983	1983–[a] 1984
131	159	231	114	118	111	106
168	160	157	108	163	157	105
109	117	145	147	106	107	115
61	48	22	78	689	4,821	4,244
70	39	90	96	92	127	167
301	376	448	128	189	184	137
157	150	141	85	88	81	84
397	486	473	130	129	110	92
633	719	693	126	119	105	114
168	180	199	108	110	117	113

TABLE 11.9 The Composition of India's Exports
(in percentages)

SITC Category	Commodity Group	1970–71	1973–74	1977–78	1980–81	1984–85
	Primary Commodities of which:	47.0	46.1	41.1	40.6	46.9
0+1	Food, beverages and tobacco	29.2	29.8	31.0	27.7	22.3
2+4	Raw Materials	17.0	15.7	9.6	12.5	9.0
3	Fuels	0.8	0.6	0.5	0.4	15.6
	Manufactures of which:	52.7	52.7	58.6	59.1	52.9
5	Chemicals	2.4	2.3	2.3	3.5	4.1
6	Manufactured Goods	40.4	39.7	40.6	34.7	30.8
7	Machinery and Transport Equipment	4.9	4.6	6.2	7.9	5.6
8	Miscellaneous Manufactured Articles	5.0	7.1	9.5	13.0	12.4
	Total[a]	100.0	100.0	100.0	100.0	100.0

[a] The columns do not add up to 100 as the cateogry of unclassified exports (SITC 9) is not included in the above figures.

Source: DGCI&S, Calcutta.

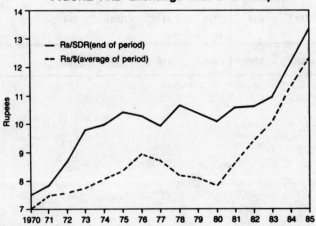

FIGURE 11.2 Exchange Rate of the Rupee

Rs/SDR(end of period)
Rs/$(average of period)

TABLE 11.10 Exchange Rate of the Rupee

Year	Rupees per U.S. Dollar (average of period)	Rupees per SDR (end of period)	Nominal Effective Exchange Rate (1975=100)	Real Effective Exchange Rate[a] (1975=100)
1970	7.50	7.50	127.39	112.96
1971	7.50	7.83	125.42	113.24
1972	7.59	8.70	116.90	110.92
1973	7.74	9.81	106.34	105.13
1974	8.10	9.98	104.12	107.83
1975	8.38	10.46	100.00	100.00
1976	8.96	10.32	98.70	89.93
1977	8.74	9.97	98.52	90.46
1978	8.19	10.67	93.79	82.88
1979	8.13	10.42	91.81	82.66
1980	7.86	10.11	94.19	90.32
1981	8.66	10.59	94.50	94.44
1982	9.46	10.63	94.81	92.34
1983	10.10	10.99	92.88	95.15
1984	11.36	12.21	87.36	93.82
1985	12.37	13.36	82.99	92.44

[a] The effective exchange rate of the rupee, computed as an annual average, is measured in relation to the ten industrialized countries, among the developed market economies, with the largest shares in India's visible exports, leading to a ten-country bilateral export-weighted index.

Source: For the exchange values of the rupee see: IMF International Financial Statistics. For the nominal and real effective exchange rate of the rupee see: Joshi, "The Nominal and Real Effective Exchange Rate of the Indian Rupee," and "Exchange Rate Policy."

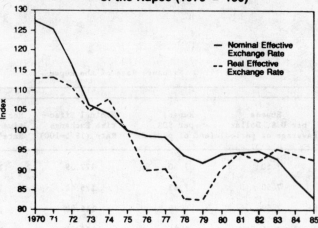

FIGURE 11.3
Nominal and Real Effective Exchange Rate
of the Rupee (1975 = 100)

— Nominal Effective
   Exchange Rate
-- Real Effective
   Exchange Rate

TABLE 11.11 Trends in the Import Intensity of Exports

	1972–73	1977–78	1980–81	1984–85
1. Import replenishment licenses[a] for exports[b] as a percentage of the value of total exports	6.9	13.7	21.2	23.5
(excluding gems and jewelery)	(4.4)[c]	(8.3)	(15.7)	(15.3)
2. Import replenishment licenses[a] for exports[b] as a percentage of the value of exports eligible for such licenses	10.4	18.6	29.5	35.5
(excluding gems and jewelery)	(6.8)[c]	(11.7)	(22.7)	(24.5)

[a] The figures on the value of import replenishment licenses include all import licenses issued on the basis of export performance: REP licenses, Advance licenses, Imprest licenses, Special imprest licenses, and Additional licenses.

[b] It is assumed that all exports except for tea, coffee, sugar, rice, raw cotton, oil cakes, iron ore, jute manufactures and crude oil and petroleum products are eligible for import replenishment facilities.

[c] The estimated percentages in parentheses exclude gems and jewelery both from the numerator and the denominator as the import intensity of these exports is much higher than the average for exports.

Sources: For data on the value of import replenishment licenses see Office of the Chief Controller of Imports and Exports (CCI&E) and Ministry of Commerce, Report of the Committee on Trade Policies (New Delhi: Government of India, December 1984).

12

India's Foreign Borrowing

C. Rangarajan

It is almost axiomatic that countries in the early stages of development will need resources from abroad to accelerate economic growth. External sources supplement domestic savings to achieve a higher level of investment. However, these external resources need to be made available on terms and conditions which will enable the recipient countries to repay the foreign liabilities over a period of time. The strategy of economic growth adopted by the recipient countries must incorporate this compulsion to repay the foreign obligations besides providing a sound base for faster growth. At the same time, the donor countries and the multilateral financial institutions have a responsibility to ensure that the terms on which these resources are provided are reasonable so that the process of economic growth is not retarded.

The focus of this chapter is on India's foreign borrowing and how it meshed with the development strategy of the country. India's attitude to foreign borrowing besides being influenced by domestic considerations is also naturally conditioned by the external environment. This chapter is thus divided into three sections. The first section deals with changes in the international environment in relation to the transfer of real resources. The second section discusses India's attitude to foreign borrowing and how the current account deficit was financed. The third section raises some issues in the context of India's need for external financing during the Seventh Five-Year Plan covering the period 1985–90.

Changes in the International Environment

The post-Second World War period till the advent of the first oil shock in 1973–74 was marked by a substantial transfer of real resources to developing countries on concessional terms. There was a broad consensus

The opinions expressed in this chapter are those of the author and do not necessarily represent those of the Reserve Bank of India, with which he is associated. The author is grateful to K. L. Deshpande for his help in writing this chapter.

among industrial countries with surplus resources that real transfer of resources from this group to developing countries was of mutual benefit to the donors as well as the recipients. Multilateral and regional development finance institutions made rapid strides, and this was the period in which the world community was convinced of the need to agree upon a target for the official development assistance of 0.7 percent of GNP.

The two oil shocks of the seventies, the deep and long recession of the early eighties and the international responses to meet these difficult challenges dramatically changed the international environment in a number of ways. Sustained economic and trade growth still eludes the world. The need for adequate transfer of resources on concessional terms to developing countries is being openly questioned and the international community has so far failed to evolve a common strategy to resolve the external debt crisis that remains a real threat to the smooth functioning of the international monetary system. Policies of individual major powers have exhibited a kind of independence which is unique to this recent period. The mix of monetary and fiscal policies pursued by industrial countries after 1979 resulted in interest rates steeply rising and at a time when export prices for many developing countries were declining.

The two major oil price increases shifted substantial resources from nonoil exporting countries. Reflecting the investment preferences of oil exporters, international banks acquired a central position in international finance. The financing gap experienced by nonoil developing countries was so large that several of them had to resort to external borrowing on a substantial scale. The initiatives of international and regional financial institutions to fill the gap fell short of the requirements. In the end, the nonoil developing countries resorted to bank finance on a large scale.

As the financing gap widened during the seventies, the outstanding debt of developing countries rose sharply. Total debt outstanding (both medium- and long-term debt and including International Monetary Fund credit but excluding short-term debt) increased tenfold from $67 billion in 1970 to $699 billion in 1984. Besides, short-term debt increased from $78 billion in 1978 to $170 billion in 1982 before declining to $129 billion in 1984. The ratio of debt to exports of goods and services rose from 119.9 percent in 1970 to 154.5 percent in 1983. As can be seen from Table 12.1, significant changes occurred with respect to the quantum as well as the pattern of financing of current account deficits. In 1973 nondebt creating flows constituted approximately 47.7 percent of the total financing need. This ratio came down to 21.6 percent in 1981. Short-term borrowings, which were almost negligible in 1973, constituted over 17 percent of the total financing need in 1981. International banks, which emerged as an important supplier of credit to developing countries, almost withdrew from the scene between 1981 and 1984, leading to a sudden drop in the resources available to the developing countries. The procyclical behavior of the international banks aggravated the difficulties of some of the economies. With growth in private lending, the average maturity of the external debt of developing countries in respect of new commitments significantly shortened from 20.5 years in 1970 to 15.0 years in 1984. Between 1975 and 1984, the proportion of floating interest rate loans in the public debt of these countries increased from 20.1 percent to 44.9 percent, and this along with the increase in interest rates since 1980 meant a steep escalation in debt-servicing costs from $15 billion in 1975 to $77 billion in 1984. A marked variability in the exchange rates of major international currencies coupled with serious misalignments, which became prominent features since the fixed exchange rate system was abandoned in 1973, added to the burden of borrowers in servicing debt besides adversely affecting investment activity.

The crash in oil prices in the first half of 1986 and continued weaknesses in oil prices have meant a transfer of resources estimated at about $60–70 billion from oil-exporting to oil-importing countries, and the major beneficiaries have been the industrial countries with large oil import bills. The new situation is similar to the one that prevailed in the sixties with industrial countries achieving large external surpluses but with one marked difference. The United States, in recent years, has been a net absorber of resources on a massive scale with a current account deficit running above $100 billion. Thus, in the last few years, the nonoil developing countries at times have had to compete with industrial countries for real resources. Given their inherent limitations and weaknesses, the nonoil developing countries were at a disadvantage in relation to strong borrower countries. Mid-1986, however, witnessed a downward movement in interest rates and this should provide some relief to debtors, depending on the relative weightage of debt at flexible interest rates and the relative decline in the international interest rates.

In the past few years, in the discussions on the problems of developing countries, one finds more often references to "adjustment" than to "growth." Obviously, "growth" without "adjustment" is not sustainable. Equally, "adjustment" without "growth" lacks purpose. A program of adjustment that calls for a sharp and sudden decline in growth and investment may not even pave the way for long-run growth. Adjustment ultimately requires moving resources into the export sector in order to reduce current account deficits and to investment in general to accelerate growth. Both these require time. The speed of adjustment will depend on the structural characteristics of the economy and external flows will help to provide the needed time and also to avoid the adverse effects of sudden changes in policy which will otherwise be required. An optimal path of adjustment must therefore be chosen, bearing in mind the adverse consequences, economic and social. The negative attitude towards transfer of real resources on the part of the industrially advanced countries and multilateral financial institutions must give way to a more positive approach. The objective must be optimization of global economic welfare. One sees hardly any evidence of this at the present moment. It is ironic that there was a net flow of resources from developing countries of the order of the $14 billion in 1983 and $20 billion in 1984.

India's Approach to Foreign Borrowing

Like all developing countries, India needs external resources to accelerate economic growth. But India's development plans since 1951, when the First Five-Year Plan was launched, have emphasized the goal of self-reliance and the need for development to rest primarily on sources mobilized domestically. India's gross savings rate which stood at 10 percent of GNP in the early fifties is now around 23 percent. This is a substantial achievement considering the low level of per capita income of the country. Inflow of real resources from abroad, essential as they are, not only to supplement domestic savings but also to provide the needed technology, have constituted only 5 percent to 8 percent of the country's total investments. India's current account deficit as a proportion to GDP averaged around 1.6 percent during the Sixth Five-Year Plan (1980–85). It reached the peak level of 1.9 percent once in 1981–82 and again in 1985–86 (see Appendix Statement 12.1). These figures are lower than the deficit of nonoil developing countries as a group in relation to their GDP, which ranged from 2 percent to 5 percent over this period. As a result of the cautious policy adopted towards foreign borrowing, the average ratio of debt outstanding to GNP in India was 16.7 percent as against the average ratio of 49.2 percent at the end of 1984 for all countries in the World Debt Tables. Thus, the ratio for India was about one-third of the ratio for all countries taken together.

India's balance of payments came under a severe strain in the seventies as a result of the two oil shocks. It would be of interest to examine India's response and adjustment in the wake of the two steep increases in oil prices (see Appendix Statement 12.2). After the first oil shock, the deficit on current account rose from 0.8 percent of GDP in 1973–74 to 1.1 percent in 1974–75. India too, like many nonoil developing countries, suffered a deterioration in the terms of trade which weakened by 44 percent during the three years 1973–74 to 1975–76. In absolute terms, the deficit in 1974–75 was $963 million (see Appendix Statement 12.3). The following year saw a substantial adjustment to the oil shock as the deficit dropped to $93 million or less than 0.1 percent of GDP. In 1976–77, there emerged a current account surplus of 1.4 percent of GDP. This swift adjustment was due to a combination of factors. There was basically a strong growth in exports (in U.S. dollar terms) of nearly 20 percent per annum during both 1975–76 and 1976–77. The international trade environment was also conducive as world trade rose by over 8 percent a year in value terms during this period. In volume terms, world trade declined by 4 percent in 1975 but rebounded next year with a rise of 11 percent. India's export effort was also aided by the fact that after the sharp increase in prices during 1973–74 and 1974–75, price increases were modest in the following four years. The average rate of increase in wholesale prices between 1975–76 and 1978–79 in India was only 1.5 percent per annum (see Appendix Statement 12.4).

There was also a substantial rise in private transfers during this period while imports remained more or less unchanged, partly because of improvement in oil production and only a modest rise in consumption and contraction in fertilizer imports as a result of higher domestic production. Aid receipts were reasonably buoyant and India drew on various International Monetary Fund facilities including oil facilities during the years

1973–74 to 1975–76. Over the next three years, by the time of the second oil shock, India had already repurchased the Fund drawings.

Thus, the Indian economy adjusted to the first oil shock rather quickly. The vigorous anti-inflationary policies pursued in 1974–75 and 1975–76 helped to accelerate exports by making Indian goods more competitive because of the moderate increase in domestic price levels. They also resulted in some initial decline in investment. Nonoil imports adjusted for changes in the unit values showed a decline. The growth rate of the economy was nevertheless maintained at a high level because of a good agricultural performance in three out of the four years following 1974–75.

The scenario was in many ways different after the second oil shock. Between 1978–79 and 1980–81 Indian imports rose by $6.8 billion or by over three-fourths. The current account deficit rose ninefold, from less than $300 million in 1978–79 to over $2,800 million in 1980–81 and to a peak of $3,142 million in 1981–82. The terms of trade deteriorated sharply by over 35 percent during 1979–80 and 1980–81. Total imports stagnated at around $15.5 billion between 1980–81 and 1983–84. With domestic production of oil increasing from 11.6 million tons in 1978–79 to 16.2 million tons in 1981–82, there were substantial savings on oil imports. Nonoil imports, on the other hand, grew by over 11 percent a year in three out of the four years so that overall imports remain unchanged. There was also a strong increase in private transfers and current invisibles. But export growth was subdued and nowhere close to the remarkable performance after the first oil shock. This was partly a reflection of the international trade environment. As is well-known, in terms of volume growth this was the leanest period for world trade during the last three decades. The magnitude of financing required was of a much larger order and, given the poor response of concessional assistance, India first drew down its foreign exchange reserves and later turned to Fund resources as well as to borrowings on commercial terms. However, India's balance of payments improved to the extent that it did not fully utilize the drawings contracted under the Extended Fund Facility.

The decline in the ratio of current account deficit to GDP from 1.9 percent in 1981–82 to an estimated 1.3 percent in 1984–85 does point to the success of the adjustment effort, though it was not as dramatic as after the first oil shock. At the same time, in absolute amounts, the deficit remained above $2 billion throughout the period. The sustained growth in nonoil imports helped to maintain the tempo of growth in income and investment. Between 1980 and 1985 the Indian economy grew at an average rate of 5.2 percent per annum with fixed capital formation growing at a rate of 5.8 percent a year.

The pattern of financing of the current account deficit of India is given in Table 12.2. Prior to 1973–74, India relied exclusively on debt on concessional terms. Debt to official creditors constituted roughly 95 percent of the gross external liabilities of India in 1970. The proportion of public external debt at variable interest rates was also low at just 0.4 percent even as late as in 1978. The average maturity period on loan commitments by the official creditors was 44.8 years (with 9.3 years as grace period) in 1978. In 1981–82, when there was a sharp increase in the current account deficit, India met 50 percent of the financing need by drawing down its reserves. In that year, while external assistance met 36.1 percent of the financing need, use of Fund credit and nonresident deposits accounted for 18.7 percent and 2.2 percent respectively. In 1983–84, external assistance, use of Fund credit and nonresident deposits met 36.5 percent, 33.8 percent and 17.0 percent, respectively, of the financing needs. Other capital transactions, including commercial borrowings, for the first time accounted for a significant proportion of the total financial requirements. By the end of 1984, the proportion of public external debt at variable interest rates rose to 7.9 percent of the total liabilities. The average rate of interest on loan commitments from official creditors which had been 1.8 percent in 1978 moved to 6 percent in 1984. Similarly, the maturity period on loan commitments by the official creditors contracted from 44.8 years (with 9.3 years as grace period) in 1978 to 31.2 years (with 7.5 years as grace period) in 1984. As a result, the grant element in respect of loan commitments by official creditors came down drastically from 72.4 percent to 34.3 percent over the six years ending 1984.

It may be useful to look at the nature and significance of some of the inflows on capital account. The inflow of nonresident bank deposits remained relatively small during 1980–81 and 1981–82 but picked up rapidly thereafter. These attracted as much as $1,150 million during 1985–86, contributing close to 30 percent of the estimated current account deficit in that year. Most of these deposits have been in longer-term maturities, and an analysis of the behavior of these deposits indicates that most of these deposits are renewed at the time of maturity. Further, the proportion of deposits under the Non-Resident External Rupee Account, which are denominated in rupees and most of which are expected to be utilized in India, formed over three-fifths of outstanding nonresident deposits at the end of March 1986. Interest rates on these deposits, particularly under the Foreign Currency Non-Resident Account Scheme, which are denominated in U.S. dollars or pounds sterling, are adjusted from time to time, taking into account the trend of interest rates in the international markets in order to avoid interest arbitrage and the flow of "hot" money. Though these deposits may not necessarily show, in the coming period, the degree of buoyancy they had shown in the last two years, nevertheless they will constitute of fairly steady flow of funds into the country.

India has used the resources available through the International Monetary Fund from time to time. Use of Fund resources (including the Trust Fund loan) contributed to a substantial extent to the financing of the current account deficit during 1980–81 to 1983–84. In 1982–83, 69 percent of the current account deficit was financed through Extended Fund Facility drawings and the proportion was 50 percent during the next year. However, as indicated earlier, in 1984–85, because of the improved situation in the balance of payments, India terminated the Extended Fund Facility before fully utilizing the amount originally contemplated. India approached the Fund early in the process of adjustment, and tried to avoid a critical balance-of-payments situation that might have arisen later. This was consistent with the Fund policy to encourage members to approach the Fund at an early stage of balance-of-payments difficulties so that adjustment efforts could succeed with minimal hardships.

Till the end of 1980, India had not made any substantial borrowings on commercial terms. During the next three years, India entered the international capital market and contracted commercial borrowings. These borrowings took the form of suppliers' credit, syndicated Euro Credits, floating rate notes, fixed rate bonds and revolving underwriting facility. During the period 1980–81 to 1984–85, the total quantum of proposals approved by the Government of India aggregated approximately over $7 billion. The net drawings have, however, been lower. Drawings depend upon the progress of the project for which the loans have been granted. Because of the fairly strong performance of the Indian economy, the low level of outstanding international debt and an impeccable record of debt servicing, India has been able to borrow with very low margins over LIBOR. Two years ago, India was able to avail herself of a large syndicated loan of $980 million in relation to a single unit. The interest rate was 0.5 percent over LIBOR.

Indian policy towards commercial borrowings has always been one of caution. External commercial borrowings are generally not approved for financing rupee costs. Borrowings for financing the import of capital goods are approved only for projects capable of generating surplus to repay the loans. The overall level of commercial borrowings is guided by the total picture in relation to the balance of payments.

Within the overall policy framework and objectives, India has encouraged direct and portfolio investment with and without repatriation facilities. As in the case of several other low-income countries, this source of funds has provided very little fresh capital to India. However, during the last two years there has been a noticeable response from nonresident Indians. Available data on direct foreign investment indicate that during the period 1976–77 to 1979–80 branches of foreign companies in India disinvested to the tune of $140 million. In each of these years, gross inflow of equity capital into foreign-controlled rupee companies was less than $12 million. According to the World Development Report, more than one-half of the quantified flow of direct investment in developing countries took the form of reinvested earnings. In India, during the above period, reinvested earnings exceeded the net inflow by about a quarter, implying a new outflow of capital if retained earnings were excluded.

Seventh Five-Year Plan and Some Issues

India's Seventh Five-Year Plan covering the period April 1985–March 1990 aims at achieving an annual growth rate of 5 percent. The growth rate of agricultural output is expected to be around 4 percent and that of industrial production 8.3 percent. The Plan projects a current account deficit of $16.8 billion at 1984–85 prices (and exchange rates). After allowing for a terms-of-trade loss and some increase in reserves, the financing requirements are placed at $17.6 billion. The average ratio of current account deficit to GDP for the Plan period is worked out at 1.6

percent with the ratio for the last year of the Plan being postulated at
1.4 percent. The debt service to current receipts ratio, again average for
the Plan period, is estimated at 17.6 percent.

Imports during the Seventh Plan period are projected to increase at
an annual rate of 5.8 percent or only a little more rapidly than the pace
of growth of the economy. Bulk imports, which include, among others,
petroleum, oil and lubricants, fertilizers, metals and edible oils, are expected
to increase slightly faster than GDP, while nonbulk imports have been
projected on the assumption of an import elasticity of 1.2, implying an
average annual growth of 6 percent in real terms. This elasticity is much
lower than the import elasticity of 2.2 recorded between 1973–74 and
1981–82. The volume of exports is projected to increase annually by
about 7 percent during 1985–90. Though this projection is based upon
an aggregation of estimates made with respect to individual commodities,
the order of increase envisaged is much higher than what had been
experienced in the previous five years. The trade deficit projected for
the Plan period comes to $29.2 billion, which would approximately be
2.8 percent of GDP.

The most significant change that has occurred since the Plan projections
were originally formulated has been the steep fall in the price of oil.
India, being an oil-importing country, should derive considerable benefit
from this fall. Domestic production of crude oil during the Seventh Plan
period is not expected to show the kind of dramatic increase that was
witnessed during the Sixth Plan period. Domestic production, which
constituted only 27 percent of the total consumption in 1980–81, rose
to 69 percent in 1984–85. This proportion is likely to go down rather
than increase during the Seventh Plan. However, the fall in oil prices
should reduce the import bill in the immediate short run. India may also
benefit by the fall in the price of fertilizers of which also the country is
an important importer. However, in view of greater emphasis that is being
placed on modernization of industry and upgrading of technology, nonbulk
imports may show a higher rise than what was indicated in the Seventh
Plan document. In fact, in 1985–86, which is the first year of the Seventh
Plan, imports of capital goods both on project and nonproject accounts
have shown a substantial rise. On the export front, while India's exports
to Gulf countries may be affected adversely, the country's exports to the
industrially advanced countries may increase to the extent their growth
rates have been spurred by the fall in oil prices. Thus, taking into account
both the positive and negative impact, perhaps the trade deficit may
remain at the level as indicated in the Plan document.

Expatriate remittances constitute an important element of India's invisible earnings. A substantial proportion of expatriate remittances orig-
inates from the oil-producing countries of West Asia. The recent decline
in oil prices may have an adverse effect on these remittances. Even under
the original projections, the nominal level of expatriate remittances were
expected to remain more or less unchanged, thus implying some decline
in real terms. On the whole, invisible earnings are expected to offset
somewhat less than half of the deficit on merchandise account or a much
smaller proportion of it than in the Sixth Plan period.

The World Debt Tables (1985–86) projected repayments to official and private creditors during the period 1985–89 (which broadly corresponds with the Seventh Plan period) at $9.0 billion. During the Seventh Plan, repurchases from the International Monetary Fund are estimated at $3.2 billion, yielding total repayments of $12.2 billion over the Plan period. With net financing requirements of $17.6 billion indicated earlier, gross financing needs during the Seventh Plan may be placed at $29.8 billion.

If we turn to the modes of financing, external assistance in the pipeline, at the end of March 1986, is estimated at $14.6 billion. The Aid India Consortium has agreed to provide assistance of $4.5 billion during 1986–87, as against $3.9 billion during 1985–86. If aid authorizations during the remaining three years of the Plan aggregate $14–15 billion, available external assistance for the Plan as a whole would be around $35 billion. It is the progress in utilization of this assistance which would determine the order of resources that need to be mobilized through other sources.

During 1985–86, gross utilization of external assistance is estimated at $2.0 billion as against authorizations of $4.5 billion from Consortium and other sources. If utilization is speeded up to reach $4.5 billion in the last year of the Plan, gross aid utilization during the Plan period may work out to around $16 billion.

Net inflow under nonresident deposits during 1985–86, as mentioned earlier, exceeded $1.1 billion. For the Plan period these deposits may be expected to amount to $4.5 billion, implying some decline in the rate of growth in the coming years, which would partly be a reflection of the slowdown in economic activity in the Middle East.

Fresh inflow of capital in the form of direct and portfolio investment may average $100 million a year during the Plan period, providing $0.5 billion in total.

The residual amount of $8.8 billion would be required to be raised through external commercial borrowing; the annual average requirement would work out to about $1.7 billion, not much higher than what has been raised recently.

During the Seventh Plan, the various parameters governing the balance of payments will remain manageable and under control. The current account deficit at 1.6 percent of GDP and the debt service ratio of 17.6 percent can be regarded as reasonable. No official projections of balance of payments have been made beyond 1990. However, certain estimates are available on the long-term growth prospects of the country in the Seventh Plan document. The document envisages that the country would continue to grow at 5 percent per annum till the end of the century. The rate of capital formation has been projected to increase from 25.9 percent of GDP in 1989–90 to 26.4 percent at the end of the century and that of domestic savings from 24.5 percent to 25.8 percent. The contribution of foreign savings is expected to decline from 1.4 percent of GDP in 1989–90 to 0.6 percent in the year 2000. This order of decline would be necessary to keep the debt service ratio at a reasonable and comfortable level. Given the postulated growth in income of 5 percent per annum, an improvement in the current account of the order envisaged would require much better performance in exports and import substitution than in the recent past. The developments in domestic oil production and the success in the conservation of energy, particularly of hydrocarbons, would be of crucial importance in respect of balance-of-payments outturn during the fifteen years.

India's effort to keep the balance-of-payments position on an even keel also depends upon the international economic environment. The growth in international capital markets is by itself not a justification for asking low-income countries to resort to commercial borrowings. Also a country should not be prematurely pushed into larger high-cost borrowings because it has managed its affairs well in the past. The flow of resources from the developed surplus countries to developing countries has shown a decline. This is true not only of official external assistance but also of the resources made available by the multilateral financial institutions. Funds made available by the International Monetary Fund have come down from $13.0 billion in 1983 to $5.9 billion in 1984 and rather sharply to $0.6 billion in 1985. Far from expanding the scope of finance, the access rights of the member countries to the Fund facilities have been cut down year after year. There has been a notable reluctance to make fresh allocation of special drawing rights (SDRs). During the fourth basic period, which will come to an end soon, there has been no allocation and recent discussions on the subject do not hold out much hope. The rationale that justified the allocation during the third basic period—steady rise in demand for international liquidity, a part of which could and should be met through allocation of SDRs—continues to be valid today also. Availability of owned reserves through SDR allocation would avoid deflationary policies for generating current account surplus to ensure adequate level of reserves on the part of the developing countries. A greater availability of finance which takes into account not only problems of highly indebted countries but also of other developing countries for concessional finance is of paramount importance. While India's efforts to generate a higher growth would rest largely on her own resources, a more encouraging international economic setting would prove to be of immense help. The balance-of-payments scenario for the Seventh Plan period and beyond as sketched earlier would require a fairly substantial volume growth in India's exports. Here again, the international trade environment will play a crucial factor. India cannot afford to follow a liberal policy with respect to imports if her exports encounter strong protectionist walls. The developed countries, far from reducing the degree of protection, have increased various forms of protection, open and disguised. An improved international environment with respect to aid and trade is a must. India will continue to pursue a policy of prudence and caution as far as foreign borrowing is concerned so that foreign borrowing facilitates and does not become a constraint on growth.

TABLE 12.1 Financing of Deficits: Nonoil Developing Countries
(in billions of U.S. dollars)

	1973	1981	1984
1. Current Account Deficit	11.5	108.3	37.9
2. Errors and Omissions	0.6	16.5	5.3
3. Reserve Accumulation	9.7	3.7	19.3
4. Total Financing Need (1+2+3)	21.8	128.5	62.5
Financed By:			
5. Nondebt Creating Flows	10.4 (47.7)[a]	27.8 (21.6)	22.1 (35.4)
Official Transfers	5.6	13.3	13.0
Direct Investment Flows	4.4	13.5	8.6
SDR Allocation, Valuation Change, etc.	0.4	1.0	0.5
6. Asset Transactions	–	– 14.3	– 5.1
7. Net External Borrowings	11.4 (52.3)	115.0 (89.5)	45.3 (72 5)
a) Reserve-Related Liabilities	–	8.9	6.0
i) Of Which Use of Fund Credit	–	6.0	5.3
b) Long-Term Borrowing from Official Creditors	5.7 (26.1)	25.1 (19.5)	25.8 (41.3)
c) Other Net External Borrowing	5.7 (26.1)	81.0 (63.0)	13.5 (21.6)
i) Long-Term	5.7	58.7	22.9
A) From Banks	9.0[b]	30.8	21.8
B) Others	– 3.3	27.9	1.1
ii) Short-Term	–	22.3	– 9.4

[a] Figures within parentheses show percentages to total financing need.
[b] From financial institutions.

Source: International Monetary Fund World Economic Outlook 1985 and previous issues.

TABLE 12.2 Financing of Deficits: India
(in millions of U.S. dollars)

	1973–74	1981–82	1983–84
1. Current Account Deficit	571	3,142	2,606
2. Current Account Deficit as a Proportion of GDP	0.8	1.9	1.4
3. Errors and Omissions	264	441	474
4. Reserve Accumulation	95	–	748
5. Financing Need (1+3+4)	930	3,583	3,828
6. Financing Need as a Proportion of GDP	1.3	2.2	1.0
Financed By:			
7. External Assistance (net)	795 (85.5)	1,292 (36.1)	1,396 (36.5)
8. Use of Fund Credit	75 (8.1)	691 (18.7)	1,294 (33.8)
9. Nonresident Deposits	– (2.2)	79 (17.0)	651
10. Use of Reserves	–	1,805 (50.3)	—
11. Other Capital Transactions (including Commercial borrowings)	60 (6.4)	–264 (–7.3)	487 (12.7)

a Figures within parentheses against items 7 to 11 show percentages
to financing need (item 5).

Source: Reserve Bank of India, Department of Economic Analysis and Policy.

APPENDIX

STATEMENT 12.1 India: Current Account Balance as a Proportion of GDP at Current Market Prices

Year	Current Account Balance (millions of U.S. $)	Percentage of GDP
1971–72	−772	−1.3
1972–73	−519	−0.8
1973–74	−571	−0.8
1974–75	−963	−1.1
1975–76	−93	−0.1
1976–77	1,271	1.4
1977–78	1,538	1.5
1978–79	−298	−0.3
1979–80	−946	−9.7
1980–81	−2,806	−1.7
1981–82	−3,142	−1.9
1982–83	−2,841	−1.7
1983–84	−2,606	−1.4

STATEMENT 12.2 India's Foreign Exchange Reserves (1971–72 to 1985–86)
(in millions of U.S. dollars)

End of Fiscal Year	Total Reserves[a]
1971–72	1,277
1972–73	1,311
1973–74	1,417
1974–75	1,379
1975–76	2,172
1976–77	3,747
1977–78	5,824
1978–79	7,357
1979–80	7,579
1980–81	7,228
1981–82	4,795
1982–83	5,289
1983–84	6,167
1984–85	6,435
1985–86	7,074

[a] Consist of foreign current assets, SDRs, gold and reserve position in the Fund. Gold is valued at 1 oz = 35 SDRs.

STATEMENT 12.3   India: Balance of Payments (1971–72 to 1983–84)
(in millions of U.S. $)

		1971–72	1972–73	1973–74	1974–75	1975–76	1976–77
1.	Imports	2,678	2,882	3,487	5,237	5,472	5,371
2.	Exports	2,091	2,587	3,014	4,003	4,795	5,717
3.	Trade Balance (2–1)	−587	−335	−473	−1,234	−677	346
4.	Invisibles and Nonmonetary Gold	−185	−184	−98	271	584	925
5.	Current Account (net)	−772	−519	−571	−963	−93	1,271
6.	External Assistance (net) (Gross) (Repayments)	702 (1,038) (−336)	539 (921) (−382)	795 (1,175) (−380)	1,128 (1,468) (−340)	1,526 (1,895) (−369)	1,355 (1,758) (−403)
7.	IMF (net)	—	—	75	611	237	−335
8.	Allocation of SDRs	103	—	—	—	—	—
9.	Other Capital (net)	188	−23	60	−393	−495	−369
10.	Errors and Omissions	−86	−42	−264	−368	−255	−362
11.	Change in Reserves (− Increase)	−135	45	−95	−15	−920	−1,560

STATEMENT 12.3 (Continued)

		1977–78	1978–79	1979–80	1980–81	1981–82	1982–83	1983–
1.	Imports	6,458	8,989	11,822	15,862	15,484	15,429	15,5
2.	Exports	6,333	6,750	7,656	8,316	8,659	9,453	9,8
3.	Trade Balance (2–1)	−125	−2,239	−4,166	−7,546	−6,825	−5,976	−5,6
4.	Invisibles and Nonmonetary Gold	1,663	1,941	3,220	4,740	3,683	3,135	3,0
5.	Current Account (net)	1,538	−298	−946	−2,806	−3,142	−2,841	−2,6
6.	External Assistance (net)	1,010	931	1,184	1,272	1,292	1,518	1,3
	(Gross)	(1,579)	(1,495)	(1,844)	(2,140)	(2,021)	(2,235)	(2,1
	(Repayments)	(−561)	(−564)	(−660)	(−868)	(−729)	(−717)	(−7
7.	IMF (net)	−337	−251	−102	1,026	671	1,958	1,2
8.	Allocation of SDRs	—	153	156	152	—	—	-
9.	Other Capital (net)	−381	−36	152	−97	−185	−199	1,1
10.	Errors and Omissions	−18	715	13	−200	−441	210	−4
11.	Change in Reserves (− Increase)	−1,812	−1,214	−456	653	1,805	−646	−7

STATEMENT 12.4   India — Selected Indicators

Year	GDP at Constant Factor	Index of Agricultural Production	Index of Industrial Production	Gross Domestic Saving	Gross Capital Formation
				(as a proportion of gross domestic production at current market prices)	
(1)	(2)[a]	(3)[a]	(4)[a]	(5)	(6)
1971–72	1.6	−0.3	5.7	17.3	18.4
1972–73	−1.0	−8.0	3.9	16.2	16.9
1973–74	4.8	9.9	0.8	19.3	20.0
1974–75	0.9	−3.2	3.2	18.2	19.1
1975–76	9.7	15.2	7.2	20.1	19.9
1976–77	0.6	−7.0	9.6	22.5	20.8
1977–78	8.7	14.3	3.3	22.5	20.9
1978–79	5.8	3.8	7.6	24.7	24.8
1979–80	−4.9	−15.2	−1.4	23.0	23.5
1980–81	7.4	15.6	4.0	22.8	24.5
1981–82	5.5	5.6	8.6	23.0	24.8
1982–83	2.9	−3.8	3.9	22.6	24.2
1983–84	7.8	13.7	5.4	22.1	23.4
1984–85	3.6	−0.9	5.8	22.1	23.4

[a] Percentage change over the previous year in respect of columns 2, 3, 4, 7 and 8.

STATEMENT 12.4 (Continued)

Year	Wholesale Price Index (average)	M$_3$	Overall Budgetary Deficit as a Proportion of GDP at Current Market Prices
	(7)[a]	(8)[a]	(9)
1971–72	5.6	15.2	1.7
1972–73	10.0	18.3	1.8
1973–74	20.2	17.4	0.9
1974–75	25.2	10.9	0.8
1975–76	−1.1	15.0	0.4
1976–77	2.1	23.6	0.2
1977–78	5.2	18.4	1.1
1978–79	--	21.9	0.6
1979–80	17.1	17.7	2.5
1980–81	18.2	18.1	2.7
1981–82	9.3	12.5	1.7
1982–83	2.6	16.1	1.4
1983–84	9.5	18.1	1.1
1984–85	7.1	18.9	2.8

13

Some Aspects of India's Export Policy and Performance

Charan D. Wadhva

India's exports in value terms recorded rapid rates of growth even during the periods of widespread recession in the international economy following the two oil price shocks. Thus, India's exports recorded an average annual growth rate in nominal rupee terms of 27.2 percent during the period 1973–74 to 1976–77 and of 13.7 percent during 1981–82 to 1983–84 (see Table 13.1). However, the deceleration in the rate of growth of Indian exports to an average rate of growth of 5.5 percent during the period 1977–78 and 1978–79, when the international economy had largely recovered from the aftereffects of the recessions of 1974 and 1975, created doubts regarding the ability of the Indian economy to generate self-sustaining rapid growth of its exports. These doubts have always existed throughout the history of planned economic development in India despite the increased intensity and range of export promotion policy measures undertaken by the Government of India in recent years in order to manage its external balance.

The balance-of-payments position which appeared to be manageable until recently no longer appears to be as comfortable for the current and the remaining years of the Seventh Five-Year Plan (1985–90). This is so for a number of reasons. Firstly, the rate of growth of India's exports has shown signs of deceleration in 1985–86 and the prospects for growth in exports of several of our commodities appear none too bright for the coming years.[1] Secondly, the rate of growth of imports which was lower than the rate of growth of exports throughout the 1980s (Table 13.1) threatens to revert to the old pattern of the 1970s in the coming years. This would undoubtedly occur largely due to the more intensive import

---

I would like to thank Vijay Joshi for discussing with me his work on the exchange rate of the Indian rupee. I would like to acknowledge the assistance provided by Mohd Saqib in the compilation and processing of statistical data used in this chapter. I also thank the participants of the Boston Conference on the Indian Economy for their comments and suggestions for revising this chapter.

liberalization policies being followed by the present Government. The imports of capital goods, raw materials and components in volume terms registered a growth of about 9 percent per annum during the period 1980–84.

If the present trends continue, the balance-of-payments position is likely to become more difficult and may even turn to be critical by the year 1990 unless exports grow at a much faster rate. Acceleration of the rate of growth of exports in real terms has been recognized as a "key element of the foreign trade and payments strategy retained in the Seventh Plan."[2] The Planning Commission has suggested a target rate of growth of exports of 7 percent per annum to meet the projected requirements of imports for the Seventh Five-Year Plan period without unduly aggravating the balance-of-payments position.[3] The actual rate of growth in the value of exports in 1970–71 prices during the years 1981–82 to 1984–85 has been disappointingly low—around 4.5 percent only (see Table 13.2). The rate of inflow of remittances from nonresident Indians has declined in view of the sharp fall in world oil prices being currently experienced. While this same fall in international oil prices will give us a breather for some time on the import side, oil prices are bound to go up in the future. There is a squeeze on concessional aid flows to India by the International Development Association (the soft loans window of the World Bank) as such flows have fallen from the average of U.S. $1,200 million annually to near $600 million annually. The debt service ratio (including repayments due to the International Monetary Fund) is likely to go up from about 15 percent for 1984–85 to over 20 percent by 1988–89. The Seventh Five-Year Plan has also postulated an import growth rate of 5.8 percent per annum and borrowing U.S. $9.5 billion (or U.S. $1.9 billion annually) from commercial markets over the next five years.

The critical need for stepping up the rate of growth of exports in real terms to 7 percent per annum (or more) can hardly be exaggerated. The World Bank in its 1986 report on the Indian Economy has termed "export performance" as the *most critical* factor in maintaining a viable balance-of-payments position. The World Bank has calculated that if the growth of India's volume of exports were to grow only at the existing rate of 4.8 percent per annum (as achieved in the 1980–84 period) and all other requirements of foreign exchange projected by the Seventh Plan remain valid, India would have to borrow approximately U.S. $6.1 billion more (making a total of U.S. $15.6 billion) in commercial markets up to 1990 to maintain the GDP growth rate of 5 percent per annum and industrial growth rate of 6.6 percent per annum. This would push up the current account deficit to GDP ratio to about 2.4 percent (compared to 1.2 percent at present) and the debt service ratio to 26.4 percent in 1989–90. This will adversely affect India's credit rating in the international capital markets. There is an imperative need for formulating innovative policy supportive programs which will help to achieve a minimum of 7 percent annual growth in exports in quantum terms. This would help in managing the external balance without further adverse effects on the Indian economy.

Having established the critical need for accelerating the growth of exports, we proceed to examine a few specific aspects of performance of policy and India's exports in quantitative terms. These aspects are analyzed under the following four sections: (1) India's exports and income in world markets; (2) the relationship between India's exports and exchange rate measures; (3) a micro view of export performance; (4) concluding remarks

India's Exports and Income in World Markets

This section is divided into two subsections: (1) the empirical relationship between India's global exports (in real terms) and the world income (GDP in real terms); and (2) the empirical relationship between India's "regional" (real) exports and the relevant regional (real) income. Our purpose in undertaking such empirical exercises is to examine how sensitive India's exports are to changes in "world" income. Through these exercises, we are directly testing whether "global" recessions would seriously affect our exports.

India's Global Exports Related to World Income

The following double log relationship has been estimated between India's global exports (in real terms) X_w and the index number of GDP of the world (Y_w):[4]

$$\text{(1) Log } X_w = -2.68 + 2.16 \text{ Log } Y_w. \ldots$$
$$(12.75)*$$
$$R^2 = 0.92 \text{ ; DW } = 1.54$$

Equation (1) shows that India's exports are highly elastic (the elasticity coefficient being 2.16) with respect to global income. A continued high rate of growth of output in the world economy indeed benefits India through enlarging its (real) exports. The logic should work the other way also. Prolonged recession would lead to a sizable effect in reducing India's (real) exports.[5]

India's Exports and Regional Income

We attempt to test the empirical relationship between India's exports and "regional" income with respect to the following regions: (1) the group of oil-exporting countries; and (2) the Asian developing countries.

India's Exports to the Group of Oil-Exporting Countries Related to the Income of This Group. Equation (2) presents the relationship between India's (real) exports to the group of oil-exporting countries (X_{OFC}) and indices of the group's (real) income (Y_{OFC}) measured in terms to GDP:

$$\text{(2) Log } X_{OFC} = -13 + 3.9 \text{ Log } Y_{OFC}. \ldots$$
$$(13.03)*$$
$$R^2 = 0.91; \text{ DW } = 1.21$$

Thus, we see from equation (2) that India's exports are highly elastic with respect to the income levels in the oil-exporting countries. In fact, a comparison of equations (1) and (2) shows that the coefficient of elasticity of India's exports with respect to the income levels in the oil-exporting countries (3.9) is higher than with respect to the global income (2.16). This is not surprising as the Gulf and countries of the Middle East belonging to the group of oil-exporting countries constitute significant markets for Indian goods. Thus, any fall in oil prices which results in reduction of real income of the oil-exporting countries of the Gulf and the Middle East would most likely reduce the exports from India to them in real terms. Besides, such a fall in real income of the oil-exporting countries would lead to dimming the prospects of labor migration to them and also of remittances from the nonresident Indians from these countries into India.

India's Exports and Income Levels in the Group of Asian Developing Countries. We have also carried out a similar analysis with respect to the relation of India's (real) exports to the income indices of the group of Asian developing countries. The corresponding elasticity coefficient in this case was estimated to be 3.03.

The above results reconfirm that (growth in) income levels in the group of developing countries, illustrated with reference to the Asian countries, also exert a positive influence in increasing India's exports (in real terms) and vice versa.

The Relationship Between India's Exports and Exchange Rate Measures

Increasing attention is being paid currently to discussing the question whether India should consider devaluing the rupee in response to its current (and even more the impending) balance-of-payments problems. In order to examine the desirability or otherwise of such a measure, it is important to examine the role that changes in exchange rates can play in promoting India's exports. The protagonists of the devaluation measure mainly base their case on the beneficial effect this measure would have for increasing India's (real) exports. We examine this very limited question in a partial equilibrium framework using an OLS technique. Three exchange rate measures are explored: (1) nominal effective exchange rate (NER); (2) effective relative prices; and (3) the real effective exchange rate (RER).[6] Two alternative dependent variables are also explored, namely, exports measured in constant prices and a quantum index of exports. The regression results, which include other independent variables besides the exchange rate, are presented in Table 13.4 (the additional data for these regressions are reproduced in Tables 13.5 and 13.6).

As may be seen from Table 13.3, the nominal effective exchange rate as well as the real effective exchange rate with base year (1975 = 100) on the whole declined to numbers below 100 during the years 1975 to 1984, showing a policy-induced "depreciation" of the Indian rupee. Thus, we would a priori expect the sign of the coefficients of NER and RER to be negative since India's (real) exports have been going up throughout the period from 1970 to 1984. The results presented in Table 13.4 indeed confirm this. The results in Table 13.4 show that *other things remaining constant:*

1. India's (real) exports are highly elastic with respect to the NER (with a coefficient of elasticity of 2.61).
2. Similarly, India's exports with respect to the RER are highly elastic (with a coefficient of elasticity of 2.28).
3. When India's exports are regressed on both world income and the RER, the elasticity coefficient with respect to RER comes out to be 1.31, though this estimate is not statistically significant, and the elasticity coefficient with respect to world income turns out to be 0.82.
4. If the quantum index is adopted as dependent variable instead, and its logarithm regressed on world income as well as the price index for India relative to world price level, the resultant price elasticity is −0.014 which is insignificant statistically but correct in sign.

We have also tried to examine the impact of the exchange rate on India's export performance at a more *disaggregate* level for a few products. We report the results, in elasticity form, for five products, namely: (1) cotton fabrics; (2) engineering goods; (3) coffee; (4) fish and fish preparations; and (5) handicrafts. (The additional data are reported in Table 13.7.) The results for other products were found not to be worth reporting at this stage.

Table 13.8 presents the econometric results of the exercise relating the nominal effective exchange rate (NER) to the nominal values of exports. These results confirm that exchange rate depreciation has an important effect in increasing India's exports of all five selected products, including both traditional products and the nontraditional products such as engineering goods. The coefficients of the NER are all much above unity and are of appropriate sign and statistically significant at a 5 percent level of significance. These lead to the conclusion that Indian's exports of these selected products are highly elastic with respect to the nominal effective exchange rate.

The econometric results in Table 13.8 are based on similar data but for the real magnitudes of the variables involved. Thus we examine the impact of the real effective exchange rate (RER) and the incentives adjusted real effective exchange rate (IRER) on the value of exports of five selected product measures in constant prices. The results in Table 13.9 confirm that for the five selected products, exports in real terms are highly elastic with respect to both the RER and IRER. The signs of the coefficients are correct and are also much above unity. We therefore conclude that the real effective exchange rate does influence the growth of real exports of the selected products. We presume that this result would hold for most of the nontraditional products exported by India.

A look at the simple econometric results presented in Tables 13.4, 13.8, and 13.9 reveals that there is definite role which depreciation of the Indian rupee can play, subject to other things being constant, in increasing India's exports in real terms in line with economic theory.

It would be naive to suggest from the above analysis that the exchange rate instrument should be considered in isolation, or without regard to the several other preconditions which economic theory itself lays down for the success of devaluation, namely:

1. The sum of the relevant demand elasticities for exports and imports be greater than unity;
2. There should be no supply bottlenecks in the domestic economy so that exportable output does go up on response to the change in the exchange rate;
3. The domestic price level does not rise relative to the international price level;
4. That exports are not much affected by nonprice factors (such as nontariff barriers; quality, delivery schedules, brand loyalties, terms of export credit and the like) and affected largely by the price factor;
5. That there is no retaliatory exchange rate change from competing exporting countries (no competitive devaluation).

It is debatable whether all these conditions can be satisfied in the case of Indian exports for deriving maximum benefit from the decision to devalue the Indian rupee. With the changing composition of India's exports more and more in favor of manufactured goods and price-elastic non-traditional goods, the chances of devaluation producing the desirable effect on India's exports have increased today compared to, say, 1966. In any case, through a managed exchange rate, the Reserve Bank of India has gradually and with some regularity effected substantial depreciation of the Indian rupee during the last few years without any disastrous effects and, if anything, some beneficial effects on the price competitiveness of India's manufactured exports. However, the decision to devalue the Indian rupee in a single step by say 20 percent (over and above the existing arrangement gradually to depreciate the rupee against leading currencies) cannot be taken only by considering its effects on India's exports. An in-depth and comprehensive study of the costs and benefits of such a policy decision needs to be launched.

A Micro View of Export Performance

The macro view on constraints on Indian exports—both international and domestic—has been dealt with effectively by the Abid Hussain Committee (Report of the Committee on Trade Policies).[7] This committee had based its analysis on the feedback provided by the captains of industries and entrepreneurs belonging to small-scale industries in India. My earlier work on the subject of micro perspectives on exports confirms the findings of the Abid Hussain Committee.[8] Basically, the real constraints on the expansion of Indian exports are internal and not external, though at the margin, the difficulties posed by the external constraints are increasing over time in selected sectors (such as quotas on garments). The internal constraints are based on both the supply side and demand side. The supply-side constraints within India work through infrastructural bottlenecks (via shortage of inputs such as power) which limit the growth of output for exports. The demand-side constraints work through pressure of internal demand and reduce the exportable output significantly. This is due to much higher prices of exportables prevailing in India and consequently higher profitability of sales in the home market compared to exports. The real constraint is actually imposed by clearly lower profitability of exports compared to domestic sales. All the export incentives put together still fall far short of the effective protection for import substitution, notwithstanding the gradual but sure moves to reduce protection to Indian industries. Unless this basic problem of lower profitability of Indian manufactured exports is solved, no self-sustaining momentum can be imparted to Indian exports in the highly competitive international markets.

International competitiveness in manufactured products (without prejudice to the expansion of agro-based exports) is a function of both price and nonprice factors. It is better to conceive of international competitiveness under present conditions as a function of *comparative "marketing" advantage* instead of the traditional comparative production cost advantage. Perhaps the weakest link in the management chain of India's international business is the lack of an adequate marketing planning system based on up-to-date and reliable marketing information.

In this connection, I would like to reiterate the need for urgently implementing the scheme already accepted by the Government of India for setting up a National Center for Trade Information. This would greatly assist the small- and medium-scale industries to plan for and successfully implement schemes for internationalizing their business.

I would further plead for microlevel planning for exports as a supplement to macrolevel planning for export promotion. The large-scale units, the subsidiaries of foreign multinationals, and export and trading houses must evolve precise plans and annual targets for exports and other forms of international business. This should be done in consultation with, and with the full cooperation of, the Government of India and Government agencies within India, as well as our commercial representatives abroad. A jointly programmed action plan, with much greater involvement, policy support, procedure simplification and efficient monitoring from the Government of India is essential. This would go a long way in building an appropriate export culture for self-sustaining growth of India's exports in the years to come.

Concluding Remarks

This chapter has primarily focused on selected aspects of India's export performance largely at the aggregative level and in the process commented on some of the desirable elements of a national policy for self-sustaining growth of India's exports in the future. The critical importance of the need for substantially accelerating the rate of growth of Indian exports has been highlighted in the context of the emerging, adverse balance-of-payments scenario. A real diagnosis of the problems can be undertaken only by conducting specific product market studies at the disaggregated level. This will enable policymakers to identify selected thrust areas where India can have and must develop a "comparative marketing advantage" and must nurture and "protect" these areas at all costs. There will be a need for research-based, periodic reviews to confirm the longer-run economic viability of the selected thrust products as well as thrust markets. The appropriate institutional model which would support such an approach would be based upon a "Government-Industry Partnership." Building an appropriate export culture would not be easy but should be possible provided there is a *will* for this purpose among the partners.

Notes

1. The Commerce Ministry (Government of India) in its Annual Report 1985–86 cites the international environment as one of the reasons for this assessment. To quote, "The international environment for trade continues to be precarious for many of our commodities and manufactures in the wake of slowing down in the growth of some of the major economies of the world and protectionist measures faced by our exporters in several countries". (ibid., 3).

2. *Seventh Five Year Plan 1985–90* (New Delhi: Government of India, Planning Commission, 1985), vol. 1, chap. 5.

3. Ibid.

4. Through this chapter, the figures within the parentheses indicate t-values for a zero null hypothesis for the relevant coefficients.

5. It may also be noted that the corresponding elasticity coefficient with respect to the (real) income of the group of developed countries for India's exports was as high as 5.12. The developed market economies constitute the largest single group as markets for India's exports. Thus, India's exports are seriously affected by prolonged recession in the developed countries in particular.

6. The exchange rate series follow measures developed by Vijay Joshi which are reproduced in Table 13.3 in this chapter. For methodology and other details, the main source is Vijay Joshi, "The Nominal and Real Effective Exchange Rate of the Indian Rupee 1971–83," *Reserve Bank of India Occasional Papers* 5, no. 1 (June 1984):28–87. This has been supplemented by his paper on "Exchange Rate Policy," *Economic Times* (Bombay), 31 January 1986, 5. Joshi's preferred series, based on a basket of ten currencies, are adopted for present purposes. The ten countries in the basket are the United States, Japan, the United Kingdom, West Germany, Italy, the Netherlands, France, Belgium, Switzerland, and Australia.

7. Report of the Committee on Trade Policies (New Delhi: Government of India, Ministry of Commerce, December 1984), 13–19.

8. This section is based on my earlier work and is subjective in nature as far as its extrapolation to the present conditions is concerned. In view of my work on this subject having been published earlier, I have kept this section brief. See Charan D. Wadhva, "Export Development Policies and Plans: Macro and Micro Perspectives," in C. Rangarajan, et al. *Strategy for Industrial Development in the 80's* (New Delhi: Oxford University Press, 1981), chap. 5.

TABLE 13.1   Trends in India's Foreign Trade 1970–71 to 1984–85

	Exports (Rs crores[a])	Percentage Change (%)	Imports (Rs crores)	Percentage Change (%)	B.O.T. (Rs crores)
1970–71	1,535	8.63	1,634	3.29	−99
1971–72	1,608	4.76	1,824	11.63	−216
1972–73	1,971	22.57	1,867	2.36	104
1973–74	2,523	28.01	2,955	58.28	−432
1974–75	3,329	31.95	4,519	52.93	−1,190
1975–76	4,026	20.94	5,265	16.51	−1,239
1976–77	5,143	27.74	5,074	−3.63	69
1977–78	5,408	5.15	6,020	18.64	−612
1978–79	5,726	5.88	6,811	13.14	−1,085
1979–80	6,418	12.09	9,143	34.24	−2,725
1980–81	6,711	4.57	12,549	37.25	−5,838
1981–82	7,806	16.32	13,608	8.44	−5,802
1982–83	8,834	13.17	14,360	5.53	−5,526
1983–84	9,865	11.67	15,762	9.76	−5,897
1984–85	11,555	17.13	17,092	8.44	−5,537

[a]Rs. 1 crore = Rs 10 million.

Sources: Directorate General of Commercial Intelligence and Statistics
(Calcutta); Reserve Bank of India Bulletin (various issues); Economic Survey
1985–86 (New Delhi: Government of India, 1986).

TABLE 13.2   India's Exports 1970–71 to 1984–85

	Exports (Rs crores)	Percentage Change (%)	Quantum Index	Percentage Change (%)	Exports at 1970–71 (Rs crores)	Percentage Change (%)
1970–71	1,535	8.63	106	—	1,535	—
1971–72	1,608	4.76	107	0.94	1,576	2.67
1972–73	1,971	22.57	120	12.15	1,744	10.66
1973–74	2,523	28.01	125	4.17	1,828	4.82
1974–75	3,329	31.95	133	6.40	1,924	5.25
1975–76	4,026	20.94	147	10.53	2,165	12.53
1976–77	5,143	27.74	174	18.37	2,597	19.95
1977–78	5,408	5.15	168	−3.45	2,425	−6.62
1978–79	5,726	5.88	180	7.14	2,591	6.85
1979–80	6,418	12.09	199	10.56	2,878	11.08
1980–81	6,711	4.57	238	19.60	3,442	19.60
1981–82	7,806	16.32	198	−16.81	2,870	−16.62
1982–83	8,834	13.17	210	6.06	3,057	6.52
1983–84	9,865	11.67	218	3.81	3,413	11.65
1984–85	11,555	17.13	235	7.80	3,998	17.14

Source: UN Statistical Yearbook, National Accounts Statistics (New York:
United Nations, various years).

TABLE 13.3 Nominal and Real Effective Exchange Rates of Indian Rupee

	Nominal Effective Exchange Rate	Real Effective Exchange Rate	Effective Relative Prices
1970–71	100	100	100
1971–72	98	100	102
1972–73	92	98	107
1973–74	83	93	111
1974–75	82	95	117
1975–76	78	89	113
1976–77	77	80	103
1977–78	77	80	104
1978–79	74	73	100
1979–80	72	73	102
1980–81	74	80	108
1981–82	74	84	113
1982–83	74	82	110
1983–84	73	84	116
1984–85	70	83	117

Source: Based on Joshi, "The Nominal and Real Effective Exchange Rate of the Indian Rupee, 1971–83," 50.

TABLE 13.4 India's (Total) Exports Related to Exchange Rate and Other Variables

Dependent Variable	Intercept	Independent Variables				R^2	D.W.
Ln (X)	19.69	Ln (NER)	−2.61 (9.47)			0.87	1.32
Ln (X)	18.18	Ln (RER)	−2.28 (4.44)			0.60	0.75
Ln (X)	−6.02	Ln (RER)	−1.31 (0.48)	Ln (GDP)	0.82 (9.23)	0.91	2.58
X	−3588	ERP	−17.52 (0.59)	GDP Wld	−41.06 (8.68)	0.88	1.55
Ln (QX)	−4.82	Ln (PIPW)	−0.014 (0.15)	LN(GDPWld)	2.05 (15.66)	0.95	2.19

Notes:
X   denotes exports at constant (1970–71) prices
QX   denotes quantum index of exports
NER   denotes nominal exchange rate
RER   denotes real effective exchange rate
GDP   denotes gross domestic product at 1970–71 prices
Wld   denotes world
PIPW   denotes Indian prices over world price
ERP   denotes effective relative prices

TABLE 13.5 Data on Income and Price Indices

	GDP at 1970–71 Prices	Price Index for India	Price Index for World	Index of World Income
1970–71	36,736	100	100	100
1971–72	37,312	105	104	104
1972–73	36,940	114	99	110
1973–74	38,722	133	112	116
1974–75	39,080	171	171	118
1975–76	42,890	178	219	119
1976–77	43,160	174	177	125
1977–78	46,920	187	203	131
1978–79	49,619	187	246	136
1979–80	47,191	208	236	141
1980–81	50,705	251	275	144
1981–82	53,469	281	298	145
1982–83	55,032	288	255	145
1983–84	59,319	311	224	148
1984–85	61,473	338	239	148

Source: IMF Statistics, Economic Survey 1985–86.

TABLE 13.6 Movement of Indices: India

	Indian Prices/ World Prices	Rupees per Dollar	Wholesale Price Index	Unit Value of Exports
1970–71	1.0	7.57	100	100
1971–72	1.01	7.53	106	102
1972–73	1.15	7.59	116	113
1973–74	1.19	7.74	140	138
1974–75	1.0	8.1	175	173
1975–76	0.81	8.38	173	186
1976–77	0.98	8.37	177	198
1977–78	0.92	8.37	186	223
1978–79	0.76	8.96	186	221
1979–80	0.88	8.74	217	223
1980–81	0.91	8.19	257	195
1981–82	0.94	8.13	281	272
1982–83	1.13	7.86	288	289
1983–84	1.39	8.66	316	289
1984–85	1.41	9.46	338	294

Source: IMF Statistics, Economic Survey 1985–86.

TABLE 13.7 India's Exports at Current Prices[a]
(Rs crores)

			Commodity		
	Cotton Fabrics	Engineering Goods	Coffee	Fish Preparations	Handi-crafts
1970–71	75.3	130.4	25.11	30.5	69.86
1971–72	67.93	123.79	28.4	45.39	84.52
1972–73	100.9	87.4	32.9	54.5	119.7
1973–74	194.7	118.3	46.0	89.2	137.1
1974–75	158.9	215.5	51.6	66.2	186.6
1975–76	161.2	259.6	66.7	127.2	224.11
1976–77	267.3	302.2	126.0	180.6	263.1
1977–78	224.7	337.2	194.4	174.3	455.7
1978–79	224.3	399.4	144.0	226.3	751.8
1979–80	287.4	448.8	163.3	253.4	832.49
1980–81	276.5	525.9	214.2	217.0	935.40
1981–82	294.6	617.9	146.3	284.9	1,200.38
1982–83	271.47	799.22	184.2	364.16	1,312.65
1983–84	276.6	691.39	182.5	327.3	1,599.33
1984–85	412.87	738.39	198.13	335.82	1,521.41

[a]The data in Table 13.7 have been converted to constant prices (base 1970–71 = 100) by using the series of general wholesale price index of India (reproduced in Table 13.5).

Source: Economic Survey (various issues).

TABLE 13.8 Impact of the Real Effective Exchange Rate and Incentive
Adjusted Exchange Rate on India's Exports of Selected Products
(at constant prices)

Commodity (Exports)	Intercept	Ln RER	Ln IRER[a]	R^2	D.W.
1. Ln Cotton Fabrics	22.9	-3.97 (5.04)		0.66	1.58
2. Ln Cotton Fabrics	20.41		-3.39 (3.77)	0.52	0.85
3. Ln Engineering Goods	14.88	-3.17 (5.83)		0.724	1.30
4. Ln Engineering Goods	13.26		-2.79 (4.48)	0.607	0.68
5. Ln Coffee	17.38	-4.08 (6.1)		0.74	2.06
6. Ln Coffee	15.73		-3.68 (4.98)	0.656	1.22
7. Ln Fish and Preparations	16.19	-3.71 (5.44)		0.694	1.62
8. Ln Fish and Preparations	13.39		-3.06 (3.07)	0.51	0.92
9. Ln Handicrafts	29.77	-6.53 (6.96)		0.79	0.65
10. Ln Handicrafts	24.63		-5.33 (4.16)	0.57	0.34

[a]IRER - Incentive adjusted Real Effective Exchange Rate.

TABLE 13.9 Impact of the Nominal Effective Exchange Rate
on India's Exports of Selected Products
(at constant prices)

	Intercept	Ln NER	R^2	D.W.
1. Ln Cotton	24.51	−4.39 (8.7)	0.85	2.28
2. Ln Engineering Goods	33.4	−6.25 (8.9)	0.86	0.97
3. Ln Coffee	35.6	−7.09 (9.27)	0.87	1.03
4. Ln Fish and Preparations	36.96	−7.32 (14.41)	0.94	2.17
5. Ln Handicrafts	49.98	−10.04 (13.44)	0.93	0.75

PART SIX

Domestic Savings, Taxation and Aggregate Demand

14

India's Fiscal Policy

Shankar Acharya

Introduction

In a mixed economy, pursuing planned economic development, fiscal policy plays a central and multidimensional role. To quote the Seventh Five-Year Plan (1985–90):

> Through it [fiscal policy] the Government creates and sustains the public economy consisting of the provision of public services and public investment; at the same time it is an instrument for reallocation of resources according to national priorities, redistribution, promotion of private savings and investments, and the maintenance of stability.[1]

The purpose of this chapter is to attempt a summary assessment of India's past fiscal policy in terms of the fundamental objectives of growth and social justice and to highlight some of the major themes which appear to underlie the spate of fiscal policy initiatives launched since mid-1985. The chapter also outlines some of the likely priorities for policy concern in the future.[2]

The principal way in which fiscal policy influences growth in a country at India's stage of development is through the efficacy, or otherwise, of mobilizing resources for development. The second section deals with this aspect. Fiscal policy also affects growth by influencing the efficiency of resource allocation, both within the public economy and without. This aspect is dealt with in the third section. In the fourth section we turn to comment on the equity dimension of India's fiscal policy. The fifth section focuses on the main themes underlying recent initiatives in India's fiscal policy. The chapter ends with a final section pointing to some of the key areas of policy concern for the future.

The responsibility for the views expressed in this chapter rests solely with the author and cannot be attributed to the Ministry of Finance with which he is affiliated as Economic Advisor. The author is grateful to Amaresh Bagchi and M. P. Aggarwal for their assistance and comments, though neither is implicated in the views expressed here.

Fiscal Policy and Resource Mobilization

In this section we offer an appraisal of resource mobilization efforts according to a set of alternative criteria.

Performance According to Tax Effort

As Table 14.1 shows, India has done rather well to raise the tax-GDP ratio from under 7 percent in 1950–51 to around 17 percent in 1984–85. For a country which began this period with a very low per capita income and achieved only a modest increase of 1–2 percent per year, on average, over the period, this record in mobilizing taxes is clearly commendable. This strong, intertemporal revenue performance is also borne out by the buoyancy shown by almost all major taxes. As Table 14.2 indicates, all major taxes, except noncorporate income tax and land revenue, have recorded buoyancy greater than unity. In the context of Five-Year Plans, targets set for additional resource mobilization (ARM) have usually been overfulfilled, at least in nominal terms. Table 14.3 highlights the importance of taxation in ARM over the last three-and-a-half decades.

Performance in Relation to Plan Targets for Public Savings

Tax revenues constitute only one, though admittedly critical, dimension of resource mobilization. Other aspects include generation of nontax revenues, control over current Government expenditure and performance of public sector enterprises. And, in India's federal structure, each of these dimensions needs to be assessed at both the Central and State levels. Perhaps the best summary assessment of resource mobilization performance may be obtained by focusing on trends in overall public savings, especially in relation to plan targets.

Ever since the Fourth Five-Year Plan, ending in 1973–74, Plan documents have explicitly specified target rates of public savings (relative to GDP) for the terminal year of the respective Five-Year Plan. Table 14.4 compares actual performance with plan targets.

A glance at the table shows that public savings performance in the terminal year fell short of target in the Fourth (1969–74) and Sixth Five-Year (1980–85) Plans. The target was exceeded in the Fifth Five-Year Plan (1974–79), but even this is subject to a qualification. The initial version of the Fifth Plan had proposed a target of 6.0 percent of GDP for the terminal year for public savings. The oil shock of 1973–74 led to a revision of the Plan, with the final document, which emerged midway in the Plan period, having scaled down the public savings target to 4.6 percent of GDP. Thus, in overall terms, it is difficult to avoid the conclusion that public savings performance has fallen markedly below planned levels in the past fifteen years.

Part of the explanation for the lackluster public savings performance may be gleaned from an examination of the disaggregated picture of public savings, provided in Table 14.5. The data clearly highlight the declining contribution of Government savings to overall public savings in recent years. The share of Government savings in total public savings has declined from a peak of 63 percent in 1975–76 to a *negative* 10 percent in 1984–85. What is more, as Table 14.6 shows, this decline in Government savings is attributable less to any weakness in mobilizing revenues and more to a rapid growth in current Government expenditures. Total current receipts of the Government have increased, as a ratio of GDP, fairly steadily from under 14 percent in 1970–71 to nearly 20 percent in 1984–85. And this buoyancy in current receipts has been mainly due to the strong performance in mobilizing tax revenues, whose share has risen from 12.3 percent of GDP in 1970–71 to 17.3 percent in 1984–85. The real problem for Government savings has been the outpacing of current receipts by current expenditures. Over the same period, current expenditures grew from 12.3 percent to 20 percent of GDP. Table 14.6 also suggests that the main elements fueling the growth of current expenditures have been subsidies and interest payments.

The decline in the share of Government savings, in total public savings, highlighted in Table 14.5, has meant a corresponding increase in the relative contribution of public sector enterprises (PSEs). But this statistical tautology cannot be taken as an unqualified tribute to the surplus generation performance of these units. Even the doubling of PSE savings ratio from 1.7 percent of GDP in 1970–71 to 3.5 percent in 1984–85 has to be interpreted with caution. It is necessary to emphasize that each year public investment augments, by substantial amounts, the capital stock employed by PSEs. The real issue is what has been PSE savings performance in relation to potential.

A serious answer to this question would require a major exercise, well beyond the scope of this bird's-eye review of fiscal policy. However, some pieces of information are suggestive. At the Central level, the capital employed in some 207 enterprises in 1984–85 is estimated to have been about Rs 364 billion, at historical cost. Of this, about half was in the form of equity. If this equity were to yield a modest return of 10 percent after tax, then after-tax profits would have amounted to about Rs 18 billion. In fact, the return was only Rs 9.3 billion, or about half as much. Furthermore, net after-tax profits of a handful of petroleum companies amounted to about Rs 11.2 billion, indicating that, but for these companies, the Central PSEs would have shown a net loss after tax in 1984–85.

At the State level, the PSE record is distinctly worse. The most important units are the State Electricity Boards, which were estimated to account for over Rs 13.0 billion of capital employed in 1984–85. But these units are estimated to have turned in a commercial loss of Rs 11 billion in that year. Another important set of State-level PSEs is constituted by the State Road Transport Undertakings. Preliminary estimates suggest that these units ran a net loss of about Rs 2 billion in 1984–85.

Taken together, this piecemeal evidence suggests that savings performance of PSEs has been well short of potential in recent years.

To sum up, public savings have generally fallen short of Plan targets in the last fifteen or so years. Despite a strong performance in raising current receipts, especially tax revenues, Government savings have fallen sharply because of a sustained increase in current Government expenditures, especially on account of interest payments and subsidies. Though, in relation to GDP, savings of public sector enterprises have shown a significant increase, the results fall substantially short of the potential implicit in the massive and growing stock of productive assets at the disposal of these units.

Performance in Relation to Private Savings

No assessment of fiscal policy with respect to resource mobilization can be complete, even superficially, without considering the effects of fiscal policy on private savings. However, in contrast to the case of public savings, the links between fiscal policy and private savings are less direct and more debatable. To begin with, fiscal policy clearly plays an important role in determining the disposable income in the hands of private entities, whether these are households, corporations or unincorporated enterprises. And, in most theories of private savings behavior, disposable income is a leading actor. Fiscal policy is also important in influencing the rates of return to savings and investment and such rates of return are generally believed to play a significant part in determining the savings of households and enterprises. Fiscal policy influences rates of return both directly, through tax incentives/disincentives, and indirectly, through its effects on overall profitability and price stability.

In India, fiscal (more particularly) tax policy has been used extensively for giving special inducements for savings. Subject to certain limits, savings out of current income if invested in life insurance, provident fund or certain "small" saving schemes like the National Savings Certificates of specified categories are allowed to be deducted from taxable income. Interest income from certain investments like bank deposits, dividends from Indian company shares and income from units of the United Trust of India is exempt from income tax, again subject to certain limits. Investments in life insurance or provident fund are exempt from wealth tax without any limit, while those in certain other assets like bank deposits and shares (stocks) of Indian companies are exempt up to certain limits. These limits have been revised upward from time to time. Investments in equities of newly created industrial companies have also enjoyed tax concessions in various forms.

Concessions in income and wealth taxes are provided also for encouraging investment in specified areas like housing. Income from new houses is exempt up to certain limits. The value of one house is exempt also from wealth tax. Recently, imputed income from owner-occupied houses has been exempted from tax. The area of tax benefits for saving in general and in housing in particular is proposed to be expanded further. Payments made by a taxpayer towards the cost of a new residential property including repayment of loan and interest are proposed to be made tax deductible, if the borrowings for this investment are made from specified sources. There are also "rollover provisions" for relief from capital gains tax in the case of investment in housing.

An adequate consideration of the impact of these concessions and the more general question about the impact of fiscal policy on private savings is quite beyond the scope of this chapter.[3] Here we limit ourselves to summarizing the record on private and economywide savings in relation to terminal-year Plan targets.

Table 14.7 underscores several obvious points. First, in each of the last three Five-Year Plans, the private savings rate for the terminal year has exceeded the Plan target, with the overfulfillment being quite dramatic in the Fourth and Fifth Five-Year Plans. Second, this remarkable buoyancy in private savings has been entirely due to the strong savings performance of the household sector (including unincorporated enterprises).

Resource Mobilization and the Black Economy

In recent years the phenomenon of tax evasion and the "black economy" has commanded growing attention, in India and abroad.[4] While the bulk of the analytical work has focused on efforts at quantifying the scale of the black economy,[5] there is growing recognition of the need to assess and analyze the economic *consequences* of a substantial black economy. In this section we briefly touch upon some of the consequences for the fiscal system and fiscal policy, insofar as they relate to resource mobilization.

But before doing so, we note the obvious point that fiscal policy plays an important causal role in generating and sustaining a black economy. A recent review of the underlying causes of the black economy has grouped causal factors under eight heads and emphasized that the itemized causes act in *concert,* not as isolated elements.[6] The study reviews the extensive theoretical literature on determinants of tax evasion and notes the remarkable paucity of *empirical* work on this subject in India. At the end of the review it asks and answers a rhetorical question in the following terms:

> So where does this leave us? Essentially with our judgments and prejudices. And to put those on the table, we side with those who believe that high effective rates of taxation are a major contributing factor to tax evasion and black income generation in India. Improved tax compliance *can* result from significant and sustained reductions in the effective burdens of those who are liable to tax.

The study also draws attention to the growing potential for black income generation offered by the expenditure side of the fiscal system.

The most immediate, and also the most obvious, consequence of widespread tax evasion is the loss of revenue that should have accrued to the exchequer. The long-run consequence of such revenue loss is to reduce the built-in elasticity of the tax system. Most studies of major taxes in India indicate that such elasticities are disappointingly low, though this may not be attributable solely to tax evasion.[7] To meet revenue targets in the face of large-scale evasion the Government, until recently, relied on raising tax rates or expanding the range of commodities subject to tax. The first option had the undesirable effect of increasing the inducements for avoidance and evasion (and thus became an increasingly self-defeating route), while the second added to the complexity of an already complex tax structure, entailing a number of undesirable consequences for equity and allocative efficiency.

In a longer view, widespread tax evasion has constrained the scope of tax reform. To give just one example, the economic rationale of a last-stage, single-point sales tax is widely acknowledged: it avoids cascading and other distortionary allocative effects and can be designed to approximate a general tax on consumption. Yet, the administrative difficulties of stemming evasion under such a tax have been an influential argument against substituting this form of sales tax for the present (economically more "irrational") sales tax structures in many Indian States.

A less obvious manner in which the black economy has frustrated resource mobilization relates to black incomes reaped through "siphoning off" from public programs and projects. In essence, these leakages add to the expenditure claims on the exchequer, since a given project or program costs much more than it should because of the "provision" for siphoning off. Such leakages may be seen as additional (and illegal) transfer payments, which effectively reduce the value of resources mobilized.[8]

Domestic resource mobilization is also, probably, constrained by the likely bias in favor of consumption associated with black incomes. Consumption expenditure, especially on "luxury services" (including expensive wedding festivities and the "five-star hotel culture"), is a way of spending black income which carries far less risk of detection and penalty than accumulation of financial or real assets. Hence, it can be plausibly argued, a large black economy imparts a downwards bias to the economy's savings propensity.

Fiscal Policy and Allocational Efficiency

As we observed earlier, fiscal policy also influences economic growth through its effect on the efficiency of resource allocation and use. In this section we briefly consider some of the issues involved. But first an aside.

Our focus here, as in previous sections, is on the effects of fiscal policy on the *supply side* of the economy. This is in sharp contrast to the preoccupation (at least until recently) in industrialized economies with the output effects of fiscal policy operating through changes in *aggregate demand* (that is, loosely speaking, the Keynesian perspective). It is interesting that the traditional concern of development economics with issues of *aggregate supply* have, of late, become remarkably fashionable in the economic policy debate of industrialized countries.

Efficiency in the Public Economy

The proportion of India's GDP accounted for by the public sector has increased substantially since the introduction of planned economic development. Furthermore, this increase is almost wholly accounted for by the proliferation and growth of nondepartmental PSEs (the "departmental enterprises" are basically railways, posts and telegraph). These points are highlighted by the summary Table 14.8.

This growth in the role of the public sector is directly traceable to the preponderant share in total Plan outlay allocated to the public sector Plan expenditures (investment and current development outlay) in the various Five-Year Plans. In the Third, Fourth and Fifth Plans, this share was well in excess of 60 percent (Table 14.9). Even after the decline in the next two Plans, the public sector was still allocated just over half of total planned outlay in the Seventh Plan.

Commensurate with the growth in relative significance of the public sector in producing goods and services, there has been increasing interest and concern about the efficiency of resource use within this sector. In view of the especially rapid growth in the share of investment and output accounted for by nondepartmental PSEs, this burgeoning interest has quite naturally focused on these enterprises.

Though studies of individual enterprises and sectors/subsectors abound, it is difficult to come by rigorous appraisals of the efficiency of resource use by the PSEs, taken as a whole. As a matter of research priority, it is very important to address this lacuna since purely financial indicators are obviously inadequate yardsticks of performance when enterprises are explicitly charged with objectives other than the maximization of commercial profits.

Nonetheless, despite the absence of such rigorous and comprehensive appraisals, the abundance of studies at the enterprise, subsector and sectoral levels, the indifferent financial performance of PSEs alluded to earlier and available data on physical input-output ratios and productivity indices all suggest that the efficiency of resource use in PSEs is well below potential. Partly in response to this widely held perception of the problem, the Government has recently advanced, in its paper on Administered Price Policy, a number of proposals for giving greater weight to cost cutting and productivity increases in setting PSE administered prices.[9]

Tax Structure and Allocational Efficiency

Tax policy is, of course, a key determinant of the efficiency of resource use in the economy. The evolution of India's tax structure, in terms of contribution to total tax revenue is summarized in Table 14.10. Several points stand out. First, the share of direct taxes has fallen from 37 percent in 1950–51 to 15 percent in 1984–85. Correspondingly, the share of indirect taxes has risen from 63 percent to 85 percent. Thus, the sustained increase in the tax-GDP ratio, noted earlier, has essentially been fueled by the growth of indirect taxes. Second, within the ambit of indirect taxes, the preponderant role has been played by three taxes: customs and excise duties at the Central Government level and sales taxes at the State level. Hence, it is commodity taxation which has basically accounted for the growth of tax revenues over the last three-and-a-half decades. Third, an issue which we take up below in the discussion of the equity dimensions of fiscal policy, the share of personal income tax has fallen markedly from 21 percent in 1950–51 to 5 percent in 1984–85.

The heavy reliance on commodity taxation has had important consequences for the efficiency of resource allocation in the economy, many of which had not been fully appreciated when the tax policies were being framed, mainly on the basis of revenue-raising considerations. First, a number of studies have pointed out that India's structure of customs duties, coupled with the regime of quantitative restrictions, has conferred high and widely divergent rates of effective protection to different lines of industrial activity.[10] This has been interpreted as prima facie evidence of efficiency losses due to, in large part, the customs tariff structure.

Second, as emphasized by the report of the Jha Committee on indirect taxes,[11] a readiness to levy indirect taxes on inputs has led to the problem of "cascading" of tax and interest costs, distorted the incentive structure for investment and production, penalized exports and made it extremely difficult to assess the burden of indirect taxation. Furthermore, both the Jha Committee, as well as its predecessors, such as the Venkatappiah Committee,[12] have criticized the sheer complexity of the indirect tax structure for contributing to evasion and for compounding administrative problems.

Third, Acharya and Associates have drawn attention to the loss due to "rent-seeking," not only from the usual price-quantity controls, but also from the complexity of the tax structure.[13] Estimates of losses due to rent seeking are both scarce and questionable. Some recent—and very high—estimates have been presented for India by Mohammed and Whalley,[14] but they suffer from some serious qualifications, as pointed out by Acharya and Associates. Nevertheless, it is difficult to refute the presumption that there are significant real economic losses, not least because of diversion of the time and attention of industrial managers and entrepreneurs to issues of tax avoidance and evasion, because of the sheer complexity of the tax structure.

Fiscal Policy and the Black Economy: Allocative Aspects

In an earlier section we have touched on some of the ways in which tax evasion and the black economy impede resource mobilization. A sizable black economy also poses serious problems for the allocative dimensions of fiscal policy. To begin with, widespread tax evasion blunts the allocative signals of the tax system. When, in the case of a large number of manufacturers and traders, the tax dues are believed to be the end product of a complicated interaction between the tax statutes, the evasion opportunities, the enforcement machinery and its susceptibility to corruption, it is idle to pretend that only the first of these factors, namely, the tax laws, is solely responsible for the resource allocation implications of tax system. In arriving at decisions on investment, production and sale, a rational economic agent will consider not only the tax code but also the possibilities for reducing its bite through legal and illegal methods. To complicate matters, this sort of weakening of the allocational signals of taxes is not uniformly spread across different tax instruments for the simple reason that the extent of evasion varies very substantially from one kind of tax to another.

The allocative impact of fiscal policy is also weakened on the expenditure side by the presence of a large black economy. We have alluded earlier to the problem of illicit leakages from public expenditure programs. As in the case of taxes, the potential and scope for leakages vary across different kinds of public expenditure programs. What this means in practice is that efficiency of public expenditure, on the ground, can be quite different across different sectors even if the anticipated returns were more or less uniform. Furthermore, the ex ante pattern of public expenditure may sometimes be distorted by the relative possibilities for "siphoning off." For example, it has been suggested that important public sector investment decisions are sometimes biased in favor of new "greenfield plants" and against consolidation and expansion of existing units because the former offer much greater scope for illicit cuts and commissions on large foreign contracts. Furthermore, the posts where such illegal cuts and commissions can be most easily arranged come to acquire a market price. Postings, transfers and promotions in respect of these posts become increasingly influenced by corrupt practices at the expense of more regular considerations such as experience and competence. Not surprisingly, the concern for quality and accountability in public expenditure declines. The predictable consequence of all these factors is a decline in the efficiency of public projects and programs.[15]

Of course, to the extent that the black economy is fueled by pervasive price and quantity controls which spawn economic rents that are either competed away through rent-seeking behavior or are enjoyed as illegal premia, there are substantial opportunities for fiscal policy to mop up such illegal rents to the benefit of exchequer. This potential has sometimes been exploited in India, for example, through the combined deployment of partial decontrol and higher excise levies for the hitherto price-controlled cement industry in 1982. However, it can probably be argued that fiscal policy for mopping up illicit rents has not been used as effectively and frequently as it might have been.

Fiscal Policy and Equity

It is important to distinguish between the static and dynamic effects of fiscal policy on equity. From the vantage point of comparative statistics the key issues are who bears the tax burden of fiscal policy and who benefits from public expenditure. Of course, even answering these relatively "simple" questions raises knotty theoretical problems of identifying the appropriate counterfactual, not to mention the enormous empirical effort (and here we are abstracting from the equity consequences of a large population of PSEs).

These problems are multiplied when one approaches the issue in a dynamic framework and asks: What has been the effect on, say, the size distribution of income, over a specified period of time, which can be attributed to fiscal policy? After all, fiscal policy affects growth. And, depending on the structural characteristics of the economy as well as the policy frame, that growth can be associated with more or less equity in the distribution of income or consumption or wealth. Though interesting, this set of issues is virtually unanswerable (at least, satisfactorily), with the present state of the art in modeling dynamic, distributional consequences of alternative fiscal policies in India. Given these limitations, we restrict this section to a brief survey of more "typical" issues.

Direct Versus Indirect Taxes

We observed earlier that the share of direct taxes, in total tax revenues, has fallen from 37 percent in 1950–51 to 15 percent in 1984–85. And the share of personal income tax collections has dropped from 21 percent to 5 percent over the same period. Empirically, these trends run counter to the general experience of other countries in the course of development.[16] A recent review of tax structure change in India in the post-Independence era comes to the conclusion that, contrary to the historical experience of countries like Japan, no correlation is noticeable between the share of direct taxes—or of personal income taxes—with per capita income, which is chosen as the index of development.[17] The "outlier" Indian experience is sought to be explained by Chelliah by the proposition that the share of income tax or direct taxes can be expected to rise with the growth of per capita income (or economic development) *only after* per capita income has reached a certain threshold level and grown fairly fast after that.

The concern with the declining and low share of direct taxes stems from the widely accepted view that direct taxes, and specially personal income taxes, constitute potent instruments in the armory of tax policy to secure distributive justice. To quote the Government's recent Long Term Fiscal Policy (LTFP):[18]

> While the predominance of indirect taxes in the present situation is unavoidable, it cannot be gainsaid that a certain balance has to be maintained between direct and indirect taxes. Taxes like the personal income tax have an important role in the tax structure and cannot be substituted by taxes on commodities. It is not easy to tailor commodity taxes to the circumstance of tax-payers in the same way as is possible with the personal income tax. Hence, although reliance on indirect taxation cannot be avoided in the foreseeable future, it is necessary to make a transition to a system whereby income tax makes a larger contribution to revenue. Such transition is not possible without a distinct improvement in the buoyancy of the income tax in response to growth in incomes. An important objective of fiscal policy must be to reverse the decline in the share of direct taxes over the long term.
>
> The lack of buoyancy in income tax revenue is attributable to several factors, including narrow coverage of the working population, numerous exemptions and deductions and widespread evasion. The total number of income tax payers has remained at about 4 million or so for many years. Bringing unincorporated enterprises under taxation has proved difficult. With a narrow base, revenue needs led to the imposition of high nominal rates of tax. There is a reason to believe that a broader base of taxation, resulting from healthy growth of the economy, combined with moderate rates of taxes and strict enforcement can yield better revenue results. It is this approach which underlies the changes made in the structure of income tax rates this year and the overhaul of the administration and procedures currently under way.

So far this strategy seems to be paying dividends, though it may be a little too early to arrive at a definitive judgment. In 1985–86, the ratio of direct taxes to GDP is estimated to have increased from 2.25 percent to 2.44 percent of GDP.[19] However, net of States' share in direct taxes, the ratio hardly changed from 1.66 percent of GDP in 1984–85 to 1.64 percent in 1985–86 (this was essentially because the surcharge on income tax, which was not subject to sharing with States, was abolished effective 1985–86). But, as noted by Bagchi,[20] this uptrend in the ratio of direct taxes to GDP may well be reversed in 1986–87. Assuming a further 10 percent nominal increase in GDP, the budget estimates imply a ratio of 2.27 percent (gross of States' share) and 1.48 percent (net of States' share). As Bagchi has noted, the latter number also falls short of the Long Term Fiscal Policy's target of 1.7 percent for 1986–87. Clearly, sustained efforts are required to increase the ratio of direct taxes to GDP and overcome some of the strong social, administrative and political factors inhibiting the growth of direct tax collections.

One of the direct tax measures taken of late, however, might have an adverse impact on equity, namely, the abolition of estate duty. The principal justification was that, in actual operation, the estate duty was administratively cumbersome and took a heavy toll of assessees in terms of harassment. However, its abolition does weaken the equity of the tax system with respect to the issue of intergenerational transfers. It should be pointed out that gift and wealth taxes remain still in operation and, if effectively implemented, these might help to counter accumulation. But for these taxes to perform this task effectively, it would be necessary to keep in check tendencies towards permissiveness in the matter of exemptions and valuation.

Incidence of Indirect Taxes

A redeeming feature of the Indian tax system is that despite a strong tilt towards indirect taxes, the overall incidence in all probability has remained progressive. The study of tax incidence by Chelliah and Lal[21] showed that the indirect taxes as a proportion of household expenditure show a steady increase with a rise in expenditure levels. However, a more recent study by Ahmad and Stern,[22] which takes into account the tax/subsidy incidence on inputs used indirectly through interindustry linkages, shows less progressivity than the earlier study. In the new study, although most taxes are still found to be more or less progressive, they are not invariably so. And for urban areas, the tax burdens for most of the taxes were found to be roughly uniform across expenditure classes.

Studies on tax incidence are known to suffer from many deficiencies. One important drawback of these studies arises from the difficulty of measuring the effective incidence of taxes in a system where taxes are levied on practically all commodities including inputs at almost all stages of production and at different levels of government. Also, the assumptions regarding full forward shifting of the commodity taxes which is common to these studies may be questionable in the case of several products because of the market structure. The recent reforms in the structure of excise duties levied by the Central Government aimed at generalizing the system of setoffs for duty paid on inputs (called MODVAT) should greatly facilitate the assessment of the effective incidence of excise duties.

Benefits from Government Expenditure

Thus far, there have been no comprehensive assessments of who benefits from public expenditure (and how much) for India comparable to the studies carried out by Meerman for Malaysia and Selowsky for Colombia.[23] Such studies are clearly necessary for a fuller assessment of the equity implications of fiscal policy. In their absence any empirical appraisal of these issues is inevitably constrained to a partial picture. Here, we confine ourselves to a few observations on the major programs which have spearheaded the Government's direct attack on the poverty problem.

But before making these observations, it is important to reiterate the usual caveats, namely: that India's poverty problems are both complex and deep-seated; that efforts at poverty alleviation must embrace both direct approaches as well as policies and programs aimed at accelerating overall growth in output and employment in the economy; and that even within the limited domain of public expenditure and quite apart from specific antipoverty programs, particular emphasis needs to be accorded to sectors such as agriculture, irrigation, education and other social services, which are most conducive to broad-based growth of incomes, employment and welfare, especially in rural areas.[24]

While the Government's antipoverty programs have a long history, they have gathered momentum (and higher financial allocations) in recent years.[25] At present the three most important nationwide programs are the Integrated Rural Development Program (IRDP), the National Rural Employment Program (NREP) and the Rural Landless Employment Guarantee Program (RLEGP). Of these, the first, IRDP, has invited the greatest analytical and research scrutiny, and we briefly discuss it here for illustrative purposes. The basic thrust of IRDP is to channel income-earning assets to households below the poverty line in order to achieve a sustained increase in the income-generating capacity of the poor.

The available appraisals of IRDP range from partial assessments based on village-level studies to more comprehensive State and national surveys of beneficiaries. Among the better known in the latter category are the studies by the Institute for Financial Management and Research, the Reserve Bank of India, the Program Evaluation Organization of the Planning Commission and the National Bank for Agriculture and Rural Development. Over the past year, the Ministry of Agriculture (Department of Rural Development) has initiated an extremely ambitious program of Concurrent Evaluation, based on surveys of beneficiaries carried out by twenty-nine reputed research institutions in thirty-six districts every month on a random rotating sample basis since October 1985.[26]

Based on the data collected under the Concurrent Evaluation program for the period October 1985 to March 1986, it is interesting to summarize some of the main positive and negative findings. The positive ones include:

1. Fifty-eight percent of the families selected for IRDP assistance belong to the destitute category (Rs 1–2,265 per year per family) and 41 percent to the very, very poor (Rs 2,266–3,500). Thus the thrust of IRDP is on the poorest of the poor.
2. As regards repayment of IRDP loans, 45 percent of sample families had no overdues and 34 percent had overdues up to Rs 1,000 only. So, the repayment picture is far better than some of the more critical accounts would suggest.
3. About 70 percent of the assets supplied (over time) under IRDP were found to be intact.
4. In about 25 percent of cases the assets generated incremental income of more than Rs 2,000 per year; in another 22 percent of cases, such increase was between Rs 1,001 to Rs 2,000.

Among the most noteworthy negative aspects highlighted by the Concurrent Evaluation are the following:

1. The incremental income generated by IRDP-provided assets was zero in 23 percent of cases and Rs 1–1,000 in 29 percent of cases.
2. In about 25 percent of cases, the difference between the assessed (by sample survey) and recorded value of IRDP-provided assets was found to be significant, that is, more than Rs 250. This suggests that the "leakage" problem, through the manipulation of the asset price, is significant, though not overwhelming.
3. On the basis of the revised poverty line of Rs 6,400 per family only 11 percent of old beneficiaries have crossed this line. Of course, in large part, this reflects the program's concentration on the poorest families.

The data generated by the ongoing Concurrent Evaluations will clearly require careful analysis. But the preliminary evidence noted above suggests that IRDP is a basically sound antipoverty program with room for improvement.

Equity, Tax Evasion and the Black Economy

Quite obviously, large-scale tax evasion undermines the equity of the tax system. "Horizontal" equity is breached since the effective burden of taxation differs widely across the assessees with comparable levels of economic income. For example, it is common knowledge that salaried individuals, who have their income tax deducted at the source, bear a disproportionately high burden of this tax compared to the self-employed, who have far greater opportunities for evasion. "Vertical equity" or the progressivity of the income tax structure also becomes a casualty when an assessee's tax liability has less to do with his ability to pay and more to do with his ability to evade. Indeed, a possible explanation for the declining role, until recently, of personal income taxation in India was the extent to which evasion had undermined its administration.

Turning to a broader issue, we may ask whether the presence of a sizable black economy implies that the distribution of income is more or less equal than it would have been in its absence. We do not have the wherewithal to explore this counterfactual comparison systematically. All we can do is to assess, heuristically, whether, given the existence of the black economy, the actual distribution of household incomes is likely to be more or less egalitarian than that shown by the recorded data.

It is widely believed that in responding to household surveys of income and consumption, households with a higher proportion of black income are more likely to understate their true incomes and to do so to a greater degree. In judging the nature of the bias embedded in survey data on income distribution we have to assess where, in the size distribution of incomes, black incomes are more likely to accrue.

To begin with, given the progressive structure of income taxation, the incentive to reap black incomes through understatement of legal-source incomes is clearly positively related with income. So we should expect richer households to earn proportionately greater black incomes through this means. As for illegal-source black income, whether through illegal economic activity such as smuggling or illegal transfers such as bribes, on balance, we suggest that the opportunities for earning such black incomes are skewed in favor of the "haves" (such as industrialists, traders, real estate operators, contractors, lawyers, accountants, politicians, bureaucrats and artists) rather than "have nots," such as small-holder farmers, rural labor and casual labor. And, in most of these cases, it is at least plausible that the secondary effects associated with expenditure from black incomes do not compensate for the initially greater skewedness in the opportunities for making these incomes. Hence, our tentative judgment would be that the distribution of *actual* household income (from all sources) is likely to be even more skewed in favor of the rich (say, the top decile) than is indicated by the standard surveys such as those carried out by the National Sample Survey (NSS) and independent research organizations such as the National Council for Applied Economic Research (NCAER).

Fiscal Policy: New Thrusts

Perception of Key Problems in 1984–85

The latter months of 1984 and the early months of 1985 witnessed the coincidence of a number of trends and events which highlighted some key problems of fiscal policy and set the stage for an array of bold new initiatives. These trends and events included:

- The final stages of completing the Seventh Five-Year Plan and the associated debate, within and outside official circles, on the resources position;
- The submission of a number of influential reports prepared under Government auspices, including the Report of the Committee to Examine Principles of a Possible Shift from Physical to Financial

Controls (the Narasimham Committee), the Report of the Committee on Trade Policies (the Abid Hussain Committee), a series of reports prepared by the Economic Administration Reforms Commission under the leadership of L. K. Jha, the Report of the Committee to Review the Working of the Monetary System (the Chakravarty Committee) and the Report on Black Money by the National Institute of Public Finance and Policy;

- Perhaps most importantly, the coming to power of the Rajiv Gandhi Government, following a sweeping electoral victory.

This impressive spate of official and semiofficial reports addressed a wide range of economic concerns and policies. Insofar as fiscal policy is concerned, it is possible to distill the perceptions regarding the key fiscal problems facing the nation.[27] At some cost in terms of oversimplification, these perceptions may be summarized as follows:

1. The tax structure and tax statutes had become far too complex.
2. A combination of reasonably high tax rates and ineffective administration had greatly compounded the problems of tax evasion and the black economy.
3. Tax policy had been unduly ad hoc and unpredictable. The dominant concern for raising revenue had led to a relative neglect of consequences of the tax structure for resource allocation and equity.
4. With the growth in size and diversity of the Indian economy, economic management through discretionary physical controls was becoming increasingly difficult and counterproductive. Greater reliance on nondiscretionary fiscal and financial rules was necessary.
5. The tight resources position for financing the Seventh Plan was, in large measure, due to rapid growth in non-Plan expenditure commitments.
6. The Central Government's budget deficit played a key role in determining the rate of growth of money supply and hence, at one remove, the rate of inflation.

It is interesting, and important, to note that most of the reports/documents, from which these perceptions of fiscal problem have been distilled, were completed (or in final draft) before the advent of the Rajiv Gandhi Government. In that sense, the emerging consensus on the need for fiscal policy reform predates the ascension of the new administration. This point can be adduced in support of the view, frequently voiced by official spokesmen and others, that the economic policies of the new Government represented a judicious mix of "continuity with change." They were not, as some alleged, wholly novel policy directions grafted onto the economic scene.

Main Themes of the "New Fiscal Policy"

The growing consensus on the need for fiscal policy reform combined with the advent of the new Government to usher in a remarkable array of fiscal policy initiatives in the relatively brief period between March 1985 and August 1986. Whatever one's view on the merits and demerits of individual initiatives, it is difficult to find any other period in India's post-Independence fiscal history in which so much policy change was compressed into such a brief time span. While it is possible to discern the antecedents of the fiscal policy changes in pre-1985 trends, official documents and reports (and thus stress the element of continuity), there is little doubt that the *acceleration* in the pace of fiscal policy reforms was unprecedented and drew attention to the "change" portion of the catch-phrase "continuity with change."

The main themes of the "New Fiscal Policy" flow quite naturally from the perceptions highlighted earlier. In our view, the principal themes are:

1. A systematic effort to *simplify* both the tax structure and the tax laws;
2. A deliberate shift to a regime of *"reasonable" direct tax rates, combined with better administration* and enforcement, to improve compliance and raise revenues;
3. The fostering of a *stable and predictable* tax policy environment;
4. Greater recognition and *weight given to the resource allocation and equity* consequences of taxation;
5. More reliance on *nondiscretionary fiscal and financial instruments* in managing the economy, as compared to ad hoc, discretionary physcial controls;
6. Concerted efforts to *improve tax administration* and reduce the scope for arbitrary harassment;
7. Growing appreciations of the *links between fiscal and monetary* policy;
8. Fresh initiatives to *strengthen methods of expenditure control.*

Each of these major themes merits some elaboration and illustration in terms of the policy actions taken in the last eighteen months or so.

Major Themes and Policy Initiatives

Simplification of Tax Structure and Statutes. The far-reaching efforts at simplification were kicked off by the 1985 budget, which, inter alia, reduced the number of slabs in personal income taxation from nine to five, abolished the administratively cumbersome estate duty, provided for clubbing of separate limits for exemption from wealth tax available for one house and specificed financial assets into one consolidate exemption and weeded out several exemptions and deductions from the company tax.

These were followed, in the 1986 budget (and in line with the Long Term Fiscal Policy announced in December 1985), by major simplifications of the gift tax and capital gains taxation. The depreciation provisions for corporate taxation were also rendered more simple and liberal. The 1986 budget also brought a sweeping reform of the central excise tax, the most important single tax in terms of revenue and, arguably, effects on resource allocation and equity. In the process, the number of rates of excise were sharply reduced to multiples of 5 percent. The slab system of excise concessions for small-scale industrial units were also made simpler and more growth oriented.

As a measure of simplification and rationalization, the Government also enacted a revised nomenclature for the central excise tariff, which is broadly in conformity with the harmonized system of classifications adopted for the customs tariff. This massive effort at matching the classifications of the two most important indirect taxes is expected to remove a long-standing grievance of industry.

More recently, in August 1986, the Government has published a discussion paper on "Simplification and Rationalisation of Direct Tax Laws."[28] The goal is to further simplify direct tax laws and procedures to encourage voluntary compliance and ease the task of administration. After comments and suggestions are taken into account, the aim is to introduce a comprehensive Taxation Laws (Amendment) Bill by the next Budget Session of Parliament. The ultimate goal is to have a single Direct Taxes Code (in place of separate statutes for income tax, wealth tax and gift tax) by the end of the financial year 1987–88.

More "Reasonable" Tax Rates and Better Administration. This theme is exemplified by the substantial reductions in the marginal tax rates for personal income and wealth and corporate incomes (as well as more generous exemptions) carried out in the 1985 budget. The marginal tax rate for personal income was brought down from 62 percent to 50 percent, and that for personal wealth was sharply reduced from 5 percent to 2 percent. At the same time, the basic rate of tax for widely held companies was reduced by five percentage points to 50 percent. It should be noted, in passing, that the tax rate reductions were by no means unprecedented in the Indian context. The marginal rate of tax (including surcharge) on personal income had stood at a confiscatory 97.75 percent during most of the first half of the 1970s, before being brought down to the 60–70 percent range through sharp cuts in 1974–75 and 1976–77.

At the same time that direct tax rates were being made more reasonable, measures were launched to tone up administration and enforcement. Tax administrators of doubtful integrity were retired, transferred or sidelined. A well-publicized series of search and seizure operations was launched to heighten the perceived cost of tax evasion. Administrative procedures were streamlined to reduce harassment of honest taxpayers and encourage compliance. A limited form of tax amnesty was introduced to encourage tax evaders to come into the fold of a "reasonable rates" regime.

While it may be too early to evaluate the overall success of the strategy, the initial revenue results certainly belie the fears expressed by critics. In 1985–86, personal income tax collections increased by an unprecedented *30 percent*. Even allowing for a nonrepeatable element attributable to the amnesty program, the initial returns to the strategy were clearly favorable.

Fostering a Stable and Predictable Economic Environment. Tax policy is, of course, only one element, albeit an important one, of the overall economic environment. But at least in repsect of this element, the Government's announcement of its Long Term Fiscal Policy marked a landmark in India's fiscal history.[29] Indeed, we are hard put to find other examples where a major nation has formally committed itself to such a comprehensive program of tax policy reforms in a medium-term framework.

Against the backdrop of the financing requirements of the Seventh Plan, the LTFP chalked out in considerable detail, the directions of change in direct and indirect tax policies. In doing so, it imparted a definite direction and coherence to the sequence of annual budgets and thus greatly reduced the uncertainty and suspense which is typically associated with a government's tax policy intentions.

The significance of the LTFP can be fully appreciated when one compares the policy intentions it announced with the actions taken thus far. Where the LTFP promised to keep the tax structure unchanged, for instance with respect to the post-1985 budget rates of tax on personal income and wealth, the promise has been kept. In the more typical context of the large menu of tax policy changes presaged in the LTFP, the overwhelming majority have been enacted through the 1986 budget and subsequently.

Allocative and Equity Dimensions of Tax Policy. In the past, India's tax policy was often indicted for excessive concern with revenue raising and insufficient regard for the consequences of resource allocation and equity. Though this underlying bias may still be present (and it is hardly surprising given the imperative of Plan funding), there is little doubt that allocational and equity dimensions of tax policy have received growing attention in recent times.

The overhaul of central excise taxation through the introduction of MODVAT exemplifies these concerns. Prior to the introduction of MOD-VAT, excise taxes were frequently levied on inputs, leading to distortions in the production structure, "cascading" of taxes and making it very difficult to assess the incidence of the tax burden across different income classes. The MODVAT system of providing pro forma credit for taxes paid on inputs (as announced in the LTFP and introduced in the 1986 budget) basically aims to progressively relieve inputs from excise and countervailing duties. This administratively complex and far-reaching reform is driven by concerns about allocative efficiency and equity. To quote the LTFP:

> shifting the effective burden of excise taxation away from inputs and on to final products is at the heart of the proposed reform. Aside from reducing distortionary effects on production and thus increasing the competitiveness of Indian industry, the shifting of excise to final products will help in tailoring excise duties in such a manner that the well-off bear a higher proportionate burden than the poor.

Of course, it is too early to judge the extent to which a more "transparent" system of indirect taxation will be actually deployed to move towards a more progressive tax structure. The hikes in excise duties on luxury items (for the Indian context), such as passenger cars and color televisions, carried out in the 1986 budget indicate some use of this potential. For the moment, the important point is that the design of tax policy appears to have given substantial weight to considerations of allocational efficiency and equity.[30]

A second example, where recent tax reform has been driven by allocational considerations, relates to the investment allowance for companies. It was felt that the investment allowance encouraged capital intensity, favored large, well-established companies and did not do enough to encourage savings by corporate entities. The new "funding scheme," which is being phased in to replace the investment allowance, is believed to be superior in these respects. Up to 20 percent of profits will be fully deductible from taxable income if deposited in an interest-bearing account of the Industrial Development Bank of India. These deposits can then be used for investments in plant and machinery.

Allocational considerations are also dominant in the thrust of customs tariff reform proposed in the LTFP. However, movement in this area has been perceptibly slower than in virtually all other areas covered by the LTFP, not least because of the intrinsic difficulty of managing a transition to tariff-based control of imports against a background of balance-of-payments pressures.

Greater Reliance on Fiscal/Financial Instruments. At a general level, the remarkable resurgence of tax policy initiatives can be taken to reflect the Government's preference for fiscal instruments over physical ones in pursuing socioeconomic objectives. The greater weight being given to allocational and equity dimensions in the design of tax policy can also be viewed as indicative of the growing recognition of the potential of fiscal policy in serving these dimensions. In a different time and context when physical controls were the preferred option, fiscal policy may have been less active.

Viewed from another angle, the recent loosening of industrial licensing controls and the cumulative, incremental liberalization of import policy has clearly enhanced the role of fiscal and financial instruments in guiding resource allocation. It remains a moot point as to the extent to which, in specific contexts, fiscal measures are being deliberately calibrated to substitute for physical controls. Recent reforms of customs duties for capital goods imports provide a significant example of such conscious substitution.

Tax Administration. We have already alluded to some of the measures taken to tighten up tax administration and increase the perceived cost of tax evasion to the potential evader. In addition, the Income Tax Department is shifting to a system of random sampling for selecting returns (of personal taxable income below Rs 100,000) for scrutiny, and, in this way, freeing more administrative resources for detection and follow-up of "big fish" tax evaders. Certain weaknesses in the laws which hinder effective prosecution of tax evaders, are being amended.[31] With respect to both direct and indirect taxes, data systems are being increasingly computerized for ready retrieval and analysis.

The recent discussion paper on simplification of direct tax laws has proposed substituting a simple system of mandatory interest in place of provisions which give tax-assessing authorities discretionary powers to levy penalties and charge interest for certain defaults on the part of the assessee. The discussion paper also proposed to substitute present provisions prescribing penalties for concealment of income by a simple system of additional tax equal to 30 percent of the amount by which the returned income falls short of the assessed income.

The thrust of these and other proposals is to substitute quasi-automatic monetary penalties in place of discretionary procedures subject to multistage appeals and litigation, wherever possible, in the determination of tax liability, concealment of income, etc.

Fiscal and Monetary Links. In recent years there has been growing appreciation of the links between the Government's fiscal operations, money supply and inflation. This appreciation has been heightened by the recent Report of the Committee to Review the Working of the Monetary System (Chakravarty Committee Report).[32] This report has pointed out that credit extended to the Government by the Reserve Bank of India (RBI) has been the principal source of reserve money. As a proportion of reserve money the net RBI credit to the Government has increased from 83 percent in 1970–71 to 92 percent in 1983–84. Other studies have also shown that changes in the stock of reserve money can largely be explained in terms of changes in net RBI credit to the Government. Furthermore, as noted by the Chakravarty Committee Report, the relationship between reserve money and money stock has been quite strong in 1970s.[33]

Thus, the fiscal operations of the Government, especially the Central Government, strongly influence money supply in the economy. While there is an extensive literature on the determinants of inflation in India and the debate about the relative role of money and credit policies continues, the Chakravarty Committee Report has reinforced the view that money supply is an important determinant of inflation.

Recognizing these links, the Government has recently accepted the Chakravarty Committee's recommendation for setting overall monetary targets, which can be monitored and which will help bring about better coordination between fiscal and monetary policies. The setting and monitoring of internal monetary targets is being conducted on an experimental basis.

New Initiatives for Expenditure Control. Against the background of rapidly rising expenditure claims and growing appreciation of the destabilizing potential of large fiscal deficits, the Government has undertaken several important initiatives in the field of strengthening expenditure control. To begin with, a very firm line has been taken with the perennial problems of overdrafts by States. At the Central Government level a system of quarterly budgeting in respect of major projects has been introduced with a view to identifying projects where funds are lying idle and diverting them to other well-implemented projects where funds are most needed. A program of commitment budgeting is being evolved for ensuring that ongoing projects are not starved of funds. In the search for effective prioritization and control over Government expenditures, a system of zero-base budgeting is being introduced to assure proper assessment and allocation of funds according to accepted priorities.

Fiscal Policy: Some Challenges Ahead

In this section we briefly outline some of the challenges that lie ahead for India's fiscal policy.

Resources for Financing the Plan

The Government's Long Term Fiscal Policy has highlighted the importance of improving public savings performance if the Seventh Plan is to be financed in a noninflationary manner. The three elements which are crucial to improving public savings are assuring buoyancy in tax revenues, containing current expenditure and enhancing the efficiency of operation and surplus generation by the PSEs.

By the second year of the Seventh Plan, a substantial measure of success had been attained in augmenting tax revenues through the Government's strategy of combining tax reform and simplification with better enforcement and administration. However, there had been much less success in respect of the other two dimensions. Current Government expenditure continued to grow apace and surplus generation by the PSEs was well below initial Plan targets.

In its recent paper on administered price policy the Government outlined some approaches for linking pricing with productivity and for injecting more cost consciousness in the operational environment of PSEs. These and other measures are urgently required to increase the real productivity of PSEs and thus ensure that their real contribution to public savings improves markedly. The prospect for containing current Government expenditures is, at best, uncertain in the light of the recent Pay Commission award for Central Government employees and a noticeable deterioration in the external security environment.

If, because of the difficulties, public savings fail to improve enough, the consequences will become manifest in additional recourse by the Government to borrowed funds with attendant pressure on interest rates and possible crowding out of private investment, excessive monetization of public debt with its inflationary implications, a reduction in the size of the Plan, or some combination of all these possibilities.

Fiscal Policy and External Balance

The consequences of any persistent fiscal imbalance may not remain limited to the domestic sphere. In macro terms, India's fiscal and monetary policy has traditionally been focused on issues of domestic balance, notably price stability. Price stability clearly has an important bearing on India's competitiveness in external markets. There is also reason to believe that the relatively conservative stance of Indian fiscal and monetary policy has, in the past, assisted the management of external balance. Thus, I. J. Ahluwalia[34] attributes some of India's success in accelerating real export growth in the period 1972–79 to the strongly deflationary stance of fiscal and monetary policy adopted in the wake of the first oil shock of 1974.

The converse is that a persistent shortfall in public savings performance could result in a secularly expansionary fiscal policy, which, in turn, could inhibit improvements in the foreign trade balance and aggravate the problem of overall balance-of-payments management. Against this background, it is important to ensure that India avoids the Latin American syndrome of borrowing externally to meet *domestic* financing pressures. Down that road looms the specter of serious and chronic *external* debt management problems.

Issues of Federal Finance

The federal structure of India's polity spawns a host of issues for fiscal policy which are beyond the scope of this chapter. But one general issue is likely to pose a significant challenge in the years ahead. In the past, the expenditure obligations of the States have typically exceeded their capacity to satisfy them from their own resources. As a result, the States have been substantially dependent on a variety of transfers from the Center including: devolution from Central taxes, share in small savings, non-Plan assistance and Plan assistance. In the context of increasing fiscal stringency being experienced by the Center, maintaining the pattern of growing transfers from the Center to States is going to become increasingly difficult. This, in turn, is likely to put more pressure on the States to mobilize their own resources to meet a higher proportion of their expenditure commitments.

Another area of general concern relates to municipal finances. Recent studies of this neglected area of India's fiscal landscape have pointed to the parlous state of municipal finances in most cities and townships.[35] The already difficult municipal finance situation is likely to be substantially compounded, in future, by the rapid growth of urban population and the high cost of urban infrastructure.[36] Solutions to this set of emerging strains are likely to require far-reaching reforms in existing systems of municipal taxation and cost recovery practices for urban infrastructure.

The Tax Policy Agenda

Returning to the prime actor on the fiscal scene, the Central Government, the main items on the tax policy reform agenda are:

1. Implementation of further measures to simplify and rationalize direct tax laws, in the wake of public debate on the Government's discussion paper on the subject;[37]
2. Progressive extension of the MODVAT reform to the remaining chapters of the central excise tariff (with the exception of tobacco, petroleum products and textiles, which were specifically excluded from the reform in the Long Term Fiscal Policy);
3. Continued rationalization of the customs tariff structure, with a view to placing greater reliance on tariffs, instead of quantitative restrictions, for regulating imports.

The first two of these tax policy reforms can be expected to be implemented in the next two or three years. However, in view of the recent increase in India's trade deficit and the resultant pressure on the overall balance of payments, the transition from quantitative restrictions to tariffs could well become attenuated.

Notes

1. *Seventh Five Year Plan 1985–90* (New Delhi: Government of India, Planning Commission, 1985).

2. We are painfully aware that owing to limitations of time, resources and (perhaps most important) abilities, this chapter falls far short of doing justice to the vast subject at hand.

3. Interesting recent papers on these issues in the Indian context are S. Madhur, "Taxation and Household Savings in India: An Empirical Study" (Working Paper No. 17) (New Delhi: Indian Council for Research on International Economic Relations, 1984); and J. V. M. Sharma, "Taxation and Savings Behaviour of Private Corporate Sector in India" (Working Paper No. 16) (New Delhi: Indian Council for Research on International Economic Relations, 1984).

4. See S. Acharya and Associates, *Aspects of the Black Economy in India* (1985; reprint, New Delhi: National Institute of Public Finance and Policy, 1986), and references cited therein.

5. S. Acharya, "Unaccounted Economy in India: A Critical Review of Some Recent Estimates," *Economic and Political Weekly* (3 December 1983), provides a systematic critical review of past quantification efforts relating to India. Acharya and Associates, *Aspects of the Black Economy in India*, provides a fresh set of estimates.

6. See Acharya and Associates, *Aspects of the Black Economy in India*.

7. See, for example, I. K. Khadye, "The Responsiveness of Tax Revenues to National Income in India (1960–61—1978–79)," *Reserve Bank of India Occasional Papers* 2, no. 1 (1981); and National Institute of Public Finance and Policy (NIPFP), "Income and Price Elasticities of Central and State Taxes" (November 1984, Mimeographed).

8. See Acharya and Associates, *Aspects of the Black Economy in India*, for consideration of these issues.

9. *Administered Prices Policy: A Discussion Paper* (New Delhi: Government of India, Ministry of Finance, 1986).

10. See, for example, J. N. Bhagwati and P. Desai, *India: Planning for Industrialization: Industrialization and Trade Policies Since 1951* (New Delhi: Oxford University Press, 1970); and J. N. Bhagwati and T. N. Srinivasan, *Foreign Trade Regimes and Economic Development: India* (New York: Columbia University Press, 1975).

11. *Report of the Indirect Taxation Enquiry Committee* (New Delhi: Government of India, Ministry of Finance, 1978).

12. *Report of the Central Excise (Self Removal Procedure) Review Committee* (New Delhi: Government of India, Ministry of Finance, 1974).

13. The seminal article on rent seeking is A. O. Krueger, "The Political Economy of the Rent-Seeking Society," *American Economic Review* (June 1974). R. D. Tollinson, "Rent-Seeking: A Survey," *Kyklos* 35 (1982), provides a recent survey of this literature while J. N. Bhagwati, "Directly Unproductive Profit Seeking (DUP) Activities," *Journal of Political Economy* (October 1982), presents a synthesis in which rent seeking of Krueger's variety is seen as a special case of "directly unproductive, profit-seeking activities."

14. S. Mohammad and J. Whalley, "Rent Seeking in India: Its Costs and Policy Significance," *Kyklos* 37 (1984).

15. See Acharya and Associates, *Aspects of the Black Economy in India,* for a fuller discussion.

16. See, for example, H. H. Hinrichs, *A General Theory of Tax Structure Change During Economic Development* (Cambridge, Mass.: Harvard Law School, 1966).

17. R. J. Chelliah, "Changes in Tax Revenue Structure—A Case Study of India" (Paper presented at the 42nd Congress of International Institute of Public Finance, Athens, August 1986).

18. *Long Term Fiscal Policy* (New Delhi: Government of India, Ministry of Finance, 1985).

19. Taking the revised estimates for 1985–85 and assuming a 10 percent increase in GDP at market prices in nominal terms over the Central Statistical Organization's quick estimates for 1984–85.

20. A. Bagchi, "Budget and Long Term Fiscal Policy," *Economic and Political Weekly* (12 April 1986).

21. R. J. Chelliah and R. N. Lal, *Incidence of Indirect Taxation in India, 1973–74* (New Delhi: National Institute of Public Finance and Policy, 1981).

22. E. Ahmad and N. Stern, "Effective Taxes and Tax Reform in India" (University of Warwick, Development Economics Research Centre, Discussion Paper No. 25, January 1983).

23. J. Meerman, *Public Expenditure in Malaysia: Who Benefits and Why* (New York: Oxford University Press, 1979); M. Selowsky, *Who Benefits from Government Expenditure—A Case Study of Colombia* (New York: Oxford University Press, 1979).

24. On this last point, it is heartening that the recent 1986–87 Central Government budget has increased Plan allocations for agriculture, irrigation and allied activities by 30 percent and for education by 60 percent, as compared to corresponding allocations in the previous year.

25. For example, the recent 1986–87 Central Government budget increased the Plan allocation for antipoverty programs by about 65 percent, as compared to budget estimates for the previous year.

26. *Concurrent Evaluation of IRDP: The Main Findings of the Survey for October, 1985-March, 1986* (New Delhi: Government of India, Ministry of Agriculture, 1986).

27. It is not our case that each of the reports/documents voiced all of these concerns, though there was, undoubtedly, a substantial domain of shared ground.

28. *Simplification and Rationalisation of Direct Tax Laws: Discussion Paper* (New Delhi: Government of India, Ministry of Finance, 1986).

29. *Long Term Fiscal Policy* (New Delhi: Government of India, Ministry of Finance, 1985).

30. It should be emphasized that the basic idea of MODVAT, as well as its rationale, was forcefully advocated by the Report of the Indirect Taxation Enquiry Committee (New Delhi: Government of India, Ministry of Finance, 1978).

31. Acharya and Associates, *Aspects of the Black Economy in India,* provides a detailed account in Chapter 10 of the lacunae in past procedures and regulations relating to penalties and prosecution of tax evasion.

32. *Report of the Committee to Review the Working of the Monetary System* (Bombay: Reserve Bank of India, 1985).

33. C. Rangarajan and A. Singh, "Reserve Money: Concepts and Policy Implication for India," *Reserve Bank of India Occasional Papers* (June 1984).

34. M. S. Ahluwalia, "Balance of Payments Adjustment in India, 1970–71 to 1983–84" (UN Document UNCTAD/MFD/TA/32/Add.2) (New York: United Nations, 1985).

35. See, for example, *Financing of Urban Development: Report of a Task Force* (New Delhi: Government of India, Planning Commission, 1983); and *Report of the West Bengal Municipal Finance Commission,* Supplementary Volume 2: *Study on Property*

Tax Reform in West Bengal by National Institute of Public Finance and Policy (Calcutta: Government of West Bengal, 1982).

36. The high cost of urban infrastructure requirements is highlighted by Acharya and Mohan, "Projections of Investment Requirements in Urban Infrastructure."

37. *Simplification and Rationalization of Direct Taxes: Discussion Paper* (New Delhi: Government of India, Ministry of Finance, 1986).

TABLE 14.1 Tax Revenue as Percentage of GDP
at Current Market Prices[a]

Year	Direct Taxes	Indirect Taxes	Total Tax Revenue
1950–51	2.4	4.1	6.5
1960–61	2.7	6.3	9.0
1970–71	2.7	9.6	12.3
1971–72	3.0	10.4	13.4
1972–73	3.1	10.8	13.9
1973–74	2.8	10.0	12.8
1974–75	2.8	10.8	13.6
1975–76	3.6	11.9	15.5
1976–77	3.5	12.4	15.9
1977–78	3.2	11.9	15.1
1978–79	3.1	13.0	16.1
1979–80	3.1	13.7	16.8
1980–81	2.8	13.1	15.9
1981–82	3.0	13.6	16.7
1982–83	2.9	14.0	16.9
1983–84	2.8	13.8	16.6
1984–85	2.8	14.4	17.3

[a] Central and State government revenues combined are shown.

Source: National Accounts Statistics (New Delhi: Government of India, Central Statistical Organization).

TABLE 14.2 Elasticity and Buoyancy of India's Tax System

	Elasticity[a]		Buoyancy[b]	
	1966–67 to 1983–84	1970–71 to 1983–84	1966–67 to 1983–84	1970–71 to 1983–84
Corporate Tax	1.0621	1.0841	1.1662	1.1931
Income Tax	0.8827	0.7967	0.9306	0.7983
Union Excise	1.0542	1.1749	1.4190	1.5086
Sales Tax	1.3140	1.3020	1.4241	1.4144
State Excise	1.1292	1.1044	1.3389	1.2994
Stamps and Registration	0.8869	0.9111	1.0253	1.0629
Land Revenue	0.2909	0.2746	0.4714	0.4977
Tax Revenue (Center)	0.8857	0.8891	1.2071	1.1699
Tax Revenue (States)	1.1192	1.1077	1.2869	1.2838
Total Tax Revenue	0.9608	0.9598	1.2329	1.2071

[a] "Elasticity" takes account of other variables such as changes in tax rates.

[b] "Buoyancy" is the change in the tax revenues/change in GNP.

Source: National Institute of Public Finance and Policy, New Delhi.

TABLE 14.3 Additional Resources Mobilized (ARM)
by the Center and States During the Plans

		ARM (at current prices)	ARM Through Taxation	Share of ARM Taxation to Total ARM (percentage)
		(billion Rs)		
First Plan	(1951–56)	3.95	2.44	61.77
Second Plan	(1956–61)	12.16	10.22	84.05
Third Plan	(1961–66)	28.91	26.17	90.52
Annual Plans	(1966–69)	8.35	6.81	81.56
Fourth Plan	(1969–74)	49.97	43.13	86.31
Fifth Plan	(1974–79)	138.91	82.03	59.05
Sixth Plan	(1980–85)			

Source: Indian Economic Statistics, Public Finance, Part 2 (New Delhi:
Government of India, Ministry of Finance, 1981); and various Plan documents
(New Delhi: Government of India, Planning Commission).

TABLE 14.4 Terminal Year Public Savings: Plan
Target Versus Actual[a]
(as percent of GDP)

	Plan Target	Actual
1973–74 (Fourth Plan)	4.5	1.9
1978–79 (Fifth Plan)	4.6	4.9
1984–85 (Sixth Plan)	6.0	3.2
1989–90 (Seventh Plan)	5.1	—

[a] The ratios shown are of gross public savings to GDP, except for 1973–74,
when the relevant concept is net public savings to net national product
(NNP).

TABLE 14.5 Structure of Public Sector Gross Savings[a]
(as percent of GDP at market prices)

Years	Gov't Admin.	Public Sector Enterprises			Total	Percent Distribution	
		Dept.	Non–Dept.	Total (Cols. 3+4)	(Cols. 2+5)	Govt. Admin.	Public Sect. Enterprises
(1)	(2)	(3)	(4)	(5)	(6)	(7)	(8)
1970–71	1.4	0.7	1.0	1.7	3.1	46.0	54.0
1971–72	1.2	0.8	1.0	1.7	3.0	41.5	58.5
1972–73	1.1	0.6	1.1	1.7	2.8	38.7	61.3
1973–74	1.6	0.3	1.2	1.5	3.1	51.9	48.1
1974–75	2.1	0.3	1.4	1.7	3.8	55.1	44.9
1975–76	2.8	0.5	1.2	1.7	4.5	62.7	37.3
1976–77	2.7	0.8	1.8	2.6	5.2	50.9	49.1
1977–78	2.3	0.8	1.5	2.3	4.6	50.4	49.6
1978–79	2.6	0.7	1.6	2.3	4.9	52.7	47.3
1979–80	2.4	0.7	1.5	2.2	4.6	52.1	47.9
1980–81	1.7	0.5	1.4	1.9	3.6	47.7	52.3
1981–82	2.3	0.6	2.1	2.7	4.9	46.0	54.0
1982–83	1.5	0.7	2.6	3.3	4.8	32.1	67.9
1983–84	0.6	0.6	2.5	3.1	3.7	16.4	83.6
1984–85	(–)0.3	0.6	2.8	3.5	3.2	(–)10.2	110.2

[a] Total may not add due to rounding.

Source: National Accounts Statistics (various issues) (New Delhi: Government of India, Central Statistical Organization).

TABLE 14.6 Government Current Receipts and Expenditure
(as percent of GDP at market prices)

Years	Current Receipts		Current Expenditures			
	Total	of which: Tax Receipts	Total	of which:		
				Defense	Interest	Subsidies
(1)	(2)	(3)	(4)	(5)	(6)	(7)
1970–71	13.7	12.3	12.3	3.1	0.5	0.8
1971–72	15.0	13.4	13.8	3.6	0.6	1.0
1972–73	15.2	13.9	14.1	3.5	0.7	1.1
1973–74	13.9	12.8	12.3	3.0	0.8	1.2
1974–75	14.9	13.6	12.8	3.1	0.5	1.7
1975–76	16.8	15.5	14.0	3.5	0.7	1.5
1976–77	17.6	15.9	15.0	3.4	0.7	1.7
1977–78	16.7	15.1	14.4	3.1	0.8	2.0
1978–79	17.8	16.1	15.2	3.0	1.0	2.3
1979–80	18.5	16.8	16.1	3.3	0.9	2.4
1980–81	17.6	15.9	15.9	3.2	1.2	2.2
1981–82	18.4	16.7	16.1	3.3	1.3	2.2
1982–83	19.0	16.9	17.5	3.4	1.6	2.3
1983–84	18.4	16.6	17.7	3.4	1.9	2.6
1984–85	19.6	17.3	20.0	3.5	2.5	3.3

Source: National Accounts Statistics (various issues) (New Delhi: Government of India, Central Statistical Organization).

TABLE 14.7 Terminal—Year Savings Rates: Plan Targets Versus Actuals
(as percent of GDP)

	Fourth Plan[a] (1973–74)		Fifth Plan (1978–79)		Sixth Plan (1984–85)		Seventh Plan (1989–90)
	Target	Actual	Target	Actual	Target	Actual	Target
1. Private	8.7	13.0	11.3	19.8	18.4	19.0	19.2
of which:							
Households	7.6	12.1	9.8	18.2	16.4	17.3	16.9
Corporations	1.1	0.9	1.5	1.6	2.0	1.7	2.3
2. Public	4.5	1.9	4.6	4.9	6.0	3.2	5.1
3. Total	13.2	14.9	15.9	24.7	24.4	22.1	24.3

[a] Refers to net savings.

TABLE 14.8 Percent Share of Public Sector in GDP (Current Prices)

	1970–71	1977–78	1983–84
Administrative Departments	6.5	6.9	7.8
Department Enterprises	4.0	4.1	3.9
Nondepartmental Enterprises	4.4	8.4	11.4
Total	14.9	19.4	23.6

Source: National Accounts Statistics (various issues) (New Delhi: Government of India, Central Statistical Organization).

TABLE 14.9 Share in India's Total Plan Outlay
from Second to Seventh Plan
(original estimates)

	Second Plan 1956–61	Third Plan 1961–66	Fourth Plan 1969–74	Fifth Plan 1974–79	Sixth Plan 1980–85	Seventh Plan 1985–90
1. Public Sector	54.07	64.66	63.92	69.57	56.62	51.70
a. Current Development Outlay	—	10.35	9.02	10.95	7.84	7.40
b. Investment	54.07	54.31	54.90	58.62	48.78	44.30
2. Private Sector Investment[a]	45.93	35.34	36.08	30.43	43.38	48.30
3. Total Plan Outlay	100.00	100.00	100.00	100.00	100.00	100.00

[a] Excludes investment financed by capital transfers from the public sector on Plan account.

Source: Plan documents.

TABLE 14.10   India's Tax Structure (Center, States and
Union Territories) 1950–51 to 1984–85
(percentage to total tax revenue)

	1950–51	1960–61	1970–71	1980–81	1984–85
Direct Taxes	36.79	29.77	21.23	16.47	15.18
Corporation Tax	6.28	8.12	7.80	6.61	7.85
Income Tax	21.37	12.49	9.95	7.59	5.03
Wealth Tax	—	0.60	0.32	0.34	0.27
Land Revenue	8.22	7.24	2.54	0.79	0.91
Agriculture Income Tax	0.57	0.71	0.22	0.23	0.13
Indirect Taxes	63.21	70.23	78.76	83.53	84.82
Customs	25.07	12.59	11.03	17.18	19.73
Union Excise	10.78	30.83	37.00	32.76	31.03
State Excise	7.95	4.07	4.24	4.46	5.26
Sales Tax	9.29	12.14	16.55	20.25	20.42
Stamps and Registration	4.43	3.49	2.84	2.20	1.97
Motor Vehicles	1.24	2.53	2.36	2.14	1.97
Center's Taxes[a]	64.59	66.30	67.47	66.41	65.84
States' "Own" Taxes	33.41	33.70	32.53	33.59	34.16

[a] Gross of taxes transferred to States.

Source: Indian Economic Statistics, Public Finance (New Delhi: Government of
India, Ministry of Finance).

15

Uses and Abuses of Instruments for Resource Mobilization: The Indian Experience

Mihir Rakshit

> *Faust. If feeling fails you, vain will be your course,*
> *And idle what you plan unless your art*
> *Springs from the soul with elemental force*
>
> —Goethe, *Faust*

Two contrasting currents of thought mark the official documents and pronouncements on economic planning in India today. First, there is a sense of euphoria and self-congratulation at the near attainment of the growth rate envisaged in the Sixth Five-Year Plan (1980–85) and at the relative stability of prices in recent years. Second, financing of the Seventh Five-Year Plan (1985–90) has become a major problem in spite of the sharp rise in the ratios of gross domestic savings and revenue collection to gross domestic product (from 10.2 percent and 6.83 percent at the beginning of the Plan period to around 23.0 percent and 18.5 percent respectively at the end of the Sixth Plan), and the Government is busy devising means for the mobilization of resources—with drives for stepping up tax collections, hikes in administered prices and large-scale borrowing from the market by public sector enterprises figuring prominently in the policy package adopted so far. In the present chapter we try to make sense of this apparent contradiction and examine the efficacy of the various instruments of resource mobilization used by the Government. However, before that, it may be useful to draw attention to some features of growth, saving, taxation and capital formation in India—features that highlight both the strengths and the weaknesses of the macroeconomic performance of India and may serve as a background for our discussion on the scope and methods of resource mobilization.

Saving, Investment and Growth in India:
Myths and Reality

India's effort in respect of mobilization of savings appears commendable, but the steep rise in the saving and investment ratios has not been matched by her record in respect of growth, there being no perceptible trend in the overall rate of growth of the economy between the First Five-Year Plan (1951–56) and the Sixth Plan (1980–85) (see Table 15.1). Indeed, even if we ignore 1979–80, characterized by high saving and investment ratios with a negative growth rate, the figures relating to the Third (1961–66), the Fourth (1969–74) or even the Sixth Plan periods underline the existence of the "Saving-Investment Puzzle" in the Indian economy. Elsewhere[1] we have discussed at some length the nature and probable magnitude of the upward bias inherent in the Central Statistical Organization (CSO) method of estimation of aggregate saving and investment. On the present occasion, however, we propose to suspend our disbelief in the dramatic figures produced by the CSO and to concentrate on those aspects of the behavior of output, saving and investment which throw some light on the nature of the problem confronting the policymakers.

First, it is of some importance to realize that the macroeconomic performance of India in recent years is not as impressive as it may appear at first sight. Thus if we compare the figures of the two four-year periods—one preceding 1979–80 and the other beginning with 1982–83[2]—the average annual rate of growth in the latter is found to be lower than that in the former by more than one percentage point (which is very large in the context of an average growth of 3.7 percent during the entire Plan period). What is of more significance, while the yearly growth rates of agriculture and manufacturing in 1975–79 exceeded those in 1982–86 by 2.25 and 1.75 percentage points respectively, the contribution of public administration and defense to GDP (in real terms) grew at the rate of 11 percent per annum during the Sixth Plan against 5 percent during the earlier Plan.[3] There is thus no room for complacency in respect either of the magnitude or of the content of growth in recent years.

Second, while we do not propose to explore in detail the nature and sources of the so-called mismatch between the changes in the investment (saving) ratio and the growth rate of the Indian economy during the Plan period, it is worth recording that there is a significant difference in the time trend of the investment ratio depending on whether it is estimated at current or constant prices: the ratio measured at current prices records a sharp rise from 6.8 in 1950–51 to 16.6 in 1979–80, but the increase is far less dramatic (from 9.3 to 14.7) when the estimates are at 1970–71 prices (see Table 15.2). Note also that the ratio of net capital formation at constant prices appeared to have reached a plateau in the mid-sixties with practically no trend thereafter. This feature is of course related to the change in the prices of investment relatively to those of consumption goods, which in its turn is the outcome of the process of price formation in the two sectors and the development policies pursued by the Government.

In fact, as we shall presently see, the myth in respect of India's saving ratio is related to a similar myth regarding her tax ratio, and the wide gap between the appearance and the reality in both the cases is largely due to the way the Government has wielded the instruments of resource mobilization. Be that as it may, the fact remains that even by the CSO statistics the ratio of capital formation to income in real terms is not as high as is generally supposed.[4]

From the analytical and policy point of view, however, the important variable to consider in this connection is not the investment or the saving ratio, but the *level* of investment in relation to "capacity" output of the economy. Indeed, one of the most remarkable features of the macrobehavior of the Indian economy that has not been adequately examined is the close link between *changes* in the *absolute* levels of investment in real terms and variations in the rate of capital formation (as a percentage of GDP). As shown in Table 15.2, between 1950–51 and 1979–80 in all the nine years when the level of real investment registered a decline, there was a fall in the saving and investment ratios as well, with real income rising (moderately) in six years. There were altogether twelve years, however, during which the investment ratio (at current prices) fell; but in the three years when this fall was accompanied with a rise in the absolute level of investment (in real terms), the extent of rise was relatively moderate and (what is of no less significance) the ratio at constant prices in fact declined in only one year (1977–78). There is thus a prima facie case for shifting the focus of analysis to the level and the growth of investment in real terms, and for subscribing to the Keynesian view that if one takes care of investment, saving will take care of itself.

Resource Mobilization Without Tears

Indeed the salient features of the behavior of the Indian economy in recent years appear to make the Keynesian case almost open and shut. The industrial sector in India, especially the basic and capital goods industries, have been working with substantial excess capacity. While the average rate of capacity utilization in major industries has been around 70 percent, in the basic and capital goods sectors the rates are of the order of 58 percent and 65 percent respectively.[5] The irony of the situation is that the recessionary conditions faced by the capital goods sector have become acute over the last year and a half due to the Government policy of liberalizing imports of projects and equipments—a policy that promotes the use of the most scarce resource of the economy at the moment, viz, foreign exchange, in lieu of domestic resources with zero opportunity cost to the society. What is more curious, in many cases (e.g., fertilizer equipment, heavy electrical machinery, railway wagons, etc.) underutilization in public sector units is due largely to inadequate Government investment itself.[6] Add to that the fact that wages in these units form a part of fixed costs and the basic inputs (e.g., steel) required for the production of these goods are also supplied by other public sector units, and it is not very difficult to see that the usual argument advanced for limiting development expenditure, viz, "paucity of resources," involves nothing short of a fallacy of composition.

Nor does the constraint on a step-up in Plan expenditure appear to operate from the supply side of the labor or the food market. Over the last few years while substantial stocks of food grains have been accumulated by the Food Corporation of India,[7] the number of people in the live register of employment exchanges has recorded a yearly growth rate of 7 percent (with employment in the organized sector growing at the rate of only 1.3 percent per annum). Even these figures do not reflect properly the extent of growing underutilization of labor. Since the rise in employment in the organized sector is due mostly to additional recruitment in Government services, there is a strong likelihood that this added primarily to the magnitude of disguised employment in the economy.

To a traditional Keynesian the prevailing conditions thus cannot but appear propitious for a step-up in investment (or development) expenditure without imposing any significant burden on the Ministry of Finance to devise ways and means for Additional Resource Mobilization (ARM). Estimates in respect of the capacity output may even yield, under the existing tax structure and propensities to spend, the figure for additional Plan expenditure that can be undertaken without generating any serious inflationary pressure.[8] And given the favorable factors noted above, the figure should not be of a minor order. This does not mean that a substantial across-the-board increase in the level of development expenditure is feasible without creating acute scarcity conditions and/or steep price increases. There are, we should note, certain crucial sectors of the economy, e.g., power and transport, where supply constraints are in fact binding, and these (together with the scarcity of imported inputs) limit production in some other sectors of the economy.

The Indian economy has indeed been characterized quite often by the simultaneous coexistence of demand and supply constraints though they have shifted across sectors over different periods.[9] Hence the sectoral distribution of development expenditure, and not simply its scale, will affect significantly the mobilization of resources in real terms and the associated inflationary pressure: the "resource crunch"—to borrow jargon currently popular with the Indian economists—would appear more severe, the greater the concentration of expenditure on sectors where the constraint on output operates on the supply side. This line of reasoning suggests that, under the present conditions prevailing in India, a sizable increase in development expenditure that will generate demand for domestic capital foods and food grains is quite feasible, provided the Government is prepared to impose restrictions (through fiscal or other means) on imports and the use of power for "nonessential" purposes.

Such a policy package, while eminently sensible, would still leave untapped a substantial amount of resources in the economy. Village surveys, especially in the Northeastern States and backward regions, indicate that there is not only unemployed labor, but also underutilized land along with idle water and other local resources in many rural areas. This underutilization may be traced to demand deficiency (coupled with the imperfect link between the local and the national markets); to the nonavailability of production loans; or to the scarcity of outside inputs like fertilizer, pesticides, diesel oil or purely technical know-how. A major constituent of the art of resource mobilization in a large country like India should thus be identification of areas with unemployed resources and allocation of larger (local-resource-intensive) development expenditure in these regions. Such measures need generally to be backed up by the provision of additional credit facilities and the injection of some outside inputs in these areas. To the extent extension of production loans promotes the utilization of idle resources, such measures are wholly disinflationary.[10] Even when the input injected from outside is in short supply and required to be diverted from other regions, aggregate output is likely to increase because of the operation of the supply-side multiplier, as a small dose of outside input results in a significant increase in the employment of idle local resources.

Development Expenditure, Employment and "Saving" Potential

Considering the current state of the availability of resources, we have suggested the feasibility of an increase in two types of development expenditure: first, on domestic capital goods; and second, on rural development programs, especially in backward regions with idle resources. While the former will generate little additional employment in the short run, the number of jobs created per unit of expenditure should be fairly large under the latter. This is precisely what is required for containing inflation: the additional consumption demand will then be mostly for food grains (given the differences in the consumption propensities of the rural poor and workers in the organized sector). Note also that the extra expenditure on domestic capital goods will automatically generate almost an equivalent amount of saving in the public sector itself (without any inflationary pressure) since money wages constitute an element of fixed costs in state enterprises and almost all industries producing basic and capital goods belong to the public sector.

But what of the alleged low saving potential of the additional income generated through rural development programs? Even apart from the fact that such programs would reduce the cost of holding large stocks by the Food Corporation of India (FCI), the sharp rise in household savings[11] following the rapid expansion of credit to agriculture, small-scale industries and other activities in the priority sector suggests that the marginal propensity to save out of incomes generated from these activities is not as low as is generally assumed. There are, let us emphasize, basic differences between the behavior of savings in an advanced and a subsistence economy. Many a development economist has drawn attention to the preponderance in the latter of personalized consumption loans through which savings of one section of the population are used for sustaining the consumption of people with inadequate incomes.[12] Under these conditions expansion of productive activity and employment opportunities in depressed regions will automatically generate extra savings as the newly employed try to free themselves from the clutches of the moneylenders.[13]

Indeed, in the cases just considered even if the whole of the extra income is consumed, the rise in the productive capacity of the economy could be substantial due to the consumption-productivity nexus a la Smith, Ricardo, Marshall and Leibenstein.[14] Marshall makes a clear distinction between "necessary" and nonessential consumption that appears to be of great relevance for countries like India: "Any increase in consumption that is strictly necessary to efficiency pays its own way and adds, as much as it draws from, the national dividend. But an increase in consumption, that is not thus necessary, can be afforded only through an increase in man's command over nature."[15] Marshall goes on to suggest that the salutary effect of the provision of necessary consumption—on workers' efficiency, industrial faculties, building of character and willingness to limit the size of the family and make sacrifices for their children—are cumulative and extend over generations.[16] It appears one of the strongest cases for state intervention to set the economy to a course of self-sustained growth in both material and moral spheres. Given the substantial stock of food grains lying with the Food Corporation of India, the Indian economy appears particularly well placed at the moment to undertake such investment on an enhanced scale through a massive drive for expansion of employment opportunities, especially in backward regions.

On Plugging the Leakage and Augmenting the Pool of Investable Resources

If we look beyond the immediate policy options before the planners, it is clear that the problem of resource mobilization (in the conventional sense) is bound to surface once we want to sustain a high rate of growth. Even in the short run, as we have seen, shortage of specific resources may limit certain types of development expenditure. We propose to discuss the implications of such constraints for policy purposes at a later stage and concentrate for the moment on the ways and means of resource mobilization in terms of an aggregative framework.

The basic problem in this regard is of course to induce or force people to release resources that can be used for development purposes. This objective is somewhat different from that of a step-up in the level of saving and investment in the economy, since "development" expenditure is at once a broader and a narrower concept than investment in the conventional sense. This difference and the essence of resource mobilization in a developing economy are underlined by the Marshallian (and the Kaleckian) criterion of the economic and wasteful use of resources: all uses of resources that do not contribute to present or future "necessary" consumption constitute a leakage from the "development potential" of the economy,[17] and the scope and efficacy of different instruments of resource mobilization have to be judged in the context of this cardinal principle. Even at the risk of laboring the obvious, it appears necessary to emphasize in the Indian context that resource mobilization consists not so much in the collection of revenue, but more in the curtailment of superfluous consumption, of investment that does not raise the production potential of wage goods, as also of wasteful business and Government expenses which more often than not are disguised private consumption, producing public "bads" rather than "goods."

The Two Faces of Borrowing

If judged by the above criterion, what role does borrowing by the Government play in the mobilization of resources? The question assumes importance in the context of the heavy reliance on borrowing[18] for financing the successive Five-Year Plans. Its contribution was as high as 48 percent of the total public sector Plan outlay in the First Plan; shot up to 66 percent during the Annual Plans (1966–69); and came down to 46 percent during the Sixth Plan. This mode of financing development expenditure has resulted in a hugh public debt which totaled Rs 10,557,200 million in 1984 and put substantial burden on the Exchequer by way of interest payments. Let us, however, follow the advice of the seers and count the blessings in this dark scenario. The total debt of the Union and State governments taken together (net of intergovernmental loans) as a percentage of GDP has nonetheless not displayed any upward trend: in fact it came down slightly from 56 percent to 54 percent[19] between 1971 and 1984. Second and more important, external debt as a proportion of GDP fell substantially, from 16.1 percent to 7.8 percent during the same period.

However, though the relative decline in the burden of indebtedness to the outside world is no doubt a welcome phenomenon, the other side of the coin is that (unlike loans from abroad) domestic borrowings generally constitute a transfer of resources from the private to the public sector, and not a net addition to the investable surplus of the economy. The contribution of such transfers lies in (1) attaining the Plan allocation of resources between the two sectors; and (2) reducing nonessential investment. In assessing the role of internal borrowing in resource mobilization it is necessary to take note of some features of the financial system in general and the structure of public debt in particular.

The major part of Government borrowing has been from financial institutions which themselves belong almost exclusively to the public sector. In fact one of the most encouraging developments of the Indian economy since the nationalization of commercial banks is the rapid growth of savings mobilized through financial institutions of which banks are by far the most important. Thus, while in 1966–69 only 32.4 percent of household savings were held in the form of (net) financial assets, the ratio jumped to 56 percent in 1981–84.[20] No less significant is the fact that around 90 percent of households' financial assets are held in the form of claims on the public sector (in which bank deposits account for more than 40 percent of the total.[21]

This development is encouraged on two counts. First, it has made the task of the Government much easier to meet the pattern of Plan expenditure in *both* the public and the private sectors. The quantitative significance of this factor is underlined by the fact that between 1968–69 and 1983–84 while gross domestic savings as a percentage of GDP rose from 14.1 to 22.6, the Government's command over savings registered a much faster rate of growth. Direct savings of the public sector rose from 2.6 percent to 4.1 percent of GDP; but with greater mobiization of household savings through the financial sector investible resources controlled by the Government registered an increase from 8.3 percent of GDP to more than 19 percent. Hence it has become possible for the planners to use credit policy as an alternative of (or a supplement to) fiscal measures in order to influence decisively the pattern of both investment and current production.[22] Such a policy has indeed been pursued to a certain extent by way of rapid expansion of bank loans to priority sectors in the absence of which adoption of new technology in agriculture would have been impossible. But the instrument of credit rationing has not been employed with sufficient vigor to prevent the leakage of resources in the form of nonessential consumption and investment.

Again, the decisive command over the community's saving now being enjoyed by the public sector can make the interest rate policy an extremely potent instrument of both allocation and mobilization of resources. In India the interest rate has hardly been used as an allocative device with the result that the system of credit rationing has become rather complex.[23] This has also involved subsidy on credit and hence a transfer of incomes from the public to the private sector. The resource drain on this count has to some extent been balanced through fixation of relatively low borrowing rates of interest for the public sector over the greater part of the Plan period. But there has been a sharp rise over the last decade in interest rates on Government borrowings—from 5 percent to 8.5 percent on medium-term securities, from 6.25 percent to 10.50 percent on long-term securities, and from 8.25 percent to 12 percent on National Savings Certificates—with the result that interest payments have emerged as an important factor contributing to the budget deficit (on revenue account). Given the failure of our fiscal machinery to mop up private gains from public investment, it is of course essential to limit interest payments by the public sector. However, for mobilization of larger resources it is not the interest charges on public debt, but the interest receipts of *households* from financial institutions and the Government taken together that are required to be contained. So far, (despite the interest hikes noted above) the Government policy of maintaining a low ratio of direct to indirect[24] borrowing from households has kept the effective interest cost of development expenditure at around 9 percent (as against the current rate of 15 percent paid on debentures and company deposits). But the Government appears bent on throwing this advantage away and reducing the overall saving ratio of the economy in the none too distant future: it has effected a substantial rise in interest rates on internal loans in the recent budget and proposes to rely more and more on direct borrowing from households through issue of debentures with a net return of no less than 15 percent. The full impact of the new policy will be felt only after seven to eight years. But the magnitude of its burden on resource mobilization may be indicated by the fact that, were the current policy in respect of borrowing pursued from, say, the early seventies, the present interest obligations of the public sector would have been 50 percent more and constituted roughly 8 percent of GDP[25]—with the result that all the Seventh Five-

Year Plan (1985–90) "enterprises of great pitch and moment / With this regard their currents turn awry, / And lose the name of action. . . ."

The burden of our argument is fairly simple. In a developing economy with an ineffective system of direct taxes, interest payments to consumers must be regarded a necessary evil—necessary only if household savings are positively related to interest rates.[26] However, though saving in the form of a particular financial asset is found to be responsive to the relative return on that asset, there is no firm evidence to suggest that *aggregate* saving is interest elastic.[27] Again, even if households reduce their current consumption with an increase in the rate of interest, the marginal interest cost to the society will be higher than the rate paid to individuals because of the difference between the marginal and average (interest) costs and due to the rising resource costs of additional tax collections for servicing the payments. Thus an interest rate policy for effective mobilization of resources and their deployment for development purposes must be characterized by (1) relatively low interest rates to private lenders; (2) a tax on interest rates to deprive producers of cheap credit (in the form of company deposits or debentures); and (3) a differential interest rate to support credit rationing in order to attain the Plan allocation of resources.

Resource Demobilization Through Inflow of Foreign Funds

Inflow of foreign capital is recognized as an important means of supplementing domestic saving for rapid capital accumulation in an LDC. However, the (foreign) debt trap into which many third-world countries find themselves caught at the moment suggests that while tapping external sources of finance we need to be extremely wary, if not follow strictly Polonius's advice[28] to Laertes. In India external loans have not been very important in financing domestic investment (which on an average has exceeded domestic saving by around 1.5 percent of GDP). Even so, foreign debt currently forms over 8 percent of GDP and the proportion is likely to go up if the Government policy of project imports through foreign collaboration and of attracting funds from nonresident Indians is successful.

Development economists have been acutely aware of the crowding-out effect of the easy availability of foreign loans—as "borrowing dulls the edge of husbandry" of the Government and gives rise to the problem of amortization due to slow growth reinforced by restrictive import policies of developed countries. In the Indian case the most important source of leakage opened up by the inflow of foreign funds is the rise in nonessential consumption and investment. While an easy balance-of-payments position has almost invariably led to liberalization of imports of raw materials and components for supporting superfluous items of consumption, Indian companies have been permitted, even encouraged, to undertake nonessential investment if they can find a collaborator ready to bear the foreign exchange component of the project cost. Such ventures not only use up current domestic inputs (like cement, steel, technical manpower or transport) but also form a permanent source of resource drain as they start yielding goods and services.

Neither have large-scale remittances by Indians living abroad been an unmixed blessing. Even if we assume that all the foreign exchange accruing to the economy has been used to support the import of essential goods, the additional resource mobilization on this count need not have been positive. These remittances have in general financed nonessential consumption, purchase of land and luxury construction. In areas (e.g., Kerala) from where migration of labor to the Middle East has taken place on a large scale, gaudy buildings have come up, land prices have soared, but investment in industries and agriculture has remained negligible and unemployment widespread. What is more, the steep rise in the price of land has perhaps tended to reduce saving through the Pigou effect,[29] so that it is not clear whether the remittances from abroad have made any significant contribution to resource mobilization for the Plans. Similarly, against the additional volume of imports made possible by investment on the part of the nonresident Indians in domestic companies must be set the leakage in the form of nonessential investment and extra consumption through the Pigou effect, especially since "investments" in the old shares of *existing* companies generate increases in share prices out of all proportion to the magnitude of such investments.

The deleterious effects noted above are due not to the inflow of foreign funds as such, but to the ineffectiveness of domestic policies in limiting nonessential uses of resources. Hence while it is necessary to ensure that all the available foreign exchange is used for sustaining only essential production and investment, the objective is unlikely to be attained in the absence of an effective system of credit control and taxation for the deployment of domestic resources according to Plan priorities.

On How to Tax and Not Release Resources

The major instrument of resource mobilization in a developing economy, it is unanimously agreed, should be taxation, and India's record in this regard appears highly impressive. Between 1950–51 and 1984–85 total tax revenue as a percentage of GDP rose sharply from 6.83 to 18.70 (Table 15.3). What is also heartening, during the same period the cost of collection of taxes—an unavoidable leakage in the process of resource mobilization—came down from 5.2 percent to approximately 2.4 percent of the total tax revenue. However, these figures give a gross overestimate of the extent of resource mobilization through the tax machinery, and even at the risk of some repetition we propose to indicate briefly the reasons for our contention.

Note, first, that in spite of the rise in the ratio of taxes to GDP between the beginning of the First and the end of the Sixth Plan, tax collections as a percentage of total Government expenditure fell from 73.27 to 65.59. Second and more important, the steep rise in the total tax revenue is due entirely to indirect taxes which as a percentage of GDP recorded an increase from 4.32 to 16.03 (over the period mentioned), while collections from direct taxes crawled from 2.51 percent to 2.68 percent of GDP. Third, there has been a structural change in the revenue from direct taxes during the Plan period with corporation tax gaining in importance at the expense of personal income tax: in 1950–51 corporation tax formed 17 percent of direct taxes, but in 1984–85 the figure shot up to 51 percent (Table 15.4). Finally, most of the indirect taxes—in the form of customs, excise duties and sales taxes—are on intermediate and capital goods, and not on items of final consumption.

Not only has tax revenue failed to keep pace with Government expenditure, the effectiveness of the tax system in mobilizing resources has also fallen over the Plan period. In 1950–51 almost all direct taxes were borne by the private sector and (given the low corporation tax) gave a good approximation of their impact on household disposable income. With the sharp decline in the importance of personal income tax and larger proportions of corporation tax paid by public sector enterprises, the picture has altered radically in recent years: for every rupee of direct tax collected now, the household disposable income declines by only around fifty paise.

This trend has been sought to be reversed in the last two budgets through (following the Laffer principle!) a fairly sharp reduction in the rates of personal income tax; complete exemption of imputed income of owner-occupied houses; abolition of the estate duty; and substantial concessions in respect of capital gains and wealth tax. Direct tax collections have indeed risen at a rate faster than that of GDP over the last year and a half (though the ratio of direct taxes to the gross tax revenue of the Union Government is expected to go down from 21 percent in 1984–85 to 18.4 percent in 1986–87).[30] But what has escaped the notice of the Ministry of Finance is that the current increase in the direct tax revenue is due in all probability to large-scale raids conducted by the tax authority coupled with the lenient treatment promised to people declaring before 31 March 1987 their black income and wealth or violation of The Foreign Exchange Regulation Act.[31] If so, the spurt in direct tax collections cannot but be temporary and the avowed policy of not raising the rates of income and other direct taxes over the next five years is bound to make the problem of resource mobilization more difficult. What is no less important, these concessions contributed in no small measure to the sharp rise in the prices of shares and real estate, and hence to the leakage of investible resources of the economy through the Pigou effect.

We present in the appendix to this chapter a few tentative results in respect of the relative efficacy of direct and indirect taxes as instruments of resource mobilization in an economy where factor prices are inflexible in the downward direction, product prices are fixed on a cost-plus basis, and money wages (through dearness allowances) are linked to the cost of living index—assumptions which appear reasonably appropriate in the Indian context. It is not very difficult to see that, while the personal income tax is generally the most effective in releasing resources, the efficiency of indirect taxes will be less when they form a higher proportion of GDP; when adjustments in dearness allowances are greater with respect to movements in the cost of living index; and when the ratio of wages in the value added is larger.[32] It is for this reason that one cannot but have serious misgivings regarding the pattern of taxes that has evolved over the Plan period.

True, the ease of administering corporation and indirect taxes (especially customs and excise duties on intermediate inputs produced in the organized sector) has kept the cost of tax collections at a relatively low level. But there are other costs associated with our pattern of taxation that may not be quite inconsequential. It is a common complaint that the Indian economy is replete with numerous subsidies, quantitative controls and rationing which lead to widespread corruption and require an elaborate machinery for their administration. Add to these the inefficiency in the use of resources because of indirect taxes, those on intermediate inputs in particular, and the soft option of putting an overwhelming premium on administrative convenience and leaving the existing inequalities in income and wealth completely untouched cannot but appear myopic and contrary to the basic principles of development planning.

In the Indian context there is another important reason which makes our indirect taxes ineffective as a means of raising resources. The reason lies basically in the fact that Government expenditure itself forms an important part of aggregate demand[33] and to the extent these taxes (or a price increase by public sector enterprises) require additional expenditure on the part of the Government to keep its command over goods and services in real terms unchanged, no extra resource has been released for development purposes. To see the point most clearly, consider the case where an additional excise tax is imposed on the products of the Bharat Heavy Electricals or where public sector undertakings are to pay steeper customs duties on their essential imports of machinery and equipment. The additional tax revenue of the Government in this case will exactly equal the extra expenditure (in nominal terms) required for carrying through the Plan investment (in real terms) of the State Electricity Boards or other public sector units: the figure supplied by the Ministry of Finance under the head "Additional Taxation" will be wholly illusory in that though tax collections may mount, or even rise as a ratio of GDP, resources (in real terms) at the disposal of the Government are left unchanged!

The major source of the so-called resource crunch in the face of a steep rise in tax revenue may thus be traced to the pattern of taxes the Government has relied upon. A large part of direct tax collections, as we have seen, leaves the disposable income of households completely untouched. Nor has the public sector, contrary to the popular notion, been able to mobilize substantial resources through indirect taxes and hikes in administered prices since (1) their impact is mostly on capital and intermediate goods, and (2) the Government itself is the most important user of the goods and services the prices of which are jacked up through these measures. A preliminary investigation regarding the burden of indirect taxes suggests that in 1984–85, while out of the total excise and customs collections the shares of capital goods, intermediate goods and consumption goods were 30 percent, 40 percent and 30 percent respectively, the corresponding shares in general sales tax were of the order of 23 percent, 28 percent and 48 percent.[34] Assuming that 50 percent of the burden of duties on intermediate inputs are ultimately borne by investors and the Government and that this ratio is the same for indirect taxes other than customs, Union excise and general sales tax (which anyway, as Table 15.4 shows, account for nearly 85 percent of total indirect tax collections in 1984–85), there may be said to be no net release of resources corresponding to 50 percent of the duties imposed on goods and services—a figure which incidentally corresponds to that found for direct taxes as well. Consider hence the differential impact of direct and indirect taxes on private consumption for the remaining part of the tax revenue,[35] and the resource crunch should not appear as much of a puzzle.

A Minimum Needs Approach to Fiscal Planning

In any restructuring of the system of indirect taxes[36] the focus would thus have to be not on the amount of revenue collected, but rather on who are made to pay the taxes and what type and amount of resources are released thereby. If it is possible to identify industries producing nonessential goods, indirect taxes (along with credit rationing and other measures) can be used to plug partially, if not wholly, these sources of resource leakage. There are, to be sure, "productive" activities which can be singled out for such penalties, or even prohibition. But the problem is that (1) output of a large number of industries caters to both essential and nonessential needs, and (2) unless the excess purchasing power of the rich can somehow be siphoned off, its diversion to other channels may create new and greater sources of leakage that may be more difficult to plug.

Under the present conditions the feasibility of two sets of measures for tackling the problems just noted may be employed. The first relates to the Basic Needs Approach under which (1) production of goods for satisfying these needs is encouraged through a high procurement price[37] and/or subsidized inputs; (2) a minimum amount of these goods and services is provided at subsidized prices to families whose incomes fall below a certain level; and (3) high rates of taxes are imposed on goods and services sold outside the public distribution system (so that the relatively affluent are left with less purchasing power). Under this system intra-middle-cum-upper-class distribution of income will tend to become more unequal. But such distress to the middle class should perhaps be regarded as the necessary price for the removal of hunger and poverty. Indeed if the Government administrators—the most influential members of the middle class—may then be induced in their own class interest to devise and implement an effective system of direct taxes, a major impediment to development planning and transformation of the society will be removed!

But pending such a transformation, and given the inadequate control of the Government over different lines of production, we have to live with the inevitability of resource leakage by way of nonessential consumption and investment, and a second set of measures is required to minimize such wastes. The problem here is to reduce as far as possible the amount of resources used in meeting the demand of the relatively affluent. The solution to the problem lies both in imposing taxes and diverting their demand to those goods and services which draw relatively less on inputs required for supporting essential investment and consumption. The theoretically inclined may conduct along these lines a cost-benefit analysis of the production of "nonessential" goods for the rich and indicate the optimum level of their output: (to adapt Shakespeare once again) the principle here is to use the bait of (resource-light) luxury goods to catch the carp of scarce resources.

So far the value of the bait appears to have been much larger than that of the catch, and it is time we change the pattern of our resource use with the above objective in view. The important point to recognize in this connection is that fashion can be easily molded and the sense of "exclusiveness" plays a dominant role in respect of the demand for luxury items. Thus instead of subsidizing handicrafts and handloom products to promote their sale among the masses, the Government should perhaps (along with a vigorous drive for their export) try to improve their quality and market them mostly for the rich. A policy of severely curtailing the domestic production of passenger cars, color TV sets or VCRs, and auctioning every year a limited number of imported items of these goods should release a considerable amount of net resources in the economy. So would auctioning of a limited number of plots of urban land and luxury flats,[38] and channeling all sales of urban property through the Government. The least expensive means (though perhaps not the most suitable for a democratic society) will, however, be to create a demand among the rich for honorific titles conferred by the state for their large contributions (through the Government) towards providing the poor education, health, water and other basic requirements[39]

Summary and Conclusions

1. In recent years the Indian economy has been characterized by a high saving ratio as also a high saving ratio of taxes to GDP, rising unemployment, excess capacity in capital goods industries, a fairly large stock of food grains lying with the Food Corporation of India, and relatively poor utilization of resources in many backward regions. Still there is said to be a "resource crunch" and the Government is busy contemplating various devices for Additional Resource Mobilization in order to finance the Plan. We have tried to indicate that (a) the so-called resource crunch is largely illusory and appears due to the focus on the *aggregate* demand and supply conditions rather than on the constraints operating in various regions and sectors; (b) there is large scope for increasing development expenditure through a change in its sectoral and spatial allocation and extension of credit facilities or provisions of outside inputs in selected areas; and (c) investment in the form of credit, marketing and other extension networks in backward regions—which form a substantial part of the total—will yield large dividends by making possible utilization of local resources lying idle in these areas.

2. A sustained increase in development expenditure will, of course, give rise sooner or later to the problem of additional resource mobilization. In this context it is useful to distinguish, following Marshall and Kalecki, between "essential" and "nonessential" consumption and investment (both

private and public) and to underline the fact that resource mobilization for development planning in a country like India should consist basically in releasing resources from their nonessential uses. It is from this point of view that one has to judge the efficacy of the financial system, taxation or the pricing and the export-import policy of the Government.

3. One of the most encouraging developments of the Indian economy, especially since the nationalization of commercial banks in 1969, has been the overwhelming command over the economy's saving gained by the public sector, primarily through financial institutions. This has made the task of preventing the leakage of resources much simpler (than at the beginning of the Plan period) and opened up the possibility of using differential lending and borrowing rates as a potent tool for reallocation of resources and mopping up excess purchasing power in private hands. However, the Government has not taken full advantage of this development for arresting the wastage of resources and appears bent on reducing the investible surplus of the economy by its recent moves in respect of interest rates and of financing public sector investment by the issue of high-yield debentures.

4. An important source of resource demobilization has been the employment of foreign capital for nonessential investment in the domestic sector and additional consumption due to soaring land and share prices that remittances and portfolio investment by nonresident Indians have led to. In order that inflow of foreign funds contributes effectively to resources available for "development," it is essential to exercise strict vigilance on the pattern of resource use in the domestic sector.

5. The task of preventing the wastage of resources has been made extremely difficult by the declining importance of direct taxes in general and personal income tax in particular, and the heavy reliance on indirect taxes on intermediate inputs and capital goods for meeting Government expenditure. Under this system tax collections do not add significantly to the investible surplus, especially since their impact very often falls precisely on goods used by the Government itself. Again, in order to counter, at least partially, the distortions produced by the unequal distribution of income the Government has to employ a whole host of measures, e.g., price control-cum-rationing of essential articles and other quantitative restrictions, all of which use up resources, directly or indirectly.

6. Hence the necessity of devising an effective system of direct taxes and of using indirect taxes primarily as an instrument of sectoral real-location of resources to meet the Plan objectives. While the goal in respect of direct taxes appears remote at the moment, it is possible in the meantime to extend the Basic Needs Approach to planning for indirect taxes and administered prices. The thrust of the policy should be to provide a minimum amount of basic goods and services to the poorer sections of the community; to use high procurement price or other devices to ensure their supply to the public distribution system; and to employ indirect taxes or administered prices to reduce the purchasing power of middle and upper classes. There is a general feeling in India that the middle class, politically the most articulate section of the community, has so far joined forces with the upper income groups and has left in the lurch the

unemployed, the landless laborers and workers in the unorganized sector.[40] The Minimum Needs Approach to fiscal and administrative planning, by forcing the middle and the upper income groups to fight it out among themselves for the share of the cake outside the control of the Government, will perhaps contribute in no small measure to the evolution of an effective system of direct taxes.

Notes

1. M. Rakshit, *The Labour Surplus Economy* (New Delhi: Macmillan, 1982); M. Rakshit, "On Assessment and Interpretation of Saving-Investment Estimates in India," *Economic and Political Weekly* Annual Number (1983).

2. When the economy may be taken to have recovered from the shock of 1979–80. See *Economic Survey 1985–86* (New Delhi: Government of India, 1986), 1.

3. Ibid., 1, 106.

4. Hence the popular belief that in view of India's high saving ratio the planners need to pay attention only to the efficiency of industrial enterprises seems to be based not only on an inadequate appreciation of the data base of the Indian economy, but even on a superficial reading of official statistics.

5. See Industrial Development Bank of India, *Annual Reports* (Bombay). Though in some cases the shortfall in production can be accounted for by the erratic supply of power, there is no doubt that in the majority of cases, in capital goods industries in particular, demand deficiency has been the decisive factor.

6. The classic case is that of the 25 percent decline in the production of railway wagons in 1984–85 as the Indian Railways—a public sector unit—"have been curtailing their orders on the wagon manufacturers due to the *paucity of resources*" (*Economic Survey 1985–86*, 42–43); At the same time wagon shortage was constraining the movement of goods!

7. Which is trying to dispose of it in the international market. This, in the context of large-scale hunger and malnutrition in the country, suggests that something is wrong with both the head and the heart of Indian planners.

8. The Indian experience suggests that though money wages in the organized sector are linked with the cost-of-living index and sticky in the downward direction, the Phillips' curve-type phenomenon is conspicuous by its absence. This, however, may have been due to the slow growth of employment in the organized sector.

9. Development economists, especially those emphasizing the structural features in less developed countries (LDCs), have drawn attention to the necessity of a disaggregative approach in respect of demand management in view of the differences in the working of the agricultural and the industrial sectors, and often of their subsectors. See, in this connection, L. Taylor, *Structuralist Macroeconomics* (New York: Basic Books, 1983), and Rakshit, *The Labour Surplus Economy*.

10. A theme we elaborated at some length elsewhere. See M. Rakshit, "Monetary Policy in a Developing Economy" (Paper presented at the Conference on Global Macroeconomic Policies, WIDER, Helsinki, August 1986).

11. There are no reliable statistics in respect of rural savings or savings generated in unincorporated enterprises: CSO gives savings figures for only the public, the private corporate and household sectors, and all private producers outside the corporate sector are treated as "households."

12. See A. Bhaduri, *The Economic Structure of Backward Agriculture* (London: Academic Press, 1983); *All India Debt and Investment Survey, 1971–72* (Bombay: Reserve Bank of India, 1978); and Rakshit, *The Labour Surplus Economy*.

13. As we have emphasized elsewhere (Rakshit, "Monetary Policy in a Developing Economy") because of the personalized nature of these loans, the moneylenders will not divert the amount released to other borrowers.

14. A. Smith, *An Enquiry into the Nature and Causes of the Wealth of Nations* (1776; New York: Modern Library, n.d.); D. Ricardo, *Principles of Political Economy and Taxation* (1817; London: Everyman, 1948); Marshall, *Principles of Economics*; and Harvey Liebenstein (1957).

15. Marshall, *Principles of Economics*, 553.

16. Ibid., 464–66. One may go further and draw on the modern physiological and psychological evidence to suggest that high living of the affluent saps their energy and enterprise and costs them and the nation dearly in terms of medicine and health care (especially since such expenses are borne by the company and often incurred in foreign currency). In view of the reverse U-shaped relation between consumption and efficiency, redistribution of income and wealth in a developing economy may thus be deemed an act of investment that promotes universal welfare!

17. Under an efficient system of development planning the problem of choice between current consumption and investment should come in only when the wastage in the form of superfluous consumption and investment has been largely eliminated. The rhetoric of the politicians and the economists to restrain current consumption for the benefit of future generations cannot but ring insincere, or even seem a poor joke in doubtful taste, to the unemployed and people in the low income groups. I remember one of my friends quipping after the last year's Budget that the Government appeared determined to fight poverty to the last morsel of the poor man's meal.

18. Exclusive of deficit financing.

19. Computed from Table 1, p. 20, of *Report of the Committee to Review the Workings of the Monetary Reserve System* (Bombay: Reserve Bank of India, 1985).

20. Ibid., 45.

21. Ibid., 48.

22. Through reallocation of the supply of credit for financing working capital (Rakshit, "Monetary Policy in a Developing Economy").

23. We have examined elsewhere how an interest rate policy can effectively support credit rationing (Rakshit, "Monetary Policy in a Developing Economy").

24. Through the intermediation of banks and other financial institutions.

25. Unless we believe that high interest charges would have stimulated Government administrators and managers of public sector undertakings to give of their best! By the same logic a stiff dose of taxes should also shake the managers off their indolence. Anyway, the argument in the text relates to interest payments to *households*, not to what is charged from enterprises for the use of funds.

26. Since the degree of inequality of income is less than that of assets, larger interest incomes tend to make the distribution of income more unequal.

27. Very often the household saving ratio has risen in the face of a decline in *real* interest rates (in India variations in nominal interest rates have been slow and discontinuous).

28. "Neither a borrower, nor a lender be" (*Hamlet* I, iii, 74).

29. Note that the Pigou effect operates (1) because prices of land and shares rise at a faster rate than that of consumer goods, and (2) for *all* holders of land and shares, and not only for those who actually sell these assets. In fact, a small dose of new funds can lead to a sharp rise in asset prices with very little actual transactions of shares or land (see J. M. Keynes, *A Treatise on Money*, vol. 1 [London: Macmillan, 1930]).

30. *Economic Survey 1985–86*, 2.

31. Our argument is strengthened by the fact that tax raids have also contributed towards a rise in indirect tax collections in excess of what may be estimated in terms of changes in GDP and customs or other duties.

32. Since under these conditions the price increase (following indirect taxes) will be greater and hence the amount of resources released smaller. See the appendix in this connection.

33. In 1983–84, for example, total Government expenditure was no less than 31 percent of GNP. See, in this connection, Rakshit, "Monetary Policy in a Developing Economy," and K. Sundaram and S. Tendulkar, "Financing the Step-up in Plan Investment," *Economic and Political Weekly* (June 1986).

34. A. Bagchi, "Fiscal Policy for Development—The Indian Experience" (Delhi: National Institute of Public Finance and Policy, 1986).

35. Along the lines suggested in the appendix.

36. Which we shall have to rely on heavily in the foreseeable future, given the failure of direct taxes.

37. Which should also help the Government gain command over these goods (especially when they are produced outside the organized sector).

38. With a clampdown on their production in the private sector.

39. This will remove the stigma of a commercial good from the titles conferred and give universal satisfaction to the wealthy irrespective of whether they value earthly or heavenly honor. Meanwhile the materially inclined planner should limit the supply of titles for revenue maximization which may require price discrimination of the second degree.

40. P. Bardhan, *The Political Economy of Development in India* (London: Basil and Blackwell, 1984).

TABLE 15.1 Saving, Investment and Growth

Plan Period	Annual Growth in GNP at 1970–71 Prices	Gross Domestic Saving Ratio (current prices)	Gross Investment Ratio (current prices)
First Plan (1951–52 to 1955–56)	3.6	10.4	10.8
Second Plan (1955–56 to 1960–61)	4.0	12.3	15.3
Third Plan (1961–62 to 1965–66)	2.5	14.3	16.7
Three Annual Plans (1966–67 to 1968–69)	4.1	14.8	17.2
Fourth Plan (1969–70 to 1973–74)	3.5	17.2	18.0
Fifth Plan (1974–75 to 1978–79)	5.2	21.7	21.9
Annual Plan (1979–80)	(−) 4.7	23.0	23.5
Sixth Plan (1980–81 to 1984–85)	5.3	22.5[a]	24.0[a]
Average over the Plan Period	3.7		

a The figures are simple averages of the annual ratios. However, the resultant bias is insignificant since fluctuations in the annual saving and investment ratios were minor over this period.

Sources: Economic Survey. 1985–86 (New Delhi: Government of India, 1986); Report of the Committee to Review the Working of the Monetary System (Bombay: Reserve Bank of India, 1985) (hereinafter cited as Reserve Bank of India Report).

TABLE 15.2 Net Capital Formation and Saving in India

Year	Net Capital Formation (Rs, crores[a] at 1970-71 prices)	Net Saving (percent of NDP at current prices)	Rate of Net Capital Formation (percent of NDP)	
			At Current Prices	At 1970-71 Prices
1950-51	1,641	7.0	6.8	9.3
1951-52	2,049	6.7	8.6	11.3
1952-53	1,054	4.5	4.1	5.6
1953-54	1,321	5.3	5.1	6.6
1954-55	1,501	6.8	6.9	7.3
1955-56	2,422	10.0	10.4	11.3
1956-57	3,329	9.8	13.0	14.7
1957-58	3,082	7.3	11.4	13.8
1958-59	2,298	6.1	9.0	9.5
1959-60	2,615	8.3	10.0	10.6
1960-61	3,349	9.3	12.7	12.9
1961-62	2,886	8.4	10.7	10.7
1962-63	3,388	9.6	12.3	12.2
1963-64	3,616	9.8	12.1	12.3
1964-65	3,990	9.2	12.0	12.6
1965-66	4,482	11.2	13.8	14.8
1966-67	4,892	11.8	15.4	16.3
1967-68	4,264	9.6	12.3	13.0
1968-69	3,811	9.5	10.8	11.3
1969-70	4,567	11.8	12.5	12.7
1970-71	4,960	12.0	13.0	13.0
1971-72	5,262	12.4	13.6	13.5
1972-73	4,667	11.3	11.9	12.1
1973-74	6,629	15.0	15.7	16.6
1974-75	5,850	13.8	14.8	14.6
1975-76	5,917	15.4	15.2	13.4
1976-77	6,534	17.4	15.7	14.6
1977-78	6,989	17.0	15.3	14.4
1978-79	8,680	19.2	19.0	16.8
1979-80	7,217	16.1	16.6	14.7

[a] 1 crore = Rs 10 million.

Source: Reserve Bank of India (1982).

TABLE 15.3 Combined Tax Revenue of Center, State and Union Territories

Year	Total Tax Revenue as Percent of GDP	Direct Taxes as Percent of GDP	Indirect Taxes as Percent of GDP	Total Taxes as Percent of Total Government Expenditure	Cost of Tax Collection as Percent of Tax Revenue
1950–51	6.83	2.51	4.32	73.27	5.3
1955–56	7.90	2.67	5.23	60.36	6.8
1960–61	9.60	2.86	6.74	60.07	5.4
1965–66	13.26	3.33	9.93	65.49	3.4
1970–71	12.94	2.75	10.19	67.41	3.9
1975–76	16.78	3.74	13.04	73.73	3.2
1980–81	17.40	2.87	14.54	65.23	2.5
1984–85	18.70	2.68	16.03	65.59	2.4

Sources: Report on Currency and Finance, Annual Issues (Bombay: Reserve Bank of India).

TABLE 15.4 Pattern of Direct and Indirect Taxes[a]

Year	Corporation Tax as Percent of Direct Taxes	Income Tax as Percent of Direct Taxes	Customs as Percent of Indirect Taxes	Union Excise as Percent of Indirect Taxes	General Sales Tax as Percent of Indirect Taxes
1950–51	17.05	58.07	39.67	17.05	14.69
1955–56	14.09	50.95	32.78	28.56	16.04
1960–61	27.28	41.96	17.92	43.90	17.28
1965–66	41.52	37.02	24.64	41.05	17.44
1970–71	36.72	46.89	14.00	47.00	21.01
1975–76	34.57	48.72	16.34	38.49	22.82
1980–81	40.11	46.09	20.57	39.21	24.24
1984–85	50.65	34.44	24.00	36.12	24.16

[a] Of the direct taxes not shown interest taxes stand on the same footing as corporation tax.

Sources: Reserve Bank of India Report on Currency and Finance, Annual Issues.

APPENDIX [1]

Taxes As Instruments of Resource Mobilization

A.1 Consider an economy producing a given level of output.[2] Y with an initial market price of 1 per unit. The problem is to find out the additional investment (or development) expenditure in real terms, dR, that may be undertaken corresponding to a given amount of tax revenue, dT, (in nominal terms) without creating an excess demand in the commodity market. Assume that money wages are inflexible in the downward direction and product prices are fixed on a cost-plus basis. If the collection of direct taxes amounts to dT_i and the entire sum is realized from households, the amount of dR will be given by the relation

(1) $dR = c.dT_i$
where c = households' marginal propensity to consume.

If, however, a fraction δ of direct taxes is collected from the corporate sector (including public sector enterprises), this part has little impact on household disposable income. The extent of resource mobilization then equals

(2) $dR = c.(1 - \delta) dT_i$

A.2 In the economy we have been considering indirect taxes release resources only through the price effect. If dT_n is the amount of additional indirect taxes collected, with given factor costs, GDP (consisting of a homogeneous output) at market prices goes up by dT_n. Hence prices now rise to $(Y + dT_n)/Y$ and the fall in household disposable incomes will be $dT_n/(1 + dT_n/Y)$, provided all incomes initially accrued to households. Resources released through indirect taxes now amount to

(3) $dR = c.\dfrac{dT_n}{(1 + dT_n/Y)}$

Thus the larger the amount of indirect tax collections as a proportion of GDP, the less will be the value of dR. The conclusion is strengthened when money wages are linked to the cost-of-living index. Let T_n be the initial amount of indirect tax collected (which we take to be small for simplicity). The initial price relation is

(4) $P(price) = \omega + \pi \dfrac{T_n}{Y} = 1$ (by choice of units)
where ω = per unit wage costs; π = surplus per unit; and T_n/Y = per unit indirect taxes.

Let β be the ratio of wages to nonwage incomes (under the cost-plus rule of pricing) and α the fraction by which money wages are adjusted for every unit increase in the cost-of-living index. Hence

(5) $\qquad \pi = \dfrac{\omega}{\beta}$

and

(6) $\qquad d\omega = \alpha dP$

Hence

(7) $\qquad d\pi = \dfrac{d\omega}{\beta} = \dfrac{\alpha}{\beta} dP$

From (4), (6), and (7) we then obtain

$$dP = d\omega + d\pi + \dfrac{dT_n}{Y} \quad \text{(real output being given)}$$

$$= \alpha.dP + \dfrac{\alpha}{\beta}.dP + \dfrac{dT_n}{Y} \quad \text{(from (6) and (7))}$$

Or

(9) $\qquad dP = \dfrac{dT_n/Y}{[1-\alpha(1+\beta)/\beta]}$

Since the new price level is now $(1 + dP)$, the fall in household disposable income is approximated by $dT_n/(1 + dP)$. Hence equation (3) now becomes

(10) $\qquad dR = c.\dfrac{dT_n}{1+(dT_n/Y/[1-\alpha(1+\beta)/\beta]}$

Thus indirect taxes become completely ineffective as an instrument of resource mobilization if α exceeds $\beta/(1+\beta)$: with wages forming say 70 percent of the value added, no additional resources will be released if money wages adjust by 70 percent of the change in the cost of living index.

A.3 The relations (3) and (10) are based on the assumption that all incomes initially accrue to households. If, however, households receive only a fraction h of Y in the initial situation, the two relations, it may easily be verified, will change respectively to

(3a) $\qquad dR = c.h.\dfrac{dT_n}{(1 + dT_n/Y)}$

and

(10a) $\qquad dR = c.h.\dfrac{dT_n}{(1 + dT_n/Y)/[1-\alpha(1+\beta)/\beta]}$

A.4 So far we have assumed all goods to be homogeneous. What if production conditions and indirect taxes imposed are different in the investment and the consumption goods sectors? Let the initial prices of both goods be unity, the initial amount of consumption C, and the fraction of total indirect taxes collected from consumption goods λ. It will suffice if we work out the resultant modification in (3). Note that imposition of dT_n raises the market value of consumption goods to $(C + \lambda.dT_n)$ and consumption goods prices to $(1 + \lambda.dT_n)$ and consumption goods prices to $(1 + \lambda.dT_n/C)$. Hence the fall in consumption at base prices, i.e., dR, is given by

$$(3b) \qquad dR = C - c.\frac{Y}{(1 + \lambda dT_n/C)} - \frac{\lambda.dT_n}{1 + \lambda dT_n/C}$$

where c also approximates the average propensity to consume.

However, since the production conditions in the two sectors are different, the marginal rate of transformation (say σ) between the two goods (measured at base prices) will be less than unity. Hence the additional investment made possible (dI) by indirect taxes will be a fraction of what is shown under (3b):

$$(3c) \qquad dI = \sigma.\lambda.\frac{dT_n}{1 + \lambda dT_n/C}$$

Notes

1. This is an extension of the analysis in M. Rakshit, "A Primer on Budgetary Policy," *Economic and Political Weekly* (Budget Issue, 9 April 1983).
2. Taxes are required for resource mobilization only in this case, not if resources are unemployed.

Development Strategy for the Future

16

India's Economic Performance, Policies and Prospects

Montek S. Ahluwalia

The chapters in this volume provide a comprehensive review of almost all important aspects of the Indian economy. They also convey much of the flavor of the current debate on economic issues in India, with its usual diversity of views. In this chapter I propose to examine what this review adds up to in terms of the present state and future prospects of the Indian economy and the evolution of economic policies in India.

A particular objective of this chapter is to provide the total perspective in which some of the recent initiatives in India's economic policy need to be viewed. These initiatives, usually characterized by the catchall phrase "economic liberalization," have been the special focus of international attention directed at India. They are certainly important, but they must be seen as one element of the total economic policy package, addressed especially at improving performance in the industrial sector. Economic policy must also deal with many other aspects of performance where the key issues do not relate to economic liberalization. It is also important to distinguish the Indian policy initiatives from the classical "liberalization packages" which are ardently advocated in many quarters. There are important differences in approach, and perhaps also in underlying philosophy, and these differences are brought out in this chapter.

Objectives of Policy

Both performance and policy are in some sense best judged in terms of the objectives of development policy, the more so in an economy in which objectives have been consciously set in successive national plans. The broad objectives which have guided India's development strategy are listed below. Some of them are obviously common to all developing countries, but others are not so, at least not to the same extent.

The views expressed in the chapter are those of the author.

1. Achievement of a high rate of economic growth leading to a sustained improvement in the levels of living of the population. This is obviously a common objective of all developing countries.
2. Reduction in inequalities, and more especially an accelerated effort to remove poverty at a pace faster than would be achieved solely through the normal growth process. This objective too is commonly subscribed to in the plans of many developing countries, though the importance accorded to it varies, as do the policies adopted in its pursuit.
3. Development of a mixed economy with a strong public sector, especially in key areas of the economy. The creation of a public sector could be viewed as an instrument for achieving broader objectives of growth with equity, but India's development strategy has accorded such special importance to the public sector that it could properly be described as an independent objective of policy. The creation of a public sector was viewed not merely as an instrument to achieve other objectives. There was a more basic and widely shared sociopolitical commitment to the creation of a mixed economy, in which the state has a substantial direct control over important production sectors.
4. Achievement of a high order of "self-reliance" has been an important independent objective. The term itself is used in two senses. In one sense, self-reliance has meant that development must be financed as far as possible from domestic savings, avoiding excessive dependence upon external assistance. Self-reliance has also meant a conscious effort at developing a broad domestic production base and an indigenous technological capacity, both of which were felt to be essential requirements for building a strong industrialized economy.
5. Promotion of balanced regional development, with a narrowing of economic difference across regions. This has tended to be viewed not just as matter of promoting economic growth but more specifically as a matter of regional balance in the degree of industrialization.
6. Finally, these social and economic objectives were to be pursued in the framework of a constitutional democracy.

These broad objectives have been evident from the very early stages of planning in India. Over time they have taken more concrete shape as distinct objectives. It is evident that some of these objectives involve a potential conflict or trade-off with growth, at least in the short term. The possibility of such trade-offs in the short run was always consciously recognized, though, of course, it is always relevant to ask whether in practice the trade-off was optimized.

How has the economy performed in terms of these objectives? A summary assessment is offered in the following sections, focusing especially on recent performance and identifying some key aspects of policy and future priorities as they emerge from recent experience.

Growth Performance

The rate of growth of the economy is the most commonly used measure of overall performance and it is appropriate to begin with this indicator. Up to about the mid-seventies, India's trend growth rate of GDP, ignoring yearly fluctuations, seemed firmly anchored at about 3.5 percent per year, unforgettably characterized by the late Professor Raj Krishna as "the Hindu rate of growth." There is clear evidence that the economy broke through this constraint some time in the mid-seventies. The growth rate over the past ten years or so averages about 4.5 percent and this is an average over a period in which growth was accelerating. The underlying growth rate of the economy in the mid-eighties is nearer 5 percent per year. This is not high compared with growth rates achieved in earlier decades by the better-performing developing countries. Some countries have achieved annual growth rates as high as 10 percent over sustained periods, and many have grown at rates between 6 percent and 7 percent in the sixties and early seventies. But this comparison is not wholly fair in assessing recent economic performance in India.

An obvious point which has to be noted is that India is a relatively large economy and also among the group of low-income countries of the developing world. The size of the economy ensures that a process of averaging must be at work. India's "growth potential" cannot therefore be presumed to be equal to the fastest-growing developing countries, but closer to the average. More important, India's recent performance should not be assessed by comparing it with growth rates achieved by developing countries in an earlier period when the international environment was especially conducive to rapid growth. The growth potential of the developing world as a whole has slowed down since the mid-seventies, and when due allowance is made for this factor, India's recent growth performance and current growth prospects appear in a much better light.

In the period up to the mid-seventies India's growth rate of around 3.5 percent per year was much lower than the average of about 6.0 percent achieved by the developing countries as a whole. In the past ten years, however, India's growth rate has accelerated, while growth rates in most of the developing world have decelerated. India's growth rate in the period 1981–86 was almost 5 percent, when all developing countries taken together grew by only 2.5 percent. Admittedly the low growth of developing countries as a group was partly due to negative growth rates in the oil-exporting countries, but even if these countries are excluded, the category of non-oil-developing countries shows a growth of only 3.5 percent per year in this period. In fact, India's growth performance in the eighties is exceeded only by some of the fast-growing East Asian economies and China.

This raises the question whether the acceleration in growth is a temporary phenomenon or indicative of a more basic improvement in the economy's growth potential. The theme explored in this chapter is that India has indeed experienced a permanent acceleration in growth, accompanied by an increase in its underlying growth potential. A degree of structural maturity has been achieved in both agriculture and industry, which not only has laid the foundation for sustained growth at 5 percent but also holds out the prospect of higher growth in future. The elements of this transformation and the policy framework in which it took place are discussed in the subsequent sections of this chapter.

Turnaround in Agriculture

A key element in the improvement in aggregate performance was improved performance in agriculture. This not only contributed directly to faster growth of GDP but also stimulated industrial growth through well-known linkages between the two sectors.

Conventional wisdom identifies the beginning of the Green Revolution with the introduction of the Mexican hybrid wheat in the late sixties. The new seeds quickly led to increased wheat yields in Punjab, where agroclimatic conditions were favorable and effective water management was readily possible. But this was only the beginning of the story. To achieve an agricultural turnaround, it was necessary to spread the Green Revolution more widely, both in terms of crops and also in terms of geographical regions. This required a comprehensive strategy for agricultural change requiring active Government intervention in many dimensions. It required a sustained effort at expanding irrigation with a shift from major to medium and minor irrigation. It was necessary to push the banking system into the rural areas to provide credit for the purchase of biochemical inputs needed for high-yielding varieties (HYVs). These measures were accompanied by a policy of providing effective price support at remunerative prices. It was also necessary to strengthen research to adapt high-yielding varieties to local conditions and to develop new varieties continuously. Varietal development is particularly important in the case of rice, which is grown in widely varying agroclimatic conditions in the Gangetic basin and which requires a correspondingly larger number of varieties to ensure suitability in different local conditions.

Agricultural policy evolved along these lines in the seventies, but it took time to have a noticeable impact. Although yields and production of wheat grew rapidly in Punjab from an early stage, this was not reflected in a convincing improvement in total agricultural performance until after the mid-seventies. With the usual lags in availability of data, and also the fact that it takes time before an upswing can be statistically established with confidence, there was considerable skepticism about agricultural performance even in the late seventies. Vaidyanathan[1] found evidence that Indian agriculture may actually be decelerating, while Srinivasan[2] cautioned that the Green Revolution was as yet only a wheat revolution. By the early eighties, however, it became generally accepted that Indian agriculture had indeed entered a new phase, with a discernible acceleration in agricultural growth. The compound growth rate of production for all crops has increased from about 2.5 percent in the period 1950–51 to 1967–68, to about 3 percent after the mid-seventies. The compound annual growth rate of the index of agricultural production in the more recent period from 1980–81 to 1985–86 is about 3.2 percent. There is also clear evidence that agricultural production is becoming less vulnerable to variations in rainfall, itself an important aspect of agricultural performance.

The rate of growth achieved is still short of the 4 percent target growth of agricultural production in the Seventh Five-Year Plan (1985–90) but there are good reasons to believe that an acceleration to 4 percent growth is possible because of the structural and institutional changes which have taken place in the agricultural sector over the past ten years. The institutional system needed to deliver the necessary inputs has a much wider coverage today than it did ten years ago, but its full potential for increasing yields has yet to be realized. There has been an impressive increase in irrigation potential with the addition of about two million hectares of irrigation capacity every year. However, effective utilization of this capacity has lagged behind because of insufficient investment in the construction of field channels and drains and also because of inefficient water management practices. The area covered under high-yielding varieties shows an impressive increase from about 40 percent in 1980–81 to over 60 percent in 1986–87, but while area coverage has increased, yields have not increased as much as could be expected. The banking infrastructure has also greatly increased its penetration of rural areas and is well positioned to provide rural credit for large parts of the country. All these developments constitute a structural transformation in the making—they have increased the production potential of Indian agriculture in a way which is not yet fully reflected in actual production.

Average yields in India are still well below yields achieved by many East Asian countries, although yields achieved in the best-performing agricultural states compare favorably. The inter-State variation in yields is a good indicator of the tremendous scope for further improvement in agricultural production. Rice yields are 3,200 kilograms per hectare in Punjab and 2,800 kilograms per hectare in Haryana. By contrast they are only 1,490 kilograms per hectare in Uttar Pradesh, 1,130 kilograms per hectare in Bihar and 1,560 kilograms per hectare in West Bengal. The area under rice in these States is very large. Even modest improvement in yields, narrowing the gap between what has already been achieved in the most productive areas in the country, could produce a large impact on overall agricultural growth.

Fortunately there are definite signs that the Green Revolution is indeed spreading to those areas, and yields are increasing in Uttar Pradesh and also Bihar. The task of agricultural transformation of these areas is not easy. It will require a tremendous improvement in the ground level functioning of the development administration to provide the farmer with the full package of support needed. But the process has definitely taken off, and further acceleration can be expected.

Industrial Performance and Policies

Rapid industrialization has long been viewed as the key to sustained growth and modernization of the economy. However, industrial policies were not framed solely by the immediate requirements of growth maximization. They were also influenced by active Government intervention in pursuit of some of the other developmental objectives listed earlier in this chapter.

The results present a mixed picture. In some respects the industrial sector can be said to have achieved the objectives set for it. A substantial public sector presence has been created, laying the foundations for a mixed economy. A high degree of "self reliance" has been achieved in the sense that a highly diversified industrial base has been created, catering to the domestic needs of the economy in a very wide variety of products. The entrepreneurial base of the economy has also been widened greatly, with the emergence of a number of new large- and medium-scale industrial houses and a profusion of small-scale entrepreneurs. Finally, industry has spread into regions where industry did not exist earlier and into which it probably would not have gone for many more years but for Government intervention.

Against these achievements there are some obvious shortcomings. Industrial growth has not been as rapid as was expected. After a promising early period in the fifties and early sixties, industrial growth slowed down considerably, and from 1964–65 to 1975–76 the index of industrial production showed a growth rate of only 4 percent per year and value added in industry grew at 3.5 percent per year. There is evidence of a gradual acceleration after the mid-seventies, though with considerable year-to-year fluctuations. In the most recent period 1981–82 to 1986–87, the index of industrial production (using the new index base 1980–81 = 100) shows an average growth rate of around 7 percent per year while value-added growth is about 6 percent. This is definitely an improvement on past performance, but it still falls short of what is needed to take the economy beyond the current 5 percent growth of GDP. For the future, India should be aiming at an industrial growth rate of around 9 percent to 10 percent, with value added in the industrial sector growing at 8 percent to 9 percent.

Another major shortcoming in India's industrial sector is its lack of international competitiveness and consequent poor export performance. Export performance is obviously important in a situation in which the continued growth and modernization of the economy requires a substantial inflow of imported capital goods and other inputs into production. The industrial sector, which absorbs a large percentage of total resources available to the economy, must be able to earn the foreign exchange it needs from exports. This has not yet happened to the extent needed, and one of the major constraints is clearly lack of competitiveness in terms of both cost and quality.

These shortcomings of slow industrial growth and a high-cost uncompetitive industrial sector have been widely recognized in India and have led to critical reexamination of the industrial policy structure to see what corrective steps are necessary. The blame for slow industrial growth cannot, of course, be laid on policy alone. For example, it could be argued that the key to faster industrial growth lies in a more rapid pace of expansion in agriculture which would provide the stimulus for faster growth in industry. While this is undoubtedly true, a consensus has also emerged that the system of regulatory control that has evolved over time is not conducive to industrial efficiency and dynamism.

A number of official reports and academic studies have documented the problems created by a control system consisting of detailed, often multiple, regulation and scrutiny. This system has operated in a manner which hampered the ability of industrial units to take rational investment decisions, limited their ability to modernize existing capacities and even discouraged expansion of production beyond licensed capacity. It has also restricted competition which would have been a spur to improved quality and lower cost. Much of the problem arises because of the multiplicity of objectives to which industrial policy has been tailored, each involving an intervention which has an economic cost.

The catalogue of criticisms of the industrial policy are well-known. The original rationale for industrial licensing was to direct private investment into desired areas and also to avoid wasteful overinvestment. In practice, strict licensing often had the effect of limiting expansion by efficient units or entry by potential new units on the ground that adequate capacity had already been licensed. Inefficient producers were therefore effectively shielded from domestic competition. The objective of limiting concentration of economic power led to specially strict scrutiny and regulation of the expansion or investment plans of larger houses, with a view to ensuring that their activities were restricted to high-priority, technically more difficult industries. Consideration of maintaining regional balance often led to fragmentation of capacity, with a consequent loss of economies of sale. There was a tendency to license a larger number of small units spread over many States, where a single economic-scale plant would have been more efficient.

These and other sources of inefficiency undoubtedly contributed to the emergence of a high-cost industrial structure which slowed growth and reduced export competitiveness. Such a structure would obviously not have been sustainable in a more open economy, which allows competition from imports, but the trade policy permitted very little room for import competition. The objective of self-reliance should have meant self-reliance with efficiency. In practice, however, domestic production was protected from external competition with little regard to domestic resource costs. Protection, which should have been viewed as giving initial support for infant industries, which would in time outgrow the need for it, typically continued as an indefinite crutch, supporting industries whose costs of production were far out of line with international prices.

These problems prompted the establishment of various official committees in the early eighties to examine the structure of industrial and trade policies and make recommendations for change. On the basis of their recommendations a series of policy initiatives were taken in 1985 and 1986. The most important of these were the following:

1. The coverage of industrial licensing was reduced by delicensing twenty-five industries and eighty-two pharmaceutical products.

2. Where licensing remained in operation, procedures were simplified and industrial licensing was much more liberally operated. Furthermore, greater flexibility was provided to producers to expand capacity within

existing licensed capacity. Provisions for allowing automatic expansion in licensed capacity, which existed earlier, were liberalized. For a number of products, licenses were "broadbanded" so as to cover similar products, thus allowing flexibility in varying the product mix.

3. The minimum size of assets beyond which a unit is declared a "large house" and subjected to specially rigorous scrutiny in licensing was increased from Rs 200 million to Rs 1,000 million.

4. Twenty-seven industries were added to the list of industries for which large houses are exempted from the special scrutiny normally required.

5. A list of industries was notified where economies of scale are important, and for these industries minimum economic scales of plant were specified. Existing units below these sizes will be allowed to expand freely up to the minimum economic size, and new units will be licensed only for these or higher sizes.

6. A number of items were earlier reserved for production in the small-scale sector, defined in terms of units with investment in plant and machinery below Rs 35 lakhs.[3] In many cases, this investment limit was too low for efficient production of the reserved items. The list of reserved items has been reviewed, and a number of items have been deleted, or in some cases redefined, to enable larger-scale investment to be made for the production of a large number of items.

7. In the area of trade policy, the Government accepted the principle of shifting from quantitative controls to tariff controls. Implementation, however, was left to be determined in the light of practical possibilities. Some tariff adjustments have indeed been made along these lines.

8. No major change was made in the degree of import liberalization in 1985 and 1986, but it was reaffirmed that the liberalization that had earlier taken place over the first half of the eighties would stay in place. The affirmation that import policy would not be reversed was an important signal in a situation where the balance of payments was beginning to show strain.

9. A major step was taken towards rationalization of the indirect tax system in 1986 by introducing a modified value-added tax, covering a wide range of commodities. The system provides for adjustment of the duties paid on inputs against the tax due on output. Although tax rates on outputs were simultaneously raised to avoid any net reduction in effective taxation in the initial stages, it was nevertheless an important reform. The total burden of excise taxation on a commodity is now more apparent since earlier-stage duties are adjusted against the tax. This paves the way for restructuring of indirect taxation in the future. The Government has indicated that restructuring of indirect taxes will be attempted industry by industry.

10. Steps have also been taken to rationalize the structure of customs duties. The range of variation of tariffs for capital goods has been reduced. Tariffs were raised on a number of items earlier allowed at 55 percent duty and lowered on others where the tariff was 101 percent, and all these items now face a uniform duty of 85 percent (inclusive of a 15 percent countervailing duty which offsets the 15 percent domestic excise duty on capital goods). In addition, the customs duty structure for

components and raw materials has been both lowered, and rationalized, for selected sectors. It has also been indicated that such restructuring will continue to be made sector by sector.

11. Finally, a number of measures were taken to improve the competitive position of exporters. The procedures for giving exporters access to imports at international prices were further improved in several ways and direct tax incentives for income from exports were strengthened. Some of these measures are applicable to all exporters, but others were aimed at particular export sectors. The customs duties on capital goods for certain industries deemed to have export potential (gems and jewelery, garments, leather, etc.) were reduced to 35 percent in an effort to bring the cost of production in these industries more in line with world prices.

It is too early to evaluate quantitatively the effect of the 1985 and 1986 measures on actual industrial performance. However, there is no doubt that they have contributed to a spurt of investment proposals in these years. The volume of industrial licenses approved in 1985 and 1986 increased very substantially and there was also a large increase in industrial investment proposals in the delicensed category as measured by the number of registrations. Moreover, because of the more liberal approach to technological modernization and import of capital goods for this purpose, the more recent investment proposals embody better technology than has been allowed in the past. Many of them also represent plant sizes which are nearer to economic levels of scale. The full impact of this investment boom and the associated qualitative improvements should be evident in the next few years when the capacities to be created by these investments come on-stream.

An important determinant of industrial performance in India is the performance of the public sector. The creation of a large public sector presence in the Indian economy was one of the explicit objectives of India's development strategy and the success in achieving this objective is evident. Public sector output today accounts for about 45 percent of the output of the organized industrial sector and 30 percent of total industrial output. Its size alone ensures that an overall acceleration of industrial growth would require an improvement in public sector performance. This is all the more so since the public sector occupies a dominant position in key infrastructure industries such as power generation, coal, steel and crude oil production, and performance in these areas is crucial to the general level of industrial efficiency.

There can be no doubt that very considerable improvement is needed in public sector performance. The logic of undertaking large investments to create a public sector with a commanding presence implies that it will generate the necessary surpluses to be able to replace capital and finance investment for future growth. The record in this respect has been disappointing. There are heartening examples of very good performance by individual enterprises, but, equally, there are many cases of large and chronic loss makers. The overall generation of resources from this sector is well below the levels assumed in the Plan. If the resources contributed by the oil sector are excluded, the performance of the other public sector organizations appears in a much poorer light.

There is no easy solution to the problem of improving public sector performance. Many of the public sector enterprises suffer from earlier noneconomic decisions, which are not always the fault of management. No simple formula will overcome these problems. Many are heavily overmanned, and it is not easy to lay off surplus labor. Some suffer from wrong technology choices or product mix decisions made earlier which impose a continuing burden on the enterprise. In some cases, public sector projects become unviable even before they commence production because capital costs are allowed to escalate to unreasonable levels on account of delays in implementation, usually because the unit was short of funds at the early stages. Still other loss-making enterprises in the public sector are actually former private sector units which had become financially unviable and were taken over by the Government only to protect employment. Each of these pathologies obviously calls for its own solution.

However, a consensus is emerging on one important issue, and that is the need to give management autonomy to public sector enterprises as a key requirement for efficient functioning. There is no inherent reason why a public sector corporation should be inefficient, if it is run like a corporation. In particular, it must not be subjected to continuous interference from the Government or bureaucracy which demoralizes public sector management and dilutes accountability. Government should set out the corporate objectives of the enterprise and top management must be given the full degree of autonomy needed to achieve these corporate objectives. With this autonomy there must also be accountability. The performance of top management must be judged in terms of the achievement of agreed objectives. The Sengupta Committee, which examined the functioning of public sector enterprises and submitted its report in 1985, had recommended that the objective of ensuring autonomy and accountability could be achieved by introducing a Memorandum of Understanding (MOU) which would be jointly agreed between the Government and the top management of the enterprise each year. The MOU would set out the objectives according to which the management performance would be judged and it would also specify actions expected by the public sector enterprise from the Government. As an experiment, the system of MOUs is being implemented for six major public sector enterprises beginning in 1987.

It is important to note that the "privatization" which is often recommended as the answer to public sector inefficiency is not on the agenda. Proponents of privatization obviously regard the public sector as inherently inefficient. No such assumption underlies the policy reform being attempted in India. On the contrary, the basic approach is that a public sector enterprise can be as efficient as any other corporate sector unit, provided the relationship between Government and the public sector unit can be made to approximate the relationship between shareholders and a corporation.

The policy initiatives described above for improving industrial performance involve a considerable measure of deregulation and therefore may be called economic liberalization but they obviously differ in important respects from the usual liberalization packages often prescribed for developing countries and also undertaken in some cases (though with varying success). The familiar liberalization package focuses heavily on foreign trade liberalization and rationalization of protection. The usual formula is to recommend a first stage consisting of a switch from quantitative to tariff controls, followed by a phased reduction in both the variation in degrees of protection across sectors and also the average level of protection. The whole process is usually expected to be underpinned by an exchange rate depreciation. Often it includes a conscious policy of privatization of the public sector to overcome problems of public sector inefficiency. The differences in the Indian case are evident. Indian policy reform has focused much more on domestic industrial liberalization rather than foreign trade liberalization. There is considerable internal deregulation aimed at strengthening the more efficient domestic firms and encouraging them to invest and expand. This is expected to inject much more competition into the system, creating incentives for reducing costs. The internal liberalization has been accompanied by a policy of maintaining a sufficiently open access to imports to permit modernization and technological upgrading in Indian industry, which again will reduce costs and promote international competition. As far as foreign trade liberalization is concerned, a broad direction has been given about the desirability of switching from quantitative controls to tariffs, but the movement in this area is limited and certainly does not include imports of final consumer goods. However, significant tariff rationalization measures have been implemented in several sectors. Finally, there is no question of privatization of the public sector. The focus is on management and institutional reform of the public sector to improve its efficiency.

An important feature of the process of policy reform under way in India is that it is gradualist. The system is being subjected to much stronger pressures for efficiency and modernization, but at a controlled pace. The rationale for this gradualist approach lies in the perception that the system should be subjected to pressure commensurate with its ability to respond. Pressure beyond this point is only disruptive.

Financing Development

An important aspect of performance, which has a direct bearing on the longer-term growth potential of the economy, is the ability to mobilize resources for investment. India's recent performance in this dimension is commendable. The rate of gross domestic investment in the economy, which increased only marginally from 17 percent in 1960–61 to 18 percent in 1970–71, then increased sharply thereafter to reach 24.7 percent in 1980–81. It has stayed at that level in the eighties. This investment rate is not high compared with rates achieved in the more rapidly growing middle-income countries, but it is much higher than the rates achieved in all the other low-income countries except China. What is more, the high rate of investment is being financed almost entirely from higher domestic savings, testifying to the success of self-reliance in this sense of the term. The gross domestic savings rate which was 17 percent in 1970–71 had increased to 23 percent by 1985–86.

There is certainly need and scope for further increasing the rate of savings and thereby also the rate of investment. But the levels already achieved, and their evident sustainability, reflect on important structural transformation in the economy in terms of its resource mobilization capability. Even if the investment rate is only maintained at around 24–35 percent, it should be possible not only to maintain the present 5 percent growth rate, but perhaps even to achieve some further acceleration. This is because all available evidence suggests that the incremental capital-output ratio is higher in India than in other countries. This points to the scope for increased efficiency in resource use, a possibility which is confirmed by recent studies of total factor productivity such as Ahluwalia[4] and Goldar[5] which show slower growth in these indices of industrial productivity in India compared with other developing countries.

An important feature of the increase in the aggregate savings rate is that it has occurred entirely because of the rapid growth in private household savings as a percent of GDP. The ratios of private corporate sector savings and public sector savings to GDP have remained more or less constant at 2 percent and 3 percent of GDP respectively, while private sector savings increased from 12 percent of GDP in 1970–71 to 18 percent of GDP in 1985–86. This rapid growth reflects the cumulative impact of a conscious policy of giving strong incentives for private household savings, especially in the form of financial assets. Following nationalization of the Indian commercial banks in 1969 (foreign banks were not nationalized) there was a massive expansion of the banking system spreading bank branches to all parts of the country, including also rural areas. The spread of bank branches definitely helped to mobilize private savings for investment in the organized sector. Interest rate policy was also geared to encourage household savings and for the past ten years or so, rates paid on term deposits with banks and other Government-sponsored small savings schemes have yielded positive real rates of return for savers, especially for maturities of three years and above. More recently positive real rates of return have been available even for shorter maturities.

This favorable interest rate policy was reinforced by fiscal incentives for savings built into the direct tax structure which provide deductions from taxable income of the interest earned on a wide range of financial instruments. For certain types of long-term savings instruments, a deduction is also allowed for a part of the amount invested. These incentives, which have been steadily strengthened and expanded in the past ten years, have had the effect of raising the effective pretax return on eligible financial investments. They certainly encouraged the flow of savings into these investments and on the whole probably also stimulated total savings.

The institutional mechanisms for mobilizing household savings for productive investment have been further strengthened in the eighties by the remarkable development of the domestic capital market. Until about 1980 the volume of funds sought to be raised directly from the capital market through equity and bonds was only about Rs 500 crores[6] per year. By 1986–87 this had increased more than tenfold.

This is an impressive rate of expansion by any standard and is indicative of a structural transformation taking place in an important area, which would have very important implications for mobilizing capital and allocating it efficiently. The process is as yet far from complete. The capital market remains thin and vulnerable to manipulation. It lacks adequate depth in terms of the existence of large numbers of active participants, including institutional investors. It is also inadequately regulated in terms of rules for full disclosure and restrictions on trading malpractices, including, in particular, insider trading. These limitations are fully recognized and a number of initiatives have been taken to overcome these problems. The Unit Trust of India, until now the only mutual fund operating in India, and hitherto a conservative income-oriented operation at that, floated a second fund aimed at capital appreciation. The State Bank of India is to float a second mutual fund to compete with the Unit Trust. The term-lending financial institutions, which up to now have played only a limited role in the capital market, have been more active in it, in the past two years. The 1986 and 1987 budgets liberalized the treatment of long-term capital gains on sale of shares so that the maximum tax on capital gains on shares is only 20 percent for shares held for more than one year. The Government also proposes to set up a National Securities and Exchange Board which will serve as an agency supervising the functioning of the stock markets and setting clear rules on issues such as disclosure, insider trading, etc., to protect the investor. It will also serve as a forum for the development and implementation of ideas aimed at developing a healthy capital market.

In the area of resource mobilization therefore, the economy has shown a reasonably good performance with important structural changes taking place which have stengthened its capability to mobilize and allocate resources efficiently. The principal weak area has been the generation of investable surpluses from the public sector. This weakness has been widely recognized and it is to be hoped that the various measures being taken to improve public sector performance will correct this problem.

Equity and Social Justice

Considerations of equity and social justice have been extremely important in India's development objectives and policies and any evaluation of performance must include these dimensions also. This is not an easy task because of the multidimensional nature of the equity and social justice objective. The concern with income inequality and the need to increase incomes and levels of living for the poorest sections of the population is the most commonly discussed aspect of this objective. However, there are several other dimensions also, which call for distinct policy interventions. These include provision of basic or "minimum needs" for the bulk of the population (not just the poor) relating to health, education, drinking water and sanitation, removal of social disparities arising from caste, providing equality of opportunity at various levels of education to promote vertical mobility, and reduction in regional disparity, avoiding concentration of economic power within the private sector. A quantitative assessment of progress in each of these dimensions is beyond the scope of this chapter, but some broad features of performance and policies can be documented.

A major problem in assessing performance in reducing inequality is the lack of reliable time series data on the distribution of income. The only robust conclusions which can be asserted is that the distribution of income in India, as measured by the usual indicators of inequality, is among the more equal in the developing world. There is also no evidence of any increase in income inequality over time. Data on the distribution of consumption are more readily available and these show a decline up to the mid-seventies followed by a period in which there is year-to-year fluctuation but no trend (see Tendulkar[7]).

Success in reducing poverty is in many respects more important than trends in relative inequality, and this subject has been extensively investigated in the Indian literature, especially in the context of rural poverty, which is the bulk of the problem. A broad consensus is emerging. Studies have shown that up to about the mid-seventies the percentage of the rural population living below the poverty line has fluctuated over time, but without any underlying trend (see Ahluwalia[8] and Tendulkar[9]). The percentage appears to have increased in years of poor agricultural performance (allowing for appropriate lags) and to have declined in response to good agricultural performance. It has also been argued that the behavior of prices and inflation has an important impact on the extent of poverty with rising prices being associated with an accentuation of poverty.

Although a clear trend does not emerge from the available data up to the mid-seventies, the more recent performance is more encouraging. There was perceptible drop in the late seventies in the percentage of population living below the poverty line and this appears to have continued into the eighties. The Planning Commission has estimated that the percentage of the rural population in poverty declined by 10 percentage points in the Sixth Five-Year Plan period (1980–85) from 47 percent to 37 percent.

The pattern of no trend up to the mid-seventies followed by an improvement can be attributed to two factors. One is probably the acceleration in agricultural and nonagricultural growth which took place from the mid-seventies onward. In the earlier period, overall growth, and especially agricultural growth, was so low that after allowing for population growth, there was only a very modest growth in per capita incomes. Per capita income in the rural areas probably grew at no more than 0.5 percent per year up to the mid-seventies. With per capita incomes growing so slowly it is not surprising that rural poverty was not much reduced. In the second period, growth in rural per capita incomes was definitely higher. If more rapid growth in nonagricultural income earned by rural households is allowed for, the growth in per capita incomes in rural areas in the more recent period could well be in the range of 1.5 percent or so. These growth rates are still only modest, but they represent a definite improvement on the earlier pattern. The regional pattern of growth in the eighties also indicates a shift which would have helped reduce poverty. There is an acceleration in growth in some of the very areas where poverty has been most concentrated, e.g., Uttar Pradesh and Bihar.

These developments suggest that the twin strategy of relying on accelerated growth, especially in agriculture, together with special programs aimed at directly helping households below the poverty line, can produce significant results in a reasonable period of time. The Planning Commission has estimated that the percentage of the population below the poverty line will have declined to 25 percent by 1989–90. The next decade should see a further sharp decline if not virtual elimination in poverty as measured by the standard that has been used thus far.

As noted above, progress in other dimensions of equity and social justice is not so easily documented because of lack of data. But there is no doubt that there has been commensurate growth in most of the other indicators of minimum needs and living standards also. Perhaps the most important recent initiative in this area is the announcement of a New Education Policy aimed at upgrading the quality of education at all levels and accelerating the spread of education. A beginning in implementing this policy is being made in 1987–88 with a massive increase of almost 120 percent in Central Government expenditure on educational programs. The special focus on education, including adult education, has direct relevance not only for productivity of the labor force but also for equity and poverty removal.

Conclusion

It is appropriate to conclude this overview of India's economic performance and policies with a summary assessment of prospects. The past record shows an economy which has gained in strength and structural maturity in many dimensions. It has certainly emerged from the pattern of sluggish growth evident up to the mid-seventies, to a much better performance subsequently, especially in the most recent years. A growth rate of 5 percent is now definitely sustainable and could even be bettered in future if the considerable unutilized potential built up from past investment in the economy is effectively exploited. There is considerable scope for reaping such benefits both in agriculture and in industry, with present levels of the rate of investment or modest improvements therein. The policy initiatives being taken in the industrial sector will help to bring about this outcome.

Management of the balance of payments will remain an important problem especially if the objective is to achieve a balance which can finance the sort of growth in imports that is needed to sustain technological modernization in increasing numbers of sectors of the economy. This points to the extreme importance of exports in the years ahead. However, many of the policy initiatives taken in recent years on the industrial front and the changes made in policies towards exporters should help to strengthen India's export capability.

A major factor which will help stimulate virtuous cycles in the Indian economy in future is the expected slowdown in the rate of growth of population. With population growing at over 2 percent per year, much of the growth in production in the past has been absorbed by rising population. However, the prospect of a decline in the rate of growth in population is now at hand. Although fertility levels are declining, the age composition is such that the child-bearing population is expected to increase, and this will affect declining fertility for some time. Nevertheless, the rate of growth of population is likely to slow down from 2.2 percent in the past ten years to 1.8 percent in the next ten. Thereafter we can expect a faster deceleration.

The combined effect of a modest acceleration in economic growth and a gradual decline in population growth would put the economy on a much faster pace of per capita income growth than experienced in the past.

Notes

1. T. N. Vaidyanathan, "Performance and Prospects of Crop Production in India," *Economic and Political Weekly,* Special Number 1977.

2. T. N. Srinivasan, "Trends in Agriculture in India 1949–50—1977–78," *Economic and Political Weekly,* Special Number 1979.

3. Rs 1 lakh = Rs 100,00.

4. Isher J. Ahluwalia, *Industrial Growth in India: Stagnation since the Mid-Sixties,* (New Delhi: Oxford University Press, 1985.)

5. B. N. Goldar, "Productivity Factor Use Efficiency in Indian Industry" (Paper presented at a Seminar on Indian Industrialisation at the Centre for Development Studies, Trivandrum, June 9–12, 1987.)

6. Rs 1 crore = Rs 10 million.

7. S. D. Tendulkar, "Economic Inequalities and Poverty in India: An Interpretative Overview," in *The Development Process of the Indian Economy,* edited by P. R. Brahamananda and V. R. Panchmukhi (New Delhi: Himalaya Publishing House, 1987).

8. M. S. Ahluwalia, "Rural Poverty, Agricultural Production and Prices: A Reexamination," in *Agricultural Change and Rural Poverty: Variations on a Theme by Dharm Narain,* edited by John W. Mellor and Gunvant M. Desai (Baltimore, Md.: John Hopkins University Press, 1985).

9. Tendulkar, "Economic Inequalities and Poverty in India."

Statement:
Successes and Future Prospects
P. K. Kaul

Although it is perhaps easy to argue with hindsight that things might have been done much better, one may nonetheless justifiably feel a little proud of India's achievements and particularly how, in the last few years, the Indian system has responded to the new policy directions. Some of these successes are worthy of repetition.

We have, first of all, broken through what Raj Krishna has labeled the Hindu rate of growth of 3.5 percent per annum to achieve a recent growth of around 5 percent. While it can, of course, always be argued that others may have grown more rapidly than 5 percent, considering the circumstances in which India is placed, this recent improvement is certainly commendable.

India has also displayed a remarkable capacity to control the money supply situation and inflation. We have been condemned in some quarters for being too conservative with respect to this, but I feel that in the long run this prudence has paid off in terms of financial stability in a fashion which many others are striving to achieve today.

Another area in which we should feel very proud is our performance in the agricultural sector. When we gained Independence, we had a record of frequent and devastating famines. But today, improvements in the marketing and production of food grains have brought about a situation where the output of food grains is about 150 million tons and food availability is about marginally higher than actually necessary. This provides the requisite insurance against future shortages and even leaves some capacity for exports, provided the agricultural subsidies now maintained by the richer countries are withdrawn at some point in time. This does not mean that we can afford to be complacent, because population pressures on food grains will continue. However, the record to date is certainly praiseworthy.

In the area of health standards, while much still remains to be achieved, the fact that life expectancy has almost doubled from 33 to about 57 is naturally very satisfying.

The management of a difficult balance-of-payments position is also something with which we should feel happy. The devaluation of 1966 has been subjected to much debate, but in the end, as we subsequently saw in the 1970s, it did help India's export growth. Even thereafter in the late 1970s and the early 1980s, when we had some further difficulties, with the assistance of the Extended Fund Facility of the IMF we were able to get over these temporary problems and achieve today what may generally be described as a manageable situation, though one which requires constant vigilance.

India has an excellent record in honoring its international commitments, whatever they may be, and particularly in the financial sector. Despite all our difficulties we have maintained all the promises and commitments that we gave in connection with the extended fund facilities. Not many countries in the world have done so.

Last, but not least, must be cited India's tremendous record of democratic stability. We have been able to go through eight general elections. Governments have changed, parties have lost, and all without major disruption—a record that not many countries in the developing world have been able to demonstrate.

Having said all this on the achievements side I should mention at least three or four areas which I feel need attention in the future.

Having enough food grains in our kitty, what is now necessary is to aim for a more balanced output of food products. Instead of having too much food grain production and too little of, say, edible oils, some balancing is required in the agriculture package. Fresh technology imports will be essential in such areas as food processing and food storage. The food distribution system still needs to be tackled more carefully, especially in certain regions of the country.

A number of difficulties remain to be dealt with in regard to the public sector. India simply cannot afford to continue to invest in this sector when returns remain so poor. It is to be hoped that the reforms being implemented on the recommendations of the Sengupta Committee will prove effective.

The private sector will also now have to demonstrate that they can adjust to a more competitive environment. For too long the private sector has been used to being protected from competition. At present, area by area and sector by sector, reforms are being made leaving the private sector with more facilities for decisionmaking. The private sector will, however, have to show that they can use this facility efficiently.

There remains considerable need for technological improvement in industry. Our policy relating to technology import has been liberalized. A considerable number of facilities have been given. Broad guidelines have already been issued, procedures have been simplified, and the time taken for processing of applications is now much shorter. Overall approvals for technology imports have doubled in the last five years but industry has not yet taken full advantage of this. Here the United States has a role to play, for the U.S. has provided about 20 percent of all technology employed so far and it is important that U.S. industry continues to utilize this opportunity before someone else comes and captures it.

With regard to exports we apparently have to accept that we work in a very difficult environment. Trying to export a little of everything does not help in the long run. We have to be more selective. We have to find areas in which we are competitive, in which we have our strengths. We should then push and fight and hope that protectionist policies will not prevail.

In the area of social development we will have to continue to place importance on poverty alleviation. Our present policy for trying to upgrade the income-earning capabilities of people below the poverty line must continue. This is something we cannot just forget. In this whole process there will have to be a mechanism to ensure that those who are not so well off are provided for.

Of course, economic change cannot be divorced from politics. But in the past our political system has been able to make decisions which have quite often been difficult, which have quite often not been supported by everybody, but still the courage has been found to take such decisions and to see them through. It can always be argued that something more should have been done. My own view, however, is that there is a certain rate at which change can take place and that by pushing too hard the change may not take place at all. We have to feel our way toward an appropriate rate of change, with consistent movement in the right direction, even if this speed may be slower than some observers might prefer. It is not possible to attack all of the problems at the same time. I have now been associated with Indian policy formulation and implementation for twenty years or so. I see things happening today that I could not have imagined happening, say, in the early 1970s. I saw the political atmosphere under which we were all working at that time, when restrictions were imposed because of the experiences of the political system with the responses of industry and trade. Today the climate is quite different. It is the same Government—though composed of some different people— that has accepted the changes. There is a consistency in the direction in which changes are made, though not everything can be altered at the same time. But segment by segment, item by item, things are being handled and I believe that this is the correct thing to do.

Statement:
Observations on the State of the Economy
Manu Shroff

It has become fashionable to think primarily in terms of growth rate when assessing the economic situation and progress in India. Growth is important. But we must keep a balance while viewing the total picture. Since growth was not sufficient (or not regarded by some as the only yardstick), India did adopt the approach of supplementing growth-oriented policies by what has come to be known as the direct attack on poverty through programs such as the Integrated Rural Development Program, the National Rural Employment Program and so on. Unfortunately, these programs have been only a mixed success. Whatever may be said about growth accelerating as the result of policy changes, the fact remains that for large masses of people economic growth has not brought about the changes originally envisaged. Indeed, in evaluating past experience one can see that the policies we have adopted have created and sustained the dependence of rural people on the Government. This simply continues a fostering of dependency that began with colonial times. What is needed instead is the development of voluntary action in rural areas.

The policy changes that have taken place recently represent a definite break with the past in one important respect. The major episode of liberalization in the past, that of 1966, was quite different from that taking place recently. In 1966, the focus was not on the concept of establishing competitive efficiency in the economy. Rather, the intent was to increase output from existing capacity by mobilizing foreign exchange to alleviate the lack of imported inputs for industry. Indeed, "liberalization" in a general sense was not mentioned. Reference was made only to import liberalization. There was little attempt, for instance, to relax the industrial licensing policies—what has now come to be known as domestic liberalization in the present context. The limited import liberalization in 1966 failed because the international community did not keep its promises to make more foreign exchange available.

The exchange rate fixed in 1966, although it did involve a major change, was really a reasonably appropriate one. The export growth which took place in the 1970s would not have been feasible if the currency had remained overvalued after the 1966 devaluation. A correct perspective on what happened in the mid-1960s is necessary for an appropriate appreciation of what is happening now. The Bhagawati-Srinivasan study of the episode (National Bureau of Economic Research project) is worth recalling in this context.

In contrast to the 1960s, the Government is now trying not just to make possible the use of idle industrial capacity, but to bring about competitive efficiency. But that requires a steadiness of purpose which withstands temporary balance-of-payments problems. Such problems are bound to occur and to constrain the pace at which imports can increase. There is therefore the apprehension that the Government may be impelled to return to old policies of tight import control when next faced by balance-of-payments problems. The Government needs to clarify whether it is serious about pursuing policy changes and competitive efficiency or will be following "stop-and-go" policies on this issue.

If what the Government is *really* doing is some "tidying up" of economic regulation and no more (as M. Ahluwalia seemed to imply), then industry should be told so that it can adjust to that reality. Otherwise the Government will be creating expectations that cannot be fulfilled. On the other hand, if the reality to which industry should adjust is a long-term change in policy, then it needs to be assured that the Government will indeed stick with the changed policies and adopt new ones in the same direction.

Another issue that needs to be considered is with respect to the trend in the savings rate. It is too often taken for granted that India no longer faces the problem of adequate savings and that all that is needed is to increase the productivity of capital. True, capital output ratios have gone up and indicators of efficiency are by no means bright. But it would be wrong to underestimate the need for stepping up the savings rate. In recent years, it has in fact declined. It reached its maximum in 1978–79 at 25.3 percent and then declined to a current rate of 22–23 percent. It is true that bank nationalization gave an impetus to household savings held in financial, rather than traditional, form. However, even before the nationalization of the banks, some 56 percent of household savings were held in the form of financial assets. Just before nationalization this ratio decreased to 35 percent, but has gone back up to 54 percent in the last few years.

Comparing the period just before nationalization with the present, there has indeed been a dramatic increase in financial assets held by households, but a longer perspective is needed for a correct assessment. The point is that additional efforts are needed to augment the rate of savings. The Government has taken a number of steps to encourage equity investment and to increase activity in the capital markets. But much more needs to be done, although not necessarily a higher rate of taxation. Already a high 18 percent of GDP is taxed. Government saving is a problem, but this is due to Government profligacy, not inadequate taxation. Public enterprises, despite successive increases in prices, are not yielding adequate surplus either.

On the external side the picture is a gloomy one. Except for commercial borrowing, not used very much, with the result that our credit is good, the availability of foreign exchange remains a serious constraint.

Statement:
A U.S. Perspective
Bruce Smart

Both India and the United States are seeing rapid change in the world of trade, in which competition is far more intense than we have known and coming from sources we are not used to.

The close-knit world economy is creating great benefit for most of its participants and hopefully to all of them in due course. Each can find greater economic progress and hope through sharing ideas and through sharing commercial transactions which make up international trade.

These changes are revolutionizing manufacturing, finance, and government, as well as education and society. The world has to do business differently today from the way it did a generation ago. The era of self-contained national economies is shifting to a single global economic system. For many businesses, research and development, finance, manufacturing, marketing and distribution are planned and conducted on a worldwide basis.

Large corporations are forming global alliances to reduce costs, spread technologies and open markets—knowing that if they do not take this world view, other corporations will.

Whether we like it or not, the very concept of national sovereignty is losing some of its historic meaning as people, ideas, information, capital and goods flow across national boundaries in response to market forces.

This condition cannot be reversed, nor should it be. It offers economic efficiency that promises prosperity wherever bright and dedicated people set out to establish economic systems that put their talents to work.

Trade is no longer a limited activity, conducted to supplement national growth or to find scarce raw materials not available at home. Rather it binds all nations together in this increasingly integrated world.

India and the United States cannot abstain from participating in the world economy. Each has a responsibility and a role in making the world trading system work.

It is heartening to see how much Indo-U.S. relations have improved in the past several years. Both governments have made strong efforts to develop a greater sense of mutual trust and interest.

The commercial aspects of this relationship are particularly promising. Bilateral trade was a little over $4 billion last year, a 34 percent increase in five years; reasonable progress, but considerably less than the potential for our large and complementary economies. Seen from America, India's new economic policies to encourage increased private production and investment are keys to unleashing India's economic potential and to fostering closer ties with the United States and other nations.

During Secretary Malcolm Baldrige's visit to India in 1985, he made the point that expanded commercial relations between our countries depended on U.S. business seeing more reasons for doing business in

India. If commercial opportunities exist and the economic climate is favorable, U.S. technology and investment will flow to India.

The Commerce Department has been working to make sure that American businesses are aware of the promising new policy directions in India. We have sponsored seminars throughout the United States on how to do business in India. We have intensified our program of trade events in India. Increased numbers of American business leaders have been exposed to India on trade missions sponsored by Commerce and individual states.

Last year, we signed a Memorandum of Understanding on technology transfer with India to facilitate the approval of U.S. export licenses for American technology to India. The execution of this program still leaves something to be desired, and my own Department has a job to do in getting our interagency process to move a little faster.

The U.S. Generalized System of Preferences (GSP) also fosters trade. India ranks eighth among beneficiaries of this program, and in 1985 the GSP allowed $286 million of Indian exports to enter the United States duty free.

One of the satisfying events in recent months was to work closely with the Indian delegation at Punta del Este in launching the new Uruguay Round of multilateral trade negotiations. Despite great initial differences, we found through quiet conversations, principally between Secretary Baldrige and Minister V. P. Singh, that we were on less diverse ground than we had thought. As a result, we were able to find a consensus with seventy-four other nations to launch new General Agreement on Tariffs and Trade (GATT) negotiations under conditions that satisfied all, but were ideal for none.

This experience showed that if we talk to each other and if delegations develop mutual respect, we can find ways to accomplish things that might not seem possible from a distance. I look on Punta del Este as a milestone on the road of friendship which our two countries are traveling.

While the liberalizing changes in India have caused enthusiasm in America, there are still problems—bureaucratic procedures, controls and restrictive practices—that delay ventures that could contribute to the Indian economy.

We are also concerned about pressures from India's industries that have been protected and now fear foreign competition. These pressures and balance-of-payments problems could adversely affect or perhaps reverse India's liberalization. It was dissatisfaction with the competitiveness of India's industry that set liberalization in process. It would be a shame if liberalization were to be jeopardized and a new generation of industries emerging in response to more open policies disadvantaged.

President Ronald Reagan has repeatedly opposed protectionist proposals in the United States. So far we have been successful; no protectionist legislation has been passed by the Congress. At the same time, we have taken trade actions to open foreign markets to goods from the United States and other countries.

Protectionism is a threat to the world trading system. For example, the main victims of agricultural protectionism are smaller, agrarian economies that cannot compete with massive export subsidies nor penetrate import barriers.

The openness of the United States market has allowed many countries to enjoy export-led economic growth. Yet, many still maintain restrictive trade regimes and practices which prevent American firms from exporting to them. Our massive trade deficits result in part from these practices. The United States—just like India, Japan or any other nation—needs some means of paying for its imports. There is no way that we can be a market without exporting goods and services to pay for what we buy. The best antidote to protectionism in the United States is more open markets abroad.

The new GATT round is a promising step. It will require compromises on all sides to reconcile divergent national interests on complex issues such as agriculture, tropical products, natural resources, services, investment and intellectual property protection. Let us not deceive ourselves. Protectionism will be working to undermine our efforts to breathe new life into the multilateral trading system.

All of us here today understand the relationship of trade to economic development and the need for a viable multilateral trade system. India's efforts to stimulate economic growth and develop modern, competitive industries would be difficult—if not impossible—if our world trading system fails to respond to changing times.

Closer Indo-U.S. commercial ties can best flourish in a positive international trading environment. Just as free and fair trade supports economic hope and progress, so a healthy economy supports political stability and provides the will and the means to defend our democratic freedoms.

As the world's two largest democracies, India and the United States have a special responsibility to work together for a better and more open trading system. It is a cause worthy of our best efforts.

About the Contributors

Shankar N. Acharya is Economic Adviser to the Ministry of Finance, Government of India. Previous appointments include Senior Fellow, National Institute of Public Finance and Policy, New Delhi, and Research Adviser to the World Bank. Fields of interest and publication include public finance, economic development and international economics.

Isher Judge Ahluwalia is Professor of Indian Economy at the Centre for Policy Research, New Delhi, and a nonofficial consultant to the Planning Commission, Government of India. Fields of interest and publication include industrial growth, macroeconometric modeling and agriculture-industry linkages.

Montek S. Ahluwalia is Additional Secretary to the Prime Minister in the Government of India. Previous appointments include Economic Adviser to the Ministry of Finance, Government of India, and Division Chief in the Research Department, World Bank. Fields of interest and publication include macroeconomic policy and income distribution.

Yoginder K. Alagh is Member, Planning Commission, Government of India, on leave from a professorial position at the Sardar Patel Institute of Economic and Social Research, Ahmedabad. Fields of interest and publication include development policy, planning and agricultural development.

V. M. Dandekar is Professor Emeritus, Gokhale Institute of Politics and Economics, Pune, President of the Indian Society of Agricultural Economics and President of the Indian School of Political Economy. Previous appointments include Director, Gokhale Institute of Politics and Economics. Fields of interest and publication include poverty and agriculture.

Ashok V. Desai is Visiting Professor in Industrial Economics at the Delhi School of Economics. Previous appointments include Coordinator of the Energy Research Group. Fields of interest and publication include technology development and market structure.

P. N. Dhar is Chairman of the Institute of Economic Growth, Delhi. Previous appointments include: Assistant Secretary General of the United Nations, in charge of Development Research and Policy Analysis; Adviser and Secretary to the Prime Minister of India; Director, Institute of

Economic Growth; Reader in Industrial Economics, Delhi School of Economics. Fields of interest and publication include economic development of India.

David Hopper is Senior Vice President for Policy, Planning and Research in the World Bank. Previous appointments include Vice President for the South Asia Region, World Bank, and President of the International Development Research Centre, Ottawa, Canada. Fields of interest and publication include agricultural economics and development economics.

P. K. Kaul is Ambassador of India to the United States of America. Previous appointments include Cabinet Secretary, Finance Secretary and Defence Secretary in the Government of India. Fields of interest and publication include development economics.

A. M. Khusro is Chairman, National Institute of Public Finance and Policy, New Delhi. Previous appointments include Member of the Indian Planning Commission, Ambassador of India to West Germany, Vice-Chancellor, Aligarh University, and Director, Institute of Economic Growth, Delhi. Fields of interest and publication include public finance, income distribution and development economics.

Robert E.B. Lucas is Professor of Economics, Boston University. Fields of interest and publication include human resources, industrial economics and international trade.

Fredie A. Mehta is Director, Tata Economic Consultancy Services, and Chairman, Investment Corporation of India. Fields of interest and publication include industrial economics and economic management.

John W. Mellor is Director of the International Food Policy Research Institute, Washington, and a Fellow of the American Academy of Arts and Sciences and of the American Agricultural Economics Association. Previous appointments include Chief Economist for the United States Agency for International Development and Professor of Agricultural Economics, Economics, and Asian Studies at Cornell University. Fields of interest and publication include agricultural economics and growth economics.

Deepak Nayyar is Professor of Economics at the Centre for Economic Studies and Planning, Jawaharlal Nehru University, New Delhi. Previous appointments include Economic Adviser to the Ministry of Commerce, Government of India. Fields of interest and publication include international economics and development economics.

Gustav F. Papanek is Professor of Economics and Director of the Center for Asian Development Studies at Boston University. Previous appointments include Director of the Development Advisory Service, Harvard University.

Fields of interest and publication include income distribution and development economics.

Mihir K. Rakshit is Professor of Economics at the Centre for Economic Studies, Presidency College, Calcutta. Fields of interest and publication include monetary economics and macroeconomic problems of developing countries.

C. Rangarajan is Deputy Governor of the Reserve Bank of India and a Member of the Economic Advisory Council of the Prime Minister of India. Previous appointments include Professor of Economics at the Indian Institute of Management, Ahmedabad. Fields of interest and publication include monetary theory, financial institutions, industrial economics and planning.

Manu Shroff is Editor of The Economic Times, Bombay. Previous appointments include Additional Secretary to the Ministry of Finance, Government of India, and India's Alternate Executive Director on the World Bank, Assistant Executive Secretary, Development Committee, IMF/World Bank, and Professor, Indian Institute of Management, Ahmedabad. Fields of interest and publication include industrial economics.

Bruce Smart is Under Secretary for International Trade, United States Department of Commerce. Previous appointments include Chief Executive Officer of the Continental Group.

A. Vaidyanathan is Professor of Economics, Madras Institute of Development Studies, Madras, India. Fields of interest and publication include agriculture, income distribution and macro aspects of development strategy and planning.

Charan D. Wadhva is Research Professor of Political Economy at the Centre for Policy Research, New Delhi. Previous appointments include Director of the Indian Council for Research on International Economic Relations, New Delhi, and Professor at the Indian Institute of Management, Ahmedabad. Fields of interest and publication include international economics, macroeconomic policy, economic development, international business, public policy and corporate planning.

Conference Participants

Acharya, Shankar, Economic Adviser, Ministry of Finance, Government of India.

Ahluwalia, Isher Judge, Professor, Centre for Policy Research, New Delhi.

Ahluwalia, Montek S., Additional Secretary, Prime Minister's Office, Government of India. Formerly Economic Adviser, Ministry of Finance, Government of India.

Alagh, Yoginder K., Chairman, Bureau of Industrial Costs and Prices, Government of India. Formerly Adviser, Planning Commission, Government of India.

Arunachalam, M. V., Chairman, E.I.D. Parry India Ltd. Formerly President, Federation of Indian Chambers of Commerce and Industry.

Banerjee, S., Chairman, Sandoz Co. of India.

Bardhan, Pranab K., Professor, Economics Department, University of California, Berkeley.

Bhagwati, Jagdish N., Professor, Economics Department, Columbia University.

Binswanger, Hans, Chief, Agriculture Research Unit, World Bank.

Chenery, Hollis, Professor, Economics Department, Harvard University. Formerly Vice President, Economics and Research, World Bank.

Dandekar, V. M., Director, Indian School of Political Economy. Formerly Chairman, National Sample Survey, Governing Council.

Desai, Ashok V., Visiting Professor, Delhi School of Economics.

Dhar, P. N., Chairman, Indian Council for Social Science Research. Formerly Assistant Secretary General, United Nations.

Eckaus, Richard, Professor, Economics Department, MIT.

Galbraith, J. Kenneth, Professor Emeritus, Economics Department, Harvard University. Formerly U.S. Ambassador to India.

Ganguly, S., Chairman, Indian Petrochemicals Corp., and of Engineers India Ltd.

Ghosh, Dhruba N., Chairman, State Bank of India. Formerly Secretary, Department of Defence Production, Government of India.

Grawe, Roger, Senior Economist, World Bank.

Hemming, Richard, Economist, International Monetary Fund.

Holsen, John, Chief Economist, South Asia Regional Office, World Bank.

Hopper, David, Senior Vice President, World Bank.

Jagannathan, N. S., Editor, Financial Express, New Delhi.

Kanbur, Ravi, Professor, Department of Economics, University of Warwick.

Kaul, P. K., Indian Ambassador to the United States. Formerly Cabinet Secretary and Finance Secretary, Government of India.

Kauzlarich, Richard, Deputy Director (Economics), Policy Planning Staff, U.S. Department of State.

Kendall, Donald, Chairman of Pepsico, and Chairman, India-U.S. Business Council.

Khusro, A. M., Chairman, Institute of Public Finance and Public Policy, New Delhi.

Klein, Lawrence, Nobel Laureate and Professor of Economics, University of Pennsylvania.

Krishnamurty, V., Chairman, Steel Authority of India. Formerly Secretary, Ministry of Industry, Government of India.

Krugman, Paul, Professor, Economics Department, MIT.

Kumar, Lovraj, Consultant, Advisory Board on Energy, Government of India. Formerly Secretary, Ministry of Steel, Government of India.

Lewis, John, Professor, Economics Department, Princeton University. Formerly Chairman, Development Advisory Committee, O.E.C.D.

Little, Ian M.D., Professor, Oxford University.

Lucas, Robert E.B., Professor, Economics Department, Boston University.

Madhur, Srinivas, Fellow, Institute of Public Finance and Public Policy, New Delhi.

Malhotra, Ram Nath, Governor, Reserve Bank of India.

Mazumdar, Dipak, Senior Economist, World Bank.

Mehta, Fredie A., Chairman, Investment Corporation of India, and Director, Tata Economic Consulting Service.

Mellor, John W., Director, International Food Policy Research Institute.

Morse, Bradford, President, The Salzburg Seminar. Formerly Member, U.S. House of Representatives, and Administrator, U.N. Development Program.

Nadkarni, S. S., Chairman, Industrial Development Bank of India. Formerly Chairman, Industrial Credit and Investment Corporation of India.

Nayyar, Deepak, Professor, Economics Department, Jawaharlal Nehru University. Formerly Economic Adviser, Ministry of Commerce, Government of India.

Ohlin, Goran, Assistant Secretary General, United Nations. Formerly Secretary, Brandt Commission.

Papanek, Gustav F., Director, Center for Asian Development Studies, and Professor (Economics), Boston University. Formerly Director, Development Advisory Service, Harvard University.

Rakshit, Mihir, Professor, Presidency College, Calcutta University.

Rangarajan, C., Deputy Governor, Reserve Bank of India.

Roy, Prannoy, Economic Adviser, Ministry of Finance, Government of India. Formerly Executive Director, World Bank.

Sen, S. R., Member, Commission on Centre-State Relations, Government of India. Formerly Special Secretary, Planning Commission, Government of India.

Sengupta, Arjun, Executive Director, International Monetary Fund. Formerly Secretary (Economics), Prime Minister's Office, Government of India.

Shroff, Manu, Editor, Economic Times, Bombay. Formerly Additional Secretary, Ministry of Finance, Government of India.

Smart, Bruce, Under Secretary, International Trade, U.S. Department of Commerce. Formerly Chief Executive Officer, Continental Group.

Streeten, Paul, Director, World Development Institute, and Professor (Economics), Boston University.

Sule, B. R., Chairman, Associated Chambers of Commerce and Industry, and Managing Director, Mahindra and Mahindra.

Talbot, Phillips, President Emeritus, The Asia Society. Formerly Assistant Secretary for the Near East and South Asia, U.S. Department of State.

Taylor, Lance, Professor, Economics Department, MIT.

Vaidyanathan, A., Senior Fellow, Madras Institute of Development Studies.

Veit, Lawrence, Manager and International Economist, Brown Brothers Harriman.

Vyas, Vijay, Senior Adviser, Agriculture and Rural Development, World Bank.

Wadhva, Charan D., Director, Indian Council for Research in International Economic Relations.

Waide, E. Bevan, Chief, Resident Mission, World Bank, India.